Centenary Edition

THE COMPLETE WORKS OF
RALPH WALDO EMERSON

WITH

A BIOGRAPHICAL

INTRODUCTION AND NOTES

BY EDWARD WALDO EMERSON AND

A GENERAL INDEX

VOLUME

XI

MISCELLANIES

BY

RALPH WALDO EMERSON

BOSTON AND NEW YORK
HOUGHTON MIFFLIN COMPANY
The Riverside Press Cambridge

PREFACE

THE year after Mr. Emerson's death, Mr. Cabot, in editing his works, gathered into a volume the occasional writings which had never been included in previous editions, although six of them had been printed, either as pamphlets or in periodicals, long before, by the author. These were the Sermon on The Lord's Supper, the Historical Address at Concord in 1835, that at the dedication of the Soldiers' Monument there in 1867, and that on Emancipation in the British West Indies, the Essay on War, and the Editors' Address in the *Massachusetts Quarterly Review.* "American Civilization" had been a portion of the article of that name in the *Atlantic* in 1862. "The Fortune of the Republic" also had been printed as a pamphlet in 1874. Mr. Cabot said in his prefatory note, " In none was any change from the original form made by me, except in the ' Fortune of the Republic,' which was made up of several lectures, for the occasion upon which it was read." This was after Mr. Emerson was no longer able to arrange his work and his friends had come to his aid.

The speeches at the John Brown, the Walter Scott, and the Free Religious Association meetings had been printed, probably with Mr. Emerson's consent. The other pieces included by Mr. Cabot, namely, the speeches on Theodore Parker, the Emancipation Proclamation, Abraham Lincoln, at the Harvard Commemoration, "Woman," the addresses to Kossuth, and at the Burns Festival, had not been published.

All that were in Mr. Cabot's collection will be found here, although the order has been slightly changed. To these I have added Mr. Emerson's letter to President Van Buren in 1838, his speech on the Fugitive Slave Law in Concord soon after its enactment, that on Shakspeare to the Saturday Club, and his remarks at the Humboldt Centennial, and at the dinner to the Chinese Embassy; also the addresses at the consecration of Sleepy Hollow Cemetery and at the opening of the Concord Free Public Library. The oration before the New England Society of New York in 1870, printed by them in their recent volume, is not included, as most of the matter may be found in the Historical Discourse at Concord and in the essay " Boston," in *Natural History of Intellect*.

I have given to the chapters mottoes, the most of them drawn from Mr. Emerson's writings.

EDWARD W. EMERSON.

CONTENTS

		PAGE
I.	THE LORD'S SUPPER	1
II.	HISTORICAL DISCOURSE AT CONCORD	27
III.	LETTER TO PRESIDENT VAN BUREN	87
IV.	EMANCIPATION IN THE BRITISH WEST INDIES	97
V.	WAR	149
VI.	THE FUGITIVE SLAVE LAW — ADDRESS AT CONCORD	177
VII.	THE FUGITIVE SLAVE LAW — LECTURE AT NEW YORK	215
VIII.	THE ASSAULT UPON MR. SUMNER	245
IX.	SPEECH ON AFFAIRS IN KANSAS	253
X.	JOHN BROWN — SPEECH AT BOSTON	265
XI.	JOHN BROWN — SPEECH AT SALEM	275
XII.	THEODORE PARKER	283
XIII.	AMERICAN CIVILIZATION	295

CONTENTS

XIV. THE EMANCIPATION PROCLAMA-

TION   313

XV. ABRAHAM LINCOLN   327

XVI. HARVARD COMMEMORATION

SPEECH   339

XVII. DEDICATION OF THE SOLDIERS'

MONUMENT IN CONCORD   347

XVIII. EDITORS' ADDRESS   381

XIX. ADDRESS TO KOSSUTH   395

XX. WOMAN   403

XXI CONSECRATION OF SLEEPY

HOLLOW CEMETERY   427

XXII. ROBERT BURNS   437

XXIII SHAKSPEARE   445

XXIV. HUMBOLDT   455

XXV. WALTER SCOTT   461

XXVI. SPEECH AT BANQUET IN HONOR

OF CHINESE EMBASSY   469

XXVII. REMARKS AT ORGANIZATION OF

FREE RELIGIOUS ASSOCIATION   475

XXVIII. SPEECH AT SECOND ANNUAL

MEETING OF FREE RELIGIOUS

ASSOCIATION   483

CONTENTS

XXIX. ADDRESS AT OPENING OF CON-
     CORD FREE PUBLIC LIBRARY   493
XXX. THE FORTUNE OF THE REPUBLIC   509
     NOTES   545

THE LORD'S SUPPER

SERMON DELIVERED BEFORE THE SECOND CHURCH IN
BOSTON, SEPTEMBER 9, 1832

I LIKE a church; I like a cowl,
I love a prophet of the soul;
And on my heart monastic aisles
Fall like sweet strains, or pensive smiles:
Yet not for all his faith can see
Would I that cowlèd churchman be.
Why should the vest on him allure,
Which I could not on me endure?

THE word unto the prophet spoken
Was writ on tables yet unbroken;
The word by seers or sibyls told,
In groves of oak, or fanes of gold,
Still floats upon the morning wind,
Still whispers to the willing mind.

THE LORD'S SUPPER

The Kingdom of God is not meat and drink; but righteousness, and peace, and joy in the Holy Ghost. — ROMANS xiv. 17.

IN the history of the Church no subject has been more fruitful of controversy than the Lord's Supper. There never has been any unanimity in the understanding of its nature, nor any uniformity in the mode of celebrating it. Without considering the frivolous questions which have been lately debated as to the posture in which men should partake of it; whether mixed or unmixed wine should be served; whether leavened or unleavened bread should be broken;— the questions have been settled differently in every church, who should be admitted to the feast, and how often it should be prepared. In the Catholic Church, infants were at one time permitted and then forbidden to partake; and since the ninth century the laity receive the bread only, the cup being reserved to the priesthood. So, as to the time of the solemnity. In the Fourth Lateran Council, it was decreed that any believer should communicate at least once in a year,— at Easter. Afterwards it was determined that this Sacrament should be received three times in the year, — at Easter, Whitsuntide and Christmas. But more important controversies have arisen respecting its nature. The famous question of the Real Presence was the main controversy between the Church of England and the Church of Rome. The doctrine of the Consubstantiation taught by Luther was denied by Calvin. In the Church of England, Archbishops Laud and Wake maintained that the elements were an Eucharist, or sacrifice of Thanksgiving to God; Cudworth and Warburton, that this was not a sacrifice, but a sacrificial feast; and Bishop Hoadley, that it was neither a sacrifice nor a feast after sacrifice, but a simple commemoration. And finally, it is now near two hundred years since the Society of Quakers denied the authority of the rite altogether, and gave good reasons for disusing it.

I allude to these facts only to show that, so far from the Supper being a tradition in which men are fully agreed, there has always been the widest room for difference of opinion upon this particular. Having recently given particular attention to this subject, I was led to the conclusion that Jesus did not intend to establish an institution for perpetual observance when he ate the Passover with his disciples; and further, to the opinion that it is not expedient to celebrate it as we do. I shall now endeavor to state distinctly my reasons for these two opinions.

I. The authority of the rite.

An account of the Last Supper of Christ with his disciples is given by the four Evangelists, Matthew, Mark, Luke and John.

In St. Matthew's Gospel (Matt. xxvi. 26–30) are recorded the words of Jesus in giving bread and wine on that occasion to his disciples, but no expression occurs intimating that this feast was hereafter to be commemorated. In St. Mark (Mark xiv. 22–25) the same words are recorded, and still with no intimation that the occasion was to be remembered. St. Luke (Luke xxii. 19), after relating the breaking of the bread, has these words: "This do in remembrance of me." In St. John, although other occurrences of the same evening are related, this whole transaction is passed over without notice.

Now observe the facts. Two of the Evangelists, namely, Matthew and John, were of the twelve disciples, and were present on that occasion. Neither of them drops the slightest intimation of any intention on the part of Jesus to set up anything permanent. John especially, the beloved disciple, who has recorded with minuteness the conversation and the transactions of that memorable evening, has quite omitted such a notice. Neither does it appear to have come to the knowledge of Mark, who, though not an eye-witness, relates the other facts. This material fact, that the occasion was to be remembered, is found in Luke alone, who was not present. There is no reason, however, that we know, for rejecting the account of Luke. I doubt not, the expression was used by Jesus. I shall presently consider its meaning. I have only brought these accounts together, that you may judge whether it is likely that a solemn institution, to be continued to the end of time by all mankind, as they should come, nation after nation, within the influence of the Christian religion, would have been established in this slight manner — in a manner so slight, that the intention of commemorating it should not appear, from their narrative, to have caught the ear or dwelt in the mind of the only two among the twelve who wrote down what happened.

Still we must suppose that the expression, "This do in remembrance of me," had come to the ear of Luke from some disciple who was present. What did it really signify? It is a prophetic and an affectionate expression. Jesus is a Jew, sitting with his countrymen, celebrating their national feast. He thinks of his own impending death, and wishes the minds of his disciples to be prepared for it. "When hereafter," he says to them, "you shall keep the Passover, it will have an altered aspect to your eyes. It is now a historical covenant of God with the Jewish nation. Hereafter it will remind you of a new covenant sealed with my blood. In years to come, as long as your people shall come up to Jerusalem to keep this feast, the connection which has subsisted between us will give a new meaning in your eyes to the national festival, as the anniversary of my death." I see natural feeling and beauty in the use of such language from Jesus, a friend to his friends; I can readily imagine that he was willing and desirous, when his disciples met, his memory should hallow their intercourse; but I cannot bring myself to believe that in the use of such an expression he looked beyond the living generation, beyond the abolition of the festival he was celebrating, and the scattering of the nation, and meant to impose a memorial feast upon the whole world.

Without presuming to fix precisely the purpose in the mind of Jesus, you will see that

many opinions may be entertained of his intention, all consistent with the opinion that he did
not design a perpetual ordinance. He may have
foreseen that his disciples would meet to remember him, and that with good effect. It may
have crossed his mind that this would be easily
continued a hundred or a thousand years, — as
men more easily transmit a form than a virtue,
— and yet have been altogether out of his purpose to fasten it upon men in all times and all
countries.

But though the words, " Do this in remembrance of me," do not occur in Matthew, Mark
or John, and although it should be granted us
that, taken alone, they do not necessarily import so much as is usually thought, yet many
persons are apt to imagine that the very striking
and personal manner in which the eating and
drinking is described, indicates a striking and
formal purpose to found a festival. And I admit that this impression might probably be left
upon the mind of one who read only the passages under consideration in the New Testament.
But this impression is removed by reading any
narrative of the mode in which the ancient or
the modern Jews have kept the Passover. It is
then perceived that the leading circumstances

in the Gospels are only a faithful account of that ceremony. Jesus did not celebrate the Passover, and afterwards the Supper, but the Supper was the Passover. He did with his disciples exactly what every master of a family in Jerusalem was doing at the same hour with his household. It appears that the Jews ate the lamb and the unleavened bread and drank wine after a prescribed manner. It was the custom for the master of the feast to break the bread and to bless it, using this formula, which the Talmudists have preserved to us, " Blessed be Thou, O Lord, our God, who givest us the fruit of the vine," — and then to give the cup to all. Among the modern Jews, who in their dispersion retain the Passover, a hymn is also sung after this ceremony, specifying the twelve great works done by God for the deliverance of their fathers out of Egypt.

But still it may be asked, Why did Jesus make expressions so extraordinary and emphatic as these — " This is my body which is broken for you. Take ; eat. This is my blood which is shed for you. Drink it " ? — I reply they are not extraordinary expressions from him. They were familiar in his mouth. He always taught by parables and symbols. It was the national

way of teaching, and was largely used by him.
Remember the readiness which he always showed
to spiritualize every occurrence. He stopped
and wrote on the sand. He admonished his
disciples respecting the leaven of the Pharisees.
He instructed the woman of Samaria respecting living water. He permitted himself to be
anointed, declaring that it was for his interment.
He washed the feet of his disciples. These are
admitted to be symbolical actions and expressions.
Here, in like manner, he calls the bread his
body, and bids the disciples eat. He had used
the same expression repeatedly before. The
reason why St. John does not repeat his words
on this occasion seems to be that he had reported a similar discourse of Jesus to the people
of Capernaum more at length already (John vi.
27-60). He there tells the Jews, " Except ye
eat the flesh of the Son of Man and drink his
blood, ye have no life in you." And when the
Jews on that occasion complained that they did
not comprehend what he meant, he added for
their better understanding, and as if for our
understanding, that we might not think his body
was to be actually eaten, that he only meant we
should live by his commandment. He closed
his discourse with these explanatory expressions:

"The flesh profiteth nothing; the words that I speak to you, they are spirit and they are life."

Whilst I am upon this topic, I cannot help remarking that it is not a little singular that we should have preserved this rite and insisted upon perpetuating one symbolical act of Christ whilst we have totally neglected all others, — particularly one other which had at least an equal claim to our observance. Jesus washed the feet of his disciples and told them that, as he had washed their feet, they ought to wash one another's feet; for he had given them an example, that they should do as he had done to them. I ask any person who believes the Supper to have been designed by Jesus to be commemorated for-ever, to go and read the account of it in the other Gospels, and then compare with it the account of this transaction in St. John, and tell me if this be not much more explicitly author-ized than the Supper. It only differs in this, that we have found the Supper used in New England and the washing of the feet not. But if we had found it an established rite in our churches, on grounds of mere authority, it would have been impossible to have argued against it. That rite is used by the Church of Rome, and by the Sandemanians. It has been very properly

dropped by other Christians. Why? For two
reasons : (1) because it was a local custom, and
unsuitable in western countries; and (2) because
it was typical, and all understood that humility
is the thing signified. But the Passover was
local too, and does not concern us, and its bread
and wine were typical, and do not help us to
understand the redemption which they signified.
These views of the original account of the Lord's
Supper lead me to esteem it an occasion full of
solemn and prophetic interest, but never intended by Jesus to be the foundation of a perpetual institution

It appears, however, in Christian history that
the disciples had very early taken advantage of
these impressive words of Christ to hold religious
meetings, where they broke bread and drank
wine as symbols. I look upon this fact as very
natural in the circumstances of the Church. The
disciples lived together; they threw all their
property into a common stock, they were bound
together by the memory of Christ, and nothing
could be more natural than that this eventful
evening should be affectionately remembered by
them; that they, Jews like Jesus, should adopt
his expressions and his types, and furthermore,
that what was done with peculiar propriety by

them, his personal friends, with less propriety should come to be extended to their companions also. In this way religious feasts grew up among the early Christians. They were readily adopted by the Jewish converts, who were familiar with religious feasts, and also by the Pagan converts, whose idolatrous worship had been made up of sacred festivals, and who very readily abused these to gross riot, as appears from the censures of St. Paul. Many persons consider this fact, the observance of such a memorial feast by the early disciples, decisive of the question whether it ought to be observed by us. There was good reason for his personal friends to remember their friend and repeat his words. It was only too probable that among the half-converted Pagans and Jews, any rite, any form, would find favor, whilst yet unable to comprehend the spiritual character of Christianity.

The circumstance, however, that St. Paul adopts these views, has seemed to many persons conclusive in favor of the institution. I am of opinion that it is wholly upon the Epistle to the Corinthians, and not upon the Gospels, that the ordinance stands. Upon this matter of St. Paul's view of the Supper, a few important considerations must be stated.

The end which he has in view, in the eleventh chapter of the first Epistle, is not to enjoin upon his friends to observe the Supper, but to censure their abuse of it. We quote the passage now-adays as if it enjoined attendance upon the Supper; but he wrote it merely to chide them for drunkenness. To make their enormity plainer, he goes back to the origin of this religious feast to show what sort of feast that was, out of which this riot of theirs came, and so relates the transactions of the Last Supper "I have received of the Lord," he says, "that which I delivered to you" By this expression it is often thought that a miraculous communication is implied; but certainly without good reason, if it is remembered that St. Paul was living in the lifetime of all the apostles who could give him an account of the transaction; and it is contrary to all reason to suppose that God should work a miracle to convey information that could so easily be got by natural means. So that the import of the expression is that he had received the story of an eye-witness such as we also possess.

But there is a material circumstance which diminishes our confidence in the correctness of the Apostle's view; and that is, the observation that his mind had not escaped the prevalent error of the primitive Church, the belief, namely, that the second coming of Christ would shortly occur, until which time, he tells them, this feast was to be kept. Elsewhere he tells them that at that time the world would be burnt up with fire, and a new government established, in which the Saints would sit on thrones ; so slow were the disciples, during the life and after the ascension of Christ, to receive the idea which we receive, that his second coming was a spiritual kingdom, the dominion of his religion in the hearts of men, to be extended gradually over the whole world. In this manner we may see clearly enough how this ancient ordinance got its footing among the early Christians, and this single expectation of a speedy reappearance of a temporal Messiah, which kept its influence even over so spiritual a man as St. Paul, would naturally tend to preserve the use of the rite when once established.

We arrive, then, at this conclusion : first, that it does not appear, from a careful examination of the account of the Last Supper in the Evangelists, that it was designed by Jesus to be perpetual ; secondly, that it does not appear that the opinion of St. Paul, all things considered, ought to alter our opinion derived from the Evangelists.

One general remark before quitting this branch of this subject. We ought to be cautious in taking even the best ascertained opinions and practices of the primitive Church for our own. If it could be satisfactorily shown that they esteemed it authorized and to be transmitted forever, that does not settle the question for us. We know how inveterately they were attached to their Jewish prejudices, and how often even the influence of Christ failed to enlarge their views. On every other subject succeeding times have learned to form a judgment more in accordance with the spirit of Christianity than was the practice of the early ages.

II. But it is said: " Admit that the rite was not designed to be perpetual. What harm doth it ? Here it stands, generally accepted, under some form, by the Christian world, the undoubted occasion of much good : is it not better it should remain?" This is the question of expediency.

I proceed to state a few objections that in my judgment lie against its use in its present form.

1. If the view which I have taken of the history of the institution be correct, then the claim of authority should be dropped in administering it. You say, every time you celebrate the

rite, that Jesus enjoined it; and the whole language you use conveys that impression. But if you read the New Testament as I do, you do not believe he did.

2. It has seemed to me that the use of this ordinance tends to produce confusion in our views of the relation of the soul to God. It is the old objection to the doctrine of the Trinity, — that the true worship was transferred from God to Christ, or that such confusion was introduced into the soul that an undivided worship was given nowhere. Is not that the effect of the Lord's Supper? I appeal now to the convictions of communicants, and ask such persons whether they have not been occasionally conscious of a painful confusion of thought between the worship due to God and the commemoration due to Christ. For the service does not stand upon the basis of a voluntary act, but is imposed by authority. It is an expression of gratitude to Christ, enjoined by Christ. There is an endeavor to keep Jesus in mind, whilst yet the prayers are addressed to God. I fear it is the effect of this ordinance to clothe Jesus with an authority which he never claimed and which distracts the mind of the worshipper. I know our opinions differ much respecting the nature and offices of

Christ, and the degree of veneration to which he is entitled I am so much a Unitarian as this: that I believe the human mind can admit but one God, and that every effort to pay religious homage to more than one being goes to take away all right ideas. I appeal, brethren, to your individual experience. In the moment when you make the least petition to God, though it be but a silent wish that he may approve you, or add one moment to your life, — do you not, in the very act, necessarily exclude all other beings from your thought? In that act, the soul stands alone with God, and Jesus is no more present to your mind than your brother or your child.

But is not Jesus called in Scripture the Mediator? He is the mediator in that only sense in which possibly any being can mediate between God and man, — that is, an instructor of man. He teaches us how to become like God. And a true disciple of Jesus will receive the light he gives most thankfully , but the thanks he offers, and which an exalted being will accept, are not compliments, commemorations, but the use of that instruction.

3. Passing other objections, I come to this, that the use of the elements, however suitable

to the people and the modes of thought in the East, where it originated, is foreign and unsuited to affect us. Whatever long usage and strong association may have done in some individuals to deaden this repulsion, I apprehend that their use is rather tolerated than loved by any of us. We are not accustomed to express our thoughts or emotions by symbolical actions. Most men find the bread and wine no aid to devotion, and to some it is a painful impediment. To eat bread is one thing; to love the precepts of Christ and resolve to obey them is quite another.'

The statement of this objection leads me to say that I think this difficulty, wherever it is felt, to be entitled to the greatest weight. It is alone a sufficient objection to the ordinance. It is my own objection. This mode of commemorating Christ is not suitable to me. That is reason enough why I should abandon it. If I believed it was enjoined by Jesus on his disciples, and that he even contemplated making permanent this mode of commemoration, every way agreeable to an Eastern mind, and yet on trial it was disagreeable to my own feelings, I should not adopt it. I should choose other ways which, as more effectual upon me, he would approve more. For I choose that my remembrances of him should be pleasing, affecting, religious. I will love him as a glorified friend, after the free way of friendship, and not pay him a stiff sign of respect, as men do those whom they fear. A passage read from his discourses, a moving provocation to works like his, any act or meeting which tends to awaken a pure thought, a flow of love, an original design of virtue, I call a worthy, a true commemoration.

4. The importance ascribed to this particular ordinance is not consistent with the spirit of Christianity. The general object and effect of the ordinance is unexceptionable. It has been, and is, I doubt not, the occasion of indefinite good, but an importance is given by Christians to it which never can belong to any form. My friends, the Apostle well assures us that " the kingdom of God is not meat and drink, but righteousness, and peace, and joy in the Holy Ghost " I am not so foolish as to declaim against forms. Forms are as essential as bodies ; but to exalt particular forms, to adhere to one form a moment after it is outgrown, is unreasonable, and it is alien to the spirit of Christ. If I understand the distinction of Christianity, the reason why it is to be preferred over all other systems

and is divine is this, that it is a moral system;
that it presents men with truths which are their
own reason, and enjoins practices that are their
own justification ; that if miracles may be said
to have been its evidence to the first Christians,
they are not its evidence to us, but the doctrines
themselves ; that every practice is Christian
which praises itself, and every practice unchris-
tian which condemns itself. I am not engaged
to Christianity by decent forms, or saving ordinances ; it is not usage, it is not what I do not
understand, that binds me to it, — let these be
the sandy foundations of falsehoods. What I
revere and obey in it is its reality, its boundless
charity, its deep interior life, the rest it gives to
mind, the echo it returns to my thoughts, the
perfect accord it makes with my reason through
all its representation of God and His Providence; and the persuasion and courage that
come out thence to lead me upward and onward. Freedom is the essence of this faith. It
has for its object simply to make men good and
wise. Its institutions then should be as flexible
as the wants of men. That form out of which
the life and suitableness have departed should
be as worthless in its eyes as the dead leaves
that are falling around us.

And therefore, although for the satisfaction
of others I have labored to show by the history
that this rite was not intended to be perpetual;
although I have gone back to weigh the expressions of Paul, I feel that here is the true
point of view. In the midst of considerations as
to what Paul thought, and why he so thought,
I cannot help feeling that it is time misspent
to argue to or from his convictions, or those of
Luke and John, respecting any form. I seem
to lose the substance in seeking the shadow.
That for which Paul lived and died so glori-
ously; that for which Jesus gave himself to be
crucified; the end that animated the thousand
martyrs and heroes who have followed his steps,
was to redeem us from a formal religion, and
teach us to seek our well-being in the formation
of the soul. The whole world was full of idols
and ordinances. The Jewish was a religion of
forms; it was all body, it had no life, and the
Almighty God was pleased to qualify and send
forth a man to teach men that they must serve
him with the heart; that only that life was religious which was thoroughly good; that sacrifice was smoke, and forms were shadows. This
man lived and died true to this purpose; and
now, with his blessed word and life before us,

Christians must contend that it is a matter of
vital importance, — really a duty, to commemorate him by a certain form, whether that form
be agreeable to their understandings or not. Is
not this to make vain the gift of God? Is not
this to turn back the hand on the dial? Is not
this to make men, — to make ourselves, — forget that not forms, but duties; not names, but
righteousness and love are enjoined; and that in
the eye of God there is no other measure of the
value of any one form than the measure of its
use?

There remain some practical objections to the
ordinance, into which I shall not now enter.
There is one on which I had intended to say a
few words; I mean the unfavorable relation in
which it places that numerous class of persons
who abstain from it merely from disinclination
to the rite.

Influenced by these considerations, I have
proposed to the brethren of the Church to drop
the use of the elements and the claim of authority in the administration of this ordinance, and
have suggested a mode in which a meeting for
the same purpose might be held, free of objection.

My brethren have considered my views with

patience and candor, and have recommended,
unanimously, an adherence to the present form.
I have therefore been compelled to consider
whether it becomes me to administer it. I am
clearly of opinion I ought not. This discourse
has already been so far extended that I can only
say that the reason of my determination is
shortly this: It is my desire, in the office of
a Christian minister, to do nothing which I
cannot do with my whole heart. Having said
this, I have said all. I have no hostility to
this institution; I am only stating my want of
sympathy with it. Neither should I ever have
obtruded this opinion upon other people, had
I not been called by my office to administer it.
That is the end of my opposition, that I am
not interested in it I am content that it stand
to the end of the world, if it please men and
please Heaven, and I shall rejoice in all the
good it produces.

As it is the prevailing opinion and feeling
in our religious community that it is an indispensable part of the pastoral office to administer
this ordinance, I am about to resign into your
hands that office which you have confided to
me. It has many duties for which I am feebly
qualified. It has some which it will always be

my delight to discharge according to my ability, wherever I exist. And whilst the recollection of its claims oppresses me with a sense of my unworthiness, I am consoled by the hope that no time and no change can deprive me of the satisfaction of pursuing and exercising its highest functions.[1]

II

HISTORICAL DISCOURSE

AT CONCORD, ON THE SECOND CENTENNIAL ANNI-
VERSARY OF THE INCORPORATION OF THE
TOWN, SEPTEMBER 12, 1835

BULKELEY, Hunt, Willard, Hosmer, Merriam, Flint,
Possessed the land which rendered to their toil
Hay, corn, roots, hemp, flax, apples, wool and wood.
Each of these landlords walked amidst his farm
Saying, ' 'T is mine, my children's and my name's.'

Where are these men ? Asleep beneath their grounds:
And strangers, fond as they, their furrows plough.
Earth laughs in flowers, to see her boastful boys
Earth-proud, proud of the earth which is not theirs.

I will have never a noble,
No lineage counted great,
Fishers and choppers and ploughme
Shall constitute a state

Lo now! if these poor men
Can govern the land and sea
And make just laws below the sur
As planets faithful be

I cause from every creature
His proper good to flow:
As much as he is and doeth,
So much he shall bestow.

HISTORICAL DISCOURSE

FELLOW CITIZENS: The town of Concord begins, this day, the third century of its history. By a common consent, the people of New England, for a few years past, as the second centennial anniversary of each of its early settlements arrived, have seen fit to observe the day. You have thought it becoming to commemorate the planting of the first inland town. The sentiment is just, and the practice is wise. Our ears shall not be deaf to the voice of time. We will review the deeds of our fathers, and pass that just verdict on them we expect from posterity on our own.

And yet, in the eternity of Nature, how recent our antiquities appear! The imagination is impatient of a cycle so short. Who can tell how many thousand years, every day, the clouds have shaded these fields with their purple awning? The river, by whose banks most of us were born, every winter, for ages, has spread its crust of ice over the great meadows which, in ages, it had formed. But the little society of men who now, for a few years, fish in this river, plough the fields it washes, mow the grass and

reap the corn, shortly shall hurry from its banks
as did their forefathers. "Man's life," said the
Witan to the Saxon king, "is the sparrow that
enters at a window, flutters round the house,
and flies out at another, and none knoweth
whence he came, or whither he goes." ' The
more reason that we should give to our being
what permanence we can; — that we should
recall the Past, and expect the Future.

Yet the race survives whilst the individual
dies. In the country, without any interference
of the law, the agricultural life favors the permanence of families. Here are still around me
the lineal descendants of the first settlers of
this town. Here is Blood, Flint, Willard, Mer-
iam, Wood, Hosmer, Barrett, Wheeler, Jones,
Brown, Buttrick, Brooks, Stow, Hoar, Hey-
wood, Hunt, Miles, — the names of the inhabitants for the first thirty years; and the family
is in many cases represented, when the name is
not. If the name of Bulkeley is wanting, the
honor you have done me this day, in making
me your organ, testifies your persevering kindness to his blood.'

I shall not be expected, on this occasion, to
repeat the details of that oppression which drove
our fathers out hither. Yet the town of Con-

cord was settled by a party of non-conformists,
immediately from Great Britain. The best friend
the Massachusetts colony had, though much
against his will, was Archbishop Laud in England. In consequence of his famous proclamation setting up certain novelties in the rites of
public worship, fifty godly ministers were suspended for contumacy, in the course of two
years and a half. Hindered from speaking, some
of these dared to print the reasons of their dissent, and were punished with imprisonment or
mutilation.[1] This severity brought some of the
best men in England to overcome that natural
repugnance to emigration which holds the serious and moderate of every nation to their own
soil. Among the silenced clergymen was a distinguished minister of Woodhill, in Bedford-
shire, Rev. Peter Bulkeley, descended from a
noble family, honored for his own virtues, his
learning and gifts as a preacher, and adding to
his influence the weight of a large estate.[2] Per-
secution readily knits friendship between its
victims. Mr. Bulkeley, having turned his estate
into money and set his face towards New England, was easily able to persuade a good number
of planters to join him. They arrived in Boston
in 1634.[3] Probably there had been a previous

correspondence with Governor Winthrop, and an agreement that they should settle at Musketaquid. With them joined Mr. Simon Willard, a merchant from Kent in England. They petitioned the General Court for a grant of a township, and on the 2d of September, 1635, corresponding in New Style to 12th September, two hundred years ago this day, leave to begin a plantation at Musketaquid was given to Peter Bulkeley, Simon Willard, and about twelve families more.' A month later, Rev. John Jones and a large number of settlers destined for the new town arrived in Boston.'

The grant of the General Court was but a preliminary step The green meadows of Musketaquid or *Grassy Brook* were far up in the woods, not to be reached without a painful and dangerous journey through an uninterrupted wilderness. They could cross the Massachusetts or Charles River, by the ferry at Newtown; they could go up the river as far as Watertown. But the Indian paths leading up and down the country were a foot broad. They must then plunge into the thicket, and with their axes cut a road for their teams, with their women and children and their household stuff, forced to make long circuits too, to avoid hills and swamps. Edward

Johnson of Woburn has described in an affecting narrative their labors by the way. "Sometimes passing through thickets where their hands
are forced to make way for their bodies' passage,
and their feet clambering over the crossed trees,
which when they missed, they sunk into an uncertain bottom in water, and wade up to their
knees, tumbling sometimes higher, sometimes
lower. At the end of this, they meet a scorching plain, yet not so plain but that the ragged
bushes scratch their legs foully, even to wearing
their stockings to their bare skin in two or three
hours. Some of them, having no leggins, have
had the blood trickle down at every step. And
in time of summer, the sun casts such a reflecting heat from the sweet fern, whose scent is very
strong, that some nearly fainted." ' They slept on
the rocks, wherever the night found them. Much
time was lost in travelling they knew not whither,
when the sun was hidden by clouds ; for " their
compass miscarried in crowding through the
bushes," and the Indian paths, once lost, they
did not easily find.

Johnson, relating undoubtedly what he had
himself heard from the pilgrims, intimates that
they consumed many days in exploring the country, to select the best place for the town. Their

first temporary accommodation was rude enough.
" After they have found a place of abode, they
burrow themselves in the earth for their first
shelter, under a hillside, and casting the soil aloft
upon timbers, they make a fire against the earth,
at the highest side. And thus these poor servants
of Christ provide shelter for themselves, their
wives and little ones, keeping off the short show-
ers from their lodgings, but the long rains penetrate through, to their great disturbance in the
night season. Yet in these poor wigwams they
sing psalms, pray and praise their God, till they
can provide them houses, which they could not
ordinarily, till the earth, by the Lord's blessing,
brought forth bread to feed them. This they
attain with sore travail, every one that can lift a
hoe to strike into the earth standing stoutly to
his labors, and tearing up the roots and bushes
from the ground, which, the first year, yielded
them a lean crop, till the sod of the earth was
rotten, and therefore they were forced to cut
their bread very thin for a long season. But the
Lord is pleased to provide for them great store
of fish in the spring-time, and especially, alewives,
about the bigness of a herring " ' These served
them also for manure. For flesh, they looked
not for any, in those times, unless they could

barter with the Indians for venison and raccoons.
"Indian corn, even the coarsest, made as pleasant meal as rice."¹ All kinds of garden fruits
grew well, "and let no man," writes our pious
chronicler, in another place, "make a jest of
pumpkins, for with this fruit the Lord was
pleased to feed his people until their corn and
cattle were increased."²

The great cost of cattle, and the sickening of
their cattle upon such wild fodder as was never
cut before; the loss of their sheep and swine by
wolves; the sufferings of the people in the great
snows and cold soon following; and the fear of
the Pequots; are the other disasters enumerated
by the historian.

The hardships of the journey and of the first
encampment are certainly related by their contemporary with some air of romance, yet they
can scarcely be exaggerated. A march of a number of families with their stuff, through twenty
miles of unknown forest, from a little rising
town that had not much to spare, to an Indian
town in the wilderness that had nothing, must
be laborious to all, and for those who were new
to the country and bred in softness, a formidable
adventure. But the pilgrims had the preparation
of an armed mind, better than any hardihood of

body. And the rough welcome which the new
land gave them was a fit introduction to the life
they must lead in it

But what was their reception at Musketaquid?
This was an old village of the Massachusetts
Indians. Tahattawan, the Sachem, with Waban
his son-in-law, lived near Nashawtuck, now Lee's
Hill.¹ Their tribe, once numerous, the epidemic
had reduced. Here they planted, hunted and
fished. The moose was still trotting in the country, and of his sinews they made their bowstring.
Of the pith elder, that still grows beside our
brooks, they made their arrow. Of the Indian
hemp they spun their nets and lines for summer
angling, and, in winter, they sat around holes in
the ice, catching salmon, pickerel, breams and
perch, with which our river abounded.² Their
physical powers, as our fathers found them, and
before yet the English alcohol had proved more
fatal to them than the English sword, astonished
the white men.³ Their sight was so excellent,
that, standing on the seashore, they often told
of the coming of a ship at sea, sooner by one
hour, yea, two hours' sail, than any Englishman
that stood by, on purpose to look out.⁴ Roger
Williams affirms that he has known them run
between eighty and a hundred miles in a sum-

mer's day, and back again within two days. A
little pounded parched corn or no-cake sufficed
them on the march. To his bodily perfection,
the wild man added some noble traits of character. He was open as a child to kindness and
justice. Many instances of his humanity were
known to the Englishmen who suffered in the
woods from sickness or cold. " When you came
over the morning waters," said one of the Sa-
chems, " we took you into our arms. We fed
you with our best meat. Never went white man
cold and hungry from Indian wigwam."

The faithful dealing and brave good will,
which, during the life of the friendly Massasoit,
they uniformly experienced at Plymouth and at
Boston, went to their hearts. So that the peace
was made, and the ear of the savage already
secured, before the pilgrims arrived at his seat of
Musketaquid, to treat with him for his lands.

It is said that the covenant made with the
Indians, by Mr. Bulkeley and Major Willard,
was made under a great oak, formerly standing
near the site of the Middlesex Hotel.' Our
Records affirm that Squaw Sachem, Tahattawan,
and Nimrod did sell a tract of six miles square to
the English, receiving for the same, some fath-
oms of Wampumpeag, hatchets, hoes, knives,

cotton cloth and shirts. Wibbacowet, the hus
band of Squaw Sachem, received a suit of cloth,
a hat, a white linen band, shoes, stockings and
a greatcoat, and, in conclusion, the said Indians
declared themselves satisfied, and told the Englishmen they were welcome. And after the bargain was concluded, Mr. Simon Willard, pointing
to the four corners of the world, declared that
they had bought three miles from that place,
east, west, north and south.'

The Puritans, to keep the remembrance of
their unity one with another, and of their
peaceful compact with the Indians, named their
forest settlement CONCORD. They proceeded to build, under the shelter of the hill that
extends for a mile along the north side of the
Boston road, their first dwellings The labors
of a new plantation were paid by its excitements.
I seem to see them, with their pious pastor,
addressing themselves to the work of clearing
the land. Natives of another hemisphere, they
beheld, with curiosity, all the pleasing features
of the American forest. The landscape before
them was fair, if it was strange and rude. The
little flower which at this season stars our woods
and roadsides with its profuse blooms, might at-
tract even eyes as stern as theirs with its humble

beauty. The useful pine lifted its cones into the frosty air. The maple, which is already making the forest gay with its orange hues, reddened over those houseless men. The majestic summits of Wachusett and Monadnoc towering in the horizon, invited the steps of adventure westward.

As the season grew later, they felt its inconveniences. " Many were forced to go barefoot and bareleg, and some in time of frost and snow, yet were they more healthy than now they are." [1] The land was low but healthy; and if, in common with all the settlements, they found the air of America very cold, they might say with Higginson, after his description of the other elements, that " New England may boast of the element of fire, more than all the rest; for all Europe is not able to afford to make so great fires as New England. A poor servant, that is to possess but fifty acres, may afford to give more wood for fire as good as the world yields, than many noblemen in England." [2] Many were their wants, but more their privileges. The light struggled in through windows of oiled paper,[3] but they read the word of God by it. They were fain to make use of their knees for a table, but their limbs were their own. Hard labor and spare diet they had, and off wooden

trenchers, but they had peace and freedom, and
the wailing of the tempest in the woods sounded
kindlier in their ear than the smooth voice of
the prelates, at home, in England. " There is no
people," said their pastor to his little flock of
exiles, " but will strive to excel in something.
What can we excel in, if not in holiness? If we
look to number, we are the fewest; if to strength,
we are the weakest; if to wealth and riches, we
are the poorest of all the people of God through
the whole world. We cannot excel nor so much
as equal other people in these things; and if we
come short in grace and holiness too, we are the
most despicable people under heaven. Strive
we, therefore, herein to excel, and suffer not this
crown to be taken away from us." ' The sermon
fell into good and tender hearts ; the people
conspired with their teacher. Their religion was
sweetness and peace amidst toil and tears. And,
as we are informed, " the edge of their appetite
was greater to spiritual duties at their first coming, in time of wants, than afterwards."

The original Town Records, for the first
thirty years, are lost. We have records of mar-
riages and deaths, beginning nineteen years after
the settlement; and copies of some of the doings
of the town in regard to territory, of the same

date. But the original distribution of the land,
or an account of the principles on which it was
divided, are not preserved. Agreeably to the
custom of the times, a large portion was reserved
to the public, and it appears from a petition of
some newcomers, in 1643, that a part had been
divided among the first settlers without price,
on the single condition of improving it.[1] Other
portions seem to have been successively divided
off and granted to individuals, at the rate of
sixpence or a shilling an acre. But, in the first
years, the land would not pay the necessary
public charges, and they seem to have fallen
heavily on the few wealthy planters. Mr. Bulkeley, by his generosity, spent his estate, and,
doubtless in consideration of his charges, the
General Court, in 1639, granted him 300 acres
towards Cambridge; and to Mr. Spencer, probably for the like reason, 300 acres by the Ale-
wife River. In 1638, 1200 acres were granted
to Governor Winthrop, and 1000 to Thomas
Dudley, of the lands adjacent to the town, and
Governor Winthrop selected as a building spot
the land near the house of Captain Humphrey
Hunt.[2] The first record now remaining is that
of a reservation of land for the minister, and
the appropriation of new lands as commons or

pastures to some poor men. At the same date,
in 1654, the town having divided itself into three
districts, called the North, South and East
quarters, ordered, "that the North quarter are
to keep and maintain all their highways and
bridges over the great river, in their quarter,
and, in respect of the greatness of their charge
thereabout, and in regard of the ease of the East
quarter above the rest, in their highways, they
are to allow the North quarter £3 " '

Fellow citizens, this first recorded political
act of our fathers, this tax assessed on its inhabitants by a town, is the most important event
in their civil history, implying, as it does, the
exercise of a sovereign power, and connected with
all the immunities and powers of a corporate
town in Massachusetts. The greater speed and
success that distinguish the planting of the human
race in this country, over all other plantations
in history, owe themselves mainly to the new
subdivisions of the State into small corporations
of land and power. It is vain to look for the inventor No man made them. Each of the parts
of that perfect structure grew out of the necessities of an instant occasion. The germ was formed
in England. The charter gave to the freemen
of the Company of Massachusetts Bay the elec-

tion of the Governor and Council of Assistants.
It moreover gave them the power of prescribing
the manner in which freemen should be elected;
and ordered that all fundamental laws should be
enacted by the freemen of the colony. But the
Company removed to New England; more than
one hundred freemen were admitted the first
year, and it was found inconvenient to assemble
them all.' And when, presently, the design of
the colony began to fulfil itself, by the settlement of new plantations in the vicinity of Boston, and parties, with grants of land, straggled
into the country to truck with the Indians and
to clear the land for their own benefit, the Governor and freemen in Boston found it neither
desirable nor possible to control the trade and
practices of these farmers. What could the body
of freemen, meeting four times a year, at Boston,
do for the daily wants of the planters at Musketaquid? The wolf was to be killed; the Indian to be watched and resisted; wells to be dug;
the forest to be felled; pastures to be cleared;
corn to be raised; roads to be cut; town and farm
lines to be run. These things must be done,
govern who might. The nature of man and his
condition in the world, for the first time within
the period of certain history, controlled the forma-

tion of the State. The necessity of the colonists wrote the law. Their wants, their poverty, their manifest convenience made them bold to ask of the Governor and of the General Court, immunities, and, to certain purposes, sovereign powers. The townsmen's words were heard and weighed, for all knew that it was a petitioner that could not be slighted; it was the river, or the winter, or famine, or the Pequots, that spoke through them to the Governor and Council of Massachusetts Bay. Instructed by necessity, each little company organized itself after the pattern of the larger town, by appointing its constable, and other petty half-military officers. As early as 1633,[1] the office of townsman or *selectman* appears, who seems first to have been appointed by the General Court, as here, at Concord, in 1639. In 1635, the Court say, "whereas particular towns have many things which concern only themselves, it is Ordered, that the freemen of every town shall have power to dispose of their own lands, and woods, and choose their own particular officers."[2] This pointed chiefly at the office of constable, but they soon chose their own selectmen, and very early assessed taxes; a power at first resisted,[3] but speedily confirmed to them.

Meantime, to this paramount necessity, a milder and more pleasing influence was joined. I esteem it the happiness of this country that its settlers, whilst they were exploring their granted and natural rights and determining the power of the magistrate, were united by personal affection. Members of a church before whose searching covenant all rank was abolished, they stood in awe of each other, as religious men. They bore to John Winthrop, the Governor, a grave but hearty kindness. For the first time, men examined the powers of the chief whom they loved and revered. For the first time, the ideal social compact was real. The bands of love and reverence held fast the little state, whilst they untied the great cords of authority to examine their soundness and learn on what wheels they ran. They were to settle the internal constitution of the towns, and, at the same time, their power in the commonwealth. The Governor conspires with them in limiting his claims to their obedience, and values much more their love than his chartered authority. The disputes between that forbearing man and the deputies are like the quarrels of girls, so much do they turn upon complaints of unkindness, and end in such loving reconciliations. It was on doubts concerning their own power, that, in 1634, a committee repaired to him for counsel, and he advised, seeing the freemen were grown so numerous, to send deputies from every town once in a year to revise the laws and to assess all monies.' And the General Court, thus constituted, only needed to go into separate session from the Council, as they did in 1644,' to become essentially the same assembly they are this day.

By this course of events, Concord and the other plantations found themselves separate and independent of Boston, with certain rights of their own, which, what they were, time alone could fully determine, enjoying, at the same time, a strict and loving fellowship with Boston, and sure of advice and aid, on every emergency. Their powers were speedily settled by obvious convenience, and the towns learned to exercise a sovereignty in the laying of taxes; in the choice of their deputy to the house of representatives; in the disposal of the town lands; in the care of public worship, the school and the poor; and, what seemed of at least equal importance, to exercise the right of expressing an opinion on every question before the country In a town-meeting, the great secret of political science was uncovered, and the problem solved,

how to give every individual his fair weight in
the government, without any disorder from numbers. In a town-meeting, the roots of society
were reached. Here the rich gave counsel, but
the poor also; and moreover, the just and the
unjust. He is ill informed who expects, on running down the Town Records for two hundred
years, to find a church of saints, a metropolis
of patriots, enacting wholesome and creditable
laws. The constitution of the towns forbid it.
In this open democracy, every opinion had utterance; every objection, every fact, every acre of
land, every bushel of rye, its entire weight. The
moderator was the passive mouth-piece, and the
vote of the town, like the vane on the turret
overhead, free for every wind to turn, and always
turned by the last and strongest breath. In these
assemblies, the public weal, the call of interest,
duty, religion, were heard; and every local
feeling, every private grudge, every suggestion
of petulance and ignorance, were not less faithfully produced. Wrath and love came up to
town-meeting in company. By the law of 1641,
every man — freeman or not — inhabitant or
not — might introduce any business into a public
meeting. Not a complaint occurs in all the
volumes of our Records, of any inhabitant being

hindered from speaking, or suffering from any
violence or usurpation of any class. The negative ballot of a ten-shilling freeholder was as
fatal as that of the honored owner of Blood's
Farms or Willard's Purchase. A man felt himself at liberty to exhibit, at town-meeting, feelings and actions that he would have been
ashamed of anywhere but amongst his neighbors. Individual protests are frequent. Peter
Wright [1705] desired his dissent might be recorded from the town's grant to John Shepard.'
In 1795, several town-meetings are called, upon
the compensation to be made to a few proprietors
for land taken in making a bridle-road; and one
of them demanding large damages, many offers
were made him in town-meeting, and refused;
"which the town thought very unreasonable."
The matters there debated are such as to invite
very small considerations. The ill-spelled pages
of the Town Records contain the result. I shall
be excused for confessing that I have set a value
upon any symptom of meanness and private
pique which I have met with in these antique
books, as proof that justice was done; that if
the results of our history are approved as wise
and good, it was yet a free strife; if the good
counsel prevailed, the sneaking counsel did not

fail to be suggested; freedom and virtue, if they triumphed, triumphed in a fair field. And so be it an everlasting testimony for them, and so much ground of assurance of man's capacity for self-government.

It is the consequence of this institution that not a school-house, a public pew, a bridge, a pound, a mill-dam, hath been set up, or pulled down, or altered, or bought, or sold, without the whole population of this town having a voice in the affair. A general contentment is the result. And the people truly feel that they are lords of the soil. In every winding road, in every stone fence, in the smokes of the poor-house chimney, in the clock on the church, they read their own power, and consider, at leisure, the wisdom and error of their judgments.

The British government has recently presented to the several public libraries of this country, copies of the splendid edition of the Domesday Book, and other ancient public records of England. I cannot but think that it would be a suitable acknowledgment of this national munificence, if the records of one of our towns, — of this town, for example, — should be printed, and presented to the governments of Europe; to the English nation, as

XI

a thank-offering, and as a certificate of the progress of the Saxon race; to the Continental nations as a lesson of humanity and love. Tell
them, the Union has twenty-four States, and
Massachusetts is one. Tell them, Massachusetts has three hundred towns, and Concord is
one; that in Concord are five hundred ratable
polls, and every one has an equal vote.

About ten years after the planting of Concord, efforts began to be made to civilize the
Indians, and " to win them to the knowledge of
the true God." This indeed, in so many words,
is expressed in the charter of the colony as one
of its ends; and this design is named first in
the printed " Considerations," that inclined
Hampden, and determined Winthrop and his
friends, to come hither. The interest of the
Puritans in the natives was heightened by a
suspicion at that time prevailing that these were
the lost ten tribes of Israel. The man of the
woods might well draw on himself the compassion of the planters. His erect and perfect
form, though disclosing some irregular virtues,
was found joined to a dwindled soul. Master
of all sorts of wood-craft, he seemed a part of
the forest and the lake, and the secret of his
amazing skill seemed to be that he partook of

the nature and fierce instincts of the beasts he slew. Those who dwelled by ponds and rivers had some tincture of civility, but the hunters of the tribe were found intractable at catechism. Thomas Hooker anticipated the opinion of Humboldt, and called them " the ruins of man-kind."

Early efforts were made to instruct them, in which Mr. Bulkeley, Mr. Flint, and Captain Willard, took an active part. In 1644, Squaw Sachem, the widow of Nanepashemet, the great Sachem of Concord and Mystic, with two sa-chems of Wachusett, made a formal submission to the English government, and intimated their desire, "as opportunity served, and the English lived among them, to learn to read God's word, and know God aright ; " and the General Court acted on their request.' John Eliot, in October, 1646, preached his first sermon in the Indian language at Noonantum ; Waban, Tahattawan, and their sannaps, going thither from Concord to hear him. There under the rubbish and ruins of barbarous life, the human heart heard the voice of love, and awoke as from a sleep. The questions which the Indians put betray their reason and their ignorance. " Can Jesus Christ understand prayers in the Indian language?"

"If a man be wise, and his sachem weak, must he obey him?" At a meeting which Eliot gave to the squaws apart, the wife of Wampooas propounded the question, "Whether do I pray when my husband prays, if I speak nothing as he doth, yet if I like what he saith?"— "which questions were accounted of by some, as part of the whitenings of the harvest toward."[1] Tahattawan, our Concord sachem, called his Indians together, and bid them not oppose the courses which the English were taking for their good; for, said he, all the time you have lived after the Indian fashion, under the power of the higher sachems, what did they care for you? They took away your skins, your kettles and your wampum, at their own pleasure, and this was all they regarded. But you may see the English mind no such things, but only seek your welfare, and instead of taking away, are ready to give to you. Tahattawan and his son-in-law Waban, besought Eliot to come and preach to them at Concord, and here they entered, by his assistance, into an agreement to twenty-nine rules, all breathing a desire to conform themselves to English customs.[2] They requested to have a town given them within the bounds of Concord, near unto

the English. When this question was propounded by Tahattawan, he was asked, why
he desired a town so near, when there was more
room for them up in the country? The sachem
replied that he knew if the Indians dwelt far
from the English, they would not so much care
to pray, nor could they be so ready to hear the
word of God, but would be, all one, Indians
still; but dwelling near the English, he hoped
it might be otherwise with them then. We,
who see in the squalid remnants of the twenty
tribes of Massachusetts, the final failure of this
benevolent enterprise, can hardly learn without
emotion the earnestness with which the most
sensible individuals of the copper race held on
to the new hope they had conceived, of being
elevated to equality with their civilized brother.
It is piteous to see their self-distrust in their request to remain near the English, and their unanimous entreaty to Captain Willard, to be their
Recorder, being very solicitous that what they
did agree upon might be faithfully kept without
alteration. It was remarkable that the preaching
was not wholly new to them. "Their forefathers,"
the Indians told Eliot, "did know God, but
after this, they fell into a deep sleep, and when
they did awake, they quite forgot him." [1]

At the instance of Eliot, in 1651, their desire was granted by the General Court, and Nashobah, lying near Nagog Pond, now partly in Littleton, partly in Acton, became an Indian town, where a Christian worship was established under an Indian ruler and teacher. Wilson relates that, at their meetings, "the Indians sung a psalm, made Indian by Eliot, in one of our ordinary English tunes, melodiously." Such was, for half a century, the success of the general enterprise, that, in 1676, there were five hundred and sixty-seven praying Indians, and in 1689, twenty-four Indian preachers, and eighteen assemblies.

Meantime, Concord increased in territory and population. The lands were divided; highways were cut from farm to farm, and from this town to Boston. A military company had been organized in 1636. The Pequots, the terror of the farmer, were exterminated in 1637. Captain Underhill, in 1638, declared, that "the new plantations of Dedham and Concord do afford large accommodation, and will contain abundance of people." In 1639, our first selectmen, Mr. Flint, Lieutenant Willard, and Richard Griffin were appointed. And in 1641, when the colony rate was £12, Concord was assessed £5. The country already began to yield more than was consumed by the inhabitants.¹ The very great immigration from England made the lands more valuable every year, and supplied a market for the produce. In 1643, the colony was so numerous that it became expedient to divide it into four counties, Concord being included in Middlesex.² In 1644, the town contained sixty families.

But, in 1640, all immigration ceased, and the country produce and farm-stock depreciated.³ Other difficulties accrued. The fish, which had been the abundant manure of the settlers, was found to injure the land.⁴ The river, at this period, seems to have caused some distress now by its overflow, now by its drought.⁵ A cold and wet summer blighted the corn; enormous flocks of pigeons beat down and eat up all sorts of English grain; and the crops suffered much from mice.⁶ New plantations and better land had been opened, far and near; and whilst many of the colonists at Boston thought to remove, or did remove to England, the Concord people became uneasy, and looked around for new seats. In 1643, one seventh or one eighth part of the inhabitants went to Connecticut with Reverend Mr. Jones, and settled Fairfield. Weakened by this loss, the people begged to be released from a part of their rates, to which the General Court consented. Mr. Bulkeley dissuaded his people from removing, and admonished them to increase their faith with their griefs. Even this check which befell them acquaints us with the rapidity of their growth, for the good man, in dealing with his people, taxes them with luxury. " We pretended to come hither," he says, " for ordinances ; but now ordinances are light matters with us ; we are turned after the prey. We have among us excess and pride of life ; pride in apparel, daintiness in diet, and that in those who, in times past, would have been satisfied with bread. *This is the sin of the lowest of the people* "¹ Better evidence could not be desired of the rapid growth of the settlement.

The check was but momentary. The earth teemed with fruits. The people on the bay built ships, and found the way to the West Indies, with pipe-staves, lumber and fish ; and the country people speedily learned to supply themselves with sugar, tea and molasses. The college had been already gathered in 1638. Now the school-house went up. The General Court, in 1647, " to the end that learning may not be buried in the graves of our forefathers, Ordered, that every township, after the Lord had increased them to

the number of fifty house-holders, shall appoint
one to teach all children to write and read ; and
where any town shall increase to the number of
one hundred families, they shall set up a Gram-
mar school, the masters thereof being able to
instruct youth so far as they may be fitted for
the University." With these requirements Concord not only complied, but, in 1653, subscribed
a sum for several years to the support of Harvard College.[1]

But a new and alarming public distress re-
tarded the growth of this, as of the sister towns,
during more than twenty years from 1654 to
1676. In 1654, the four united New England
Colonies agreed to raise 270 foot and 40 horse,
to reduce Ninigret, Sachem of the Niantics, and
appointed Major Simon Willard, of this town,
to the command.[2] This war seems to have been
pressed by three of the colonies, and reluctantly
entered by Massachusetts. Accordingly, Major
Willard did the least he could, and incurred the
censure of the Commissioners, who write to their
" loving friend Major Willard," " that they leave
to his consideration the inconveniences arising
from his non-attendance to his commission."[3]
This expedition was but the introduction of the
war with King Philip. In 1670, the Wampanoags

began to grind their hatchets, and mend their
guns, and insult the English. Philip surrendered
seventy guns to the Commissioners in Taunton
Meeting-house,' but revenged his humiliation a
few years after, by carrying fire and the tomahawk
into the English villages. From Narragansett
to the Connecticut River, the scene of war was
shifted as fast as these red hunters could traverse
the forest. Concord was a military post. The inactivity of Major Willard, in Ninigret's war, had
lost him no confidence. He marched from Concord to Brookfield, in season to save the people
whose houses had been burned, and who had
taken shelter in a fortified house.² But he fought
with disadvantage against an enemy who must
be hunted before every battle. Some flourishing
towns were burned. John Monoco, a formidable
savage, boasted that "he had burned Medfield
and Lancaster, and would burn Groton, Concord, Watertown and Boston;" adding, "what
me will, me do." He did burn Groton, but before he had executed the remainder of his threat
he was hanged, in Boston, in September, 1676.'

A still more formidable enemy was removed,
in the same year, by the capture of Canonchet,
the faithful ally of Philip, who was soon afterwards shot at Stonington. He stoutly declared

to the Commissioners that " he would not deliver up a Wampanoag, nor the paring of a
Wampanoag's nail," and when he was told that
his sentence was death, he said " he liked it well
that he was to die before his heart was soft, or
he had spoken anything unworthy of himself." [1]

We know beforehand who must conquer in
that unequal struggle. The red man may destroy here and there a straggler, as a wild beast
may; he may fire a farm-house, or a village; but
the association of the white men and their arts
of war give them an overwhelming advantage,
and in the first blast of their trumpet we already
hear the flourish of victory. I confess what
chiefly interests me, in the annals of that war,
is the grandeur of spirit exhibited by a few of
the Indian chiefs. A nameless Wampanoag who
was put to death by the Mohicans, after cruel
tortures, was asked by his butchers, during the
torture, how he liked the war? — he said, " he
found it as sweet as sugar was to Englishmen." [2]

The only compensation which war offers for
its manifold mischiefs, is in the great personal
qualities to which it gives scope and occasion.
The virtues of patriotism and of prodigious
courage and address were exhibited on both
sides, and, in many instances, by women. The

historian of Concord has preserved an instance
of the resolution of one of the daughters of the
town. Two young farmers, Abraham and Isaac
Shepherd, had set their sister Mary, a girl of
fifteen years, to watch whilst they threshed grain
in the barn. The Indians stole upon her before
she was aware, and her brothers were slain. She
was carried captive into the Indian country, but,
at night, whilst her captors were asleep, she
plucked a saddle from under the head of one
of them, took a horse they had stolen from
Lancaster, and having got the saddle on, she
mounted, swam across the Nashua River, and
rode through the forest to her home.'

With the tragical end of Philip, the war
ended. Beleaguered in his own country, his corn
cut down, his piles of meal and other provision
wasted by the English, it was only a great thaw
in January, that, melting the snow and opening
the earth, enabled his poor followers to come at
the ground-nuts, else they had starved. Hunted
by Captain Church, he fled from one swamp to
another; his brother, his uncle, his sister, and
his beloved squaw being taken or slain, he was
at last shot down by an Indian deserter, as he
fled alone in the dark of the morning, not far
from his own fort.'

Concord suffered little from the war. This is
to be attributed no doubt, in part, to the fact
that troops were generally quartered here, and
that it was the residence of many noted soldiers.
Tradition finds another cause in the sanctity of
its minister. The elder Bulkeley was gone. In
1659,[1] his bones were laid at rest in the forest.
But the mantle of his piety and of the people's
affection fell upon his son Edward,[2] the fame of
whose prayers, it is said, once saved Concord
from an attack of the Indian.[3] A great defence
undoubtedly was the village of Praying Indians,
until this settlement fell a victim to the envenomed prejudice against their countrymen. The
worst feature in the history of those years, is,
that no man spake for the Indian. When the
Dutch, or the French, or the English royalist
disagreed with the Colony, there was always
found a Dutch, or French, or tory party, — an
earnest minority, — to keep things from extrem-
ity. But the Indian seemed to inspire such a
feeling as the wild beast inspires in the people
near his den. It is the misfortune of Concord
to have permitted a disgraceful outrage upon
the friendly Indians settled within its limits, in
February, 1676, which ended in their forcible
expulsion from the town.[4]

This painful incident is but too just an example of the measure which the Indians have generally received from the whites. For them the heart of charity, of humanity, was stone. After Philip's death, their strength was irrecoverably broken. They never more disturbed the interior settlements, and a few vagrant families, that are now pensioners on the bounty of Massachusetts, are all that is left of the twenty tribes.

> "Alas! the tears their day is o'er,
> Their fires are out from hill and shore,
> No more for them the wild deer bounds,
> The plough is on their hunting grounds,
> The pale man's axe rings through their woods,
> The pale man's sail skims o'er their floods,
> Their pleasant springs are ... "

I turn gladly to the progress of our civil history. Before 1666, 15,... acres had been added by grants of the General Court to the original territory of the town,' so that Concord then included the greater part of the towns of Bedford, Acton, Lincoln and Carlisle.

In the great growth of the country, Concord participated, as is manifest from its increasing polls and increased rates. Randolph at this period writes to the English government, concerning the country towns; "The farmers are

numerous and wealthy, live in good houses ; are
given to hospitality; and make good advantage
by their corn, cattle, poultry, butter and cheese.''[1]
Edward Bulkeley was the pastor, until his death,
in 1696. His youngest brother, Peter, was deputy from Concord, and was chosen speaker of
the house of deputies in 1676. The following
year, he was sent to England, with Mr. Stough-
ton, as agent for the Colony ; and on his return,
in 1685, was a royal councillor. But I am sorry
to find that the servile Randolph speaks of him
with marked respect.[2] It would seem that his visit
to England had made him a courtier. In 1689,
Concord partook of the general indignation of the
province against Andros. A company marched
to the capital under Lieutenant Heald, forming
a part of that body concerning which we are
informed, " the country people came armed into
Boston, on the afternoon (of Thursday, 18th
April) in such rage and heat, as made us all
tremble to think what would follow ; for nothing
would satisfy them but that the governor must be
bound in chains or cords, and put in a more secure
place, and that they would see done before they
went away; and to satisfy them he was guarded by
them to the fort.''[3] But the Town Records of that
day confine themselves to descriptions of lands,

and to conferences with the neighboring towns to
run boundary lines. In 1699, so broad was their
territory, I find the selectmen running the lines
with Chelmsford, Cambridge and Watertown.'
Some interesting peculiarities in the manners and
customs of the time appear in the town's books.
Proposals of marriage were made by the parents
of the parties, and minutes of such private agreements sometimes entered on the clerk's records.'
The public charity seems to have been bestowed
in a manner now obsolete. The town lends its
commons as pastures, to poor men; and " being
informed of the great present want of Thomas
Pellit, gave order to Stephen Hosmer to deliver
a town cow, of a black color, with a white face,
unto said Pellit, for his present supply."'

From the beginning to the middle of the eighteenth century, our records indicate no interruption of the tranquillity of the inhabitants, either
in church or in civil affairs. After the death of
Rev. Mr. Estabrook, in 1711, it was propounded
at the town-meeting, " whether one of the three
gentlemen lately improved here in preaching,
namely, Mr. John Whiting, Mr. Holyoke and
Mr. Prescott, shall be now chosen in the work
of the ministry? Voted affirmatively.'' Mr.
Whiting, who was chosen, was, we are told in

his epitaph, "a universal lover of mankind."
The charges of education and of legislation, at
this period, seem to have afflicted the town; for
they vote to petition the General Court to be
eased of the law relating to providing a schoolmaster; happily, the Court refused; and in 1712,
the selectmen agreed with Captain James Minott,
"for his son Timothy to keep the school at the
school-house for the town of Concord, for half
a year beginning 2d June; and if any scholar
shall come, within the said time, for larning exceeding his son's ability, the said Captain doth
agree to instruct them himself in the tongues,
till the above said time be fulfilled; for which
service, the town is to pay Captain Minott ten
pounds." Captain Minott seems to have served
our prudent fathers in the double capacity of
teacher and representative. It is an article in the
selectmen's warrant for the town-meeting, "to
see if the town will lay in for a representative
not exceeding four pounds." Captain Minott
was chosen, and after the General Court was
adjourned received of the town for his services,
an allowance of three shillings per day. The
country was not yet so thickly settled but that
the inhabitants suffered from wolves and wild-
cats, which infested the woods; since bounties of

XI

twenty shillings are given as late as 1735, to Indians and whites, for the heads of these animals,
after the constable has cut off the ears.[1]

Mr. Whiting was succeeded in the pastoral
office by Rev. Daniel Bliss, in 1738. Soon after
his ordination, the town seems to have been
divided by ecclesiastical discords. In 1741, the
celebrated Whitfield preached here, in the open
air, to a great congregation.[2] Mr. Bliss heard
that great orator with delight, and by his earnest
sympathy with him, in opinion and practice, gave
offence to a part of his people. Party and mutual councils were called, but no grave charge
was made good against him. I find, in the
Church Records, the charges preferred against
him, his answer thereto, and the result of the
Council. The charges seem to have been made
by the lovers of order and moderation against
Mr. Bliss, as a favorer of religious excitements.
His answer to one of the counts breathes such
true piety that I cannot forbear to quote it. The
ninth allegation is " That in praying for himself,
in a church-meeting, in December last, he said,
' he was a poor vile worm of the dust, that was
allowed as Mediator between God and this people.' " To this Mr. Bliss replied, " In the prayer
you speak of, Jesus Christ was acknowledged as

the only Mediator between God and man; at
which time, I was filled with wonder, that such
a sinful and worthless worm as I am, was allowed
to represent Christ, in any manner, even so far
as to be bringing the petitions and thank-offer-
ings of the people unto God, and God's will
and truths to the people; and used the word
Mediator in some differing light from that you
have given it; but I confess I was soon uneasy
that I had used the word, lest some would put
a wrong meaning thereupon." ' The Council
admonished Mr. Bliss of some improprieties of
expression, but bore witness to his purity and
fidelity in his office. In 1764, Whitfield preached
again at Concord, on Sunday afternoon; Mr.
Bliss preached in the morning, and the Concord
people thought their minister gave them the
better sermon of the two. It was also his last.²

The planting of the colony was the effect of
religious principle. The Revolution was the fruit
of another principle, — the devouring thirst for
justice. From the appearance of the article in
the Selectmen's warrant, in 1765, "to see if the
town will give the Representative any instructions about any important affair to be transacted
by the General Court, concerning the Stamp
Act," ³ to the peace of 1783, the Town Records

breathe a resolute and warlike spirit, so bold from the first as hardly to admit of increase.

It would be impossible on this occasion to recite all these patriotic papers. I must content myself with a few brief extracts. On the 24th January, 1774, in answer to letters received from the united committees of correspondence, in the vicinity of Boston, the town say:

"We cannot possibly view with indifference the past and present obstinate endeavors of the enemies of this, as well as the mother country, to rob us of those rights, that are the distinguishing glory and felicity of this land; rights, that we are obliged to no power, under heaven, for the enjoyment of; as they are the fruit of the heroic enterprises of the first settlers of these American colonies. And though we cannot but be alarmed at the great majority, in the British parliament, for the imposition of unconstitutional taxes on the colonies, yet, it gives life and strength to every attempt to oppose them, that not only the people of this, but the neighboring provinces are remarkably united in the important and interesting opposition, which, as it succeeded before, in some measure, by the blessing of heaven, so, we cannot but hope it will be attended with still greater success, in future.

" *Resolved*, That these colonies have been and still are illegally taxed by the British parliament, as they are not virtually represented therein.

" That the purchasing commodities subject to such illegal taxation is an explicit, though an impious and sordid resignation of the liberties of this free and happy people.

" That, as the British parliament have empowered the East India Company to export their tea into America, for the sole purpose of raising a revenue from hence; to render the design abortive, we will not, in this town, either by ourselves, or any from or under us, buy, sell, or use any of the East India Company's tea, or any other tea, whilst there is a duty for raising a revenue thereon in America; neither will we suffer any such tea to be used in our families.

" That all such persons as shall purchase, sell, or use any such tea, shall, for the future, be deemed unfriendly to the happy constitution of this country.

" That, in conjunction with our brethren in America, we will risk our fortunes, and even our lives, in defence of his majesty, King George the Third, his person, crown and dignity; and will, also, with the same resolution, as his free-born subjects in this country, to the utmost of our power, defend all our rights inviolate to the latest posterity.

"That, if any person or persons, inhabitants of this province, so long as there is a duty on tea, shall import any tea from the India House, in England, or be factors for the East India Company, we will treat them, in an eminent degree, as enemies to their country, and with contempt and detestation.

"That we think it our duty, at this critical time of our public affairs, to return our hearty thanks to the town of Boston, for every rational measure they have taken for the preservation or recovery of our invaluable rights and liberties infringed upon; and we hope, should the state of our public affairs require it, that they will still remain watchful and persevering, with a steady zeal to espy out everything that shall have a tendency to subvert our happy constitution"'

On the 27th June, near three hundred persons, upwards of twenty-one years of age, inhabitants of Concord, entered into a covenant, "solemnly engaging with each other, in the presence of God, to suspend all commercial intercourse with Great Britain, until the act for blocking the harbor of Boston be repealed, and neither to buy nor consume any merchandise imported from Great Britain, nor to deal with those who do." [1]

In August, a County Convention met in this town, to deliberate upon the alarming state of public affairs, and published an admirable report. [2] In September, incensed at the new royal law which made the judges dependent on the crown, the inhabitants assembled on the common, and forbade the justices to open the court of sessions. This little town then assumed the sovereignty. It was judge and jury and council and king. On the 26th of the month, the whole town resolved itself into a committee of safety, " to suppress all riots, tumults, and disorders in said town, and to aid all untainted magistrates in the execution of the laws of the land." It was then voted, to raise one or more companies of minute-men, by enlistment, to be paid by the town whenever called out of town ; and to provide arms and ammunition, " that those who are unable to purchase them themselves, may have the advantage of them, if necessity calls for it " In October, the Provincial Congress met in Concord. John Hancock was President. This body was composed of the foremost patriots, and adopted those efficient

measures whose progress and issue belong to
the history of the nation.'

The clergy of New England were, for the
most part, zealous promoters of the Revolution.
A deep religious sentiment sanctified the thirst
for liberty. All the military movements in this
town were solemnized by acts of public worship. In January, 1775, a meeting was held for
the enlisting of minute-men. Reverend William
Emerson, the chaplain of the Provincial Congress, preached to the people. Sixty men enlisted and, in a few days, many more. On 13th
March, at a general review of all the military
companies, he preached to a very full assembly,
taking for his text, 2 Chronicles xiii. 12, "And,
behold, God himself is with us for our captain,
and his priests with sounding trumpets to cry
alarm against you."² It is said that all the
services of that day made a deep impression on
the people, even to the singing of the psalm.

A large amount of military stores had been
deposited in this town, by order of the Provincial Committee of Safety. It was to destroy
those stores that the troops who were attacked
in this town, on the 19th April, 1775, were sent
hither by General Gage.

The story of that day is well known. In

these peaceful fields, for the first time since a
hundred years, the drum and alarm-gun were
heard, and the farmers snatched down their
rusty firelocks from the kitchen walls, to make
good the resolute words of their town debates.
In the field where the western abutment of the
old bridge may still be seen, about half a mile
from this spot, the first organized resistance was
made to the British arms. There the Americans
first shed British blood. Eight hundred British
soldiers, under the command of Lieutenant-
Colonel Francis Smith, had marched from Boston to Concord; at Lexington had fired upon
the brave handful of militia, for which a speedy
revenge was reaped by the same militia in the
afternoon. When they entered Concord, they
found the militia and minute-men assembled
under the command of Colonel Barrett and
Major Buttrick. This little battalion, though in
their hasty council some were urgent to stand
their ground, retreated before the enemy to the
high land on the other bank of the river, to wait
for reinforcement. Colonel Barrett ordered the
troops not to fire, unless fired upon. The British
following them across the bridge, posted two
companies, amounting to about one hundred
men, to guard the bridge, and secure the return

of the plundering party. Meantime, the men of
Acton, Bedford, Lincoln and Carlisle, all once
included in Concord, remembering their parent
town in the hour of danger, arrived and fell
into the ranks so fast, that Major Buttrick
found himself superior in number to the enemy's party at the bridge. And when the smoke
began to rise from the village where the British
were burning cannon-carriages and military
stores, the Americans resolved to force their
way into town. The English beginning to pluck
up some of the planks of the bridge, the Americans quickened their pace, and the British fired
one or two shots up the river (our ancient
friend here, Master Blood,' saw the water struck
by the first ball); then a single gun, the ball
from which wounded Luther Blanchard and
Jonas Brown, and then a volley, by which Captain Isaac Davis and Abner Hosmer of Acton
were instantly killed. Major Buttrick leaped
from the ground, and gave the command to
fire, which was repeated in a simultaneous cry
by all his men. The Americans fired, and killed
two men and wounded eight. A head-stone
and a foot-stone, on this bank of the river,
mark the place where these first victims lie.'
The British retreated immediately towards the

village, and were joined by two companies of grenadiers, whom the noise of the firing had hastened to the spot. The militia and minute-men — every one from that moment being his own commander — ran over the hills opposite the battle-field, and across the great fields, into the east quarter of the town, to waylay the enemy, and annoy his retreat. The British, as soon as they were rejoined by the plundering detachment, began that disastrous retreat to Boston, which was an omen to both parties of the event of the war.

In all the anecdotes of that day's events we may discern the natural action of the people. It was not an extravagant ebullition of feeling, but might have been calculated on by any one acquainted with the spirits and habits of our community. Those poor farmers who came up, that day, to defend their native soil, acted from the simplest instincts. They did not know it was a deed of fame they were doing. These men did not babble of glory. They never dreamed their children would contend who had done the most. They supposed they had a right to their corn and their cattle, without paying tribute to any but their own governors. And as they had no fear of man, they yet did have a fear of

God. Captain Charles Miles, who was wounded in the pursuit of the enemy, told my venerable friend who sits by me, that " he went to the services of that day, with the same seriousness and acknowledgment of God, which he carried to church." [1]

The presence of these aged men who were in arms on that day seems to bring us nearer to it. The benignant Providence which has prolonged their lives to this hour gratifies the strong curiosity of the new generation. The Pilgrims are gone ; but we see what manner of persons they were who stood in the worst perils of the Revolution. We hold by the hand the last of the invincible men of old, and confirm from living lips the sealed records of time.

And you, my fathers, whom God and the history of your country have ennobled, may well bear a chief part in keeping this peaceful birthday of our town. You are indeed extraordinary heroes. If ever men in arms had a spotless cause, you had. You have fought a good fight. And having quit you like men in the battle, you have quit yourselves like men in your virtuous families ; in your cornfields ; and in society. We will not hide your honorable gray hairs under perishing laurel-leaves, but the eye of affection and veneration follows you. You are set apart—and forever—for the esteem and gratitude of the human race. To you belongs a better badge than stars and ribbons. This prospering country is your ornament, and this expanding nation is multiplying your praise with millions of tongues.'

The agitating events of those days were duly remembered in the church. On the second day after the affray, divine service was attended, in this house, by 700 soldiers. William Emerson, the pastor, had a hereditary claim to the affection of the people, being descended in the fourth generation from Edward Bulkeley, son of Peter. But he had merits of his own. The cause of the Colonies was so much in his heart that he did not cease to make it the subject of his preaching and his prayers, and is said to have deeply inspired many of his people with his own enthusiasm. He, at least, saw clearly the pregnant consequences of the 19th April. I have found within a few days, among some family papers, his almanac of 1775, in a blank leaf of which he has written a narrative of the fight;² and at the close of the month, he writes, "This month remarkable for the greatest events of the present age." To promote the same cause, he asked, and obtained of the town, leave to accept the

commission of chaplain to the Northern army,
at Ticonderoga, and died, after a few months,
of the distemper that prevailed in the camp.

In the whole course of the war the town did
not depart from this pledge it had given. Its
little population of 1300 souls behaved like a
party to the contest. The number of its troops
constantly in service is very great. Its pecuniary
burdens are out of all proportion to its capital.
The economy so rigid, which marked its earlier
history, has all vanished. It spends profusely,
affectionately, in the service. "Since," say the
plaintive records, "General Washington, at Cambridge, is not able to give but 24s. per cord for
wood, for the army; it is Voted, that this town
encourage the inhabitants to supply the army,
by paying two dollars per cord, over and above
the General's price, to such as shall carry wood
thither;" and 210 cords of wood were carried.
A similar order is taken respecting hay. Whilst
Boston was occupied by the British troops,
Concord contributed to the relief of the inhabitants, £70, in money; 225 bushels of grain,
and a quantity of meat and wood. When, presently, the poor of Boston were quartered by the
Provincial Congress on the neighboring country,
Concord received 82 persons to its hospitality.

In the year 1775, it raised 100 minute-men, and 74 soldiers to serve at Cambridge. In March, 1776, 145 men were raised by this town to serve at Dorchester Heights.[1] In June, the General Assembly of Massachusetts resolved to raise 5000 militia for six months, to reinforce the Continental army. "The numbers," say they, "are large, but this Court has the fullest assurance that their brethren, on this occasion, will not confer with flesh and blood, but will, without hesitation, and with the utmost alacrity and despatch, fill up the numbers proportioned to the several towns."[2] On that occasion, Concord furnished 67 men, paving them itself, at an expense of £622. And so on, with every levy, to the end of the war. For these men it was continually providing shoes, stockings, shirts, coats, blankets and beef. The taxes, which, before the war, had not much exceeded £200 per annum, amounted, in the year 1782, to $9544, in silver.[3]

The great expense of the war was borne with cheerfulness, whilst the war lasted; but years passed, after the peace, before the debt was paid. As soon as danger and injury ceased, the people were left at leisure to consider their poverty and their debts. The Town Records show how slowly

the inhabitants recovered from the strain of
excessive exertion. Their instructions to their
representatives are full of loud complaints of the
disgraceful state of public credit, and the excess
of public expenditure. They may be pardoned,
under such distress, for the mistakes of an extreme frugality. They fell into a common error,
not yet dismissed to the moon, that the remedy
was, to forbid the great importation of foreign
commodities, and to prescribe by law the prices
of articles. The operation of a new government
was dreaded, lest it should prove expensive, and
the country towns thought it would be cheaper
if it were removed from the capital. They were
jealous lest the General Court should pay itself
too liberally, and our fathers must be forgiven
by their charitable posterity, if, in 1782, before
choosing a representative, it was "Voted, that
the person who should be chosen representative
to the General Court should receive 6s. per day,
whilst in actual service, an account of which
time he should bring to the town, and if it should
be that the General Court should resolve, that,
their pay should be more than 6s., then the
representative shall be hereby directed to pay
the overplus into the town treasury." This was
securing the prudence of the public servants.

But whilst the town had its own full share of the public distress, it was very far from desiring relief at the cost of order and law. In 1786, when the general sufferings drove the people in parts of Worcester and Hampshire counties to insurrection, a large party of armed insurgents arrived in this town, on the 12th September, to hinder the sitting of the Court of Common Pleas. But they found no countenance here.[1] The same people who had been active in a County Convention to consider grievances, condemned the rebellion, and joined the authorities in putting it down.[2] In 1787, the admirable instructions given by the town to its representative are a proud monument of the good sense and good feeling that prevailed. The grievances ceased with the adoption of the Federal Constitution. The constitution of Massachusetts had been already accepted. It was put to the town of Concord, in October, 1776, by the Legislature, whether the existing house of representatives should enact a constitution for the State? The town answered No.[3] The General Court, notwithstanding, draughted a constitution, sent it here, and asked the town whether they would have it for the law of the State? The town answered No, by a unanimous vote. In 1780, a

constitution of the State, proposed by the Con
vention chosen for that purpose, was accepte
by the town with the reservation of some art
cles.¹ And, in 1788, the town, by its delegat
accepted the new Constitution of the Unite
States, and this event closed the whole seri
of important public events in which this tow
played a part.

From that time to the present hour, this tow
has made a slow but constant progress in popu
lation and wealth, and the arts of peace. It h
suffered neither from war, nor pestilence, no
famine, nor flagrant crime. Its population,
the census of 183 , was 2 2 souls. The pub
lic expenses, for the last year, amounted
$4290 ; for the present year, to $3 4 . If th
community stints its expense in small matters,
spends freely on great duties. The town raise
this year, $18 for its public schools ; besid
about $12 which are paid by subscriptio
for private schools. This year, it expends $8
for its poor ; the last year it expended $0
Two religious societies, of differing creed, dwe
together in good understanding, both promo
ing, we hope, the cause of righteousness an
love. Concord has always been noted for i
ministers. The living need no praise of min

Yet it is among the sources of satisfaction and
gratitude, this day, that the aged with whom
is wisdom, our fathers' counsellor and friend, is
spared to counsel and intercede for the sons.'

Such, fellow citizens, is an imperfect sketch
of the history of Concord. I have been greatly
indebted, in preparing this sketch, to the printed
but unpublished History of this town, furnished
me by the unhesitating kindness of its author,
long a resident in this place. I hope that History will not long remain unknown. The author
has done us and posterity a kindness, by the
zeal and patience of his research, and has wisely
enriched his pages with the resolutions, addresses and instructions to its agents, which from
time to time, at critical periods, the town has
voted.' Meantime, I have read with care the
Town Records themselves. They must ever be
the fountains of all just information respecting
your character and customs. They are the history of the town. They exhibit a pleasing picture
of a community almost exclusively agricultural,
where no man has much time for words, in his
search after things ; of a community of great simplicity of manners, and of a manifest love of justice. For the most part, the town has deserved
the name it wears. I find our annals marked

with a uniform good sense I find no ridiculous
laws, no eavesdropping legislators, no hanging
of witches, no ghosts, no whipping of Quakers,
no unnatural crimes. The tone of the Records
rises with the dignity of the event. These soiled
and musty books are luminous and electric
within. The old town clerks did not spell very
correctly, but they contrive to make pretty intelligible the will of a free and just community
Frugal our fathers were, — very frugal, — though,
for the most part, they deal generously by their
minister, and provide well for the schools and
the poor. If, at any time, in common with most
of our towns, they have carried this economy to
the verge of a vice, it is to be remembered that
a town is, in many respects, a financial corporation. They economize, that they may sacrifice.
They stint and higgle on the price of a pew, that
they may send 200 soldiers to General Washington to keep Great Britain at bay. For splendor,
there must somewhere be rigid economy. That
the head of the house may go brave, the members must be plainly clad, and the town must
save that the State may spend. Of late years,
the growth of Concord has been slow Without
navigable waters, without mineral riches, without
any considerable mill privileges, the natural in-

crease of her population is drained by the constant emigration of the youth. Her sons have
settled the region around us, and far from us.
Their wagons have rattled down the remote
western hills. And in every part of this country, and in many foreign parts, they plough the
earth, they traverse the sea, they engage in trade
and in all the professions.'

Fellow citizens ; let not the solemn shadows
of two hundred years, this day, fall over us in
vain. I feel some unwillingness to quit the remembrance of the past. With all the hope of
the new I feel that we are leaving the old. Every
moment carries us farther from the two great
epochs of public principle, the Planting, and the
Revolution of the colony. Fortunate and favored this town has been, in having received so
large an infusion of the spirit of both of those
periods. Humble as is our village in the circle
of later and prouder towns that whiten the land,
it has been consecrated by the presence and
activity of the purest men. Why need I remind
you of our own Hosmers, Minotts, Cumings,
Barretts, Beattons, the departed benefactors of
the town ? On the village green have been the
steps of Winthrop and Dudley ; of John Eliot,
the Indian apostle, who had a courage that in-

timidated those savages whom his love could
not melt; of Whitfield, whose silver voice melted
his great congregation into tears; of Hancock,
and his compatriots of the Provincial Congress;
of Langdon, and the college over which he presided. But even more sacred influences than
these have mingled here with the stream of
human life. The merit of those who fill a space
in the world's history, who are borne forward,
as it were, by the weight of thousands whom
they lead, sheds a perfume less sweet than do the
sacrifices of private virtue. I have had much
opportunity of access to anecdotes of families,
and I believe this town to have been the dwell-
ing-place, in all times since its planting, of
pious and excellent persons, who walked meekly
through the paths of common life, who served
God, and loved man, and never let go the
hope of immortality. The benediction of their
prayers and of their principles lingers around us.
The acknowledgment of the Supreme Being
exalts the history of this people. It brought the
fathers hither. In a war of principle, it delivered their sons. And so long as a spark of this
faith survives among the children's children so
long shall the name of Concord be honest and
venerable.

III

LETTER

TO MARTIN VAN BUREN, PRESIDENT OF THE UNITED STATES

A PROTEST AGAINST THE REMOVAL OF THE CHEROKEE INDIANS FROM THE STATE OF GEORGIA

"Say, what is Honour? 'Tis the finest sense
Of justice which the human mind can frame,
Intent each lurking frailty to disclaim,
And guard the way of life from all offence,
Suffered or done."

WORDSWORTH.

LETTER

TO MARTIN VAN BUREN, PRESIDENT OF THE UNITED STATES

CONCORD, MASS., April 23, 1838.

SIR: The seat you fill places you in a relation of credit and nearness to every citizen. By right and natural position, every citizen is your friend. Before any acts contrary to his own judgment or interest have repelled the affections of any man, each may look with trust and living anticipation to your government. Each has the highest right to call your attention to such subjects as are of a public nature, and properly belong to the chief magistrate; and the good magistrate will feel a joy in meeting such confidence. In this belief and at the instance of a few of my friends and neighbors, I crave of your patience a short hearing for their sentiments and my own: and the circumstance that my name will be utterly unknown to you will only give the fairer chance to your equitable construction of what I have to say.

Sir, my communication respects the sinister rumors that fill this part of the country concerning the Cherokee people. The interest

always felt in the aboriginal population — an
interest naturally growing as that decays — has
been heightened in regard to this tribe. Even
in our distant State some good rumor of their
worth and civility has arrived. We have learned
with joy their improvement in the social arts.
We have read their newspapers We have seen
some of them in our schools and colleges. In
common with the great body of the American
people, we have witnessed with sympathy the
painful labors of these red men to redeem their
own race from the doom of eternal inferiority,
and to borrow and domesticate in the tribe the
arts and customs of the Caucasian race. And
notwithstanding the unaccountable apathy with
which of late years the Indians have been sometimes abandoned to their enemies, it is not to
be doubted that it is the good pleasure and the
understanding of all humane persons in the
Republic, of the men and the matrons sitting
in the thriving independent families all over the
land, that they shall be duly cared for; that
they shall taste justice and love from all to
whom we have delegated the office of dealing
with them.

The newspapers now inform us that, in
December, 1835, a treaty contracting for the

exchange of all the Cherokee territory was pretended to be made by an agent on the part of the United States with some persons appearing on the part of the Cherokees; that the fact afterwards transpired that these deputies did by no means represent the will of the nation; and that, out of eighteen thousand souls composing the nation, fifteen thousand six hundred and sixty-eight have protested against the so-called treaty. It now appears that the government of the United States choose to hold the Cherokees to this sham treaty, and are proceeding to execute the same. Almost the entire Cherokee Nation stand up and say, "This is not our act. Behold us. Here are we. Do not mistake that handful of deserters for us;" and the American President and the Cabinet, the Senate and the House of Representatives, neither hear these men nor see them, and are contracting to put this active nation into carts and boats, and to drag them over mountains and rivers to a wilderness at a vast distance beyond the Mississippi. And a paper purporting to be an army order fixes a month from this day as the hour for this doleful removal.

In the name of God, sir, we ask you if this be so. Do the newspapers rightly inform us?

Men and women with pale and perplexed faces meet one another in the streets and churches here, and ask if this be so. We have inquired if this be a gross misrepresentation from the party opposed to the government and anxious to blacken it with the people. We have looked in the newspapers of different parties and find a horrid confirmation of the tale. We are slow to believe it. We hoped the Indians were misinformed, and that their remonstrance was premature, and will turn out to be a needless act of terror.

The piety, the principle that is left in the United States, if only in its coarsest form, a regard to the speech of men, — forbid us to entertain it as a fact. Such a dereliction of all faith and virtue, such a denial of justice, and such deafness to screams for mercy were never heard of in times of peace and in the dealing of a nation with its own allies and wards, since the earth was made. Sir, does this government think that the people of the United States are become savage and mad? From their mind are the sentiments of love and a good nature wiped clean out? The soul of man, the justice, the mercy that is the heart's heart in all men, from Maine to Georgia, does abhor this business.

In speaking thus the sentiments of my neighbors and my own, perhaps I overstep the bounds of decorum. But would it not be a higher indecorum coldly to argue a matter like this? We only state the fact that a crime is projected that confounds our understandings by its magnitude, — a crime that really deprives us as well as the Cherokees of a country? for how could we call the conspiracy that should crush these poor Indians our government, or the land that was cursed by their parting and dying imprecations our country, any more? You, sir, will bring down that renowned chair in which you sit into infamy if your seal is set to this instrument of perfidy; and the name of this nation, hitherto the sweet omen of religion and liberty, will stink to the world.

You will not do us the injustice of connecting this remonstrance with any sectional and party feeling. It is in our hearts the simplest commandment of brotherly love. We will not have this great and solemn claim upon national and human justice huddled aside under the flimsy plea of its being a party act. Sir, to us the questions upon which the government and the people have been agitated during the past year, touching the prostration of the currency and of

trade, seem but motes in comparison. These
hard times, it is true, have brought the discussion home to every farmhouse and poor
man's house in this town; but it is the chirping
of grasshoppers beside the immortal question
whether justice shall be done by the race of
civilized to the race of savage man, — whether all
the attributes of reason, of civility, of justice,
and even of mercy, shall be put off by the
American people, and so vast an outrage upon
the Cherokee Nation and upon human nature
shall be consummated.

One circumstance lessens the reluctance with
which I intrude at this time on your attention
my conviction that the government ought to be
admonished of a new historical fact, which the
discussion of this question has disclosed, namely,
that there exists in a great part of the Northern
people a gloomy diffidence in the *moral* character of the government.

On the broaching of this question, a general
expression of despondency, of disbelief that any
good will accrue from a remonstrance on an act
of fraud and robbery, appeared in those men to
whom we naturally turn for aid and counsel
Will the American government steal? Will it
lie? Will it kill? — We ask triumphantly. Our

counsellors and old statesmen here say that ten
years ago they would have staked their lives on
the affirmation that the proposed Indian measures could not be executed ; that the unanimous
country would put them down. And now the
steps of this crime follow each other so fast, at
such fatally quick time, that the millions of virtuous citizens, whose agents the government are,
have no place to interpose, and must shut their
eyes until the last howl and wailing of these
tormented villages and tribes shall afflict the ear
of the world.

I will not hide from you, as an indication of
the alarming distrust, that a letter addressed as
mine is, and suggesting to the mind of the
Executive the plain obligations of man, has a
burlesque character in the apprehensions of some
of my friends. I, sir, will not beforehand treat
you with the contumely of this distrust. I will
at least state to you this fact, and show you how
plain and humane people, whose love would
be honor, regard the policy of the government,
and what injurious inferences they draw as to
the minds of the governors. A man with your
experience in affairs must have seen cause to
appreciate the futility of opposition to the moral
sentiment. However feeble the sufferer and

however great the oppressor, it is in the nature of things that the blow should recoil upon the aggressor For God is in the sentiment, and it cannot be withstood. The potentate and the people perish before it, but with it, and as its executor, they are omnipotent.

I write thus, sir, to inform you of the state of mind these Indian tidings have awakened here, and to pray with one voice more that you, whose hands are strong with the delegated power of fifteen millions of men, will avert with that might the terrific injury which threatens the Cherokee tribe.

With great respect, sir, I am your fellow citizen,

RALPH WALDO EMERSON

IV

ADDRESS

DELIVERED IN CONCORD ON THE ANNIVERSARY
OF THE EMANCIPATION OF THE NEGROES
IN THE BRITISH WEST INDIES,
AUGUST 1, 1844

THERE a captive sat in chains,
Crooning ditties treasured well
From his Afric's torrid plains
Sole estate his sire bequeathed, —
Hapless sire to hapless son, —
Was the wailing song he breathed
And his chain when life was done

ADDRESS

EMANCIPATION IN THE BRITISH WEST INDIES

FRIENDS AND FELLOW CITIZENS: We are
met to exchange congratulations on the
anniversary of an event singular in the history
of civilization; a day of reason; of the clear
light; of that which makes us better than a
flock of birds and beasts; a day which gave the
immense fortification of a fact, of gross history,
to ethical abstractions. It was the settlement, as
far as a great Empire was concerned, of a question on which almost every leading citizen in it
had taken care to record his vote; one which
for many years absorbed the attention of the
best and most eminent of mankind. I might
well hesitate, coming from other studies, and
without the smallest claim to be a special laborer
in this work of humanity, to undertake to set
this matter before you; which ought rather to
be done by a strict coöperation of many well-
advised persons; but I shall not apologize for
my weakness. In this cause, no man's weakness
is any prejudice: it has a thousand sons; if one

man cannot speak, ten others can ; and, whether
by the wisdom of its friends, or by the folly of
the adversaries; by speech and by silence; by
doing and by omitting to do, it goes forward
Therefore I will speak, — or, not I, but the
might of liberty in my weakness. The subject
is said to have the property of making dull men
eloquent.

It has been in all men's experience a marked
effect of the enterprise in behalf of the African,
to generate an overbearing and defying spirit.
The institution of slavery seems to its opponent
to have but one side, and he feels that none but
a stupid or a malignant person can hesitate on a
view of the facts. Under such an impulse, I was
about to say, If any cannot speak, or cannot
hear the words of freedom, let him go hence, —
I had almost said, Creep into your grave, the
universe has no need of you! But I have thought
better: let him not go. When we consider what
remains to be done for this interest in this country, the dictates of humanity make us tender of
such as are not yet persuaded.' The hardest
selfishness is to be borne with. Let us withhold
every reproachful, and, if we can, every indignant
remark. In this cause, we must renounce our
temper, and the risings of pride. If there be any

man who thinks the ruin of a race of men a small matter, compared with the last decoration and completions of his own comfort, — who would not so much as part with his ice-cream, to save them from rapine and manacles, I think I must not hesitate to satisfy that man that also his cream and vanilla are safer and cheaper by placing the negro nation on a fair footing than by robbing them. If the Virginian piques himself on the picturesque luxury of his vassalage, on the heavy Ethiopian manners of his house-servants, their silent obedience, their hue of bronze, their turbaned heads, and would not exchange them for the more intelligent but precarious hired service of whites, I shall not refuse to show him that when their free-papers are made out, it will still be their interest to remain on his estate, and that the oldest planters of Jamaica are convinced that it is cheaper to pay wages than to own the slave.

The history of mankind interests us only as it exhibits a steady gain of truth and right, in the incessant conflict which it records between the material and the moral nature. From the earliest monuments it appears that one race was victim and served the other races. In the oldest temples of Egypt, negro captives are painted on the

tombs of kings, in such attitudes as to show that
they are on the point of being executed; and
Herodotus, our oldest historian, relates that
the Troglodytes hunted the Ethiopians in four-
horse chariots From the earliest time, the negro
has been an article of luxury to the commercial
nations So has it been, down to the day that has
just dawned on the world Language must be
raked, the secrets of slaughter-houses and infa-
mous holes that cannot front the day, must be
ransacked, to tell what negro slavery has been.
These men, our benefactors, as they are producers of corn and wine, of coffee, of tobacco, of
cotton, of sugar, of rum and brandy, gentle and
joyous themselves, and producers of comfort and
luxury for the civilized world, — there seated in
the finest climates of the globe, children of the
sun, — I am heart-sick when I read how they
came there, and how they are kept there. Their
case was left out of the mind and out of the heart
of their brothers. The prizes of society, the
trumpet of fame, the privileges of learning, of
culture, of religion, the decencies and joys of
marriage, honor, obedience, personal authority
and a perpetual melioration into a finer civility,
— these were for all, but not for them. For the
negro, was the slave-ship to begin with, in whose

filthy hold he sat in irons, unable to lie down;
bad food, and insufficiency of that; disfranchise-
ment; no property in the rags that covered him;
no marriage, no right in the poor black woman
that cherished him in her bosom, no right to
the children of his body; no security from the
humors, none from the crimes, none from the
appetites of his master: toil, famine, insult and
flogging; and, when he sank in the furrow, no
wind of good fame blew over him, no priest of
salvation visited him with glad tidings: but
he went down to death with dusky dreams of
African shadow-catchers and Obeahs hunting
him.' Very sad was the negro tradition, that the
Great Spirit, in the beginning offered the black
man, whom he loved better than the buckra, or
white, his choice of two boxes, a big and a little
one. The black man was greedy, and chose the
largest. "The buckra box was full up with
pen, paper and whip, and the negro box with
hoe and bill; and hoe and bill for negro to this
day."

But the crude element of good in human
affairs must work and ripen, spite of whips and
plantation laws and West Indian interest. Conscience rolled on its pillow, and could not sleep.
We sympathize very tenderly here with the poor

aggrieved planter, of whom so many unpleasant
things are said, but if we saw the whip applied
to old men, to tender women; and, undeniably,
though I shrink to say so, pregnant women set
in the treadmill for refusing to work; when, not
they, but the eternal law of animal nature refused to work; — if we saw men's backs flayed
with cowhides, and " hot rum poured on, super-
induced with brine or pickle, rubbed in with a
cornhusk, in the scorching heat of the sun;" —
if we saw the runaways hunted with bloodhounds
into swamps and hills; and, in cases of passion,
a planter throwing his negro into a copper of
boiling cane-juice, — if we saw these things with
eyes, we too should wince. They are not pleasant sights. The blood is moral, the blood is
anti-slavery it runs cold in the veins· the stomach rises with disgust, and curses slavery. Well,
so it happened; a good man or woman, a country boy or girl, — it would so fall out, — once
in a while saw these injuries and had the indis-
cretion to tell of them The horrid story ran
and flew; the winds blew it all over the world.
They who heard it asked their rich and great
friends if it was true, or only missionary lies.
The richest and greatest, the prime minister of
England, the king's privy council were obliged

to say that it was too true. It became plain to
all men, the more this business was looked into,
that the crimes and cruelties of the slave-traders
and slave-owners could not be overstated. The
more it was searched, the more shocking anecdotes came up, — things not to be spoken. Humane persons who were informed of the reports
insisted on proving them   Granville Sharpe was
accidentally made acquainted with the sufferings
of a slave, whom a West Indian planter had
brought with him to London and had beaten
with a pistol on his head, so badly that his whole
body became diseased, and the man useless to
his master, who left him to go whither he pleased.
The man applied to Mr. William Sharpe, a charitable surgeon, who attended the diseases of the
poor. In process of time, he was healed. Granville Sharpe found him at his brother's and pro-
cured a place for him in an apothecary's shop.
The master accidentally met his recovered slave,
and instantly endeavored to get possession of
him again. Sharpe protected the slave. In consulting with the lawyers, they told Sharpe the
laws were against him. Sharpe would not believe
it; no prescription on earth could ever render
such iniquities legal. 'But the decisions are
against you, and Lord Mansfield, now Chief

Justice of England, leans to the decisions.'
Sharpe instantly sat down and gave himself to
the study of English law for more than two
years, until he had proved that the opinions relied on, of Talbot and Yorke, were incompatible
with the former English decisions and with the
whole spirit of English law. He published his
book in 1769, and he so filled the heads and
hearts of his advocates that when he brought the
case of George Somerset, another slave, before
Lord Mansfield, the slavish decisions were set
aside, and equity affirmed.' There is a sparkle
of God's righteousness in Lord Mansfield's
judgment, which does the heart good. Very
unwilling had that great lawyer been to reverse
the late decisions; he suggested twice from the
bench, in the course of the trial, how the question might be got rid of: but the hint was not
taken; the case was adjourned again and again,
and judgment delayed. At last judgment was
demanded, and on the 22d June, 1772, Lord
Mansfield is reported to have decided in these
words:

" Immemorial usage preserves the memory of
positive law, long after all traces of the occasion,
reason, authority and time of its introduction,
are lost; and in a case so odious as the condition

of slaves, must be taken strictly (tracing the subject to *natural principles*, the claim of slavery never can be supported). The power claimed by this return never was in use here. We cannot say the cause set forth by this return is allowed or approved of by the laws of this kingdom; and therefore the man must be discharged."

This decision established the principle that the "air of England is too pure for any slave to breathe," but the wrongs in the islands were not thereby touched. Public attention, however, was drawn that way, and the methods of the stealing and the transportation from Africa became noised abroad. The Quakers got the story. In their plain meeting-houses and prim dwellings this dismal agitation got entrance. They were rich: they owned, for debt or by inheritance, island property; they were religious, tender-hearted men and women; and they had to hear the news and digest it as they could. Six Quakers met in London on the 6th of July, 1783, — William Dillwyn, Samuel Hoar, George Harrison, Thomas Knowles, John Lloyd, Joseph Woods, "to consider what step they should take for the relief and liberation of the negro slaves in the West Indies, and for the discouragement of the slave-trade on the coast of Africa." They made

friends and raised money for the slave; they
interested their Yearly Meeting; and all English and all American Quakers. John Woolman
of New Jersey, whilst yet an apprentice, was
uneasy in his mind when he was set to write a
bill of sale of a negro, for his master. He gave
his testimony against the traffic, in Maryland
and Virginia. Thomas Clarkson was a youth
at Cambridge, England, when the subject given
out for a Latin prize dissertation was, " Is it
right to make slaves of others against their will?"
He wrote an essay, and won the prize; but he
wrote too well for his own peace; he began to
ask himself if these things could be true; and
if they were, he could no longer rest. He left
Cambridge, he fell in with the six Quakers.
They engaged him to act for them. He himself
interested Mr. Wilberforce in the matter. The
shipmasters in that trade were the greatest mis-
creants, and guilty of every barbarity to their own
crews. Clarkson went to Bristol, made himself
acquainted with the interior of the slave-ships
and the details of the trade. The facts confirmed
his sentiment, " that Providence had never made
that to be wise which was immoral, and that the
slave-trade was as impolitic as it was unjust,"'
that it was found peculiarly fatal to those

employed in it. More seamen died in that trade in one year than in the whole remaining trade of the country in two. Mr. Pitt and Mr. Fox were drawn into the generous enterprise. In 1788, the House of Commons voted Parliamentary inquiry. In 1791, a bill to abolish the trade was brought in by Wilberforce, and supported by him and by Fox and Burke and Pitt, with the utmost ability and faithfulness ; resisted by the planters and the whole West Indian interest, and lost. During the next sixteen years, ten times, year after year, the attempt was renewed by Mr. Wilberforce, and ten times defeated by the planters. The king, and all the royal family but one, were against it. These debates are instructive, as they show on what grounds the trade was assailed and defended. Everything generous, wise and sprightly is sure to come to the attack. On the other part are found cold prudence, barefaced selfishness and silent votes. But the nation was aroused to enthusiasm. Every horrid fact became known. In 1791, three hundred thousand persons in Britain pledged themselves to abstain from all articles of island produce. The planters were obliged to give way ; and in 1807, on the 25th March, the bill passed, and the slave-trade was abolished.

The assailants of slavery had early agreed to limit their political action on this subject to the abolition of the trade, but Granville Sharpe, as a matter of conscience, whilst he acted as chairman of the London Committee, felt constrained to record his protest against the limitation, declaring that slavery was as much a crime against the Divine law as the slave-trade. The trade, under false flags, went on as before. In 1821, according to official documents presented to the American government by the Colonization Society, 200,000 slaves were deported from Africa. Nearly 30,000 were landed in the port of Havana alone. In consequence of the dangers of the trade growing out of the act of abolition, ships were built sharp for swiftness, and with a frightful disregard of the comfort of the victims they were destined to transport. They carried five, six, even seven hundred stowed in a ship built so narrow as to be unsafe, being made just broad enough on the beam to keep the sea. In attempting to make its escape from the pursuit of a man-of-war, one ship flung five hundred slaves alive into the sea. These facts went into Parliament. In the islands was an ominous state of cruel and licentious society; every house had a dungeon attached to it; every slave was worked

by the whip. There is no end to the tragic anecdotes in the municipal records of the colonies.
The boy was set to strip and flog his own
mother to blood, for a small offence. Looking
in the face of his master by the negro was held
to be violence by the island courts. He was
worked sixteen hours, and his ration by law, in
some islands, was a pint of flour and one salt
herring a day. He suffered insult, stripes, mutilation at the humor of the master: iron collars
were riveted on their necks with iron prongs ten
inches long; capsicum pepper was rubbed in
the eyes of the females; and they were done to
death with the most shocking levity between the
master and manager, without fine or inquiry.
And when, at last, some Quakers, Moravians,
and Wesleyan and Baptist missionaries, following in the steps of Carey and Ward in the East
Indies, had been moved to come and cheer the
poor victim with the hope of some reparation,
in a future world, of the wrongs he suffered in
this, these missionaries were persecuted by the
planters, their lives threatened, their chapels
burned, and the negroes furiously forbidden to
go near them. These outrages rekindled the
flame of British indignation. Petitions poured
into Parliament: a million persons signed their

names to these; and in 1833, on the 14th May, Lord Stanley, Minister of the Colonies, introduced into the House of Commons his bill for the Emancipation.

The scheme of the Minister, with such modification as it received in the legislature, proposed gradual emancipation; that on 1st August, 1834, all persons now slaves should be entitled to be registered as apprenticed laborers, and to acquire thereby all the rights and privileges of freemen, subject to the restriction of laboring under certain conditions. These conditions were, that the prædials should owe three fourths of the profits of their labor to their masters for six years, and the non-prædials for four years.' The other fourth of the apprentice's time was to be his own, which he might sell to his master, or to other persons; and at the end of the term of years fixed, he should be free.

With these provisions and conditions, the bill proceeds, in the twelfth section, in the following terms: " Be it enacted, that all and every person who, on the first August, 1834, shall be holden in slavery within any such British colony as aforesaid, shall upon and from and after the said first August, become and be to all intents and purposes free, and discharged of and from all manner of slavery, and shall be absolutely and forever manumitted; and that the children thereafter born to any such persons, and the offspring of such children, shall, in like manner, be free, from their birth; and that from and after the first August, 1834, slavery shall be and is hereby utterly and forever abolished and declared unlawful throughout the British colonies, plantations, and possessions abroad."

The Ministers, having estimated the slave products of the colonies in annual exports of sugar, rum and coffee, at £1,500,000 per annum, estimated the total value of the slave property at 30,000,000 pounds sterling, and proposed to give the planters, as a compensation for so much of the slaves' time as the act took from them, 20,000,000 pounds sterling, to be divided into nineteen shares for the nineteen colonies, and to be distributed to the owners of slaves by commissioners, whose appointment and duties were regulated by the Act. After much debate, the bill passed by large majorities. The apprenticeship system is understood to have proceeded from Lord Brougham, and was by him urged on his colleagues, who, it is said, were inclined to the policy of immediate emancipation.

The colonial legislatures received the act of

XI

Parliament with various degrees of displeasure; and, of course, every provision of the bill was criticised with severity. The new relation between the master and the apprentice, it was feared, would be mischievous; for the bill required the appointment of magistrates who should hear every complaint of the apprentice and see that justice was done him. It was feared that the interest of the master and servant would now produce perpetual discord between them In the island of Antigua, containing 37,000 people, 30,000 being negroes, these objections had such weight that the legislature rejected the apprenticeship system, and adopted absolute emancipation. In the other islands the system of the Ministry was accepted.

The reception of it by the negro population was equal in nobleness to the deed. The negroes were called together by the missionaries and by the planters, and the news explained to them. On the night of the 31st July, they met everywhere at their churches and chapels, and at midnight, when the clock struck twelve, on their knees, the silent, weeping assembly became men; they rose and embraced each other; they cried, they sung, they prayed, they were wild with joy, but there was no riot, no feasting. I

have never read anything in history more touching than the moderation of the negroes. Some
American captains left the shore and put to sea,
anticipating insurrection and general murder.
With far different thoughts, the negroes spent
the hour in their huts and chapels. I will not
repeat to you the well-known paragraph, in
which Messrs. Thome and Kimball, the commissioners sent out in the year 1837 by the
American Anti-Slavery Society, describe the occurrences of that night in the island of Antigua.
It has been quoted in every newspaper, and
Dr. Channing has given it additional fame. But
I must be indulged in quoting a few sentences
from the pages that follow it, narrating the
behavior of the emancipated people on the next
day.'

"The first of August came on Friday, and
a release was proclaimed from all work until the
next Monday. The day was chiefly spent by
the great mass of the negroes in the churches and
chapels. The clergy and missionaries throughout the island were actively engaged, seizing the
opportunity to enlighten the people on all the
duties and responsibilities of their new relation,
and urging them to the attainment of that higher
liberty with which Christ maketh his children

free. In every quarter, we were assured, the day was like a Sabbath. Work had ceased. The hum of business was still: tranquillity pervaded the towns and country. The planters informed us that they went to the chapels where their own people were assembled, greeted them, shook hands with them, and exchanged the most hearty good wishes. At Grace Hill, there were at least a thousand persons around the Moravian Chapel who could not get in. For once the house of God suffered violence, and the violent took it by force. At Grace Bay, the people, all dressed in white, formed a procession, and walked arm in arm into the chapel. We were told that the dress of the negroes on that occasion was uncommonly simple and modest. There was not the least disposition to gayety. Throughout the island, there was not a single dance known of, either day or night, nor so much as a fiddle played."

On the next Monday morning, with very few exceptions, every negro on every plantation was in the field at his work. In some places, they waited to see their master, to know what bargain he would make; but for the most part, throughout the islands, nothing painful occurred In June, 1835, the Ministers, Lord Aberdeen and

Sir George Grey, declared to the Parliament that the system worked well; that now for ten months, from 1st August, 1834, no injury or violence had been offered to any white, and only one black had been hurt in 800,000 negroes: and, contrary to many sinister predictions, that the new crop of island produce would not fall short of that of the last year.

But the habit of oppression was not destroyed by a law and a day of jubilee. It soon appeared in all the islands that the planters were disposed to use their old privileges, and overwork the apprentices; to take from them, under various pretences, their fourth part of their time; and to exert the same licentious despotism as before. The negroes complained to the magistrates and to the governor. In the island of Jamaica, this ill blood continually grew worse. The governors, Lord Belmore, the Earl of Sligo, and afterwards Sir Lionel Smith (a governor of their own class, who had been sent out to gratify the planters), threw themselves on the side of the oppressed, and were at constant quarrel with the angry and bilious island legislature. Nothing can exceed the ill humor and sulkiness of the addresses of this assembly.

I may here express a general remark, which

the history of slavery seems to justify, that it is
not founded solely on the avarice of the planter.
We sometimes say, the planter does not want
slaves, he only wants the immunities and the
luxuries which the slaves yield him ; give him
money, give him a machine that will yield him
as much money as the slaves, and he will thankfully let them go   He has no love of slavery,
he wants luxury, and he will pay even this price
of crime and danger for it.   But I think experience does not warrant this favorable distinction,
but shows the existence, beside the covetousness,
of a bitterer element, the love of power, the
voluptuousness of holding a human being in his
absolute control. We sometimes observe that
spoiled children contract a habit of annoying
quite wantonly those who have charge of them,
and seem to measure their own sense of well-
being, not by what they do, but by the degree
of reaction they can cause. It is vain to get rid
of them by not minding them : if purring and
humming is not noticed, they squeal and screech ;
then if you chide and console them, they find
the experiment succeeds, and they begin again.
The child will sit in your arms contented, provided you do nothing. If you take a book and
read, he commences hostile operations.   The

planter is the spoiled child of his unnatural
habits, and has contracted in his indolent and
luxurious climate the need of excitement by irri-
tating and tormenting his slave.

Sir Lionel Smith defended the poor negro
girls, prey to the licentiousness of the planters ;
they shall not be whipped with tamarind rods
if they do not comply with their master's will;
he defended the negro women; they should not
be made to dig the cane-holes (which is the very
hardest of the field work); he defended the
Baptist preachers and the stipendiary magistrates,
who are the negroes' friends, from the power of
the planter. The power of the planters, however,
to oppress, was greater than the power of the
apprentice and of his guardians to withstand.
Lord Brougham and Mr. Buxton declared that
the planter had not fulfilled his part in the
contract, whilst the apprentices had fulfilled
theirs; and demanded that the emancipation
should be hastened, and the apprenticeship abolished. Parliament was compelled to pass additional laws for the defence and security of the
negro, and in ill humor at these acts, the great
island of Jamaica, with a population of half a
million, and 300,000 negroes, early in 1838,
resolved to throw up the two remaining years of

apprenticeship, and to emancipate absolutely
on the 1st August, 1838. In British Guiana, in
Dominica, the same resolution had been earlier
taken with more good will; and the other islands
fell into the measure; so that on the 1st August,
1838, the shackles dropped from every British
slave. The accounts which we have from all
parties, both from the planters (and those too
who were originally most opposed to the measure), and from the new freemen, are of the
most satisfactory kind. The manner in which
the new festival was celebrated, brings tears to
the eyes. The First of August, 1838, was observed in Jamaica as a day of thanksgiving and
prayer. Sir Lionel Smith, the governor, writes
to the British Ministry, "It is impossible for
me to do justice to the good order, decorum and gratitude which the whole laboring
population manifested on that happy occasion.
Though joy beamed on every countenance, it
was throughout tempered with solemn thank-
fulness to God, and the churches and chapels
were everywhere filled with these happy people
in humble offering of praise."

The Queen, in her speech to the Lords and
Commons, praised the conduct of the emancipated population:' and in 1840 Sir Charles

Metcalfe, the new governor of Jamaica, in his address to the Assembly expressed himself to that late exasperated body in these terms: "All those who are acquainted with the state of the island know that our emancipated population are as free, as independent in their conduct, as well conditioned, as much in the enjoyment of abundance, and as strongly sensible of the blessings of liberty, as any that we know of in any country. All disqualifications and distinctions of color have ceased; men of all colors have equal rights in law, and an equal footing in society, and every man's position is settled by the same circumstances which regulate that point in other free countries, where no difference of color exists. It may be asserted, without fear of denial, that the former slaves of Jamaica are now as secure in all social rights, as freeborn Britons." He further describes the erection of numerous churches, chapels and schools which the new population required, and adds that more are still demanded. The legislature, in their reply, echo the governor's statement, and say, "The peaceful demeanor of the emancipated population redounds to their own credit, and affords a proof of their continued comfort and prosperity."

I said, this event is signal in the history of civilization. There are many styles of civilization, and not one only. Ours is full of barbarities. There are many faculties in man, each of which takes its turn of activity, and that faculty which is paramount in any period and exerts itself through the strongest nation, determines the civility of that age: and each age thinks its own the perfection of reason. Our culture is very cheap and intelligible. Unroof any house, and you shall find it. The well-being consists in having a sufficiency of coffee and toast, with a daily newspaper; a well glazed parlor, with marbles, mirrors and centre-table; and the excitement of a few parties and a few rides in a year. Such as one house, such are all. The owner of a New York manor imitates the mansion and equipage of the London nobleman; the Boston merchant rivals his brother of New York; and the villages copy Boston. There have been nations elevated by great sentiments. Such was the civility of Sparta and the Dorian race, whilst it was defective in some of the chief elements of ours. That of Athens, again, lay in an intellect dedicated to beauty. That of Asia Minor in poetry, music and arts; that of Palestine in piety; that of Rome in military

arts and virtues, exalted by a prodigious magnanimity ; that of China and Japan in the last
exaggeration of decorum and etiquette. Our
civility, England determines the style of, inasmuch as England is the strongest of the family
of existing nations, and as we are the expansion
of that people. It is that of a trading nation ;
it is a shopkeeping civility. The English lord
is a retired shopkeeper, and has the prejudices
and timidities of that profession. And we are
shopkeepers, and have acquired the vices and
virtues that belong to trade. We peddle, we
truck, we sail, we row, we ride in cars, we creep
in teams, we go in canals, — to market, and for
the sale of goods. The national aim and employment streams into our ways of thinking,
our laws, our habits and our manners. The
customer is the immediate jewel of our souls.
Him we flatter, him we feast, compliment, vote
for, and will not contradict. It was, or it seemed
the dictate of trade, to keep the negro down.
We had found a race who were less warlike,
and less energetic shopkeepers than we; who
had very little skill in trade. We found it very
convenient to keep them at work, since, by the
aid of a little whipping, we could get their work
for nothing but their board and the cost of

whips. What if it cost a few unpleasant scenes on the coast of Africa? That was a great way off; and the scenes could be endured by some sturdy, unscrupulous fellows, who could go, for high wages, and bring us the men, and need not trouble our ears with the disagreeable particulars. If any mention was made of homicide, madness, adultery, and intolerable tortures, we would let the church-bells ring louder, the church-organ swell its peal and drown the hideous sound. The sugar they raised was excellent: nobody tasted blood in it. The coffee was fragrant; the tobacco was incense; the brandy made nations happy; the cotton clothed the world. What! all raised by these men, and no wages? Excellent! What a convenience! They seemed created by Providence to bear the heat and the whipping, and make these fine articles.

But unhappily, most unhappily, gentlemen, man is born with intellect, as well as with a love of sugar; and with a sense of justice, as well as a taste for strong drink. These ripened, as well as those. You could not educate him, you could not get any poetry, any wisdom, any beauty in woman, any strong and commanding character in man, but these absurdities would still come flashing out, — these absurdities of a demand

for justice, a generosity for the weak and oppressed. Unhappily, too, for the planter, the
laws of nature are in harmony with each other:
that which the head and the heart demand is
found to be, in the long run, for what the gross-
est calculator calls his advantage. The moral
sense is always supported by the permanent
interest of the parties. Else, I know not how, in
our world, any good would ever get done.' It
was shown to the planters that they, as well as
the negroes, were slaves ; that though they paid
no wages, they got very poor work ; that their
estates were ruining them, under the finest climate ; and that they needed the severest monopoly laws at home to keep them from bankruptcy. The oppression of the slave recoiled
on them. They were full of vices ; their children were lumps of pride, sloth, sensuality and
rottenness. The position of woman was nearly
as bad as it could be ; and, like other robbers,
they could not sleep in security. Many planters have said, since the emancipation, that, before that day, they were the greatest slaves on
the estates. Slavery is no scholar, no improver;
it does not love the whistle of the railroad ; it
does not love the newspaper, the mail-bag, a
college, a book or a preacher who has the absurd

whim of saying what he thinks; it does not increase the white population; it does not improve
the soil; everything goes to decay. For these
reasons the islands proved bad customers to
England. It was very easy for manufacturers less
shrewd than those of Birmingham and Manches-
ter to see that if the state of things in the islands
was altered, if the slaves had wages, the slaves
would be clothed, would build houses, would
fill them with tools, with pottery, with crockery,
with hardware, and negro women love fine
clothes as well as white women. In every naked
negro of those thousands, they saw a future
customer. Meantime, they saw further that the
slave-trade, by keeping in barbarism the whole
coast of eastern Africa, deprives them of countries and nations of customers, if once freedom
and civility and European manners could get a
foothold there But the trade could not be abolished whilst this hungry West Indian market,
with an appetite like the grave, cried, ' More,
more, bring me a hundred a day ;' they could
not expect any mitigation in the madness of the
poor African war-chiefs. These considerations
opened the eyes of the dullest in Britain. More
than this, the West Indian estate was owned or
mortgaged in England, and the owner and the

mortgagee had very plain intimations that the
feeling of English liberty was gaining every hour
new mass and velocity, and the hostility to such
as resisted it would be fatal. The House of
Commons would destroy the protection of island
produce, and interfere in English politics in the
island legislation: so they hastened to make
the best of their position, and accepted the bill.

These considerations, I doubt not, had their
weight; the interest of trade, the interest of the
revenue, and, moreover, the good fame of the
action. It was inevitable that men should feel
these motives. But they do not appear to have
had an excessive or unreasonable weight. On
reviewing this history, I think the whole transaction reflects infinite honor on the people and
parliament of England. It was a stately spectacle, to see the cause of human rights argued
with so much patience and generosity and with
such a mass of evidence before that powerful
people. It is a creditable incident in the history
that when, in 1789, the first privy council report of evidence on the trade (a bulky folio
embodying all the facts which the London Committee had been engaged for years in collecting,
and all the examinations before the council) was
presented to the House of Commons, a late day

being named for the discussion, in order to give
members time, — Mr. Wilberforce, Mr. Pitt,
the Prime Minister, and other gentlemen, took
advantage of the postponement to retire into the
country to read the report. For months and
years the bill was debated, with some consciousness of the extent of its relations, by the first citizens of England, the foremost men of the earth;
every argument was weighed, every particle of
evidence was sifted and laid in the scale, and,
at last, the right triumphed, the poor man was
vindicated, and the oppressor was flung out.
I know that England has the advantage of try-
ing the question at a wide distance from the spot
where the nuisance exists; the planters are not,
excepting in rare examples, members of the legislature. The extent of the empire, and the magnitude and number of other questions crowding
into court, keep this one in balance, and prevent
it from obtaining that ascendency, and being
urged with that intemperance which a question
of property tends to acquire. There are causes
in the composition of the British legislature, and
the relation of its leaders to the country and to
Europe, which exclude much that is pitiful and
injurious in other legislative assemblies. From
these reasons, the question was discussed with

a rare independence and magnanimity. It was not narrowed down to a paltry electioneering trap ; and, I must say, a delight in justice, an honest tenderness for the poor negro, for man suffering these wrongs, combined with the national pride, which refused to give the support of English soil or the protection of the English flag to these disgusting violations of nature.

Forgive me, fellow citizens, if I own to you, that in the last few days that my attention has been occupied with this history, I have not been able to read a page of it without the most painful comparisons. Whilst I have read of England, I have thought of New England. Whilst I have meditated in my solitary walks on the magnanimity of the English Bench and Senate, reaching out the benefit of the law to the most helpless citizen in her world-wide realm, I have found myself oppressed by other thoughts. As I have walked in the pastures and along the edge of woods, I could not keep my imagination on those agreeable figures, for other images that intruded on me. I could not see the great vision of the patriots and senators who have adopted the slave's cause : — they turned their backs on me. No : I see other pictures, — of mean men ; I see very poor, very ill-clothed,

XI

very ignorant men, not surrounded by happy friends, — to be plain, — poor black men of obscure employment as mariners, cooks or stewards, in ships, yet citizens of this our Commonwealth of Massachusetts, — freeborn as we, — whom the slave-laws of the States of South Carolina, Georgia and Louisiana have arrested in the vessels in which they visited those ports, and shut up in jails so long as the vessel remained in port, with the stringent addition, that if the shipmaster fails to pay the costs of this official arrest and the board in jail, these citizens are to be sold for slaves, to pay that expense. This man, these men, I see, and no law to save them. Fellow citizens, this crime will not be hushed up any longer I have learned that a citizen of Nantucket, walking in New Orleans, found a freeborn citizen of Nantucket, a man, too, of great personal worth, and, as it happened, very dear to him, as having saved his own life, working chained in the streets of that city, kidnapped by such a process as this. In the sleep of the laws, the private interference of two excellent citizens of Boston has, I have ascertained, rescued several natives of this State from these Southern prisons. Gentlemen, I thought the deck of a Massachusetts ship was as much the

territory of Massachusetts as the floor on which
we stand. It should be as sacred as the temple
of God. The poorest fishing-smack that floats
under the shadow of an iceberg in the Northern
seas, or hunts whale in the Southern ocean,
should be encompassed by her laws with comfort and protection, as much as within the arms
of Cape Ann or Cape Cod. And this kidnapping is suffered within our own land and fed-
eration, whilst the fourth article of the Constitution of the United States ordains in terms,
that, " The citizens of each State shall be entitled to all privileges and immunities of citizens
in the several States." If such a damnable
outrage can be committed on the person of a
citizen with impunity, let the Governor break
the broad seal of the State ; he bears the sword
in vain.' The Governor of Massachusetts is a
trifler ; the State-House in Boston is a play-
house ; the General Court is a dishonored body,
if they make laws which they cannot execute.
The great-hearted Puritans have left no posterity. The rich men may walk in State Street,
but they walk without honor ; and the farmers
may brag their democracy in the country, but
they are disgraced men. If the State has no
power to defend its own people in its own

shipping, because it has delegated that power to the Federal Government, has it no representation in the Federal Government?' Are those men dumb? I am no lawyer, and cannot indicate the forms applicable to the case, but here is something which transcends all forms. Let the senators and representatives of the State, containing a population of a million freemen, go in a body before the Congress and say that they have a demand to make on them, so imperative that all functions of government must stop until it is satisfied. If ordinary legislation cannot reach it, then extraordinary must be applied. The Congress should instruct the President to send to those ports of Charleston, Savannah and New Orleans such orders and such force as should release, forthwith, all such citizens of Massachusetts as were holden in prison without the allegation of any crime, and should set on foot the strictest inquisition to discover where such persons, brought into slavery by these local laws at any time heretofore, may now be. That first; and then, let order be taken to indemnify all such as have been incarcerated. As for dangers to the Union, from such demands! — the Union already is at an end when the first citizen of Massachusetts is thus

outraged. Is it an union and covenant in
which the State of Massachusetts agrees to be
imprisoned, and the State of Carolina to im-
prison?' Gentlemen, I am loath to say harsh
things, and perhaps I know too little of politics
for the smallest weight to attach to any censure
of mine, — but I am at a loss how to character-
ize the tameness and silence of the two senators
and the ten representatives of the State at
Washington. To what purpose have we clothed
each of those representatives with the power
of seventy thousand persons, and each senator
with near half a million, if they are to sit dumb
at their desks and see their constituents captured
and sold ; — perhaps to gentlemen sitting by
them in the hall? There is a scandalous rumor
that has been swelling louder of late years, —
perhaps wholly false, — that members are bul-
lied into silence by Southern gentlemen. It is
so easy to omit to speak, or even to be absent
when delicate things are to be handled. I may
as well say, what all men feel, that whilst our
very amiable and very innocent representatives
and senators at Washington are accomplished
lawyers and merchants, and very eloquent at
dinners and at caucuses, there is a disastrous
want of *men* from New England. I would gladly

make exceptions, and you will not suffer me to
forget one eloquent old man, in whose veins the
blood of Massachusetts rolls, and who singly
has defended the freedom of speech, and the
rights of the free, against the usurpation of the
slave-holder.' But the reader of Congressional
debates, in New England, is perplexed to see
with what admirable sweetness and patience the
majority of the free States are schooled and
ridden by the minority of slave-holders. What
if we should send thither representatives who
were a particle less amiable and less innocent?
I entreat you, sirs, let not this stain attach, let
not this misery accumulate any longer. If the
managers of our political parties are too prudent
and too cold;—if, most unhappily, the ambi-
tious class of young men and political men have
found out that these neglected victims are poor
and without weight; that they have no graceful
hospitalities to offer, no valuable business to
throw into any man's hands, no strong vote to
cast at the elections, and therefore may with
impunity be left in their chains or to the chance
of chains,—then let the citizens in their primary capacity take up their cause on this very
ground, and say to the government of the State,
and of the Union, that government exists to

defend the weak and the poor and the injured
party; the rich and the strong can better take
care of themselves. And as an omen and assurance of success, I point you to the bright
example which England set you, on this day,
ten years ago.

There are other comparisons and other imperative duties which come sadly to mind, —
but I do not wish to darken the hours of this
day by crimination; I turn gladly to the rightful
theme, to the bright aspects of the occasion.

This event was a moral revolution. The history of it is before you. Here was no prodigy,
no fabulous hero, no Trojan horse, no bloody
war, but all was achieved by plain means of plain
men, working not under a leader, but under a
sentiment. Other revolutions have been the insurrection of the oppressed; this was the repentance of the tyrant. It was the masters revolting
from their mastery. The slave-holder said, ' I
will not hold slaves.' The end was noble and
the means were pure. Hence the elevation and
pathos of this chapter of history. The lives of
the advocates are pages of greatness, and the
connection of the eminent senators with this
question constitutes the immortalizing moments
of those men's lives. The bare enunciation of

the theses at which the lawyers and legislators
arrived, gives a glow to the heart of the reader
Lord Chancellor Northington is the author of
the famous sentence, " As soon as any man puts
his foot on English ground, he becomes free."
" I was a slave," said the counsel of Somerset,
speaking for his client, " for I was in America :
I am now in a country where the common rights
of mankind are known and regarded." Granville Sharpe filled the ear of the judges with the
sound principles that had from time to time been
affirmed by the legal authorities : " Derived
power cannot be superior to the power from
which it is derived :" " The reasonableness of
the law is the soul of the law " " It is better
to suffer every evil, than to consent to any "
Out it would come, the God's truth, out it
came, like a bolt from a cloud, for all the
mumbling of the lawyers. One feels very sen-
sibly in all this history that a great heart and
soul are behind there, superior to any man, and
making use of each, in turn, and infinitely attractive to every person according to the degree
of reason in his own mind, so that this cause
has had the power to draw to it every particle
of talent and of worth in England, from the
beginning. All the great geniuses of the British

senate, Fox, Pitt, Burke, Grenville, Sheridan,
Grey, Canning, ranged themselves on its side;
the poet Cowper wrote for it: Franklin, Jefferson, Washington, in this country, all recorded
their votes. All men remember the subtlety and
the fire of indignation which the " Edinburgh
Review " contributed to the cause ; and every
liberal mind, poet, preacher, moralist, statesman,
has had the fortune to appear somewhere for
this cause. On the other part, appeared the
reign of pounds and shillings, and all manner of
rage and stupidity ; a resistance which drew from
Mr. Huddlestone in Parliament the observation, " That a curse attended this trade even in
the mode of defending it. By a certain fatality,
none but the vilest arguments were brought
forward, which corrupted the very persons who
used them. Every one of these was built on the
narrow ground of interest, of pecuniary profit,
of sordid gain, in opposition to every motive
that had reference to humanity, justice, and religion, or to that great principle which compre-
hended them all." This moral force perpetually
reinforces and dignifies the friends of this cause.
It gave that tenacity to their point which has
insured ultimate triumph ; and it gave that
superiority in reason, in imagery, in eloquence,

which makes in all countries anti-slavery meetings so attractive to the people, and has made
it a proverb in Massachusetts, that "eloquence
is dog-cheap at the anti-slavery chapel."

I will say further that we are indebted mainly
to this movement and to the continuers of it,
for the popular discussion of every point of practical ethics, and a reference of every question to
the absolute standard. It is notorious that the
political, religious and social schemes, with which
the minds of men are now most occupied, have
been matured, or at least broached, in the free
and daring discussions of these assemblies. Men
have become aware, through the emancipation
and kindred events, of the presence of powers
which, in their days of darkness, they had overlooked Virtuous men will not again rely on
political agents. They have found out the dele-
terious effect of political association. Up to this
day we have allowed to statesmen a paramount
social standing, and we bow low to them as to
the great. We cannot extend this deference
to them any longer. The secret cannot be kept,
that the seats of power are filled by underlings,
ignorant, timid and selfish to a degree to destroy
all claim, excepting that on compassion, to the
society of the just and generous. What happened

notoriously to an American ambassador in
England, that he found himself compelled to
palter and to disguise the fact that he was a
slave-breeder, happens to men of state. Their
vocation is a presumption against them among
well-meaning people. The superstition respecting power and office is going to the ground. The
stream of human affairs flows its own way, and
is very little affected by the activity of legislators. What great masses of men wish done,
will be done ; and they do not wish it for a
freak, but because it is their state and natural
end. There are now other energies than force,
other than political, which no man in future
can allow himself to disregard. There is direct
conversation and influence. A man is to make
himself felt by his proper force. The tendency
of things runs steadily to this point, namely, to
put every man on his merits, and to give him
so much power as he naturally exerts, — no
more, no less. Of course, the timid and base
persons, all who are conscious of no worth in
themselves, and who owe all their place to the
opportunities which the older order of things
allowed them, to deceive and defraud men,
shudder at the change, and would fain silence
every honest voice, and lock up every house

where liberty and innovation can be pleaded for.
They would raise mobs, for fear is very cruel.
But the strong and healthy yeomen and husbands
of the land, the self-sustaining class of inventive
and industrious men, fear no competition or
superiority. Come what will, their faculty cannot
be spared.

The First of August marks the entrance of
a new element into modern politics, namely, the
civilization of the negro. A man is added to
the human family. Not the least affecting part
of this history of abolition is the annihilation of
the old indecent nonsense about the nature
of the negro. In the case of the ship Zong, in
1781, whose master had thrown one hundred
and thirty-two slaves alive into the sea, to cheat
the underwriters, the first jury gave a verdict
in favor of the master and owners: they had
a right to do what they had done. Lord Mansfield is reported to have said on the bench,
"The matter left to the jury is, — Was it from
necessity? For they had no doubt — though
it shocks one very much — that the case of
slaves was the same as if horses had been thrown
overboard. It is a very shocking case." But a
more enlightened and humane opinion began to
prevail. Mr. Clarkson, early in his career, made

a collection of African productions and manufactures, as specimens of the arts and culture of
the negro; comprising cloths and loom, weapons,
polished stones and woods, leather, glass, dyes,
ornaments, soap, pipe-bowls and trinkets. These
he showed to Mr. Pitt, who saw and handled
them with extreme interest. " On sight of these,"
says Clarkson, " many sublime thoughts seemed
to rush at once into his mind, some of which
he expressed ;" and hence appeared to arise a
project which was always dear to him, of the
civilization of Africa, — a dream which forever
elevates his fame. In 1791, Mr. Wilberforce
announced to the House of Commons, " We
have already gained one victory : we have obtained for these poor creatures the recognition of
their human nature, which for a time was most
shamefully denied them." It was the sarcasm
of Montesquieu, " it would not do to suppose
that negroes were men, lest it should turn out
that whites were not;" for the white has, for
ages, done what he could to keep the negro in
that hoggish state. His laws have been furies.
It now appears that the negro race is, more than
any other, susceptible of rapid civilization. The
emancipation is observed, in the islands, to have
wrought for the negro a benefit as sudden as

when a thermometer is brought out of the shade into the sun. It has given him eyes and ears. If, before, he was taxed with such stupidity, or such defective vision, that he could not set a table square to the walls of an apartment, he is now the principal if not the only mechanic in the West Indies ; and is, besides, an architect, a physician, a lawyer, a magistrate, an editor, and a valued and increasing political power. The recent testimonies of Sturge, of Thome and Kimball, of Gurney, of Philippo, are very explicit on this point, the capacity and the success of the colored and the black population in employments of skill, of profit and of trust ; and best of all is the testimony to their moderation. They receive hints and advances from the whites that they will be gladly received as subscribers to the Exchange, as members of this or that committee of trust They hold back, and say to each other that " social position is not to be gained by pushing."

I have said that this event interests us because it came mainly from the concession of the whites ; I add, that in part it is the earning of the blacks. They won the pity and respect which they have received, by their powers and native endowments. I think this a circumstance of the highest import. Their whole future is in it. Our planet, before the age of written history, had its races of savages, like the generations of sour paste, or the animalcules that wiggle and bite in a drop of putrid water. Who cares for these or for their wars? We do not wish a world of bugs or of birds; neither afterward of Scythians, Caraibs or Feejees. The grand style of Nature, her great periods, is all we observe in them. Who cares for oppressing whites, or oppressed blacks, twenty centuries ago, more than for bad dreams? Eaters and food are in the harmony of Nature; and there too is the germ forever protected, unfolding gigantic leaf after leaf, a newer flower, a richer fruit, in every period, yet its next product is never to be guessed. It will only save what is worth saving; and it saves not by compassion, but by power. It appoints no police to guard the lion but his teeth and claws; no fort or city for the bird but his wings, no rescue for flies and mites but their spawning numbers, which no ravages can overcome. It deals with men after the same manner. If they are rude and foolish, down they must go. When at last in a race a new principle appears, an idea, — *that* conserves it; ideas only save races. If the black man is feeble and not important to

the existing races, not on a parity with the best
race, the black man must serve, and be exterminated.' But if the black man carries in his
bosom an indispensable element of a new and
coming civilization, for the sake of that element,
no wrong nor strength nor circumstance can
hurt him : he will survive and play his part. So
now, the arrival in the world of such men as
Toussaint, and the Haytian heroes, or of the
leaders of their race in Barbadoes and Jamaica,
outweighs in good omen all the English and
American humanity. The anti-slavery of the
whole world is dust in the balance before this, —
is a poor squeamishness and nervousness : the
might and the right are here : here is the anti-
slave : here is man : and if you have man, black
or white is an insignificance. The intellect, —
that is miraculous ! Who has it, has the talis-
man : his skin and bones, though they were
of the color of night, are transparent, and the
everlasting stars shine through, with attractive
beams. But a compassion for that which is not
and cannot be useful or lovely, is degrading and
futile. All the songs and newspapers and money
subscriptions and vituperation of such as do not
think with us, will avail nothing against a tact.
I say to you, you must save yourself, black or

white, man or woman; other help is none. I esteem the occasion of this jubilee to be the proud discovery that the black race can contend with the white: that in the great anthem which we call history, a piece of many parts and vast compass, after playing a long time a very low and subdued accompaniment, they perceive the time arrived when they can strike in with effect and take a master's part in the music. The civility of the world has reached that pitch that their more moral genius is becoming indispensable, and the quality of this race is to be honored for itself. For this, they have been preserved in sandy deserts, in rice-swamps, in kitchens and shoe-shops, so long: now let them emerge, clothed and in their own form.

There remains the very elevated consideration which the subject opens, but which belongs to more abstract views than we are now taking, this, namely, that the civility of no race can be perfect whilst another race is degraded. It is a doctrine alike of the oldest and of the newest philosophy, that man is one, and that you cannot injure any member, without a sympathetic injury to all the members. America is not civil, whilst Africa is barbarous.'

These considerations seem to leave no choice

XI

for the action of the intellect and the conscience
of the country. There have been moments in
this, as well as in every piece of moral history,
when there seemed room for the infusions of a
skeptical philosophy; when it seemed doubtful
whether brute force would not triumph in the
eternal struggle. I doubt not that, sometimes, a
despairing negro, when jumping over the ship's
sides to escape from the white devils who surrounded him, has believed there was no vin-
dication of right; it is horrible to think of, but
it seemed so. I doubt not that sometimes the
negro's friend, in the face of scornful and brutal
hundreds of traders and drivers, has felt his heart
sink. Especially, it seems to me, some degree
of despondency is pardonable, when he observes
the men of conscience and of intellect, his own
natural allies and champions, — those whose
attention should be nailed to the grand objects
of this cause, so hotly offended by whatever
incidental petulances or infirmities of indiscreet
defenders of the negro, as to permit themselves
to be ranged with the enemies of the human
race ; and names which should be the alarums of
liberty and the watchwords of truth, are mixed
up with all the rotten rabble of selfishness and
tyranny.' I assure myself that this coldness

and blindness will pass away. A single noble wind of sentiment will scatter them forever. I am sure that the good and wise elders, the ardent and generous youth, will not permit what is incidental and exceptional to withdraw their devotion from the essential and permanent characters of the question. There have been moments, I said, when men might be forgiven who doubted. Those moments are past. Seen in masses, it cannot be disputed, there is progress in human society. There is a blessed necessity by which the interest of men is always driving them to the right; and, again, making all crime mean and ugly. The genius of the Saxon race, friendly to liberty; the enterprise, the very muscular vigor of this nation, are inconsistent with slavery. The Intellect, with blazing eye, looking through history from the beginning onward, gazes on this blot and it disappears. The sentiment of Right, once very low and indistinct, but ever more articulate, because it is the voice of the universe, pronounces Freedom. The Power that built this fabric of things affirms it in the heart; and in the history of the First of August, has made a sign to the ages, of his will.

V

WAR

THE archangel Hope
Looks to the azure cope,
Waits through dark ages for the morn,
Defeated day by day, but unto Victory born.

WAR

IT has been a favorite study of modern philosophy to indicate the steps of human progress, to watch the rising of a thought in one
man's mind, the communication of it to a few,
to a small minority, its expansion and general
reception, until it publishes itself to the world
by destroying the existing laws and institutions,
and the generation of new. Looked at in this
general and historical way, many things wear a
very different face from that they show near
by, and one at a time,—and, particularly, war.
War, which to sane men at the present day
begins to look like an epidemic insanity, breaking out here and there like the cholera or influ-
enza, infecting men's brains instead of their
bowels,— when seen in the remote past, in the
infancy of society, appears a part of the connection of events, and, in its place, necessary.

As far as history has preserved to us the slow
unfoldings of any savage tribe, it is not easy to
see how war could be avoided by such wild,
passionate, needy, ungoverned, strong-bodied
creatures. For in the infancy of society, when
a thin population and improvidence make the

supply of food and of shelter insufficient and
very precarious, and when hunger, thirst, ague
and frozen limbs universally take precedence
of the wants of the mind and the heart, the
necessities of the strong will certainly be satisfied at the cost of the weak, at whatever peril
of future revenge It is plain, too, that in the
first dawnings of the religious sentiment, *that*
blends itself with their passions and is oil to
the fire. Not only every tribe has war-gods,
religious festivals in victory, but *religious wars.*

The student of history acquiesces the more
readily in this copious bloodshed of the early
annals, bloodshed in God's name too, when he
learns that it is a temporary and preparatory
state, and does actively forward the culture of
man. War educates the senses, calls into action
the will, perfects the physical constitution, brings
men into such swift and close collision in critical moments that man measures man. On its
own scale, on the virtues it loves, it endures no
counterfeit, but shakes the whole society until
every atom falls into the place its specific gravity
assigns it ' It presently finds the value of good
sense and of foresight, and Ulysses takes rank
next to Achilles. The leaders, picked men of
a courage and vigor tried and augmented in fifty

battles, are emulous to distinguish themselves
above each other by new merits, as clemency,
hospitality, splendor of living. The people imi-
tate the chiefs. The strong tribe, in which war
has become an art, attack and conquer their
neighbors, and teach them their arts and virtues.
New territory, augmented numbers and extended
interests call out new virtues and abilities, and
the tribe makes long strides. And, finally, when
much progress has been made, all its secrets of
wisdom and art are disseminated by its invasions.
Plutarch, in his essay On the Fortune of Alexander, considers the invasion and conquest of
the East by Alexander as one of the most bright
and pleasing pages in history; and it must be
owned he gives sound reason for his opinion.
It had the effect of uniting into one great interest the divided commonwealths of Greece, and
infusing a new and more enlarged public spirit
into the councils of their statesmen. It carried
the arts and language and philosophy of the
Greeks into the sluggish and barbarous nations
of Persia, Assyria and India. It introduced the
arts of husbandry among tribes of hunters and
shepherds. It weaned the Scythians and Persians from some cruel and licentious practices
to a more civil way of life. It introduced the

sacredness of marriage among them. It built seventy cities, and sowed the Greek customs and humane laws over Asia, and united hostile nations under one code. It brought different families of the human race together, — to blows at first, but afterwards to truce, to trade and to intermarriage. It would be very easy to show analogous benefits that have resulted from military movements of later ages.

Considerations of this kind lead us to a true view of the nature and office of war. We see it is the subject of all history; that it has been the principal employment of the most conspicuous men; that it is at this moment the delight of half the world, of almost all young and ignorant persons; that it is exhibited to us continually in the dumb show of brute nature, where war between tribes, and between individuals of the same tribe, perpetually rages. The microscope reveals miniature butchery in atomies and infinitely small biters that swim and fight in an illuminated drop of water; and the little globe is but a too faithful miniature of the large.

What does all this war, beginning from the lowest races and reaching up to man, signify? Is it not manifest that it covers a great and

beneficent principle, which Nature had deeply
at heart? What is that principle?—It is self-
help. Nature implants with life the instinct
of self-help, perpetual struggle to be, to resist
opposition, to attain to freedom, to attain to
a mastery and the security of a permanent, self-
defended being; and to each creature these
objects are made so dear that it risks its life
continually in the struggle for these ends.

But whilst this principle, necessarily, is in-
wrought into the fabric of every creature, yet it
is but *one* instinct; and though a primary one,
or we may say the very first, yet the appearance
of the other instincts immediately modifies and
controls this; turns its energies into harmless,
useful and high courses, showing thereby what
was its ultimate design; and, finally, takes out
its fangs. The instinct of self-help is very early
unfolded in the coarse and merely brute form
of war, only in the childhood and imbecility of
the other instincts, and remains in that form
only until their development. It is the ignorant
and childish part of mankind that is the fighting
part. Idle and vacant minds want excitement,
as all boys kill cats. Bull-baiting, cockpits and
the boxer's ring are the enjoyment of the part
of society whose animal nature alone has been

developed. In some parts of this country, where the intellectual and moral faculties have as yet scarcely any culture, the absorbing topic of all conversation is whipping; who fought, and which whipped? Of man, boy or beast, the only trait that much interests the speakers is the pugnacity.' And why? Because the speaker has as yet no other image of manly activity and virtue, none of endurance, none of perseverance, none of charity, none of the attainment of truth. Put him into a circle of cultivated men, where the conversation broaches the great questions that besiege the human reason, and he would be dumb and unhappy, as an Indian in church.

To men of a sedate and mature spirit, in whom is any knowledge or mental activity, the detail of battle becomes insupportably tedious and revolting. It is like the talk of one of those monomaniacs whom we sometimes meet in society, who converse on horses, and Fontenelle expressed a volume of meaning when he said, "I hate war, for it spoils conversation."

Nothing is plainer than that the sympathy with war is a juvenile and temporary state. Not only the moral sentiment, but trade, learning and whatever makes intercourse, conspire to put it down. Trade, as all men know, is the

antagonist of war. Wherever there is no property, the people will put on the knapsack for
bread; but trade is instantly endangered and
destroyed. And, moreover, trade brings men
to look each other in the face, and gives the
parties the knowledge that these enemies over
sea or over the mountain are such men as we;
who laugh and grieve, who love and fear, as we
do. And learning and art, and especially religion
weave ties that make war look like fratricide, as
it is. And as all history is the picture of war,
as we have said, so it is no less true that it is
the record of the mitigation and decline of war.
Early in the eleventh and twelfth centuries, the
Italian cities had grown so populous and strong
that they forced the rural nobility to dismantle
their castles, which were dens of cruelty, and
come and reside in the towns. The popes, to
their eternal honor, declared religious jubilees,
during which all hostilities were suspended
throughout Christendom, and man had a breathing space. The increase of civility has abolished
the use of poison and of torture, once supposed
as necessary as navies now. And, finally, the
art of war, what with gunpowder and tactics, has
made, as all men know, battles less frequent and
less murderous.

By all these means, war has been steadily on the decline; and we read with astonishment of the beastly fighting of the old times. Only in Elizabeth's time, out of the European waters, piracy was all but universal. The proverb was, — " No peace beyond the line," and the seaman shipped on the buccaneer's bargain, " No prey, no pay." The celebrated Cavendish, who was thought in his times a good Christian man, wrote thus to Lord Hunsdon, on his return from a voyage round the world· " Sept. 1588. It hath pleased Almighty God to suffer me to circumpass the whole globe of the world, entering in at the Strait of Magellan, and returning by the Cape of Buena Esperança; in which voyage, I have either discovered or brought certain intelligence of all the rich places of the world, which were ever discovered by any Christian. I navigated along the coast of Chili, Peru, and New Spain, *where I made great spoils. I burnt and sank nineteen sail of ships, small and great. All the villages and towns that ever I landed at, I burned and spoiled* And had I not been discovered upon the coast, I had taken great quantity of treasure The matter of most profit to me was a great ship of the king's, which I took at California," etc And the good Cavendish piously begins this statement, — " It hath pleased Almighty God."

Indeed, our American annals have preserved the vestiges of barbarous warfare down to more recent times. I read in Williams's History of Maine, that " Assacombuit, the Sagamore of the Anagunticook tribe, was remarkable for his turpitude and ferocity above all other known Indians; that, in 1705, Vaudreuil sent him to France, where he was introduced to the king. When he appeared at court, he lifted up his hand and said, ' This hand has slain a hundred and fifty of your majesty's enemies within the territories of New England.' This so pleased the king that he knighted him, and ordered a pension of eight livres a day to be paid him during life." This valuable person, on his return to America, took to killing his own neighbors and kindred, with such appetite that his tribe combined against him, and would have killed him had he not fled his country forever.

The scandal which we feel in such facts certainly shows that we have got on a little. All history is the decline of war, though the slow decline. All that society has yet gained is mitigation : the doctrine of the right of war still remains.

For ages (for ideas work in ages, and animate
vast societies of men) the human race has gone
on under the tyranny — shall I so call it? —
of this first brutish form of their effort to be
men; that is, for ages they have shared so much
of the nature of the lower animals, the tiger and
the shark, and the savages of the water-drop.
They have nearly exhausted all the good and
all the evil of this form: they have held as fast
to this degradation as their worst enemy could
desire; but all things have an end, and so has
this.' The eternal germination of the better
has unfolded new powers, new instincts, which
were really concealed under this rough and base
rind. The sublime question has startled one and
another happy soul in different quarters of the
globe, — Cannot love be, as well as hate?
Would not love answer the same end, or even
a better? Cannot peace be, as well as war?

This thought is no man's invention, neither
St. Pierre's nor Rousseau's, but the rising of
the general tide in the human soul, — and rising
highest, and first made visible, in the most
simple and pure souls, who have therefore
announced it to us beforehand; but presently
we all see it. It has now become so distinct as to
be a social thought   societies can be formed on

it. It is expounded, illustrated, defined, with different degrees of clearness ; and its actualization, or the measures it should inspire, predicted according to the light of each seer.

The idea itself is the epoch ; the fact that it has become so distinct to any small number of persons as to become a subject of prayer and hope, of concert and discussion, — *that* is the commanding fact. This having come, much more will follow. Revolutions go not backward. The star once risen, though only one man in the hemisphere has yet seen its upper limb in the horizon, will mount and mount, until it becomes visible to other men, to multitudes, and climbs the zenith of all eyes. And so it is not a great matter how long men refuse to believe the advent of peace : war is on its last legs ; and a universal peace is as sure as is the prevalence of civilization over barbarism, of liberal governments over feudal forms. The question for us is only *How soon?*

That the project of peace should appear visionary to great numbers of sensible men ; should appear laughable even, to numbers ; should appear to the grave and good-natured to be embarrassed with extreme practical difficulties, — is very natural. ' This is a poor, tedious

XI

society of yours,' they say : 'we do not see
what good can come of it. Peace! why, we are
all at peace now. But if a foreign nation should
wantonly insult or plunder our commerce, or,
worse yet, should land on our shores to rob and
kill, you would not have us sit, and be robbed
and killed? You mistake the times; you overestimate the virtue of men. You forget that the
quiet which now sleeps in cities and in farms,
which lets the wagon go unguarded and the
farmhouse unbolted, rests on the perfect understanding of all men that the musket, the halter
and the jail stand behind there, ready to punish
any disturber of it. All admit that this would
be the best policy, if the world were all a church,
if all the men were the best men, if all would
agree to accept this rule. But it is absurd for
one nation to attempt it alone.' '

In the first place, we answer that we never
make much account of objections which merely
respect the actual state of the world at this moment, but which admit the general expediency
and permanent excellence of the project. What
is the best must be the true; and what is
true — that is, what is at bottom fit and agreeable to the constitution of man — must at last
prevail over all obstruction and all opposition

There is no good now enjoyed by society that was not once as problematical and visionary as this. It is the tendency of the true interest of man to become his desire and steadfast aim.

But, further, it is a lesson which all history teaches wise men, to put trust in ideas, and not in circumstances. We have all grown up in the sight of frigates and navy-yards, of armed forts and islands, of arsenals and militia. The reference to any foreign register will inform us of the number of thousand or million men that are now under arms in the vast colonial system of the British Empire, of Russia, Austria and France; and one is scared to find at what a cost the peace of the globe is kept. This vast apparatus of artillery, of fleets, of stone bastions and trenches and embankments; this incessant patrolling of sentinels; this waving of national flags; this reveille and evening gun; this martial music and endless playing of marches and singing of military and naval songs seem to us to constitute an imposing actual, which will not yield in centuries to the feeble, deprecatory voices of a handful of friends of peace.

Thus always we are daunted by the appearances; not seeing that their whole value lies at bottom in the state of mind. It is really a

thought that built this portentous war-establish-
ment, and a thought shall also melt it away.'
Every nation and every man instantly surround
themselves with a material apparatus which exactly corresponds to their moral state, or their
state of thought Observe how every truth and
every error, each a *thought* of some man's mind,
clothes itself with societies, houses, cities, language, ceremonies, newspapers. Observe the
ideas of the present day, — orthodoxy, skepti-
cism, missions, popular education, temperance,
anti-masonry, anti-slavery ; see how each of
these abstractions has embodied itself in an
imposing apparatus in the community ; and how
timber, brick, lime and stone have flown into
convenient shape, obedient to the master-idea
reigning in the minds of many persons '

   You shall hear, some day, of a wild fancy
which some man has in his brain, of the mischief of secret oaths Come again one or two
years afterwards, and you shall see it has built
great houses of solid wood and brick and mortar.
You shall see a hundred presses printing a million
sheets; you shall see men and horses and
wheels made to walk, run and roll for it   this
great body of matter thus executing that one
man's wild thought This happens daily, yearly

about us, with half thoughts, often with flimsy lies, pieces of policy and speculation. With good nursing they will last three or four years before they will come to nothing. But when a truth appears, — as, for instance, a perception in the wit of one Columbus that there is land in the Western Sea; though he alone of all men has that thought, and they all jeer, — it will build ships; it will build fleets; it will carry over half Spain and half England; it will plant a colony, a state, nations and half a globe full of men.

We surround ourselves always, according to our freedom and ability, with true images of ourselves in things, whether it be ships or books or cannons or churches. The standing army, the arsenal, the camp and the gibbet do not appertain to man. They only serve as an index to show where man is now; what a bad, ungoverned temper he has; what an ugly neighbor he is; how his affections halt; how low his hope lies. He who loves the bristle of bayonets only sees in their glitter what beforehand he feels in his heart. It is avarice and hatred; it is that quivering lip, that cold, hating eye, which built magazines and powder-houses.

It follows of course that the least change in

the man will change his circumstances ; the least
enlargement of his ideas, the least mitigation of
his feelings in respect to other men ; if, for example, he could be inspired with a tender kindness to the souls of men, and should come to
feel that every man was another self with whom
he might come to join, as left hand works with
right. Every degree of the ascendency of this
feeling would cause the most striking changes
of external things : the tents would be struck ;
the men-of-war would rot ashore ; the arms
rust , the cannon would become street-posts ,
the pikes, a fisher's harpoon ; the marching regiment would be a caravan of emigrants, *peaceful*
pioneers at the fountains of the Wabash and the
Missouri. And so it must and will be : bayonet and sword must first retreat a little from
their ostentatious prominence ; then quite hide
themselves, as the sheriff's halter does now,
inviting the attendance only of relations and
friends ; and then, lastly, will be transferred to
the museums of the curious, as poisoning and
torturing tools are at this day.

War and peace thus resolve themselves into
a mercury of the state of cultivation. At a certain stage of his progress, the man fights, if he
be of a sound body and mind. At a certain

higher stage, he makes no offensive demonstration, but is alert to repel injury, and of an unconquerable heart.' At a still higher stage, he
comes into the region of holiness ; passion has
passed away from him ; his warlike nature is
all converted into an active medicinal principle ;
he sacrifices himself, and accepts with alacrity
wearisome tasks of denial and charity ; but,
being attacked, he bears it and turns the other
cheek, as one engaged, throughout his being,
no longer to the service of an individual but to
the common soul of all men.

Since the peace question has been before the
public mind, those who affirm its right and
expediency have naturally been met with objections more or less weighty. There are cases frequently put by the curious, — moral problems,
like those problems in arithmetic which in long
winter evenings the rustics try the hardness of
their heads in ciphering out. And chiefly it is
said, — Either accept this principle for better,
for worse, carry it out to the end, and meet its
absurd consequences ; or else, if you pretend to
set an arbitrary limit, a " Thus far, no farther,"
then give up the principle, and take that limit
which the common sense of all mankind has
set, and which distinguishes offensive war as

criminal, defensive war as just. Otherwise, if you go for no war, then be consistent, and give up self-defence in the highway, in your own house. Will you push it thus far? Will you stick to your principle of non-resistance when your strong-box is broken open, when your wife and babes are insulted and slaughtered in your sight? If you say yes, you only invite the robber and assassin ; and a few bloody-minded desperadoes would soon butcher the good.

In reply to this charge of absurdity on the extreme peace doctrine, as shown in the supposed consequences, I wish to say that such deductions consider only one half of the fact. They look only at the passive side of the friend of peace, only at his passivity ; they quite omit to consider his activity. But no man, it may be presumed, ever embraced the cause of peace and philanthropy for the sole end and satisfaction of being plundered and slain. A man does not come the length of the spirit of martyrdom without some active purpose, some equal motive, some flaming love. If you have a nation of men who have risen to that height of moral cultivation that they will not declare war or carry arms, for they have not so much madness left in their brains, you have a nation of lovers,

of benefactors, of true, great and able men. Let
me know more of that nation; I shall not find
them defenceless, with idle hands swinging at
their sides. I shall find them men of love,
honor and truth ; men of an immense industry ;
men whose influence is felt to the end of the
earth ; men whose very look and voice carry the
sentence of honor and shame ; and all forces
yield to their energy and persuasion. Whenever we see the doctrine of peace embraced by a
nation, we may be assured it will not be one
that invites injury ; but one, on the contrary,
which has a friend in the bottom of the heart of
every man, even of the violent and the base ;
one against which no weapon can prosper ; one
which is looked upon as the asylum of the
human race and has the tears and the blessings
of mankind.

In the second place, as far as it respects
individual action in difficult and extreme cases,
I will say, such cases seldom or never occur to
the good and just man ; nor are we careful
to say, or even to know, what in such crises is to
be done. A wise man will never impawn his
future being and action, and decide beforehand
what he shall do in a given extreme event.
Nature and God will instruct him in that hour.

The question naturally arises, How is this new aspiration of the human mind to be made visible and real? How is it to pass out of thoughts into things?

Not, certainly, in the first place, *in the way of routine and mere forms*, — the universal specific of modern politics; not by organizing a society, and going through a course of resolutions and public manifestoes, and being thus formally accredited to the public and to the civility of the newspapers. We have played this game to tediousness. In some of our cities they choose noted duellists as presidents and officers of anti-duelling societies. Men who love that bloated vanity called public opinion think all is well if they have once got their bantling through a sufficient course of speeches and cheerings, of one, two, or three public meetings; as if *they* could do anything: they vote and vote, cry hurrah on both sides, no man responsible, no man caring a pin. The next season, an Indian war, or an aggression on our commerce by Malays; or the party this man votes with have an appropriation to carry through Congress: instantly he wags his head the other way, and cries, Havoc and war!

This is not to be carried by public opinion,

but by private opinion, by private conviction,
by private, dear and earnest love. For the only
hope of this cause is in the increased insight,
and it is to be accomplished by the spontaneous
teaching, of the cultivated soul, in its secret
experience and meditation, — that it is now time
that it should pass out of the state of beast
into the state of man ; it is to hear the voice of
God, which bids the devils that have rended and
torn him come out of him and let him now
be clothed and walk forth in his right mind.

Nor, in the next place, is the peace principle
to be carried into effect by fear. It can never
be defended, it can never be executed, by cow-
ards. Everything great must be done in the
spirit of greatness. The manhood that has been
in war must be transferred to the cause of peace,
before war can lose its charm, and peace be venerable to men.

The attractiveness of war shows one thing
through all the throats of artillery, the thunders
of so many sieges, the sack of towns, the jousts
of chivalry, the shock of hosts, — this namely,
the conviction of man universally, that a man
should be himself responsible, with goods,
health and life, for his behavior ; that he should
not ask of the state protection ; should ask

WAR

nothing of the state, should be himself a kingdom and a state; fearing no man; quite willing
to use the opportunities and advantages that
good government throw in his way, but nothing daunted, and not really the poorer if
government, law and order went by the board;
because in himself reside infinite resources;
because he is sure of himself, and never needs
to ask another what in any crisis it behooves
him to do.'

What makes to us the attractiveness of the
Greek heroes? of the Roman? What makes
the attractiveness of that romantic style of living
which is the material of ten thousand plays
and romances, from Shakspeare to Scott; the
feudal baron, the French, the English nobility,
the Warwicks, Plantagenets? It is their absolute self-dependence. I do not wonder at the
dislike some of the friends of peace have expressed at Shakspeare. The veriest churl and
Jacobin cannot resist the influence of the style
and manners of these haughty lords. We are
affected, as boys and barbarians are, by the
appearance of a few rich and wilful gentlemen
who take their honor into their own keeping,
defy the world, so confident are they of their
courage and strength, and whose appearance

is the arrival of so much life and virtue. In dangerous times they are presently tried, and therefore their name is a flourish of trumpets. They, at least, affect us as a reality. They are not shams, but the substance of which that age and world is made. They are true heroes for their time. They make what is in their minds the greatest sacrifice. They will, for an injurious word, peril all their state and wealth, and go to the field. Take away that principle of responsibleness, and they become pirates and ruffians.'

This self-subsistency is the charm of war ; for this self-subsistency is essential to our idea of man. But another age comes, a truer religion and ethics open, and a man puts himself under the dominion of principles. I see him to be the servant of truth, of love and of freedom, and immovable in the waves of the crowd. The man of principle, that is, the man who, without any flourish of trumpets, titles of lordship or train of guards, without any notice of his action abroad, expecting none, takes in solitude the right step uniformly, on his private choice and disdaining consequences, — does not yield, in my imagination, to any man. He is willing to be hanged at his own gate, rather than consent to any compromise of his freedom or the suppression of his conviction. I regard no longer those names that so tingled in my ear. This is a baron of a better nobility and a stouter stomach.

The cause of peace is not the cause of cowardice. If peace is sought to be defended or preserved for the safety of the luxurious and the timid, it is a sham, and the peace will be base. War is better, and the peace will be broken. If peace is to be maintained, it must be by brave men, who have come up to the same height as the hero, namely, the will to carry their life in their hand, and stake it at any instant for their principle, but who have gone one step beyond the hero, and will not seek another man's life; — men who have, by their intellectual insight or else by their moral elevation, attained such a perception of their own intrinsic worth that they do not think property or their own body a sufficient good to be saved by such dereliction of principle as treating a man like a sheep.

If the universal cry for reform of so many inveterate abuses, with which society rings, — if the desire of a large class of young men for a faith and hope, intellectual and religious, such as they have not yet found, be an omen to be trusted;

if the disposition to rely more, in study and in action, on the unexplored riches of the human constitution, — if the search of the sublime laws of morals and the sources of hope and trust, in man, and not in books, in the present, and not in the past, proceed; if the rising generation can be provoked to think it unworthy to nestle into every abomination of the past, and shall feel the generous darings of austerity and virtue, then war has a short day, and human blood will cease to flow.

It is of little consequence in what manner, through what organs, this purpose of mercy and holiness is effected. The proposition of the Congress of Nations is undoubtedly that at which the present fabric of our society and the present course of events do point. But the mind, once prepared for the reign of principles, will easily find modes of expressing its will. There is the highest fitness in the place and time in which this enterprise is begun. Not in an obscure corner, not in a feudal Europe, not in an antiquated appanage where no onward step can be taken without rebellion, is this seed of benevolence laid in the furrow, with tears of hope; but in this broad America of God and man, where the forest is only now falling, or yet to fall, and

the green earth opened to the inundation of
emigrant men from all quarters of oppression
and guilt ; here, where not a family, not a few
men, but mankind, shall say what shall be;
here, we ask, Shall it be War, or shall it be
Peace ?

VI

THE FUGITIVE SLAVE LAW

ADDRESS TO CITIZENS OF CONCORD
3 MAY, 1851

THE Eternal Rights,
Victors over daily wrongs.
Awful victors, they misguide
Whom they will destroy,
And their coming triumph hide
In our downfall, or our joy
They reach no term, they never sleep.
In equal strength through space abide;
Though, reigning dwarfs, they crouch and creep,
The strong they slay, the swift outstride,
Fate's grass grows rank in valley clods,
And rankly on the castled steep, —
Speak it firmly, these are gods,
Are all ghosts beside •

THE FUGITIVE SLAVE LAW

FELLOW CITIZENS: I accepted your invitation to speak to you on the great question of these days, with very little consideration of what I might have to offer: for there seems to be no option. The last year has forced us all into politics, and made it a paramount duty to seek what it is often a duty to shun. We do not breathe well. There is infamy in the air. I have a new experience. I wake in the morning with a painful sensation, which I carry about all day, and which, when traced home, is the odious remembrance of that igno miny which has fallen on Massachusetts, which robs the landscape of beauty, and takes the sunshine out of every hour. I have lived all my life in this state, and never had any experience of personal inconvenience from the laws, until now. They never came near me to any discomfort before. I find the like sensibility in my neighbors; and in that class who take no interest in the ordinary questions of party politics. There are men who are as sure indexes of the equity of legislation and of the same state of public feeling, as the barometer is of the weight

of the air, and it is a bad sign when these are
discontented, for though they snuff oppression
and dishonor at a distance, it is because they are
more impressionable : the whole population will
in a short time be as painfully affected

Every hour brings us from distant quarters
of the Union the expression of mortification
at the late events in Massachusetts, and at the
behavior of Boston. The tameness was indeed
shocking. Boston, of whose fame for spirit and
character we have all been so proud, Boston,
whose citizens, intelligent people in England
told me they could always distinguish by their
culture among Americans; the Boston of the
American Revolution, which figures so proudly
in John Adams's Diary, which the whole
country has been reading; Boston, spoiled by
prosperity, must bow its ancient honor in the
dust, and make us irretrievably ashamed. In
Boston, we have said with such lofty confidence,
no fugitive slave can be arrested, and now, we
must transfer our vaunt to the country, and say,
with a little less confidence, no fugitive man
can be arrested here, at least we can brag thus
until to-morrow, when the farmers also may be
corrupted

The tameness is indeed complete. The only

haste in Boston, after the rescue of Shadrach,¹
last February, was, who should first put his
name on the list of volunteers in aid of the marshal. I met the smoothest of Episcopal Clergymen the other day, and allusion being made to
Mr. Webster's treachery, he blandly replied,
"Why, do you know I think *that* the great
action of his life." It looked as if in the city
and the suburbs all were involved in one hot
haste of terror, — presidents of colleges, and
professors, saints, and brokers, insurers, lawyers, importers, manufacturers: not an un-
pleasing sentiment, not a liberal recollection,
not so much as a snatch of an old song for freedom, dares intrude on their passive obedience.

The panic has paralyzed the journals, with
the fewest exceptions, so that one cannot open
a newspaper without being disgusted by new
records of shame. I cannot read longer even the
local good news. When I look down the columns
at the titles of paragraphs, " Education in Massachusetts," " Board of Trade," " Art Union,"
" Revival of Religion," what bitter mockeries !
The very convenience of property, the house and
land we occupy, have lost their best value, and
a man looks gloomily at his children, and thinks,
" What have I done that you should begin life

in dishonor?" Every liberal study is discredited, — literature and science appear effeminate, and the hiding of the head. The college, the churches, the schools, the very shops and factories are discredited; real estate, every kind of wealth, every branch of industry, every avenue to power, suffers injury, and the value of life is reduced. Just now a friend came into my house and said, " If this law shall be repealed I shall be glad that I have lived; if not I shall be sorry that I was born." What kind of law is that which extorts language like this from the heart of a free and civilized people?

One intellectual benefit we owe to the late disgraces. The crisis had the illuminating power of a sheet of lightning at midnight. It showed truth. It ended a good deal of nonsense we had been wont to hear and to repeat, on the 19th of April, the 17th of June, the 4th of July. It showed the slightness and unreliableness of our social fabric, it showed what stuff reputations are made of, what straws we dignify by office and title, and how competent we are to give counsel and help in a day of trial. It showed the shallowness of leaders; the divergence of parties from their alleged grounds; showed that men would not stick to what they had said, that the resolutions of public bodies, or the pledges never so often given and put on record of public men, will not bind them. The fact comes out more plainly that you cannot rely on any man for the defence of truth, who is not constitutionally or by blood and temperament on that side. A man of a greedy and unscrupulous selfishness may maintain morals when they are in fashion : but he will not stick. However close Mr. Wolf's nails have been pared, however neatly he has been shaved, and tailored, and set up on end, and taught to say, " Virtue and Religion," he cannot be relied on at a pinch : he will say, morality means pricking a vein. The popular assumption that all men loved freedom, and believed in the Christian religion, was found hollow American brag ; only persons who were known and tried benefactors are found standing for freedom : the sentimentalists went down-stream.' I question the value of our civilization, when I see that the public mind had never less hold of the strongest of all truths. The sense of injustice is blunted, — a sure sign of the shallowness of our intellect. I cannot accept the railroad and telegraph in exchange for reason and charity. It is not skill in iron locomotives that makes so fine civility, as the jealousy of liberty. I cannot think the most judicious tubing a compensation for metaphysical debility. What is the use of admirable law-forms, and political forms, if a hurricane of party feeling and a combination of monied interests can beat them to the ground? What is the use of courts, if judges only quote authorities, and no judge exerts original jurisdiction, or recurs to first principles? What is the use of a Federal Bench, if its opinions are the political breath of the hour? And what is the use of constitutions, if all the guaranties provided by the jealousy of ages for the protection of liberty are made of no effect, when a bad act of Congress finds a willing commissioner? The levity of the public mind has been shown in the past year by the most extravagant actions. Who could have believed it, if foretold that a hundred guns would be fired in Boston on the passage of the Fugitive Slave Bill? Nothing proves the want of all thought, the absence of standard in men's minds, more than the dominion of party. Here are humane people who have tears for misery, an open purse for want, who should have been the defenders of the poor man, are found his embittered enemies, rejoicing in his rendition, — merely from party ties. I thought none, that was not ready to go on all fours, would back this law. And yet here are upright men, *compotes mentis*, husbands, fathers, trustees, friends, open, generous, brave, who can see nothing in this claim for bare humanity, and the health and honor of their native State, but canting fanaticism, sedition and "one idea." Because of this preoccupied mind, the whole wealth and power of Boston — two hundred thousand souls, and one hundred and eighty millions of money — are thrown into the scale of crime: and the poor black boy, whom the fame of Boston had reached in the recesses of a vile swamp, or in the alleys of Savannah, on arriving here finds all this force employed to catch him. The famous town of Boston is his master's hound. The learning of the universities, the culture of elegant society, the acumen of lawyers, the majesty of the Bench, the eloquence of the Christian pulpit, the stoutness of Democracy, the respectability of the Whig party are all combined to kidnap him.

The crisis is interesting as it shows the self-protecting nature of the world and of the Divine laws. It is the law of the world, — as much immorality as there is, so much misery. The greatest prosperity will in vain resist the greatest calamity. You borrow the succour of the devil and he must have his fee. He was never known to abate a penny of his rents. In every nation all the immorality that exists breeds plagues. But of the corrupt society that exists we have never been able to combine any pure prosperity. There is always something in the very advantages of a condition which hurts it. Africa has its malformation, England has its Ireland; Germany its hatred of classes, France its love of gunpowder; Italy its Pope; and America, the most prosperous country in the Universe, has the greatest calamity in the Universe, negro slavery.

Let me remind you a little in detail how the natural retribution acts in reference to the statute which Congress passed a year ago. For these few months have shown very conspicuously its nature and impracticability. It is contravened:

1. By the sentiment of duty. An immoral law makes it a man's duty to break it, at every hazard. For virtue is the very self of every man. It is therefore a principle of law that an immoral contract is void, and that an immoral statute is void. For, as laws do not make right, and are simply declaratory of a right which already existed, it is not to be presumed

that they can so stultify themselves as to command injustice.

It is remarkable how rare in the history of tyrants is an immoral law. Some color, some indirection was always used. If you take up the volumes of the " Universal History," you will find it difficult searching. The precedents are few. It is not easy to parallel the wickedness of this American law. And that is the head and body of this discontent, that the law is immoral.

Here is a statute which enacts the crime of kidnapping, — a crime on one footing with arson and murder. A man's right to liberty is as inalienable as his right to life.

Pains seem to have been taken to give us in this statute a wrong pure from any mixture of right. If our resistance to this law is not right, there is no right. This is not meddling with other people's affairs: this is hindering other people from meddling with us. This is not going crusading into Virginia and Georgia after slaves, who, it is alleged, are very comfortable where they are : — that amiable argument falls to the ground : but this is befriending in our own State, on our own farms, a man who has taken the risk of being shot, or burned alive, or

cast into the sea, or starved to death, or suffo-
cated in a wooden box, to get away from his
driver: and this man who has run the gauntlet
of a thousand miles for his freedom, the statute
says, you men of Massachusetts shall hunt, and
catch, and send back again to the dog-hutch he
fled from.

It is contrary to the primal sentiment of duty,
and therefore all men that are born are, in proportion to their power of thought and their
moral sensibility, found to be the natural enemies of this law. The resistance of all moral
beings is secured to it. I had thought, I confess, what must come at last would come at
first, a banding of all men against the authority
of this statute. I thought it a point on which
all sane men were agreed, that the law must respect the public morality. I thought that all
men of all conditions had been made sharers
of a certain experience, that in certain rare and
retired moments they had been made to see
how man is man, or what makes the essence of
rational beings, namely, that whilst animals have
to do with eating the fruits of the ground,
men have to do with rectitude, with benefit,
with truth, with something which is independent
of appearances: and that this tie makes the

substantiality of life, this, and not their plough-
ing, or sailing, their trade or the breeding of
families. I thought that every time a man goes
back to his own thoughts, these angels receive
him, talk with him, and that, in the best hours,
he is uplifted in virtue of this essence, into a
peace and into a power which the material world
cannot give : that these moments counterbalance
the years of drudgery, and that this owning of
a law, be it called morals, religion, or godhead,
or what you will, constituted the explanation of
life, the excuse and indemnity for the errors
and calamities which sadden it. In long years
consumed in trifles, they remember these moments, and are consoled. I thought it was this
fair mystery, whose foundations are hidden in
eternity, which made the basis of human society, and of law ; and that to pretend anything
else, as that the acquisition of property was
the end of living, was to confound all distinctions, to make the world a greasy hotel, and,
instead of noble motives and inspirations, and
a heaven of companions and angels around and
before us, to leave us in a grimacing menagerie
of monkeys and idiots. All arts, customs, societies, books, and laws, are good as they foster and
concur with this spiritual element : all men are

beloved as they raise us to it; hateful as they deny or resist it. The laws especially draw their obligation only from their concurrence with it

I am surprised that lawyers can be so blind as to suffer the principles of Law to be discredited. A few months ago, in my dismay at hearing that the Higher Law was reckoned a good joke in the courts, I took pains to look into a few law-books. I had often heard that the Bible constituted a part of every technical law library, and that it was a principle in law that immoral laws are void

I found, accordingly, that the great jurists, Cicero, Grotius, Coke, Blackstone, Burlamaqui, Montesquieu, Vattel, Burke, Mackintosh, Jefferson, do all affirm this. I have no intention to recite these passages I had marked: — such citation indeed seems to be something cowardly (for no reasonable person needs a quotation from Blackstone to convince him that white cannot be legislated to be black, and shall content myself with reading a single passage. Blackstone admits the sovereignty "antecedent to any positive precept, of the law of Nature," among whose principles are, "that we should live on, should hurt nobody, and should render unto every one his due," etc. "*No human laws are of any validity, if contrary to this.*" "Nay, if any human law should allow or enjoin us to commit a crime" (his instance is murder), "we are bound to transgress that human law; or else we must offend both the natural and divine." Lord Coke held that where an Act of Parliament is against common right and reason, the common law shall control it, and adjudge it to be void. Chief Justice Hobart, Chief Justice Holt, and Chief Justice Mansfield held the same.

Lord Mansfield, in the case of the slave Somerset, wherein the *dicta* of Lords Talbot and Hardwicke had been cited, to the effect of carrying back the slave to the West Indies, said, "I care not for the supposed *dicta* of judges, however eminent, if they be contrary to all principle." Even the *Canon Law* says (*in malis promissis non expedit servare fidem*), "Neither allegiance nor oath can bind to obey that which is wrong."

No engagement (to a sovereign) can oblige or even authorize a man to violate the laws of Nature. All authors who have any conscience or modesty agree that a person ought not to obey such commands as are evidently contrary to the laws of God. Those governors of places

who bravely refused to execute the barbarous
orders of Charles IX. for the famous "Massacre of St. Bartholomew," have been universally
praised ; and the court did not dare to punish
them, at least openly. "Sire," said the brave
Orte, governor of Bayonne, in his letter, " I
have communicated your majesty's command
to your faithful inhabitants and warriors in the
garrison, and I have found there only good citizens, and brave soldiers ; not one hangman .
therefore, both they and I must humbly entreat
your majesty to be pleased to employ your arms
and lives in things that are possible, however
hazardous they may be, and we will exert
ourselves to the last drop of our blood."¹

The practitioners should guard this dogma
well, as the palladium of the profession, as their
anchor in the respect of mankind. Against a
principle like this, all the arguments of Mr.
Webster are the spray of a child's squirt against
a granite wall.

2. It is contravened by all the sentiments.
How can a law be enforced that fines pity, and
imprisons charity ? As long as men have bowels,
they will disobey. You know that the Act of
Congress of September 18, 1850, is a law which
every one of you will break on the earliest occa-

sion. There is not a manly Whig, or a manly
Democrat, of whom, if a slave were hidden in
one of our houses from the hounds, we should
not ask with confidence to lend his wagon in
aid of his escape, and he would lend it. The
man would be too strong for the partisan.

And here I may say that it is absurd, what I
often hear, to accuse the friends of freedom in
the North with being the occasion of the new
stringency of the Southern slave-laws. If you
starve or beat the orphan, in my presence, and
I accuse your cruelty, can I help it? In the
words of Electra in the Greek tragedy, " 'T is
you that say it, not I. You do the deeds, and
your ungodly deeds find me the words." Will
you blame the ball for rebounding from the floor,
blame the air for rushing in where a vacuum is
made or the boiler for exploding under pressure
of steam? These facts are after laws of the
world, and so is it law, that, when justice is
violated, anger begins. The very defence which
the God of Nature has provided for the innocent against cruelty is the sentiment of indignation and pity in the bosom of the beholder.
Mr. Webster tells the President that " he has
been in the North, and he has found no man,
whose opinion is of any weight, who is opposed

XI

to the law." Oh, Mr. President, trust not the information! The gravid old Universe goes spawning on; the womb conceives and the breasts give suck to thousands and millions of hairy babes formed not in the image of your statute, but in the image of the Universe; too many to be bought off; too many than they can be rich, and therefore peaceable; and necessitated to express first or last every feeling of the heart. You can keep no secret, for whatever is true some of them will unreasonably say. You can commit no crime, for they are created in their sentiments conscious of and hostile to it; and unless you can suppress the newspaper, pass a law against book-shops, gag the English tongue in America, all short of this is futile. This dreadful English Speech is saturated with songs, proverbs and speeches that flatly contradict and defy every line of Mr. Mason's statute. Nay, unless you can draw a sponge over those seditious Ten Commandments which are the root of our European and American civilization; and over that eleventh commandment, " Do unto others as you would have them do to you," your labor is vain.

3. It is contravened by the written laws themselves, because the sentiments, of course,

write the statutes. Laws are merely declaratory
of the natural sentiments of mankind, and the
language of all permanent laws will be in con-
tradiction to any immoral enactment. And thus
it happens here : Statute fights against Statute.
By the law of Congress March 2, 1807, it is
piracy and murder, punishable with death, to
enslave a man on the coast of Africa. By law
of Congress September, 1850, it is a high crime
and misdemeanor, punishable with fine and
imprisonment, to resist the reënslaving a man
on the coast of America. Off soundings, it is
piracy and murder to enslave him. On soundings, it is fine and prison not to reënslave.
What kind of legislation is this? What kind
of constitution which covers it? And yet the
crime which the second law ordains is greater
than the crime which the first law forbids under
penalty of the gibbet. For it is a greater crime
to reënslave a man who has shown himself fit
for freedom, than to enslave him at first, when
it might be pretended to be a mitigation of his
lot as a captive in war.

4. It is contravened by the mischiefs it oper-
ates. A wicked law cannot be executed by good
men, and must be by bad. Flagitious men
must be employed, and every act of theirs is a

stab at the public peace. It cannot be executed at such a cost, and so it brings a bribe in its hand. This law comes with infamy in it, and out of it. It offers a bribe in its own clauses for the consummation of the crime. To serve it, low and mean people are found by the groping of the government. No government ever found it hard to pick up tools for base actions. If you cannot find them in the huts of the poor, you shall find them in the palaces of the rich. Vanity can buy some, ambition others, and money others. The first execution of the law, as was inevitable, was a little hesitating; the second was easier; and the glib officials became, in a few weeks, quite practised and handy at stealing men. But worse, not the officials alone are bribed, but the whole community is solicited. The scowl of the community is attempted to be averted by the mischievous whisper, "Tariff and Southern market, if you will be quiet: no tariff and loss of Southern market, if you dare to murmur." I wonder that our acute people who have learned that the cheapest police is dear schools, should not find out that an immoral law costs more than the loss of the custom of a Southern city.

The humiliating scandal of great men warp-

ing right into wrong was followed up very fast
by the cities. New York advertised in Southern markets that it would go for slavery, and
posted the names of merchants who would
not. Boston, alarmed, entered into the same
design. Philadelphia, more fortunate, had no
conscience at all, and, in this auction of the
rights of mankind, rescinded all its legislation
against slavery. And the Boston " Advertiser,"
and the " Courier," in these weeks, urge the
same course on the people of Massachusetts.
Nothing remains in this race of roguery but to
coax Connecticut or Maine to outbid us all by
adopting slavery into its constitution.

Great is the mischief of a legal crime. Every
person who touches this business is contaminated. There has not been in our lifetime another
moment when public men were personally low-
ered by their political action. But here are
gentlemen whose believed probity was the confidence and fortification of multitudes, who, by
fear of public opinion, or through the dangerous ascendency of Southern manners, have been
drawn into the support of this foul business.
We poor men in the country who might once
have thought it an honor to shake hands with
them, or to dine at their boards, would now

shrink from their touch, nor could they enter
our humblest doors. You have a law which no
man can obey, or abet the obeying, without loss
of self-respect and forfeiture of the name of
gentleman. What shall we say of the function-
ary by whom the recent rendition was made?
If he has rightly defined his powers, and has
no authority to try the case, but only to prove
the prisoner's identity, and remand him, what
office is this for a reputable citizen to hold?
No man of honor can sit on that bench. It is
the extension of the planter's whipping-post;
and its incumbents must rank with a class
from which the turnkey, the hangman and the
informer are taken, necessary functionaries, it
may be, in a state, but to whom the dislike and
the ban of society universally attaches.

5. These resistances appear in the history of
the statute, in the retributions which speak so
loud in every part of this business, that I think
a tragic poet will know how to make it a lesson for all ages. Mr. Webster's measure was,
he told us, final. It was a pacification, it was a
suppression, a measure of conciliation and adjustment. These were his words at different
times : " there was to be no parleying more ;"
it was " irrepealable." Does it look final now?

His final settlement has dislocated the foundations. The state-house shakes likes a tent. His
pacification has brought all the honesty in every
house, all scrupulous and good-hearted men, all
women, and all children, to accuse the law. It
has brought United States swords into the
streets, and chains round the court-house. " A
measure of pacification and union." What is
its effect? To make one sole subject for conversation and painful thought throughout the
continent, namely, slavery. There is not a man
of thought or of feeling but is concentrating
his mind on it. There is not a clerk but recites
its statistics ; not a politician but is watching its
incalculable energy in the elections ; not a jurist
but is hunting up precedents ; not a moralist
but is prying into its quality ; not an economist but is computing its profit and loss : Mr.
Webster can judge whether this sort of solar
microscope brought to bear on his law is likely
to make opposition less. The only benefit that
has accrued from the law is its service to education. It has been like a university to the entire
people. It has turned every dinner-table into a
debating-club, and made every citizen a student
of natural law. When a moral quality comes
into politics, when a right is invaded, the discus-

sion draws on deeper sources : general principles are laid bare, which cast light on the whole frame of society. And it is cheering to behold what champions the emergency called to this poor black boy ; what subtlety, what logic, what learning, what exposure of the mischief of the law ; and, above all, with what earnestness and dignity the advocates of freedom were inspired. It was one of the best compensations of this calamity.

But the Nemesis works underneath again. It is a power that makes noonday dark, and draws us on to our undoing ; and its dismal way is to pillory the offender in the moment of his triumph. The hands that put the chain on the slave are in that moment manacled. Who has seen anything like that which is now done ? The words of John Randolph, wiser than he knew, have been ringing ominously in all echoes for thirty years, words spoken in the heat of the Missouri debate "We do not govern the people of the North by our black slaves, but by their own white slaves. We know what we are doing. We have conquered you once, and we can and will conquer you again. Ay, we will drive you to the wall, and when we have you there once more, we will keep you there and nail you down

like base money." These words resounding
ever since from California to Oregon, from Cape
Florida to Cape Cod, come down now like the
cry of Fate, in the moment when they are fulfilled. By white slaves, by a white slave, are we
beaten.' Who looked for such ghastly fulfil-
ment, or to see what we see? Hills and Halletts,
servile editors by the hundred, we could have
spared. But him, our best and proudest, the
first man of the North, in the very moment of
mounting the throne, irresistibly taking the bit
in his mouth and the collar on his neck, and har-
nessing himself to the chariot of the planters.

The fairest American fame ends in this filthy
law. Mr. Webster cannot choose but regret
his law. He must learn that those who make
fame accuse him with one voice ; that those who
have no points to carry that are not identical
with public morals and generous civilization,
that the obscure and private who have no voice
and care for none, so long as things go well,
but who feel the disgrace of the new legislation
creeping like miasma into their homes, and blot-
ting the daylight, — those to whom his name
was once dear and honored, as the manly statesman to whom the choicest gifts of Nature had
been accorded, disown him : that he who was

their pride in the woods and mountains of New
England is now their mortification, — they have
torn down his picture from the wall, they have
thrust his speeches into the chimney. No roars
of New York mobs can drown this voice in Mr
Webster's ear. It will outwhisper all the salvos
of the "Union Committees'" cannon. But I
have said too much on this painful topic. I will
not pursue that bitter history.'

But passing from the ethical to the political
view, I wish to place this statute, and we must
use the introducer and substantial author of the
bill as an illustration of the history. I have
as much charity for Mr. Webster, I think, as
any one has. I need not say how much I have
enjoyed his fame. Who has not helped to praise
him? Simply he was the one eminent American of our time, whom we could produce as a
finished work of Nature. We delighted in his
form and face, in his voice, in his eloquence,
in his power of labor, in his concentration, in
his large understanding, in his daylight statement, simple force ; the facts lay like the strata
of a cloud, or like the layers of the crust of
the globe. He saw things as they were, and
he stated them so He has been by his clear
perceptions and statements in all these years

the best head in Congress, and the champion
of the interests of the Northern seaboard : but
as the activity and growth of slavery began to be
offensively felt by his constituents, the senator
became less sensitive to these evils. They were
not for him to deal with : he was the commercial representative. He indulged occasionally
in excellent expression of the known feeling of
the New England people : but, when expected
and when pledged, he omitted to speak, and
he omitted to throw himself into the movement
in those critical moments when his leadership
would have turned the scale. At last, at a fatal
hour, this sluggishness accumulated to down-
right counteraction, and, very unexpectedly to
the whole Union, on the 7th March, 1850, in
opposition to his education, association, and to
all his own most explicit language for thirty
years, he crossed the line, and became the head
of the slavery party in this country.

Mr. Webster perhaps is only following the
laws of his blood and constitution. I suppose
his pledges were not quite natural to him. Mr.
Webster is a man who lives by his memory, a
man of the past, not a man of faith or of hope.
He obeys his powerful animal nature ; — and
his finely developed understanding only works

truly and with all its force, when it stands for
animal good; that is, for property. He believes,
in so many words, that government exists for the
protection of property. He looks at the Union
as an estate, a large farm, and is excellent in
the completeness of his defence of it so far. He
adheres to the letter. Happily he was born
late, — after the independence had been declared, the Union agreed to, and the constitution settled. What he finds already written, he
will defend. Lucky that so much had got well
written when he came. For he has no faith in
the power of self-government; none whatever
in extemporizing a government. Not the smallest municipal provision, if it were new, would
receive his sanction. In Massachusetts, in 1776,
he would, beyond all question, have been a
refugee. He praises Adams and Jefferson, but
it is a past Adams and Jefferson that his mind
can entertain.' A present Adams and Jefferson
he would denounce. So with the eulogies of
liberty in his writings, — they are sentimentalism
and youthful rhetoric. He can celebrate it, but
it means as much from him as from Metternich
or Talleyrand. This is all inevitable from his
constitution. All the drops of his blood have
eyes that look downward. It is neither praise

nor blame to say that he has no moral perception, no moral sentiment, but in that region —
to use the phrase of the phrenologists — a
hole in the head. The scraps of morality to be
gleaned from his speeches are reflections of the
mind of others; he says what he hears said,
but often makes signal blunders in their use. In
Mr. Webster's imagination the American Union
was a huge Prince Rupert's drop, which, if so
much as the smallest end be shivered off, the
whole will snap into atoms. Now the fact is
quite different from this. The people are loyal,
law-loving, law-abiding. They prefer order, and
have no taste for misrule and uproar.

The destiny of this country is great and liberal, and is to be greatly administered. It is to
be administered according to what is, and is
to be, and not according to what is dead and
gone. The union of this people is a real thing,
an alliance of men of one flock, one language,
one religion, one system of manners and ideas.
I hold it to be a real and not a statute union.
The people cleave to the Union, because they
see their advantage in it, the added power of
each.

I suppose the Union can be left to take care
of itself. As much real union as there is, the

statutes will be sure to express; as much disunion
as there is, no statute can long conceal. Under
the Union I suppose the fact to be that there
are really two nations, the North and the
South. It is not slavery that severs them, it is
climate and temperament. The South does not
like the North, slavery or no slavery, and never
did. The North likes the South well enough,
for it knows its own advantages. I am willing
to leave them to the facts. If they continue to
have a binding interest, they will be pretty sure
to find it out: if not, they will consult their
peace in parting. But one thing appears certain
to me, that, as soon as the constitution ordains
an immoral law, it ordains disunion. The law is
suicidal, and cannot be obeyed. The Union is
at an end as soon as an immoral law is enacted.
And he who writes a crime into the statute-
book digs under the foundations of the Capitol
to plant there a powder-magazine, and lays a
train.

I pass to say a few words to the question,
What shall we do?

1. What in our federal capacity is our relation to the nation?

2. And what as citizens of a state?

I am an Unionist as we all are, or nearly all,

and I strongly share the hope of mankind in the power, and therefore, in the duties of the Union ; and I conceive it demonstrated, — the necessity of common sense and justice entering into the laws. What shall we do? First, abrogate this law ; then, proceed to confine slavery to slave states, and help them effectually to make an end of it. Or shall we, as we are advised on all hands, lie by, and wait the progress of the census? But will Slavery lie by? I fear not. She is very industrious, gives herself no holidays. No proclamations will put her down. She got Texas and now will have Cuba, and means to keep her majority. The experience of the past gives us no encouragement to lie by. Shall we call a new Convention, or will any expert statesman furnish us a plan for the summary or gradual winding up of slavery, so far as the Republic is its patron? Where is the South itself? Since it is agreed by all sane men of all parties (or was yesterday) that slavery is mischievous, why does the South itself never offer the smallest counsel of her own? I have never heard in twenty years any project except Mr. Clay's. Let us hear any project with candor and respect. Is it impossible to speak of it with reason and good nature? It is really the project fit for this country to entertain and accomplish. Everything invites emancipation. The grandeur of the design, the vast stake we hold ; the national domain, the new importance of Liberia ; the manifest interest of the slave states ; the religious effort of the free states , the public opinion of the world ; — all join to demand it.

We shall one day bring the States shoulder to shoulder and the citizens man to man to exterminate slavery. Why in the name of common sense and the peace of mankind is not this made the subject of instant negotiation and settlement? Why not end this dangerous dispute on some ground of fair compensation on one side, and satisfaction on the other to the conscience of the free states ? It is really the great task fit for this country to accomplish, to buy that property of the planters, as the British nation bought the West Indian slaves. I say buy, — never conceding the right of the planter to own, but that we may acknowledge the calamity of his position, and bear a countryman's share in relieving him ; and because it is the only practicable course, and is innocent. Here is a right social or public function, which one man cannot do, which all men must do. 'Tis said it will cost two thousand millions of dollars. Was there ever any contribution that was so enthusiastically paid as this will be ? We will have a chimney-tax. We will give up our coaches, and wine, and watches. The churches will melt their plate. The father of his country shall wait, well pleased, a little longer for his monument; Franklin for his, the Pilgrim Fathers for theirs, and the patient Columbus for his. The mechanics will give, the needle-women will give; the children will have cent-societies. Every man in the land will give a week's work to dig away this accursed mountain of sorrow once and forever out of the world.[1]

Nothing is impracticable to this nation, which it shall set itself to do. Were ever men so endowed, so placed, so weaponed? Their power of territory seconded by a genius equal to every work. By new arts the earth is subdued, roaded, tunnelled, telegraphed, gas-lighted; vast amounts of old labor disused; the sinews of man being relieved by sinews of steam. We are on the brink of more wonders. The sun paints; presently we shall organize the echo, as now we do the shadow. Chemistry is extorting new aids. The genius of this people, it is found, can do anything which can be done by men. These

XI

thirty nations are equal to any work, and are
every moment stronger. In twenty-five years
they will be fifty millions. Is it not time to do
something besides ditching and draining, and
making the earth mellow and friable? Let
them confront this mountain of poison, — bore,
blast, excavate, pulverize, and shovel it once
for all, down into the bottomless Pit. A thousand millions were cheap.

But grant that the heart of financiers, accustomed to practical figures, shrinks within them at
these colossal amounts, and the embarrassments
which complicate the problem; granting that
these contingencies are too many to be spanned
by any human geometry, and that these evils
are to be relieved only by the wisdom of God
working in ages, — and by what instrument,
whether Liberia, whether flax-cotton, whether
the working out this race by Irish and Ger-
mans, none can tell, or by what sources God
has guarded his law ; still the question recurs,
What must we do? One thing is plain, we
cannot answer for the Union, but we must
keep Massachusetts true It is of unspeakable
importance that she play her honest part. She
must follow no vicious examples. Massachusetts
is a little state: countries have been great by

ideas. Europe is little compared with Asia and
Africa; yet Asia and Africa are its ox and its
ass. Europe, the least of all the continents, has
almost monopolized for twenty centuries the
genius and power of them all. Greece was the
least part of Europe. Attica a little part of that,
— one tenth of the size of Massachusetts. Yet
that district still rules the intellect of men.
Judæa was a petty country. Yet these two,
Greece and Judæa, furnish the mind and the
heart by which the rest of the world is sus-
tained; and Massachusetts is little, but, if true
to itself, can be the brain which turns about
the behemoth.

I say Massachusetts, but I mean Massachusetts in all the quarters of her dispersion;
Massachusetts, as she is the mother of all the
New England states, and as she sees her pro-
geny scattered over the face of the land, in the
farthest South, and the uttermost West. The
immense power of rectitude is apt to be forgotten in politics. But they who have brought the
great wrong on the country have not forgotten
it. They avail themselves of the known probity
and honor of Massachusetts, to endorse the
statute. The ancient maxim still holds that
never was any injustice effected except by the

help of justice. The great game of the government has been to win the sanction of Massachusetts to the crime. Hitherto they have succeeded only so far as to win Boston to a certain extent. The behavior of Boston was the reverse of what it should have been : it was supple and officious, and it put itself into the base attitude of pander to the crime. It should have placed obstruction at every step. Let the attitude of the states be firm. Let us respect the Union to all honest ends. But also respect an older and wider union, the law of Nature and rectitude. Massachusetts is as strong as the Universe, when it does that. We will never intermeddle with your slavery, — but you can in no wise be suffered to bring it to Cape Cod and Berkshire. This law must be made inoperative. It must be abrogated and wiped out of the statute-book ; but whilst it stands there, it must be disobeyed. We must make a small state great, by making every man in it true. It was the praise of Athens, " She could not lead countless armies into the field, but she knew how with a little band to defeat those who could." Every Roman reckoned himself at least a match for a Province. Every Dorian did. Every Englishman in Australia, in South

Africa, in India, or in whatever barbarous country their forts and factories have been set up, —
represents London, represents the art, power
and law of Europe. Every man educated at
the Northern school carries the like advantages
into the South. For it is confounding distinctions to speak of the geographic sections of
this country as of equal civilization. Every nation and every man bows, in spite of himself,
to a higher mental and moral existence; and
the sting of the late disgraces is that this royal
position of Massachusetts was foully lost, that
the well-known sentiment of her people was not
expressed. Let us correct this error. In this
one fastness let truth be spoken and right done.
Here let there be no confusion in our ideas.
Let us not lie, not steal, nor help to steal, and
let us not call stealing by any fine name, such
as " Union" or " Patriotism." Let us know
that not by the public, but by ourselves, our
safety must be bought. That is the secret of
Southern power, that they rest not on meetings,
but on private heats and courages.

It is very certain from the perfect guaranties
in the constitution, and the high arguments of
the defenders of liberty, which the occasion
called out, that there is sufficient margin in the

statute and the law for the spirit of the Magistrate to show itself, and one, two, three occasions
have just now occurred, and past, in either of
which, if one man had felt the spirit of Coke or
Mansfield or Parsons, and read the law with the
eye of freedom, the dishonor of Massachusetts
had been prevented, and a limit set to these
encroachments forever.

VII

THE FUGITIVE SLAVE LAW

LECTURE READ IN THE TABERNACLE, NEW YORK CITY
MARCH 7, 1854, ON THE FOURTH ANNIVERSARY
OF DANIEL WEBSTER'S SPEECH IN FAVOR
OF THE BILL

" OF all we loved and honored, naught
 Save power remains, —
A fallen angel's pride of thought,
 Still strong in chains.

All else is gone; from those great eyes
 The soul has fled.
When faith is lost, when honor dies,
 The man is dead! "

Whittier, *Ichabod!*

We that had loved him so, followed him, honoured him
  Lived in his mind and magnificent eye,
Learned his great language, caught his clear accents,
  Made him our pattern to live and to die!
Shakspeare was of us, Milton was for us,
  Burns, Shelley, were with us, — they watch from the
     graves!
He alone breaks from the van and the freemen,
  — He alone sinks to the rear and the slaves!"
                    Browning, *The Lost Leader*

THE FUGITIVE SLAVE LAW

I DO not often speak to public questions;
— they are odious and hurtful, and it seems
like meddling or leaving your work. I have
my own spirits in prison ; — spirits in deeper
prisons, whom no man visits if I do not. And
then I see what havoc it makes with any good
mind, a dissipated philanthropy. The one thing
not to be forgiven to intellectual persons is, not
to know their own task, or to take their ideas
from others. From this want of manly rest in
their own and rash acceptance of other people's
watchwords come the imbecility and fatigue of
their conversation. For they cannot affirm these
from any original experience, and of course not
with the natural movement and total strength
of their nature and talent, but only from their
memory, only from their cramped position of
standing for their teacher. They say what they
would have you believe, but what they do not
quite know.[1]

My own habitual view is to the well-being of
students or scholars. And it is only when the
public event affects them, that it very seriously
touches me. And what I have to say is to

them. For every man speaks mainly to a class
whom he works with and more or less fully represents. It is to these I am beforehand related
and engaged, in this audience or out of it — to
them and not to others. And yet, when I say
the class of scholars or students, — that is a
class which comprises in some sort all mankind,
comprises every man in the best hours of his
life; and in these days not only virtually but
actually. For who are the readers and think-
ers of 1854? Owing to the silent revolution
which the newspaper has wrought, this class
has come in this country to take in all classes.
Look into the morning trains which, from every
suburb, carry the business men into the city to
their shops, counting-rooms, work-yards and
warehouses. With them enters the car — the
newsboy, that humble priest of politics, finance,
philosophy, and religion. He unfolds his magical sheets, — twopence a head his bread of
knowledge costs — and instantly the entire rec-
tangular assembly, fresh from their breakfast,
are bending as one man to their second breakfast. There is, no doubt, chaff enough in what
he brings; but there is fact, thought, and wisdom in the crude mass, from all regions of the
world.

I have lived all my life without suffering any known inconvenience from American Slavery. I never saw it; I never heard the whip;¹ I never felt the check on my free speech and action, until, the other day, when Mr. Webster, by his personal influence, brought the Fugitive Slave Law on the country. I say Mr. Webster, for though the Bill was not his, it is yet notorious that he was the life and soul of it, that he gave it all he had: it cost him his life, and under the shadow of his great name inferior men sheltered themselves, threw their ballots for it and made the law. I say inferior men. There were all sorts of what are called brilliant men, accomplished men, men of high station, a President of the United States, Senators, men of eloquent speech, but men without self-respect, without character, and it was strange to see that office, age, fame, talent, even a repute for honesty, all count for nothing. They had no opinions, they had no memory for what they had been saying like the Lord's Prayer all their lifetime: they were only looking to what their great Captain did: if he jumped, they jumped, if he stood on his head, they did. In ordinary, the supposed sense of their district and State is their guide, and that holds them to the part of

liberty and justice. But it is always a little difficult to decipher what this public sense is ; and
when a great man comes who knots up into
himself the opinions and wishes of the people,
it is so much easier to follow him as an expo-
nent of this. He too is responsible; they will
not be. It will always suffice to say, — " I followed him."

I saw plainly that the great show their legitimate power in nothing more than in their power
to misguide us. I saw that a great man, deserv-
edly admired for his powers and their general
right direction, was able, — fault of the total
want of stamina in public men, — when he failed,
to break them all with him, to carry parties with
him.

In what I have to say of Mr. Webster I do
not confound him with vulgar politicians before
or since. There is always base ambition enough,
men who calculate on the immense ignorance of
the masses ; that is their quarry and farm : they
use the constituencies at home only for their
shoes. And, of course, they can drive out from
the contest any honorable man. The low can
best win the low, and all men like to be made
much of. There are those too who have power
and inspiration only to do ill. Their talent or

their faculty deserts them when they undertake anything right. Mr. Webster had a natural ascendancy of aspect and carriage which distinguished him over all his contemporaries. His countenance, his figure, and his manners were all in so grand a style, that he was, without effort, as superior to his most eminent rivals as they were to the humblest ; so that his arrival in any place was an event which drew crowds of people, who went to satisfy their eyes, and could not see him enough. I think they looked at him as the representative of the American Continent. He was there in his Adamitic capacity, as if he alone of all men did not disappoint the eye and the ear, but was a fit figure in the landscape.'

I remember his appearance at Bunker's Hill. There was the Monument, and here was Webster. He knew well that a little more or less of rhetoric signified nothing : he was only to say plain and equal things, — grand things if he had them, and, if he had them not, only to abstain from saying unfit things, — and the whole occasion was answered by his presence. It was a place for behavior more than for speech, and Mr. Webster walked through his part with entire success. His excellent organization, the

perfection of his elocution and all that thereto
belongs, — voice, accent, intonation, attitude,
manner, — we shall not soon find again. Then
he was so thoroughly simple and wise in his
rhetoric ; he saw through his matter, hugged his
fact so close, went to the principle or essential,
and never indulged in a weak flourish, though
he knew perfectly well how to make such ex-
ordiums, episodes and perorations as might
give perspective to his harangues without in the
least embarrassing his march or confounding
his transitions. In his statement things lay in
daylight ; we saw them in order as they were.
Though he knew very well how to present his
own personal claims, yet in his argument he was
intellectual, — stated his fact pure of all personality, so that his splendid wrath, when his eyes
became lamps, was the wrath of the fact and
the cause he stood for.

His power, like that of all great masters, was
not in excellent parts, but was total. He had
a great and everywhere equal propriety. He
worked with that closeness of adhesion to the
matter in hand which a joiner or a chemist uses,
and the same quiet and sure feeling of right to
his place that an oak or a mountain have to
theirs. After all his talents have been described,

there remains that perfect propriety which animated all the details of the action or speech
with the character of the whole, so that his
beauties of detail are endless. He seemed born
for the bar, born for the senate, and took very
naturally a leading part in large private and in
public affairs; for his head distributed things
in their right places, and what he saw so well
he compelled other people to see also. Great
is the privilege of eloquence. What gratitude
does every man feel to him who speaks well
for the right,— who translates truth into language entirely plain and clear!

The history of this country has given a disastrous importance to the defects of this great
man's mind. Whether evil influences and the
corruption of politics, or whether original in-
firmity, it was the misfortune of his country
that with this large understanding he had not
what is better than intellect, and the source of
its health. It is a law of our nature that great
thoughts come from the heart. If his moral
sensibility had been proportioned to the force
of his understanding, what limits could have
been set to his genius and beneficent power?
But he wanted that deep source of inspiration.
Hence a sterility of thought, the want of gen-

eralization in his speeches, and the curious fact
that, with a general ability which impresses all
the world, there is not a single general remark,
not an observation on life and manners, not an
aphorism that can pass into literature from his
writings.

Four years ago to-night, on one of those
high critical moments in history when great is-
sues are determined, when the powers of right
and wrong are mustered for conflict, and it lies
with one man to give a casting vote, — Mr.
Webster, most unexpectedly, threw his whole
weight on the side of Slavery, and caused by
his personal and official authority the passage
of the Fugitive Slave Bill.

It is remarked of the Americans that they
value dexterity too much, and honor too little ;
that they think they praise a man more by
saying that he is "smart" than by saying that
he is right. Whether the defect be national or
not, it is the defect and calamity of Mr. Webster ; and it is so far true of his countrymen,
namely, that the appeal is sure to be made to
his physical and mental ability when his character is assailed. His speeches on the seventh
of March, and at Albany, at Buffalo, at Syracuse
and Boston are cited in justification   And Mr

Webster's literary editor believes that it was his wish to rest his fame on the speech of the seventh of March. Now, though I have my own opinions on this seventh of March discourse and those others, and think them very transparent and very open to criticism, — yet the secondary merits of a speech, namely, its logic, its illustrations, its points, etc., are not here in question. Nobody doubts that Daniel Webster could make a good speech. Nobody doubts that there were good and plausible things to be said on the part of the South. But this is not a question of ingenuity, not a question of syllogisms, but of sides. *How came he there?*'

There are always texts and thoughts and arguments. But it is the genius and temper of the man which decides whether he will stand for right or for might. Who doubts the power of any fluent debater to defend either of our political parties, or any client in our courts? There was the same law in England for Jeffries and Talbot and Yorke to read slavery out of, and for Lord Mansfield to read freedom. And in this country one sees that there is always margin enough in the statute for a liberal judge to read one way and a servile judge another.

But the question which History will ask is

XI

broader. In the final hour, when he was forced
by the peremptory necessity of the closing
armies to take a side, — did he take the part
of great principles, the side of humanity and
justice, or the side of abuse and oppression
and chaos?

Mr. Webster decided for Slavery, and that,
when the aspect of the institution was no longer
doubtful, no longer feeble and apologetic and
proposing soon to end itself, but when it was
strong, aggressive, and threatening an illimit-
able increase. He listened to State reasons and
hopes, and left, with much complacency we are
told, the testament of his speech to the astonished State of Massachusetts, *vera pro gratis*,
a ghastly result of all those years of experience
in affairs, this, that there was nothing better for
the foremost American man to tell his countrymen than that Slavery was now at that strength
that they must beat down their conscience and
become kidnappers for it.

This was like the doleful speech falsely
ascribed to the patriot Brutus: "Virtue, I have
followed thee through life, and I find thee but a
shadow." ' Here was a question of an immoral
law; a question agitated for ages, and settled always in the same way by every great jurist, that

an immoral law cannot be valid. Cicero, Grotius,
Coke, Blackstone, Burlamaqui, Vattel, Burke,
Jefferson, do all affirm this, and I cite them, not
that they can give evidence to what is indisput-
able, but because, though lawyers and practical
statesmen, the habit of their profession did not
hide from them that this truth was the foundation of States.

Here was the question, Are you for man and
for the good of man ; or are you for the hurt and
harm of man ? It was the question whether man
shall be treated as leather ? whether the Negro
shall be, as the Indians were in Spanish America,
a piece of money ? Whether this system, which
is a kind of mill or factory for converting men
into monkeys, shall be upheld and enlarged?
And Mr. Webster and the country went for the
application to these poor men of quadruped law.

People were expecting a totally different course
from Mr. Webster. If any man had in that hour
possessed the weight with the country which he
had acquired, he could have brought the whole
country to its senses. But not a moment's pause
was allowed. Angry parties went from bad to
worse, and the decision of Webster was accom-
panied with everything offensive to freedom and
good morals. There was something like an

attempt to debauch the moral sentiment of the
clergy and of the youth.   Burke said he "would
pardon something to the spirit of liberty."   But
by Mr. Webster the opposition to the law was
sharply called treason, and prosecuted so.   He
told the people at Boston "they must conquer
their prejudices;" that "agitation of the subject
of Slavery must be suppressed."   He did as
immoral men usually do, made very low bows
to the Christian Church, and went through all
the Sunday decorums; but when allusion was
made to the question of duty and the sanctions
of morality, he very frankly said, at Albany,
"Some higher law, something existing somewhere between here and the third heaven,— I
do not know where."   And if the reporters say
true, this wretched atheism found some laughter
in the company.

I said I had never in my life up to this time
suffered from the Slave Institution.   Slavery in
Virginia or Carolina was like Slavery in Africa
or the Feejees, for me   There was an old fugitive law, but it had become, or was fast becoming, a dead letter, and, by the genius and laws of
Massachusetts, inoperative.   The new Bill made
it operative, required me to hunt slaves, and it
found citizens in Massachusetts willing to act

as judges and captors. Moreover, it discloses
the secret of the new times, that Slavery was no
longer mendicant, but was become aggressive
and dangerous.

The way in which the country was dragged to
consent to this, and the disastrous defection (on
the miserable cry of Union) of the men of letters,
of the colleges, of educated men, nay, of some
preachers of religion, — was the darkest passage
in the history. It showed that our prosperity
had hurt us, and that we could not be shocked
by crime. It showed that the old religion and
the sense of the right had faded and gone out;
that while we reckoned ourselves a highly cultivated nation, our bellies had run away with our
brains, and the principles of culture and progress
did not exist.

For I suppose that liberty is an accurate index, in men and nations, of general progress.
The theory of personal liberty must always
appeal to the most refined communities and to
the men of the rarest perception and of delicate
moral sense. For there are rights which rest on
the finest sense of justice, and, with every degree
of civility, it will be more truly felt and defined.
A barbarous tribe of good stock will, by means
of their best heads, secure substantial liberty.

But where there is any weakness in a race, and it becomes in a degree matter of concession and protection from their stronger neighbors, the incompatibility and offensiveness of the wrong will of course be most evident to the most cultivated. For it is, — is it not? — the essence of courtesy, of politeness, of religion, of love, to prefer another, to postpone oneself, to protect another from oneself. That is the distinction of the gentleman, to defend the weak and redress the injured, as it is of the savage and the brutal to usurp and use others.

In Massachusetts, as we all know, there has always existed a predominant conservative spirit. We have more money and value of every kind than other people, and wish to keep them. The plea on which freedom was resisted was Union. I went to certain serious men, who had a little more reason than the rest, and inquired why they took this part? They answered that they had no confidence in their strength to resist the Democratic party; that they saw plainly that all was going to the utmost verge of licence; each was vying with his neighbor to lead the party, by proposing the worst measure, and they threw themselves on the extreme conservatism, as a drag on the wheel: that they knew Cuba would

be had, and Mexico would be had, and they
stood stiffly on conservatism, and as near to mon-
archy as they could, only to moderate the velocity with which the car was running down the
precipice. In short, their theory was despair;
the Whig wisdom was only reprieve, a waiting
to be last devoured. They side with Carolina,
or with Arkansas, only to make a show of Whig
strength, wherewith to resist a little longer this
general ruin.

I have a respect for conservatism. I know
how deeply founded it is in our nature, and how
idle are all attempts to shake ourselves free from
it. We are all conservatives, half Whig, half
Democrat, in our essences: and might as well
try to jump out of our skins as to escape from
our Whiggery. There are two forces in Nature,
by whose antagonism we exist; the power of
Fate, Fortune, the laws of the world, the order
of things, or however else we choose to phrase
it, the material necessities, on the one hand, —
and Will or Duty or Freedom on the other.

May and Must, and the sense of right and
duty, on the one hand, and the material necessities on the other: May and Must. In vulgar
politics the Whig goes for what has been, for
the old necessities, — the Musts. The reformer

goes for the Better, for the ideal good, for the
Mays. But each of these parties must of necessity take in, in some measure, the principles
of the other. Each wishes to cover the whole
ground; to hold fast *and* to advance. Only,
one lays the emphasis on keeping, and the other
on advancing. I too think the *musts* are a safe
company to follow, and even agreeable. But if
we are Whigs, let us be Whigs of nature and
science, and so for all the necessities. Let us
know that, over and above all the *musts* of poverty and appetite, is the instinct of man to rise,
and the instinct to love and help his brother.

Now, Gentlemen, I think we have in this
hour instruction again in the simplest lesson.
Events roll, millions of men are engaged, and
the result is the enforcing of some of those first
commandments which we heard in the nursery.
We never get beyond our first lesson, for,
really, the world exists, as I understand it, to
teach the science of liberty, which begins with
liberty from fear.

The events of this month are teaching one
thing plain and clear, the worthlessness of good
tools to bad workmen; that official papers are
of no use; resolutions of public meetings, plat-
forms of conventions, no, nor laws, nor constitu-

tions, any more. These are all declaratory of the
will of the moment, and are passed with more
levity and on grounds far less honorable than
ordinary business transactions of the street.

You relied on the constitution. It has not
the word *slave* in it; and very good argument
has shown that it would not warrant the crimes
that are done under it; that, with provisions
so vague for an object not named, and which
could not be availed of to claim a barrel of sugar
or a barrel of corn, the robbing of a man and
of all his posterity is effected. You relied on
the Supreme Court. The law was right, excellent law for the lambs. But what if unhappily
the judges were chosen from the wolves, and
give to all the law a wolfish interpretation?
You relied on the Missouri Compromise. That
is ridden over. You relied on State sovereignty
in the Free States to protect their citizens.
They are driven with contempt out of the courts
and out of the territory of the Slave States, —
if they are so happy as to get out with their
lives,' — and now you relied on these dismal
guaranties infamously made in 1850; and, before the body of Webster is yet crumbled, it is
found that they have crumbled. This eternal
monument of his fame and of the Union is

rotten in four years. They are no guaranty to
the free states. They are a guaranty to the
slave states that, as they have hitherto met with
no repulse, they shall meet with none.

I fear there is no reliance to be put on any
kind or form of covenant, no, not on sacred
forms, none on churches, none on bibles. For
one would have said that a Christian would not
keep slaves ; — but the Christians keep slaves.
Of course they will not dare to read the Bible?
Won't they? They quote the Bible, quote Paul,'
quote Christ, to justify slavery. If slavery is
good, then is lying, theft, arson, homicide, each
and all good, and to be maintained by Union
societies.

These things show that no forms, neither constitutions, nor laws, nor covenants, nor churches,
nor bibles, are of any use in themselves. The
Devil nestles comfortably into them all. There
is no help but in the head and heart and ham-
strings of a man. Covenants are of no use
without honest men to keep them ; laws of
none but with loyal citizens to obey them. To
interpret Christ it needs Christ in the heart.
The teachings of the Spirit can be apprehended
only by the same spirit that gave them forth.
To make good the cause of Freedom, you

must draw off from all foolish trust in others.
You must be citadels and warriors yourselves,
declarations of Independence, the charter, the
battle and the victory. Cromwell said, " We
can only resist the superior training of the
King's soldiers, by enlisting godly men." And
no man has a right to hope that the laws of
New York will defend him from the contamination of slaves another day until he has made
up his mind that he will not owe his protection
to the laws of New York, but to his own sense
and spirit. Then he protects New York. He
only who is able to stand alone is qualified for
society. And that I understand to be the end
for which a soul exists in this world, — to be
himself the counterbalance of all falsehood and
all wrong. " The army of unright is encamped
from pole to pole, but the road of victory is
known to the just." Everything may be taken
away ; he may be poor, he may be houseless,
yet he will know out of his arms to make a pillow, and out of his breast a bolster. Why have
the minority no influence? Because they have
not a real minority of one.[1]

I conceive that thus to detach a man and
make him feel that he is to owe all to himself,
is the way to make him strong and rich ; and

here the optimist must find, if anywhere, the benefit of Slavery. We have many teachers; we are in this world for culture, to be instructed in realities, in the laws of moral and intelligent nature; and our education is not conducted by toys and luxuries, but by austere and rugged masters, by poverty, solitude, passions, War, Slavery; to know that Paradise is under the shadow of swords; ' that divine sentiments which are always soliciting us are breathed into us from on high, and are an offset to a Universe of suffering and crime; that self-reliance, the height and perfection of man, is reliance on God ' The insight of the religious sentiment will disclose to him unexpected aids in the nature of things. The Persian Saadi said, " Beware of hurting the orphan When the orphan sets a-crying, the throne of the Almighty is rocked from side to side."

Whenever a man has come to this mind, that there is no Church for him but his believing prayer; no Constitution but his dealing well and justly with his neighbor, no liberty but his invincible will to do right, — then certain aids and allies will promptly appear: for the constitution of the Universe is on his side. It is of no use to vote down gravitation of morals.

What is useful will last, whilst that which is
hurtful to the world will sink beneath all the
opposing forces which it must exasperate. The
terror which the Marseillaise struck into oppression, it thunders again to-day, —

"Tout est soldat pour vous combattre."

Everything turns soldier to fight you down.
The end for which man was made is not crime
in any form, and a man cannot steal without
incurring the penalties of the thief, though all
the legislatures vote that it is virtuous, and
though there be a general conspiracy among
scholars and official persons to hold him up,
and to say, "*Nothing is good but stealing.*" A
man who commits a crime defeats the end of
his existence. He was created for benefit, and
he exists for harm; and as well-doing makes
power and wisdom, ill-doing takes them away.
A man who steals another man's labor steals
away his own faculties; his integrity, his humanity is flowing away from him. The habit
of oppression cuts out the moral eyes, and,
though the intellect goes on simulating the
moral as before, its sanity is gradually destroyed.
It takes away the presentiments.

I suppose in general this is allowed, that if

you have a nice question of right and wrong,
you would not go with it to Louis Napoleon,
or to a political hack, or to a slave-driver. The
habit of mind of traders in power would not be
esteemed favorable to delicate moral perception.
American slavery affords no exception to this
rule No excess of good nature or of tenderness in individuals has been able to give a new
character to the system, to tear down the whip-
ping-house. The plea in the mouth of a slave-
holder that the negro is an inferior race sounds
very oddly in my ear. " The masters of slaves
seem generally anxious to prove that they are
not of a race superior in any noble quality to
the meanest of their bondmen." And indeed
when the Southerner points to the anatomy of
the negro, and talks of chimpanzee, — I recall
Montesquieu's remark, " It will not do to say
that negroes are men, lest it should turn out
that whites are not "

Slavery is disheartening, but Nature is not
so helpless but it can rid itself at last of every
wrong.' But the spasms of Nature are centuries
and ages, and will tax the faith of short-lived
men. Slowly, slowly the Avenger comes, but
comes surely. The proverbs of the nations
affirm these delays, but affirm the arrival. They

say, " God may consent, but not forever." The
delay of the Divine Justice — this was the meaning and soul of the Greek Tragedy; this the soul
of their religion. " There has come, too, one to
whom lurking warfare is dear, Retribution, with
a soul full of wiles; a violator of hospitality;
guileful without the guilt of guile; limping,
late in her arrival." They said of the happiness
of the unjust, that " at its close it begets itself
an offspring and does not die childless, and
instead of good fortune, there sprouts forth for
posterity ever-ravening calamity : " —

> " For evil word shall evil word be said,
> For murder-stroke a murder-stroke be paid.
> Who smites must smart."

These delays, you see them now in the temper of the times. The national spirit in this
country is so drowsy, preoccupied with interest, deaf to principle. The Anglo-Saxon race
is proud and strong and selfish. They believe
only in Anglo-Saxons. In 1825 Greece found
America deaf, Poland found America deaf, Italy
and Hungary found her deaf. England main-
tains trade, not liberty; stands against Greece ·
against Hungary; against Schleswig-Holstein;
against the French Republic whilst it was a
republic.

To faint hearts the times offer no invitation, and torpor exists here throughout the active classes on the subject of domestic slavery and its appalling aggressions. Yes, that is the stern edict of Providence, that liberty shall be no hasty fruit, but that event on event, population on population, age on age, shall cast itself into the opposite scale, and not until liberty has slowly accumulated weight enough to counter vail and preponderate against all this, can the sufficient recoil come. All the great cities, all the refined circles, all the statesmen, Guizot, Palm-eiston, Webster, Calhoun, are sure to be found befriending liberty with their words, and crushing it with their votes. Liberty is never cheap. It is made difficult, because freedom is the accomplishment and perfectness of man. He is a finished man,' earning and bestowing good; equal to the world; at home in Nature and dignifying that; the sun does not see anything nobler, and has nothing to teach him. Therefore mountains of difficulty must be surmounted, stern trials met, wiles of seduction, dangers, healed by a quarantine of calamities to measure his strength before he dare say, I am free.

Whilst the inconsistency of slavery with the principles on which the world is built guarantees

its downfall, I own that the patience it requires
is almost too sublime for mortals, and seems to
demand of us more than mere hoping. And
when one sees how fast the rot spreads, — it is
growing serious, — I think we demand of superior men that they be superior in this, — that
the mind and the virtue shall give their verdict
in their day, and accelerate so far the progress
of civilization. Possession is sure to throw its
stupid strength for existing power, and appetite
and ambition will go for that. Let the aid of
virtue, intelligence and education be cast where
they rightfully belong. They are organically ours.
Let them be loyal to their own. I wish to see
the instructed class here know their own flag, and
not fire on their comrades. We should not
forgive the clergy for taking on every issue the
immoral side ; nor the Bench, if it put itself on
the side of the culprit ; nor the Government,
if it sustain the mob against the laws.'

It is a potent support and ally to a brave
man standing single, or with a few, for the right,
and out-voted and ostracized, to know that better men in other parts of the country appreciate
the service and will rightly report him to his
own and the next age. Without this assurance,
he will sooner sink. He may well say, ' If my

XI

countrymen do not care to be defended, I too
will decline the controversy, from which I only
reap invectives and hatred.' Yet the lovers of
liberty may with reason tax the coldness and
indifferentism of scholars and literary men.
They are lovers of liberty in Greece and Rome
and in the English Commonwealth, but they
are lukewarm lovers of the liberty of America in
1854. The universities are not, as in Hobbes's
time, "the core of rebellion," no, but the seat of
inertness. They have forgotten their allegiance
to the Muse, and grown worldly and political. I
listened, lately, on one of those occasions when
the university chooses one of its distinguished
sons returning from the political arena, believing
that senators and statesmen would be glad to
throw off the harness and to dip again in the
Castalian pools. But if audiences forget themselves, statesmen do not. The low bows to all
the crockery gods of the day were duly made:
— only in one part of the discourse the orator
allowed to transpire, rather against his will, a
little sober sense.' It was this: 'I am, as you see,
a man virtuously inclined, and only corrupted
by my profession of politics I should prefer
the right side. You, gentlemen of these literary
and scientific schools, and the important class

you represent, have the power to make your verdict clear and prevailing. Had you done so, you
would have found me its glad organ and champion. Abstractly, I should have preferred that
side. But you have not done it. You have not
spoken out. You have failed to arm me. I can
only deal with masses as I find them. Abstractions are not for me. I go then for such parties
and opinions as have provided me with a working apparatus. I give you my word, not without
regret, that I was first for you ; and though I am
now to deny and condemn you, you see it is not
my will but the party necessity.' Having made
this manifesto and professed his adoration for
liberty in the time of his grandfathers, he proceeded with his work of denouncing freedom
and freemen at the present day, much in the
tone and spirit in which Lord Bacon prosecuted
his benefactor Essex. He denounced every
name and aspect under which liberty and progress dare show themselves in this age and
country, but with a lingering conscience which
qualified each sentence with a recommendation
to mercy.

But I put it to every noble and generous
spirit, to every poetic, every heroic, every religious heart, that not so is our learning, our

education, our poetry, our worship to be declared. Liberty is aggressive, Liberty is the Crusade of all brave and conscientious men, the Epic Poetry, the new religion, the chivalry of all gentlemen This is the oppressed Lady whom true knights on their oath and honor must rescue and save.

Now at last we are disenchanted and shall have no more false hopes. I respect the Anti-Slavery Society. It is the Cassandra that has foretold all that has befallen, fact for fact, years ago ; foretold all, and no man laid it to heart. It seemed, as the Turks say, " Fate makes that a man should not believe his own eyes." But the Fugitive Law did much to unglue the eyes of men, and now the Nebraska Bill leaves us staring. The Anti-Slavery Society will add many members this year. The Whig Party will join it ; the Democrats will join it. The population of the free states will join it. I doubt not, at last, the slave states will join it. But be that sooner or later, and whoever comes or stays away, I hope we have reached the end of our unbelief, have come to a belief that there is a divine Providence in the world, which will not save us but through our own coöperation.

VIII

THE ASSAULT UPON MR. SUMNER

SPEECH AT A MEETING OF THE CITIZENS IN
THE TOWN HALL, IN CONCORD,
MAY 26, 1856

                    His erring foe,
Self-assured that he prevails,
Looks from his victim lying low
And sees aloft the red right arm
Redress the eternal scales.

THE
ASSAULT UPON MR. SUMNER

M R. CHAIRMAN: I sympathize heartily with the spirit of the resolutions. The events of the last few years and months and days have taught us the lessons of centuries. I do not see how a barbarous community and a civilized community can constitute one state. I think we must get rid of slavery, or we must get rid of freedom. Life has not parity of value in the free state and in the slave state. In one, it is adorned with education, with skilful labor, with arts, with long prospective interests, with sacred family ties, with honor and justice. In the other, life is a fever; man is an animal, given to pleasure, frivolous, irritable, spending his days in hunting and practising with deadly weapons to defend himself against his slaves and against his companions brought up in the same idle and dangerous way. Such people live for the moment, they have properly no future, and readily risk on every passion a life which is of small value to themselves or to others. Many years ago, when Mr. Webster was challenged in Washington to a duel by one of these mad-

caps, his friends came forward with prompt good
sense and said such a thing was not to be thought
of; Mr. Webster's life was the property of his
friends and of the whole country, and was not
to be risked on the turn of a vagabond's ball.
Life and life are incommensurate. The whole
state of South Carolina does not now offer one
or any number of persons who are to be weighed
for a moment in the scale with such a person as
the meanest of them all has now struck down.
The very conditions of the game must always
be, — the worst life staked against the best.
It is the best whom they desire to kill. It is
only when they cannot answer your reasons,
that they wish to knock you down. If, therefore, Massachusetts could send to the Senate a
better man than Mr. Sumner, his death would
be only so much the more quick and certain
Now, as men's bodily strength, or skill with
knives and guns, is not usually in proportion to
their knowledge and mother-wit, but oftener in
the inverse ratio, it will only do to send foolish
persons to Washington, if you wish them to be
safe.

The outrage is the more shocking from the
singularly pure character of its victim. Mr
Sumner's position is exceptional in its honor.

He had not taken his degrees in the caucus and
in hack politics. It is notorious that, in the long
time when his election was pending, he refused
to take a single step to secure it. He would
not so much as go up to the state house to
shake hands with this or that person whose good
will was reckoned important by his friends.
He was elected. It was a homage to character
and talent. In Congress, he did not rush into
party position. He sat long silent and studious.
His friends, I remember, were told that they
would find Sumner a man of the world like the
rest; ''t is quite impossible to be at Washington and not bend; he will bend as the rest have
done.' Well, he did not bend. He took his
position and kept it. He meekly bore the cold
shoulder from some of his New England colleagues, the hatred of his enemies, the pity of
the indifferent, cheered by the love and respect
of good men with whom he acted; and has
stood for the North, a little in advance of all
the North, and therefore without adequate support. He has never faltered in his maintenance
of justice and freedom. He has gone beyond
the large expectation of his friends in his increasing ability and his manlier tone. I have
heard that some of his political friends tax him

with indolence or negligence in refusing to
make electioneering speeches, or otherwise to
bear his part in the labor which party organization requires. I say it to his honor. But more
to his honor are the faults which his enemies
lay to his charge. I think, sir, if Mr. Sumner
had any vices, we should be likely to hear of
them. They have fastened their eyes like mi-
croscopes for five years on every act, word,
manner and movement, to find a flaw, — and
with what result? His opponents accuse him
neither of drunkenness nor debauchery, nor job,
nor speculation, nor rapacity, nor personal aims
of any kind. No; but with what? Why, beyond this charge, which it is impossible was
ever sincerely made, that he broke over the
proprieties of debate, I find him accused of publishing his opinion of the Nebraska conspiracy
in a letter to the people of the United States,
with discourtesy. Then, that he is an abolitionist; as if every sane human being were not an
abolitionist, or a believer that all men should be
free. And the third crime he stands charged
with, is, that his speeches were written before
they were spoken , which, of course, must be
true in Sumner's case, as it was true of Webster,
of Adams, of Calhoun, of Burke, of Chatham,

of Demosthenes ; of every first-rate speaker
that ever lived. It is the high compliment he
pays to the intelligence of the Senate and of
the country. When the same reproach was cast
on the first orator of ancient times by some cav-
iller of his day, he said, " I should be ashamed
to come with one unconsidered word before
such an assembly." Mr. Chairman, when I
think of these most small faults as the worst
which party hatred could allege, I think I may
borrow the language which Bishop Burnet applied to Sir Isaac Newton, and say that Charles
Sumner " has the whitest soul I ever knew."

Well, sir, this noble head, so comely and so
wise, must be the target for a pair of bullies to
beat with clubs. The murderer's brand shall
stamp their foreheads wherever they may wan-
der in the earth. But I wish, sir, that the high
respects of this meeting shall be expressed to
Mr. Sumner ; that a copy of the resolutions that
have been read may be forwarded to him. I
wish that he may know the shudder of terror
which ran through all this community on the
first tidings of this brutal attack. Let him hear
that every man of worth in New England loves
his virtues ; that every mother thinks of him
as the protector of families ; that every friend

of freedom thinks him the friend of freedom.
And if our arms at this distance cannot defend
him from assassins, we confide the defence of a
life so precious to all honorable men and true
patriots, and to the Almighty Maker of men.'

IX

SPEECH

AT THE KANSAS RELIEF MEETING IN CAMBRIDGE
WEDNESDAY EVENING, SEPTEMBER 10, 1856

AND ye shall succor men;
'T is nobleness to serve;
Help them who cannot help again:
Beware from right to swerve.

SPEECH
ON AFFAIRS IN KANSAS

I REGRET, with all this company, the absence of Mr. Whitman of Kansas, whose narrative was to constitute the interest of this meeting. Mr. Whitman is not here; but knowing, as we all do, why he is not, what duties kept him at home, he is more than present. His vacant chair speaks for him. For quite other reasons, I had been wiser to have stayed at home, unskilled as I am to address a political meeting, but it is impossible for the most recluse to extricate himself from the questions of the times.

There is this peculiarity about the case of Kansas, that all the right is on one side. We hear the screams of hunted wives and children answered by the howl of the butchers. The testimony of the telegraphs from St. Louis and the border confirm the worst details. The printed letters of border ruffians avow the facts. When pressed to look at the cause of the mischief in the Kansas laws, the President falters and declines the discussion; but his supporters in the Senate, Mr. Cass, Mr. Geyer, Mr.

Hunter, speak out, and declare the intolerable atrocity of the code. It is a maxim that all party spirit produces the incapacity to receive natural impressions from facts; and our recent political history has abundantly borne out the maxim. But these details that have come from Kansas are so horrible, that the hostile press have but one word in reply, namely, that it is all exaggeration, 'tis an Abolition lie. Do the Committee of Investigation say that the outrages have been overstated? Does their dismal catalogue of private tragedies show it? Do the private letters? Is it an exaggeration, that Mr. Hopps of Somerville, Mr. Hoyt of Deerfield, Mr. Jennison of Groton, Mr. Phillips of Berkshire, have been murdered? That Mr. Robinson of Fitchburg has been imprisoned? Rev. Mr. Nute of Springfield seized, and up to this time we have no tidings of his fate?

In these calamities under which they suffer, and the worst which threaten them, the people of Kansas ask for bread, clothes, arms and men, to save them alive, and enable them to stand against these enemies of the human race. They have a right to be helped, for they have helped themselves.

This aid must be sent, and this is not to be

doled out as an ordinary charity ; but bestowed
up to the magnitude of the want, and, as has
been elsewhere said, " on the scale of a national
action." I think we are to give largely, lavishly,
to these men. And we must prepare to do it.
We must learn to do with less, live in a smaller
tenement, sell our apple-trees, our acres, our
pleasant houses. I know people who are mák-
ing haste to reduce their expenses and pay their
debts, not with a view to new accumulations,
but in preparation to save and earn for the
benefit of the Kansas emigrants.

We must have aid from individuals, — we
must also have aid from the state. I know that
the last legislature refused that aid. I know
that lawyers hesitate on technical grounds, and
wonder what method of relief the legislature
will apply. But I submit that, in a case like
this, where citizens of Massachusetts, legal
voters here, have emigrated to national territory
under the sanction of every law, and are then
set on by highwaymen, driven from their new
homes, pillaged, and numbers of them killed
and scalped, and the whole world knows that
this is no accidental brawl, but a systematic war
to the knife, and in defiance of all laws and
liberties, — I submit that the governor and

xi

legislature should neither slumber nor sleep till they have found out how to send effectual aid and comfort to these poor farmers, or else should resign their seats to those who can. But first let them hang the halls of the state-house with black crape, and order funeral service to be said for the citizens whom they were unable to defend.

We stick at the technical difficulties. I think there never was a people so choked and stultified by forms. We adore the forms of law, instead of making them vehicles of wisdom and justice. I like the primary assembly. I own I have little esteem for governments. I esteem them only good in the moment when they are established. I set the private man first. He only who is able to stand alone is qualified to be a citizen. Next to the private man, I value the primary assembly, met to watch the government and to correct it. That is the theory of the American State, that it exists to execute the will of the citizens, is always responsible to them, and is always to be changed when it does not. First, the private citizen, then the primary assembly, and the government last.

In this country for the last few years the government has been the chief obstruction to the

common weal. Who doubts that Kansas would
have been very well settled, if the United States
had let it alone? The government armed and
led the ruffians against the poor farmers. I do
not know any story so gloomy as the politics
of this country for the last twenty years, central-
izing ever more manifestly round one spring,
and that a vast crime, and ever more plainly,
until it is notorious that all promotion, power
and policy are dictated from one source, — illustrating the fatal effects of a false position to
demoralize legislation and put the best people
always at a disadvantage ; — one crime always
present, always to be varnished over, to find
fine names for ; and we free statesmen, as ac-
complices to the guilt, ever in the power of the
grand offender.

Language has lost its meaning in the universal cant. *Representative Government* is really
misrepresentative ; *Union* is a conspiracy against
the Northern States which the Northern States
are to have the privilege of paying for ; the
adding of Cuba and Central America to the slave
marts is *enlarging the area of Freedom. Manifest
Destiny, Democracy, Freedom,* fine names for an
ugly thing. They call it otto of rose and laven-
der, — I call it bilge-water. They call it Chivalry

and Freedom; I call it the stealing all the earnings of a poor man and the earnings of his little girl and boy, and the earnings of all that shall come from him, his children's children forever.

But this is Union, and this is Democracy; and our poor people, led by the nose by these fine words, dance and sing, ring bells and fire cannon, with every new link of the chain which is forged for their limbs by the plotters in the Capitol.

What are the results of law and union? There is no Union. Can any citizen of Massachusetts travel in honor through Kentucky and Alabama and speak his mind? Or can any citizen of the Southern country who happens to think kidnapping a bad thing, say so? Let Mr. Underwood of Virginia answer. Is it to be supposed that there are no men in Carolina who dissent from the popular sentiment now reigning there? It must happen, in the variety of human opinions, that there are dissenters. They are silent as the grave. Are there no women in that country, — women, who always carry the conscience of a people? Yet we have not heard one discordant whisper.

In the free states, we give a snivelling support to slavery. The judges give cowardly interpretations to the law, in direct opposition to the known foundation of all law, that *every immoral statute is void*. And here of Kansas, the President says: " Let the complainants go to the courts ; " though he knows that when the poor plundered farmer comes to the court, he finds the ringleader who has robbed him dismounting from his own horse, and unbuckling his knife to sit as his judge.

The President told the Kansas Committee that the whole difficulty grew from " the factious spirit of the Kansas people respecting institutions which they need not have concerned themselves about." A very remarkable speech from a Democratic President to his fellow citizens, that they are not to concern themselves with institutions which they alone are to create and determine. The President is a lawyer, and should know the statutes of the land. But I borrow the language of an eminent man, used long since, with far less occasion: " If that be law, let the ploughshare be run under the foundations of the Capitol ; " — and if that be Government, extirpation is the only cure.

I am glad to see that the terror at disunion and anarchy is disappearing. Massachusetts, in its heroic day, had no government — was an anar-chy. Every man stood on his own feet, was his own governor; and there was no breach of peace from Cape Cod to Mount Hoosac. California, a few years ago, by the testimony of all people at that time in the country, had the best govern-ment that ever existed. Pans of gold lay drying outside of every man's tent, in perfect security. The land was measured into little strips of a few feet wide, all side by side. A bit of ground that your hand could cover was worth one or two hundred dollars, on the edge of your strip; and there was no dispute. Every man throughout the country was armed with knife and revolver, and it was known that instant justice would be administered to each offence, and perfect peace reigned. For the Saxon man, when he is well awake, is not a pirate but a citizen, all made of hooks and eyes, and links himself naturally to his brothers, as bees hook themselves to one another and to their queen in a loyal swarm.

But the hour is coming when the strongest will not be strong enough. A harder task will the new revolution of the nineteenth century be than was the revolution of the eighteenth cen-tury. I think the American Revolution bought its glory cheap. If the problem was new, it was simple. If there were few people, they were united, and the enemy three thousand miles off. But now, vast property, gigantic interests, family connections, webs of party, cover the land with a network that immensely multiplies the dangers of war.[1]

Fellow citizens, in these times full of the fate of the Republic, I think the towns should hold town meetings, and resolve themselves into Committees of Safety, go into permanent sessions, adjourning from week to week, from month to month. I wish we could send the sergeant-at-arms to stop every American who is about to leave the country. Send home every one who is abroad, lest they should find no country to return to. Come home and stay at home, while there is a country to save. When it is lost it will be time enough then for any who are luckless enough to remain alive to gather up their clothes and depart to some land where freedom exists.

X

REMARKS

AT A MEETING FOR THE RELIEF OF THE FAMILY CJ
JOHN BROWN, AT TREMONT TEMPLE, BOSTON
NOVEMBER 18, 1859

"JOHN BROWN in Kansas settled, like a steadfast Yankee
     farmer,
Brave and godly, with four sons — all stalwart men of
     might.
There he spoke aloud for Freedom, and the Border strife
     grew warmer
Till the Rangers fired his dwelling, in his absence, in the
     night;
               And Old Brown,
               Osawatomie Brown,
Came homeward in the morning to find his house burned
     down.

Then he grasped his trusty rifle, and boldly fought for
     Freedom,
Smote from border unto border the fierce invading band:
And he and his brave boys vowed — so might Heaven help
     and speed 'em —
They would save those grand old prairies from the curse
     that blights the land;
               And Old Brown,
               Osawatomie Brown,
Said, ' Boys, the Lord will aid us! ' and he shoved his ram
     rod down."

      EDMUND CLARENCE STEDMAN, *John Brown.*

JOHN BROWN

MR. CHAIRMAN, AND FELLOW CITIZENS: I share the sympathy and sorrow which have brought us together. Gentlemen who have preceded me have well said that no wall of separation could here exist. This commanding event which has brought us together, eclipses all others which have occurred for a long time in our history, and I am very glad to see that this sudden interest in the hero of Harper's Ferry has provoked an extreme curiosity in all parts of the Republic, in regard to the details of his history. Every anecdote is eagerly sought, and I do not wonder that gentlemen find traits of relation readily between him and themselves. One finds a relation in the church, another in the profession, another in the place of his birth. He was happily a representative of the American Republic. Captain John Brown is a farmer, the fifth in descent from Peter Brown, who came to Plymouth in the Mayflower, in 1620. All the six have been farmers. His grandfather, of Simsbury, in Connecticut, was a captain in the Revolution. His father, largely interested as a raiser of stock,

became a contractor to supply the army with
beef, in the war of 1812, and our Captain John
Brown, then a boy, with his father was present
and witnessed the surrender of General Hull.
He cherishes a great respect for his father, as a
man of strong character, and his respect is probably just. For himself, he is so transparent that
all men see him through. He is a man to make
friends wherever on earth courage and integrity
are esteemed, the rarest of heroes, a pure idealist, with no by-ends of his own. Many of you
have seen him, and every one who has heard him
speak has been impressed alike by his simple,
artless goodness, joined with his sublime courage. He joins that perfect Puritan faith which
brought his fifth ancestor to Plymouth Rock
with his grandfather's ardor in the Revolution.
He believes in two articles, — two instruments,
shall I say? — the Golden Rule and the Declaration of Independence ; and he used this expression in conversation here concerning them,
" Better that a whole generation of men, women
and children should pass away by a violent death
than that one word of either should be violated
in this country." There is a Unionist, — there
is a strict constructionist for you. He believes
in the Union of the States, and he conceives

that the only obstruction to the Union is Slavery, and for that reason, as a patriot, he works for its abolition. The governor of Virginia has pronounced his eulogy in a manner that discredits the moderation of our timid parties. His own speeches to the court have interested the nation in him. What magnanimity, and what innocent pleading, as of childhood! You remember his words: "If I had interfered in behalf of the rich, the powerful, the intelligent, the so-called great, or any of their friends, parents, wives or children, it would all have been right. But I believe that to have interfered as I have done, for the despised poor, was not wrong, but right." [1]

It is easy to see what a favorite he will be with history, which plays such pranks with temporary reputations. Nothing can resist the sympathy which all elevated minds must feel with Brown, and through them the whole civilized world; and if he must suffer, he must drag official gentlemen into an immortality most undesirable, of which they have already some disagreeable forebodings. Indeed, it is the *reductio ad absurdum* of Slavery, when the governor of Virginia is forced to hang a man whom he declares to be a man of the most integrity,

truthfulness and courage he has ever met. Is
that the kind of man the gallows is built for?
It were bold to affirm that there is within that
broad commonwealth, at this moment, another
citizen as worthy to live, and as deserving of all
public and private honor, as this poor prisoner.'

But we are here to think of relief for the
family of John Brown. To my eyes, that family looks very large and very needy of relief.
It comprises his brave fellow sufferers in the
Charlestown Jail; the fugitives still hunted in
the mountains of Virginia and Pennsylvania,
the sympathizers with him in all the states;
and, I may say, almost every man who loves
the Golden Rule and the Declaration of Independence, like him, and who sees what a tiger's
thirst threatens him in the malignity of public
sentiment in the slave states. It seems to me
that a common feeling joins the people of Massachusetts with him.

I said John Brown was an idealist. He believed in his ideas to that extent that he existed
to put them all into action, he said 'he did not
believe in moral suasion, he believed in putting
the thing through.' He saw how deceptive the
forms are. We fancy, in Massachusetts, that
we are free; yet it seems the government is

quite unreliable. Great wealth, great population, men of talent in the executive, on the
bench, — all the forms right, — and yet, life
and freedom are not safe. Why? Because the
judges rely on the forms, and do not, like John
Brown, use their eyes to see the fact behind the
forms. They assume that the United States
can protect its witness or its prisoner. And in
Massachusetts that is true, but the moment he
is carried out of the bounds of Massachusetts,
the United States, it is notorious, afford no protection at all; the government, the judges, are
an envenomed party, and give such protection
as they give in Utah to honest citizens, or in
Kansas; such protection as they gave to their
own Commodore Paulding, when he was simple
enough to mistake the formal instructions of his
government for their real meaning.' The state
judges fear collision between their two allegi-
ances; but there are worse evils than collision;
namely, the doing substantial injustice. A good
man will see that the use of a judge is to secure
good government, and where the citizen's weal
is imperilled by abuse of the federal power, to
use that arm which can secure it, viz., the local
government. Had that been done on certain
calamitous occasions, we should not have seen

the honor of Massachusetts trailed in the dust, stained to all ages, once and again, by the ill-timed formalism of a venerable bench. If judges cannot find law enough to maintain the sovereignty of the state, and to protect the life and freedom of every inhabitant not a criminal, it is idle to compliment them as learned and venerable. What avails their learning or veneration? At a pinch, they are no more use than idiots. After the mischance they wring their hands, but they had better never have been born.' A Vermont judge, Hutchinson, who has the Declaration of Independence in his heart; a Wisconsin judge, who knows that laws are for the protection of citizens against kidnappers, is worth a court-house full of lawyers so idolatrous of forms as to let go the substance. Is any man in Massachusetts so simple as to believe that when a United States Court in Virginia, now, in its present reign of terror, sends to Connecticut, or New York, or Massachusetts, for a witness, it wants him for a witness? No; it wants him for a party; it wants him for meat to slaughter and eat And your *habeas corpus* is, in any way in which it has been, or, I fear, is likely to be used, a nuisance, and not a protection: for it takes away his right reliance on himself, and the natural assistance of his friends and fellow citizens, by offering him a form which is a piece of paper.

But I am detaining the meeting on matters which others understand better. I hope, then, that, in administering relief to John Brown's family, we shall remember all those whom his fate concerns, all who are in sympathy with him, and not forget to aid h'm in the best way, by securing freedom and independence in Massachusetts.

xı

XI

JOHN BROWN

SPEECH AT SALEM, JANUARY 6, 1860

"A man there came, whence none could tell,
Bearing a touchstone in his hand,
And tested all things in the land
By its unerring spell.

A thousand transformations rose
From fair to foul, from foul to fair
The golden crown he did not spare,
Nor scorn the beggar's clothes.

.   .   .   .   .   .

Then angrily the people cried,
'The loss outweighs the profit far;
Our goods suffice us as they are.
We will not have them tried.'

And since they cou'd not so avail
To check his unrelenting quest,
They seized him, saying, 'Let him test
How real is our jail!'

But though they slew him with the sword,
And in the fire his touchstone burned,
Its doings could not be o'erturned,
Its undoings restored.

And when, to stop all future harm,
They strewed its ashes to the breeze,
They little guessed each grain of these
Conveyed the perfect charm."

WILLIAM ALLINGHAM

JOHN BROWN

MR. CHAIRMAN: I have been struck with one fact, that the best orators who have added their praise to his fame, — and I need not go out of this house to find the purest eloquence in the country, — have one rival who comes off a little better, and that is JOHN BROWN. Everything that is said of him leaves people a little dissatisfied; but as soon as they read his own speeches and letters they are heartily contented, — such is the singleness of purpose which justifies him to the head and the heart of all. Taught by this experience, I mean, in the few remarks I have to make, to cling to his history, or let him speak for himself.

John Brown, the founder of liberty in Kansas, was born in Torrington, Litchfield County, Connecticut, in 1800. When he was five years old his father emigrated to Ohio, and the boy was there set to keep sheep and to look after cattle and dress skins; he went bareheaded and barefooted, and clothed in buckskin. He said that he loved rough play, could never have rough play enough; could not see a seedy hat without wishing to pull it off. But for this it needed

that the playmates should be equal ; not one in
fine clothes and the other in buckskin ; not one
his own master, hale and hearty, and the other
watched and whipped. But it chanced that in
Pennsylvania, where he was sent by his father
to collect cattle, he fell in with a boy whom he
heartily liked and whom he looked upon as his
superior. This boy was a slave ; he saw him
beaten with an iron shovel, and otherwise mal-
treated ; he saw that this boy had nothing better
to look forward to in life, whilst he himself was
petted and made much of, for he was much considered in the family where he then stayed, from
the circumstance that this boy of twelve years
had conducted alone a drove of cattle a hundred
miles But the colored boy had no friend, and
no future. This worked such indignation in him
that he swore an oath of resistance to slavery as
long as he lived. And thus his enterprise to go
into Virginia and run off five hundred or a thousand slaves was not a piece of spite or revenge,
a plot of two years or of twenty years, but the
keeping of an oath made to heaven and earth
forty-seven years before. Forty-seven years at
least, though I incline to accept his own account
of the matter at Charlestown, which makes the
date a little older, when he said, " This was all

settled millions of years before the world was made."

He grew up a religious and manly person, in severe poverty ; a fair specimen of the best stock of New England ; having that force of thought and that sense of right which are the warp and woof of greatness.   Our farmers were Orthodox Calvinists, mighty in the Scriptures ; had learned that life was a preparation, a " probation," to use their word, for a higher world, and was to be spent in loving and serving mankind.[1]

Thus was formed a romantic character absolutely without any vulgar trait ; living to ideal ends, without any mixture of self-indulgence or compromise, such as lowers the value of benevolent and thoughtful men we know ; abstemious, refusing luxuries, not sourly and reproachfully, but simply as unfit for his habit ; quiet and gentle as a child in the house.   And, as happens usually to men of romantic character, his fortunes were romantic.   Walter Scott would have delighted to draw his picture and trace his adventurous career.   A shepherd and herdsman, he learned the manners of animals, and knew the secret signals by which animals communicate.[2]   He made his hard bed on the mountains with them ; he learned to drive his flock through thickets all but impassable; he had all the skill of a shepherd by choice of breed and by wise husbandry to obtain the best wool, and that for a course of years. And the anecdotes preserved show a far-seeing skill and conduct which, in spite of adverse accidents, should secure, one year with another, an honest reward, first to the farmer, and afterwards to the dealer. If he kept sheep, it was with a royal mind; and if he traded in wool, he was a merchant prince, not in the amount of wealth, but in the protection of the interests confided to him.

I am not a little surprised at the easy effrontery with which political gentlemen, in and out of Congress, take it upon them to say that there are not a thousand men in the North who sympathize with John Brown. It would be far safer and nearer the truth to say that all people, in proportion to their sensibility and self-respect, sympathize with him. For it is impossible to see courage, and disinterestedness, and the love that casts out fear, without sympathy. All women are drawn to him by their predominance of sentiment. All gentlemen, of course, are on his side. I do not mean by "gentlemen," people of scented hair and perfumed handkerchiefs, but men of gentle blood and generosity, "fulfilled with all nobleness," who, like the Cid, give the outcast leper a share of their bed; like the dying Sidney, pass the cup of cold water to the dying soldier who needs it more. For what is the oath of gentle blood and knighthood? What but to protect the weak and lowly against the strong oppressor?

Nothing is more absurd than to complain of this sympathy, or to complain of a party of men united in opposition to slavery. As well complain of gravity, or the ebb of the tide. Who makes the abolitionist? The slave-holder. The sentiment of mercy is the natural recoil which the laws of the universe provide to protect mankind from destruction by savage passions. And our blind statesmen go up and down, with committees of vigilance and safety, hunting for the origin of this new heresy. They will need a very vigilant committee indeed to find its birthplace, and a very strong force to root it out. For the arch-abolitionist, older than Brown, and older than the Shenandoah Mountains, is Love, whose other name is Justice, which was before Alfred, before Lycurgus, before slavery, and will be after it.'

XII

THEODORE PARKER

AN ADDRESS AT THE MEMORIAL MEETING AT THE
MUSIC HALL, BOSTON, JUNE 15, 1860

"HERE comes Parker, the Orson of parsons, a man
Whom the Church undertook to put under her ban —

  .   .   .   .   .   )   .   .

There 's a background of God to each hard-working feature,
Every word that he speaks has been fierily furnaced
In the blast of a life that has struggled in earnest.
There he stands, looking more like a ploughman than priest.
It not dreadfully awkward, not graceful at least;

  .   .   .   .

But his periods fall on you, stroke after stroke,
Like the blows of a lumberer felling an oak,
You forget the man wholly, you 're thankful to meet
With a preacher who smacks of the field and the street,
And to hear, you 're not over-particular whence,
Almost Taylor's profusion, quite Latimer's sense."
     — LOWELL, *A Fable for Critics.*

THEODORE PARKER

AT the death of a good and admirable person we meet to console and animate each other by the recollection of his virtues.

I have the feeling that every man's biography is at his own expense. He furnishes not only the facts but the report. I mean that all biography is autobiography. It is only what he tells of himself that comes to be known and believed. In Plutarch's lives of Alexander and Pericles, you have the secret whispers of their confidence to their lovers and trusty friends. For it was each report of this kind that impressed those to whom it was told in a manner to secure its being told everywhere to the best, to those who speak with authority to their own times and therefore to ours. For the political rule is a cosmical rule, that if a man is not strong in his own district, he is not a good candidate elsewhere.

He whose voice will not be heard here again could well afford to tell his experiences; they were all honorable to him, and were part of the history of the civil and religious liberty of his times. Theodore Parker was a son of the soil,

charged with the energy of New England,
strong, eager, inquisitive of knowledge, of a dil-
igence that never tired, upright, of a haughty
independence, yet the gentlest of companions ;
a man of study, fit for a man of the world; with
decided opinions and plenty of power to state
them ; rapidly pushing his studies so far as to
leave few men qualified to sit as his critics.' He
elected his part of duty, or accepted nobly that
assigned him in his rare constitution. Wonderful acquisition of knowledge, a rapid wit that
heard all, and welcomed all that came, by seeing
its bearing. Such was the largeness of his reception of facts and his skill to employ them that
it looked as if he were some president of council
to whom a score of telegraphs were ever bringing in reports ; and his information would have
been excessive, but for the noble use he made
of it ever in the interest of humanity. He had
a strong understanding, a logical method, a love
for facts, a rapid eye for their historic relations,
and a skill in stripping them of traditional lus-
tres. He had a sprightly fancy, and often
amused himself with throwing his meaning into
pretty apologues ; yet we can hardly ascribe to
his mind the poetic element, though his scholarship had made him a reader and quoter of verses.

A little more feeling of the poetic significance
of his facts would have disqualified him for some
of his severer offices to his generation. The old
religions have a charm for most minds which it
is a little uncanny to disturb. 'T is sometimes
a question, shall we not leave them to decay
without rude shocks? I remember that I found
some harshness in his treatment both of Greek
and of Hebrew antiquity, and sympathized with
the pain of many good people in his auditory,
whilst I acquitted him, of course, of any wish
to be flippant. He came at a time when, to the
irresistible march of opinion, the forms still re-
tained by the most advanced sects showed loose
and lifeless, and he, with something less of affectionate attachment to the old, or with more
vigorous logic, rejected them. 'T is objected to
him that he scattered too many illusions. Perhaps more tenderness would have been graceful;
but it is vain to charge him with perverting the
opinions of the new generation.

The opinions of men are organic. Simply,
those came to him who found themselves expressed by him. And had they not met this enlightened mind, in which they beheld their own
opinions combined with zeal in every cause of
love and humanity, they would have suspected

their opinions and suppressed them, and so sunk into melancholy or malignity — a feeling of loneliness and hostility to what was reckoned respectable. 'T is plain to me that he has achieved a historic immortality here; that he has so woven himself in these few years into the history of Boston, that he can never be left out of your annals. It will not be in the acts of city councils, nor of obsequious mayors; nor, in the state-house, the proclamations of governors, with their failing virtue — failing them at critical moments — that coming generations will study what really befell; but in the plain lessons of Theodore Parker in this Music Hall, in Faneuil Hall, or in legislative committee rooms, that the true temper and authentic record of these days will be read. The next generation will care little for the chances of elections that govern governors now, it will care little for fine gentlemen who behaved shabbily; but it will read very intelligently in his rough story, fortified with exact anecdotes, precise with names and dates, what part was taken by each actor; who threw himself into the cause of humanity and came to the rescue of civilization at a hard pinch, and who blocked its course.

The vice charged against America is the want of sincerity in leading men. It does not lie at his

door. He never kept back the truth for fear to
make an enemy. But, on the other hand, it was
complained that he was bitter and harsh, that his
zeal burned with too hot a flame. It is so difficult, in evil times, to escape this charge ! for the
faithful preacher most of all. It was his merit,
like Luther, Knox and Latimer, and John Baptist, to speak tart truth, when that was peremptory
and when there were few to say it. But his sympathy for goodness was not less energetic. One
fault he had, he overestimated his friends, — I
may well say it, — and sometimes vexed them
with the importunity of his good opinion, whilst
they knew better the ebb which follows un-
founded praise. He was capable, it must be said,
of the most unmeasured eulogies on those he esteemed, especially if he had any jealousy that they
did not stand with the Boston public as highly
as they ought. His commanding merit as a
reformer is this, that he insisted beyond all men
in pulpits — I cannot think of one rival — that
the essence of Christianity is its practical morals ;
it is there for use, or it is nothing ; and if you
combine it with sharp trading, or with ordinary
city ambitions to gloze over municipal corrup-
tions, or private intemperance, or successful
fraud, or immoral politics, or unjust wars, or the

cheating of Indians, or the robbery of frontier nations, or leaving your principles at home to follow on the high seas or in Europe a supple complaisance to tyrants, — it is a hypocrisy, and the truth is not in you ; and no love of religious music or of dreams of Swedenborg, or praise of John Wesley, or of Jeremy Taylor, can save you from the Satan which you are.

His ministry fell on a political crisis also ; on the years when Southern slavery broke over its old banks, made new and vast pretensions, and wrung from the weakness or treachery of Northern people fatal concessions in the Fugitive Slave Bill and the repeal of the Missouri Compromise. Two days, bitter in the memory of Boston, the days of the rendition of Sims and of Burns, made the occasion of his most remarkable discourses. He kept nothing back. In terrible earnest he denounced the public crime, and meted out to every official, high and low, his due portion.[1] By the incessant power of his statement, he made and held a party. It was his great service to freedom. He took away the reproach of silent consent that would otherwise have lain against the indignant minority, by uttering in the hour and place wherein these outrages were done, the stern protest.

But whilst I praise this frank speaker, I have
no wish to accuse the silence of others. There
are men of good powers who have so much sympathy that they must be silent when they are not
in sympathy. If you don't agree with them, they
know they only injure the truth by speaking.
Their faculties will not play them true, and they
do not wish to squeak and gibber, and so they
shut their mouths. I can readily forgive this,
only not the other, the false tongue which makes
the worse appear the better cause. There were,
of course, multitudes to censure and defame this
truth-speaker. But the brave know the brave.
Fops, whether in hotels or churches, will utter
the fop's opinion, and faintly hope for the salvation of his soul; but his manly enemies, who
despised the fops, honored him; and it is well
known that his great hospitable heart was the
sanctuary to which every soul conscious of an
earnest opinion came for sympathy — alike the
brave slave-holder and the brave slave-rescuer.
These met in the house of this honest man —
for every sound heart loves a responsible person,
one who does not in generous company say
generous things, and in mean company base
things, but says one thing, now cheerfully, now
indignantly, but always because he must, and

because he sees that, whether he speak or refrain
from speech, this is said over him ; and history,
nature and all souls testify to the same.

Ah, my brave brother ! it seems as if, in a
frivolous age, our loss were immense, and your
place cannot be supplied. But you will already
be consoled in the transfer of your genius, knowing well that the nature of the world will affirm
to all men, in all times, that which for twenty-
five years you valiantly spoke , that the winds
of Italy murmur the same truth over your
grave; the winds of America over these be-
reaved streets ; that the sea which bore your
mourners home affirms it, the stars in their
courses, and the inspirations of youth ; whilst
the polished and pleasant traitors to human
rights, with perverted learning and disgraced
graces, rot and are forgotten with their double
tongue saying all that is sordid for the corruption of man.

The sudden and singular eminence of Mr.
Parker, the importance of his name and influence, are the verdict of his country to his virtues. We have few such men to lose ; amiable
and blameless at home, feared abroad as the
standard-bearer of liberty, taking all the duties
he could grasp, and more, refusing to spare

himself, he has gone down in early glory to his grave, to be a living and enlarging power, wherever learning, wit, honest valor and independence are honored.[1]

XIII

AMERICAN CIVILIZATION

To the mizzen, the main, and the fore
Up with it once more! —
The old tri color,
The ribbon of power,
The white, blue and red which the nations adore!
It was down at half-mast
For a grief — that is past!
To the emblem of glory no sorrow can last!

AMERICAN CIVILIZATION

USE, labor of each for all, is the health and
virtue of all beings. *Ich dien*, I serve, is
a truly royal motto. And it is the mark of
nobleness to volunteer the lowest service, the
greatest spirit only attaining to humility. Nay,
God is God because he is the servant of all.
Well, now here comes this conspiracy of slavery,
— they call it an institution, I call it a destitu-
tion, — this stealing of men and setting them to
work, stealing their labor, and the thief sitting
idle himself; and for two or three ages it has
lasted, and has yielded a certain quantity of
rice, cotton and sugar. And, standing on this
doleful experience, these people have endeavored to reverse the natural sentiments of mankind, and to pronounce labor disgraceful, and
the well-being of a man to consist in eating the
fruit of other men's labor. Labor : a man coins
himself into his labor; turns his day, his
strength, his thought, his affection into some
product which remains as the visible sign of his
power; and to protect that, to secure that to
him, to secure his past self to his future self,
is the object of all government. There is no

interest in any country so imperative as that of
labor; it covers all, and constitutions and governments exist for that, — to protect and insure
it to the laborer. All honest men are daily striving to earn their bread by their industry. And
who is this who tosses his empty head at this
blessing in disguise, the constitution of human
nature, and calls labor vile, and insults the faithful workman at his daily toil? I see for such
madness no hellebore, — for such calamity no
solution but servile war and the Africanization
of the country that permits it.

At this moment in America the aspects of
political society absorb attention. In every
house, from Canada to the Gulf, the children
ask the serious father, — " What is the news
of the war to-day, and when will there be better
times ? " The boys have no new clothes, no
gifts, no journeys; the girls must go without
new bonnets ; boys and girls find their education,
this year, less liberal and complete.' All the
little hopes that heretofore made the year pleasant
are deferred. The state of the country fills us
with anxiety and stern duties We have attempted to hold together two states of civilization : a higher state, where labor and the tenure
of land and the right of suffrage are democrat-

ical ; and a lower state, in which the old military tenure of prisoners or slaves, and of power and land in a few hands, makes an oligarchy : we have attempted to hold these two states of society under one law. But the rude and early state of society does not work well with the later, nay, works badly, and has poisoned politics, public morals and social intercourse in the Republic, now for many years.

The times put this question, Why cannot the best civilization be extended over the whole country, since the disorder of the less-civilized portion menaces the existence of the country? Is this secular progress we have described, this evolution of man to the highest powers, only to give him sensibility, and not to bring duties with it? Is he not to make his knowledge practical? to stand and to withstand? Is not civilization heroic also? Is it not for action? has it not a will? " There are periods," said Niebuhr, " when something much better than happiness and security of life is attainable." We live in a new and exceptionable age. America is another word for Opportunity. Our whole history appears like a last effort of the Divine Providence in behalf of the human race ; and a literal, slavish following of precedents, as by a justice of the

peace, is not for those who at this hour lead the
destinies of this people. The evil you contend
with has taken alarming proportions, and you
still content yourself with parrying the blows it
aims, but, as if enchanted, abstain from striking
at the cause.'

If the American people hesitate, it is not for
want of warning or advices. The telegraph has
been swift enough to announce our disasters.
The journals have not suppressed the extent
of the calamity. Neither was there any want of
argument or of experience. If the war brought
any surprise to the North, it was not the fault
of sentinels on the watch-tower, who had furnished full details of the designs, the muster and
the means of the enemy. Neither was anything
concealed of the theory or practice of slavery.
To what purpose make more big books of these
statistics? There are already mountains of facts,
if any one wants them. But people do not want
them. They bring their opinion into the world.
If they have a comatose tendency in the brain,
they are pro-slavery while they live; if of a nervous sanguineous temperament, they are abolitionists. Then interests were never persuaded.
Can you convince the shoe interest, or the iron
interest, or the cotton interest, by reading pass-

ages from Milton or Montesquieu? You wish
to satisfy people that slavery is bad economy.
Why, the Edinburgh Review pounded on that
string, and made out its case, forty years ago.
A democratic statesman said to me, long since,
that, if he owned the state of Kentucky, he
would manumit all the slaves, and be a gainer
by the transaction. Is this new? No, everybody knows it. As a general economy it is admitted. But there is no one owner of the state,
but a good many small owners. One man owns
land and slaves; another owns slaves only.
Here is a woman who has no other property, —
like a lady in Charleston I knew of, who
owned fifteen sweeps and rode in her carriage.
It is clearly a vast inconvenience to each of
these to make any change, and they are fretful
and talkative, and all their friends are; and
those less interested are inert, and, from want
of thought, averse to innovation. It is like free
trade, certainly the interest of nations, but by no
means the interest of certain towns and districts,
which tariff feeds fat; and the eager interest of
the few overpowers the apathetic general conviction of the many. Banknotes rob the public,
but are such a daily convenience that we silence
our scruples and make believe they are gold.

So imposts are the cheap and right taxation; but, by the dislike of people to pay out a direct tax, governments are forced to render life costly by making them pay twice as much, hidden in the price of tea and sugar.

In this national crisis, it is not argument that we want, but that rare courage which dares commit itself to a principle, believing that Nature is its ally, and will create the instruments it requires, and more than make good any petty and injurious profit which it may disturb. There never was such a combination as this of ours, and the rules to meet it are not set down in any history. We want men of original perception and original action, who can open their eyes wider than to a nationality, namely, to considerations of benefit to the human race, can act in the interest of civilization. Government must not be a parish clerk, a justice of the peace. It has, of necessity, in any crisis of the state, the absolute powers of a dictator. The existing administration is entitled to the utmost candor. It is to be thanked for its angelic virtue, compared with any executive experiences with which we have been familiar. But the times will not allow us to indulge in compliment I wish I saw in the people that inspiration which, if government would not obey the same, would leave the government behind and create on the moment the means and executors it wanted. Better the war should more dangerously threaten us, — should threaten fracture in what is still whole, and punish us with burned capitals and slaughtered regiments, and so exasperate the people to energy, exasperate our nationality. There are Scriptures written invisibly on men's hearts, whose letters do not come out until they are enraged. They can be read by war-fires, and by eyes in the last peril.

We cannot but remember that there have been days in American history, when, if the free states had done their duty, slavery had been blocked by an immovable barrier, and our recent calamities forever precluded. The free states yielded, and every compromise was surrender and invited new demands. Here again is a new occasion which heaven offers to sense and virtue. It looks as if we held the fate of the fairest possession of mankind in our hands, to be saved by our firmness or to be lost by hesitation.

The one power that has legs long enough and strong enough to wade across the Potomac offers itself at this hour; the one strong enough

to bring all the civility up to the height of
that which is best, prays now at the door of Congress for leave to move. Emancipation is the
demand of civilization. That is a principle;
everything else is an intrigue. This is a progressive policy, puts the whole people in healthy,
productive, amiable position, puts every man in
the South in just and natural relations with
every man in the North, laborer with laborer

I shall not attempt to unfold the details of
the project of emancipation. It has been stated
with great ability by several of its leading advocates. I will only advert to some leading points
of the argument, at the risk of repeating the
reasons of others. The war is welcome to the
Southerner; a chivalrous sport to him, like
hunting, and suits his semi-civilized condition.
On the climbing scale of progress, he is just up
to war, and has never appeared to such advantage as in the last twelvemonth. It does not
suit us. We are advanced some ages on the
war-state, — to trade, art and general cultivation.
His laborer works for him at home, so that he
loses no labor by the war. All our soldiers are
laborers, so that the South, with its inferior
numbers, is almost on a footing in effective war-
population with the North. Again, as long as

we fight without any affirmative step taken by the government, any word intimating forfeiture in the rebel states of their old privileges under the law, they and we fight on the same side, for slavery. Again, if we conquer the enemy, — what then? We shall still have to keep him under, and it will cost as much to hold him down as it did to get him down. Then comes the summer, and the fever will drive the soldiers home ; next winter we must begin at the beginning, and conquer him over again. What use then to take a fort, or a privateer, or get possession of an inlet, or to capture a regiment of rebels?

But one weapon we hold which is sure. Congress can, by edict, as a part of the military defence which it is the duty of Congress to provide, abolish slavery, and pay for such slaves as we ought to pay for. Then the slaves near our armies will come to us ; those in the interior will know in a week what their rights are, and will, where opportunity offers, prepare to take them. Instantly, the armies that now confront you must run home to protect their estates, and must stay there, and your enemies will disappear.

There can be no safety until this step is taken.

XI

We fancy that the endless debate, emphasized
by the crime and by the cannons of this war,
has brought the free states to some conviction
that it can never go well with us whilst this
mischief of slavery remains in our politics, and
that by conceit or by might we must put an end
to it. But we have too much experience of the
futility of an easy reliance on the momentary
good dispositions of the public. There does
exist, perhaps, a popular will that the Union
shall not be broken, — that our trade, and therefore our laws, must have the whole breadth of
the continent, and from Canada to the Gulf.
But since this is the rooted belief and will of
the people, so much the more are they in danger, when impatient of defeats, or impatient of
taxes, to go with a rush for some peace; and
what kind of peace shall at that moment be
easiest attained, they will make concessions for
it, — will give up the slaves, and the whole tor-
ment of the past half-century will come back to
be endured anew

Neither do I doubt, if such a composition
should take place, that the Southerners will
come back quietly and politely, leaving their
haughty dictation. It will be an era of good
feelings There will be a lull after so loud a

storm; and, no doubt, there will be discreet men from that section who will earnestly strive to inaugurate more moderate and fair administration of the government, and the North will for a time have its full share and more, in place and counsel. But this will not last; — not for want of sincere good will in sensible Southerners, but because Slavery will again speak through them its harsh necessity. It cannot live but by injustice, and it will be unjust and violent to the end of the world.'

The power of Emancipation is this, that it alters the atomic social constitution of the Southern people. Now, their interest is in keeping out white labor; then, when they must pay wages, their interest will be to let it in, to get the best labor, and, if they fear their blacks, to invite Irish, German and American laborers. Thus, whilst Slavery makes and keeps disunion, Emancipation removes the whole objection to union. Emancipation at one stroke elevates the poor-white of the South, and identifies his interest with that of the Northern laborer.

Now, in the name of all that is simple and generous, why should not this great right be done? Why should not America be capable of a second stroke for the well-being of the human

race, as eighty or ninety years ago she was for the
first, — of an affirmative step in the interests of
human civility, urged on her, too, not by any
romance of sentiment, but by her own extreme
perils? It is very certain that the statesman who
shall break through the cobwebs of doubt, fear
and petty cavil that lie in the way, will be greeted
by the unanimous thanks of mankind. Men
reconcile themselves very fast to a bold and
good measure when once it is taken, though they
condemned it in advance. A week before the
two captive commissioners were surrendered to
England, every one thought it could not be
done: it would divide the North. It was done,
and in two days all agreed it was the right action.'
And this action, which costs so little (the parties
injured by it being such a handful that they can
very easily be indemnified), rids the world, at one
stroke, of this degrading nuisance, the cause of
war and ruin to nations. This measure at once
puts all parties right. This is borrowing, as I
said, the omnipotence of a principle. What is so
foolish as the terror lest the blacks should be
made furious by freedom and wages? It is deny-
ing these that is the outrage, and makes the
danger from the blacks. But justice satisfies
everybody, — white man, red man, yellow man

and black man. All like wages, and the appetite grows by feeding.

But this measure, to be effectual, must come speedily. The weapon is slipping out of our hands. " Time," say the Indian Scriptures, " drinketh up the essence of every great and noble action which ought to be performed, and which is delayed in the execution." [1]

I hope it is not a fatal objection to this policy that it is simple and beneficent thoroughly, which is the tribute of a moral action. An unprecedented material prosperity has not tended to make us Stoics or Christians. But the laws by which the universe is organized reappear at every point, and will rule it. The end of all political struggle is to establish morality as the basis of all legislation. It is not free institutions, it is not a republic, it is not a democracy, that is the end, — no, but only the means. Morality is the object of government. [2] We want a state of things in which crime shall not pay. This is the consolation on which we rest in the darkness of the future and the afflictions of to-day, that the government of the world is moral, and does forever destroy what is not. It is the maxim of natural philosophers that the natural forces wear out in time all obstacles, and take place : and it

is the maxim of history that victory always falls
at last where it ought to fall ; or, there is perpetual march and progress to ideas. But in either
case, no link of the chain can drop out. Nature
works through her appointed elements ; and
ideas must work through the brains and the arms
of good and brave men, or they are no better
than dreams.

Since the above pages were written, President
Lincoln has proposed to Congress that the government shall cooperate with any state that shall
enact a gradual abolishment of slavery. In the
recent series of national successes, this message
is the best. It marks the happiest day in the
political year. The American Executive ranges
itself for the first time on the side of freedom.
If Congress has been backward, the President
has advanced. This state-paper is the more
interesting that it appears to be the President's
individual act, done under a strong sense of duty.
He speaks his own thought in his own style.
All thanks and honor to the Head of the State !
The message has been received throughout the
country with praise, and, we doubt not, with
more pleasure than has been spoken. If Congress accords with the President, it is not yet too

late to begin the emancipation ; but we think it
will always be too late to make it gradual. All
experience agrees that it should be immediate.[1]
More and better than the President has spoken
shall, perhaps, the effect of this message be, —
but, we are sure, not more or better than he
hoped in his heart, when, thoughtful of all the
complexities of his position, he penned these
cautious words.

XIV

THE
EMANCIPATION PROCLAMATION

AN ADDRESS DELIVERED IN BOSTON IN SEPTEMBER, 1862

. . . . . ʼ .

To-day unbind the captive,
So only are ye unbound;
Lift up a people from the dust,
Trump of their rescue, sound!

Pay ransom to the owner
And fill the bag to the brim.
Who is the owner? The slave is owner,
And ever was. Pay him.

O North! give him beauty for rags,
And honor, O South! for his shame,
Nevada! coin thy golden crags
With freedom's image and name.

Up! and the dusky race
That sat in darkness long,—
Be swift their feet as antelopes,
And as behemoth strong.

Come, East and West and North,
By races, as snow-flakes,
And carry my purpose forth,
Which neither halts nor shakes.

My will fulfilled shall be,
For in daylight or in dark,
My thunderbolt has eyes to see
His way home to the mark.

THE EMANCIPATION
PROCLAMATION

IN so many arid forms which states encrust themselves with, once in a century, if so often, a poetic act and record occur. These are the jets of thought into affairs, when, roused by danger or inspired by genius, the political leaders of the day break the else insurmountable routine of class and local legislation, and take a step forward in the direction of catholic and universal interests. Every step in the history of political liberty is a sally of the human mind into the untried Future, and has the interest of genius, and is fruitful in heroic anecdotes. Liberty is a slow fruit. It comes, like religion, for short periods, and in rare conditions, as if awaiting a culture of the race which shall make it organic and permanent. Such moments of expansion in modern history were the Confession of Augsburg, the plantation of America, the English Commonwealth of 1648, the Declaration of American Independence in 1776, the British emancipation of slaves in the West Indies, the passage of the Reform Bill, the repeal of the Corn-Laws, the Magnetic Ocean

Telegraph, though yet imperfect, the passage
of the Homestead Bill in the last Congress,
and now, eminently, President Lincoln's Proclamation on the twenty-second of September.
These are acts of great scope, working on a long
future and on permanent interests, and honoring
alike those who initiate and those who receive
them. These measures provoke no noisy joy,
but are received into a sympathy so deep as to
apprise us that mankind are greater and better
than we know.' At such times it appears as
if a new public were created to greet the new
event. It is as when an orator, having ended
the compliments and pleasantries with which he
conciliated attention, and having run over the
superficial fitness and commodities of the measure he urges, suddenly, lending himself to some
happy inspiration, announces with vibrating
voice the grand human principles involved; —
the bravos and wits who greeted him loudly
thus far are surprised and overawed; a new
audience is found in the heart of the assembly,
— an audience hitherto passive and uncon-
cerned, now at last so searched and kindled that
they come forward, every one a representative
of mankind, standing for all nationalities.

The extreme moderation with which the Presi-

dent advanced to his design, — his long-avowed
expectant policy, as if he chose to be strictly
the executive of the best public sentiment of
the country, waiting only till it should be unmistakably pronounced, — so fair a mind that
none ever listened so patiently to such extreme
varieties of opinion, — so reticent that his decision has taken all parties by surprise, whilst
yet it is just the sequel of his prior acts, — the
firm tone in which he announces it, without
inflation or surplusage, — all these have be-
spoken such favor to the act that, great as the
popularity of the President has been, we are
beginning to think that we have underestimated
the capacity and virtue which the Divine Providence has made an instrument of benefit so
vast. He has been permitted to do more for
America than any other American man. He is
well entitled to the most indulgent construction.
Forget all that we thought shortcomings, every
mistake, every delay. In the extreme embarrassments of his part, call these endurance, wisdom, magnanimity ; illuminated, as they now
are, by this dazzling success.

When we consider the immense opposition
that has been neutralized or converted by the
progress of the war (for it is not long since the

President anticipated the resignation of a large
number of officers in the army, and the secession of three states, on the promulgation of
this policy), — when we see how the great stake
which foreign nations hold in our affairs has recently brought every European power as a client
into this court, and it became every day more
apparent what gigantic and what remote interests
were to be affected by the decision of the President, — one can hardly say the deliberation
was too long. Against all timorous counsels he
had the courage to seize the moment; and such
was his position, and such the felicity attending
the action, that he has replaced government in
the good graces of mankind. " Better is virtue
in the sovereign than plenty in the season," say
the Chinese. 'T is wonderful what power is,
and how ill it is used, and how its ill use makes
life mean, and the sunshine dark. Life in America had lost much of its attraction in the later
years. The virtues of a good magistrate undo
a world of mischief, and, because Nature works
with rectitude, seem vastly more potent than
the acts of bad governors, which are ever
tempered by the good nature in the people, and
the incessant resistance which fraud and violence
encounter. The acts of good governors work a

geometrical ratio, as one midsummer day seems to repair the damage of a year of war.

A day which most of us dared not hope to see, an event worth the dreadful war, worth its costs and uncertainties, seems now to be close before us. October, November, December will have passed over beating hearts and plotting brains : then the hour will strike, and all men of African descent who have faculty enough to find their way to our lines are assured of the protection of American law.

It is by no means necessary that this measure should be suddenly marked by any signal results on the negroes or on the rebel masters. The force of the act is that it commits the country to this justice, — that it compels the innumerable officers, civil, military, naval, of the Republic to range themselves on the line of this equity. It draws the fashion to this side. It is not a measure that admits of being taken back. Done, it cannot be undone by a new administration. For slavery overpowers the disgust of the moral sentiment only through immemorial usage. It cannot be introduced as an improvement of the nineteenth century. This act makes that the lives of our heroes have not been sacrificed in vain. It makes a victory of our defeats. Our hurts are

healed; the health of the nation is repaired.
With a victory like this, we can stand many dis
asters. It does not promise the redemption of
the black race; that lies not with us: but it
relieves it of our opposition. The President by
this act has paroled all the slaves in America;
they will no more fight against us: and it relieves
our race once for all of its crime and false position. The first condition of success is secured
in putting ourselves right. We have recovered
ourselves from our false position, and planted
ourselves on a law of Nature: —

> " If that fail,
> The pillared firmament is rottenness,
> And earth's base built on stubble." [1]

The government has assured itself of the best
constituency in the world: every spark of intellect, every virtuous feeling, every religious heart,
every man of honor, every poet, every philosopher, the generosity of the cities, the health of
the country, the strong arms of the mechanic,
the endurance of farmers, the passionate conscience of women, the sympathy of distant
nations, — all rally to its support.

Of course, we are assuming the firmness of
the policy thus declared. It must not be a paper
proclamation. We confide that Mr. Lincoln is in

earnest, and as he has been slow in making up
his mind, has resisted the importunacy of parties
and of events to the latest moment, he will be
as absolute in his adhesion. Not only will he
repeat and follow up his stroke, but the nation
will add its irresistible strength. If the ruler has
duties, so has the citizen. In times like these,
when the nation is imperilled, what man can,
without shame, receive good news from day to
day without giving good news of himself? What
right has any one to read in the journals tidings
of victories, if he has not bought them by his own
valor, treasure, personal sacrifice, or by service
as good in his own department? With this blot
removed from our national honor, this heavy
load lifted off the national heart, we shall not fear
henceforward to show our faces among mankind.
We shall cease to be hypocrites and pretenders,
but what we have styled our free institutions
will be such.'

In the light of this event the public distress
begins to be removed. What if the brokers' quotations show our stocks discredited, and the gold
dollar costs one hundred and twenty-seven
cents? These tables are fallacious. Every acre
in the free states gained substantial value on
the twenty-second of September. The cause of

disunion and war has been reached and begun to
be removed. Every man's house-lot and garden
are relieved of the malaria which the purest
winds and strongest sunshine could not penetrate and purge. The territory of the Union
shines to-day with a lustre which every European
emigrant can discern from far; a sign of inmost
security and permanence. Is it feared that taxes
will check immigration? That depends on what
the taxes are spent for. If they go to fill up this
yawning Dismal Swamp, which engulfed armies
and populations, and created plague, and neutralized hitherto all the vast capabilities of this
continent, — then this taxation, which makes the
land wholesome and habitable, and will draw all
men unto it, is the best investment in which
property-holder ever lodged his earnings.

Whilst we have pointed out the opportuneness
of the Proclamation, it remains to be said that
the President had no choice. He might look
wistfully for what variety of courses lay open to
him; every line but one was closed up with fire.
This one, too, bristled with danger, but through
it was the sole safety. The measure he has adopted
was imperative. It is wonderful to see the un-
seasonable senility of what is called the Peace
Party, through all its masks, blinding their eyes

to the main feature of the war, namely, its inevitableness. The war existed long before the cannonade of Sumter, and could not be postponed. It might have begun otherwise or elsewhere, but war was in the minds and bones of the combatants, it was written on the iron leaf, and you might as easily dodge gravitation. If we had consented to a peaceable secession of the rebels, the divided sentiment of the border states made peaceable secession impossible, the insatiable temper of the South made it impossible, and the slaves on the border, wherever the border might be, were an incessant fuel to rekindle the fire. Give the Confederacy New Orleans, Charleston, and Richmond, and they would have demanded St. Louis and Baltimore. Give them these, and they would have insisted on Washington. Give them Washington, and they would have assumed the army and navy, and, through these, Philadelphia, New York, and Boston. It looks as if the battle-field would have been at least as large in that event as it is now. The war was formidable, but could not be avoided. The war was and is an immense mischief, but brought with it the immense benefit of drawing a line and rallying the free states to fix it impassably, — preventing the whole force of Southern connection and influence throughout the North from distracting every city with endless confusion, detaching that force and reducing it to handfuls, and, in the progress of hostilities, disinfecting us of our habitual proclivity, through the affection of trade and the traditions of the Democratic party, to follow Southern leading.'

These necessities which have dictated the conduct of the federal government are overlooked especially by our foreign critics. The popular statement of the opponents of the war abroad is the impossibility of our success. " If you could add," say they, " to your strength the whole army of England, of France and of Austria, you could not coerce eight millions of people to come under this government against their will." This is an odd thing for an Englishman, a Frenchman or an Austrian to say, who remembers Europe of the last seventy years, — the condition of Italy, until 1859, — of Poland, since 1793, — of France, of French Algiers, — of British Ireland, and British India. But granting the truth, rightly read, of the historical aphorism, that " the people always conquer," it is to be noted that, in the Southern States, the tenure of land and the local laws, with slavery, give the social system not a democratic but an aristocratic complexion ; and those states have shown every year a more hostile and aggressive temper, until the instinct of self-preservation forced us into the war. And the aim of the war on our part is indicated by the aim of the President's Proclamation, namely, to break up the false combination of Southern society, to destroy the piratic feature in it which makes it our enemy only as it is the enemy of the human race, and so allow its reconstruction on a just and healthful basis. Then new affinities will act, the old repulsion will cease, and, the cause of war being removed, Nature and trade may be trusted to establish a lasting peace.

We think we cannot overstate the wisdom and benefit of this act of the government. The malignant cry of the Secession press within the free states, and the recent action of the Confederate Congress, are decisive as to its efficiency and correctness of aim. Not less so is the silent joy which has greeted it in all generous hearts, and the new hope it has breathed into the world. It was well to delay the steamers at the wharves until this edict could be put on board. It will be an insurance to the ship as it goes plunging through the sea with glad tidings to all people. Happy are the young, who find the pestilence

326 EMANCIPATION PROCLAMATION

cleansed out of the earth, leaving open to them
an honest career. Happy the old, who see Nature purified before they depart. Do not let the
dying die: hold them back to this world, until
you have charged their ear and heart with this
message to other spiritual societies, announcing
the melioration of our planet: —

> " Incertainties now crown themselves assured,
>   And Peace proclaims olives of endless age." [1]

Meantime that ill-fated, much-injured race
which the Proclamation respects will lose somewhat of the dejection sculptured for ages in their
bronzed countenance, uttered in the wailing of
their plaintive music, — a race naturally benevolent, docile, industrious, and whose very miseries
sprang from their great talent for usefulness,
which, in a more moral age, will not only defend
their independence, but will give them a rank
among nations.[2]

XV

ABRAHAM LINCOLN

REMARKS AT THE FUNERAL SERVICES HELD IN
CONCORD, APRIL 19, 1865

" Nature, they say, doth dote,
   And cannot make a man
   Save on some worn-out plan,
   Repeating us by rote:
For him her Old-World moulds aside she threw,
   And, choosing sweet clay from the breast
   Of the unexhausted West,
With stuff untainted shaped a hero new,
Wise, steadfast in the strength of God, and true.
   How beautiful to see
Once more a shepherd of mankind indeed,
Who loved his charge, but never loved to lead;
One whose meek flock the people joyed to be,
   Not lured by any cheat of birth,
   But by his clear-grained human worth,
And brave old wisdom of sincerity !
   They knew that outward grace is dust;
   They could not choose but trust
In that sure-footed mind's unfaltering skill,
   And supple-tempered will
That bent, like perfect steel, to spring again and thrust

.   .   .   .

   Nothing of Europe here,
Or, then, of Europe fronting mornward still,
   Ere any names of Serf and Peer
   Could Nature's equal scheme deface; . . .
   Here was a type of the true elder race,
And one of Plutarch's men talked with us face to face."
         Lowell, *Commemoration Ode.*

ABRAHAM LINCOLN

WE meet under the gloom of a calamity which darkens down over the minds of good men in all civil society, as the fearful tidings travel over sea, over land, from country to country, like the shadow of an uncalculated eclipse over the planet. Old as history is, and manifold as are its tragedies, I doubt if any death has caused so much pain to mankind as this has caused, or will cause, on its announcement; and this, not so much because nations are by modern arts brought so closely together, as because of the mysterious hopes and fears which, in the present day, are connected with the name and institutions of America.

In this country, on Saturday, every one was struck dumb, and saw at first only deep below deep, as he meditated on the ghastly blow. And perhaps, at this hour, when the coffin which contains the dust of the President sets forward on its long march through mourning states, on its way to his home in Illinois, we might well be silent, and suffer the awful voices of the time to thunder to us. Yes, but that first despair was brief: the man was not so to be mourned. He was the most active and hopeful of men ; and his work had not perished : but acclamations of praise for the task he had accomplished burst out into a song of triumph, which even tears for his death cannot keep down.

The President stood before us as a man of the people. He was thoroughly American, had never crossed the sea, had never been spoiled by English insularity or French dissipation ; a quite native, aboriginal man, as an acorn from the oak ; no aping of foreigners, no frivolous accomplishments, Kentuckian born, working on a farm, a flatboatman, a captain in the Black Hawk War, a country lawyer, a representative in the rural legislature of Illinois ; — on such modest foundations the broad structure of his fame was laid. How slowly, and yet by happily prepared steps, he came to his place. All of us remember — it is only a history of five or six years — the surprise and the disappointment of the country at his first nomination by the convention at Chicago. Mr. Seward, then in the culmination of his good fame, was the favorite of the Eastern States. And when the new and comparatively unknown name of Lincoln was announced (notwithstanding the report of the acclamations of that convention), we heard the result coldly and sadly. It seemed too rash, on a purely local reputation, to build so grave a trust in such anxious times ; and men naturally talked of the chances in politics as incalculable. But it turned out not to be chance. The profound good opinion which the people of Illinois and of the West had conceived of him, and which they had imparted to their colleagues, that they also might justify themselves to their constituents at home, was not rash, though they did not begin to know the riches of his worth.'

A plain man of the people, an extraordinary fortune attended him. He offered no shining qualities at the first encounter ; he did not offend by superiority. He had a face and manner which disarmed suspicion, which inspired confidence, which confirmed good will. He was a man without vices. He had a strong sense of duty, which it was very easy for him to obey. Then, he had what farmers call a long head ; was excellent in working out the sum for himself; in arguing his case and convincing you fairly and firmly. Then, it turned out that he was a great worker ; had prodigious faculty of performance ; worked easily. A good worker is so rare ; everybody has some disabling quality. In a host of young men that start together and promise so many brilliant leaders for the next age, each fails on trial ; one by bad health, one by conceit, or by love of pleasure, or lethargy, or an ugly temper, — each has some disquali- fying fault that throws him out of the career. But this man was sound to the core, cheerful, persistent, all right for labor, and liked nothing so well.

Then, he had a vast good nature, which made him tolerant and accessible to all ; fair-minded, leaning to the claim of the petitioner ; affable, and not sensible to the affliction which the innumerable visits paid to him when President would have brought to any one else.' And how this good nature became a noble humanity, in many a tragic case which the events of the war brought to him, every one will remember ; and with what increasing tenderness he dealt when a whole race was thrown on his compassion. The poor negro said of him,.on an impressive occasion, " Massa Linkum am eberywhere."

Then his broad good humor, running easily into jocular talk, in which he delighted and in which he excelled, was a rich gift to this wise man. It enabled him to keep his secret ; to

meet every kind of man and every rank in society; to take off the edge of the severest decisions; to mask his own purpose and sound his
companion; and to catch with true instinct the
temper of every company he addressed. And,
more than all, it is to a man of severe labor, in
anxious and exhausting crises, the natural re-
storative, good as sleep, and is the protection
of the overdriven brain against rancor and insanity.

He is the author of a multitude of good sayings, so disguised as pleasantries that it is certain they had no reputation at first but as jests;
and only later, by the very acceptance and adoption they find in the mouths of millions, turn
out to be the wisdom of the hour. I am sure
if this man had ruled in a period of less facility
of printing, he would have become mytho-
logical in a very few years, like Æsop or Pilpay,
or one of the Seven Wise Masters, by his fables
and proverbs. But the weight and penetration
of many passages in his letters, messages and
speeches, hidden now by the very closeness of
their application to the moment, are destined
hereafter to wide fame. What pregnant defini-
tions; what unerring common sense; what foresight; and, on great occasion, what lofty, and

more than national, what humane tone! His
brief speech at Gettysburg will not easily be
surpassed by words on any recorded occasion.
This, and one other American speech, that of
John Brown to the court that tried him, and
a part of Kossuth's speech at Birmingham, can
only be compared with each other, and with no
fourth.

His occupying the chair of state was a triumph of the good sense of mankind, and of the
public conscience. This middle-class country
had got a middle-class president, at last. Yes, in
manners and sympathies, but not in powers, for
his powers were superior. This man grew according to the need. His mind mastered the problem
of the day ; and as the problem grew, so did his
comprehension of it. Rarely was man so fitted
to the event. In the midst of fears and jealous-
ies, in the Babel of counsels and parties, this man
wrought incessantly with all his might and all his
honesty, laboring to find what the people wanted,
and how to obtain that. It cannot be said there
is any exaggeration of his worth. If ever a man
was fairly tested, he was. There was no lack of
resistance, nor of slander, nor of ridicule. The
times have allowed no state secrets ; the nation
has been in such ferment, such multitudes had

to be trusted, that no secret could be kept. Every door was ajar, and we know all that befell.

Then, what an occasion was the whirlwind of the war. Here was place for no holiday magistrate, no fair-weather sailor; the new pilot was hurried to the helm in a tornado. In four years, — four years of battle-days, — his endurance, his fertility of resources, his magnanimity, were sorely tried and never found wanting. There, by his courage, his justice, his even temper, his fertile counsel, his humanity, he stood a heroic figure in the centre of a heroic epoch. He is the true history of the American people in his time. Step by step he walked before them; slow with their slowness, quickening his march by theirs, the true representative of this continent; an entirely public man; father of his country, the pulse of twenty millions throbbing in his heart, the thought of their minds articulated by his tongue.

Adam Smith remarks that the axe, which in Houbraken's portraits of British kings and worthies is engraved under those who have suffered at the block, adds a certain lofty charm to the picture. And who does not see, even in this tragedy so recent, how fast the terror and ruin of the massacre are already burning into glory around the victim? Far happier this fate than to have lived to be wished away; to have watched the decay of his own faculties; to have seen — perhaps even he — the proverbial ingratitude of statesmen; to have seen mean men preferred. Had he not lived long enough to keep the greatest promise that ever man made to his fellow men, — the practical abolition of slavery? He had seen Tennessee, Missouri and Maryland emancipate their slaves. He had seen Savannah, Charleston and Richmond surrendered; had seen the main army of the rebellion lay down its arms. He had conquered the public opinion of Canada, England and France.' Only Washington can compare with him in fortune.

And what if it should turn out, in the unfolding of the web, that he had reached the term; that this heroic deliverer could no longer serve us; that the rebellion had touched its natural conclusion, and what remained to be done required new and uncommitted hands, — a new spirit born out of the ashes of the war; and that Heaven, wishing to show the world a completed benefactor, shall make him serve his country even more by his death than by his life? Nations, like kings, are not good by facility and complaisance. " The kindness of kings consists in justice and strength." Easy good nature has been the dangerous foible of the Republic, and it was necessary that its enemies should outrage it, and drive us to unwonted firmness, to secure the salvation of this country in the next ages.

The ancients believed in a serene and beautiful Genius which ruled in the affairs of nations; which, with a slow but stern justice, carried forward the fortunes of certain chosen houses, weeding out single offenders or offending families, and securing at last the firm prosperity of the favorites of Heaven. It was too narrow a view of the Eternal Nemesis. There is a serene Providence which rules the fate of nations, which makes little account of time, little of one generation or race, makes no account of disasters, conquers alike by what is called defeat or by what is called victory, thrusts aside enemy and obstruction, crushes everything immoral as inhuman, and obtains the ultimate triumph of the best race by the sacrifice of everything which resists the moral laws of the world.' It makes its own instruments, creates the man for the time, trains him in poverty, inspires his genius, and

XI

arms him for his task. It has given every race its own talent, and ordains that only that race which combines perfectly with the virtues of all shall endure.'

XVI

HARVARD COMMEMORATION
SPEECH

JULY 21, 1865

                  " ' Old classmate, say
Do you remember our Commencement Day ?
Were we such boys as these at twenty ? ' Nay,
God called them to a nobler task than ours,
And gave them holier thoughts and manlier powers, —
This is the day of fruits and not of flowers!
These ' boys ' we talk about like ancient sages
Are the same *men* we read of in old pages —
The bronze recast of dead heroic ages'
We grudge them not, our dearest, bravest, best, —
Let but the quarrel's issue stand confest:
'T is Earth's old slave-God battling for his crown
And Freedom fighting with her visor down."

                                 HOLMES.

* Many loved Truth, and lavished life's best oil
  Amid the dust of books to find her,
Content at last, for guerdon of their toil,
  With the cast mantle she hath left behind her.
    Many in sad faith sought for her,
    Many with crossed hands sighed for her;
    But these, our brothers, fought for her,
    At life's dear peril wrought for her,
    So loved her that they died for her,
    Tasting the raptured fleetness
    Of her divine completeness:
      Their higher instinct knew
Those love her best who to themselves are true,
And what they dare to dream of, dare to do;
    They followed her and found her
    Where all may hope to find,
Not in the ashes of the burnt-out mind,
But beautiful, with danger's sweetness round her.
    Where faith made whole with deed
    Breathes its awakening breath
    Into the lifeless creed,
    They saw her plumed and mailed,
    With sweet, stern face unveiled,
And all-repaying eyes, look proud on them in death.''
                        Lowell, *Commemoration Ode*

HARVARD
COMMEMORATION SPEECH

MR. CHAIRMAN, AND GENTLEMEN:
With whatever opinion we come here, I
think it is not in man to see, without a feeling
of pride and pleasure, a tried soldier, the armed
defender of the right. I think that in these
last years all opinions have been affected by
the magnificent and stupendous spectacle which
Divine Providence has offered us of the energies
that slept in the children of this country, — that
slept and have awakened. I see thankfully those
that are here, but dim eyes in vain explore for
some who are not.

The old Greek Heraclitus said, " War is the
Father of all things." He said it, no doubt, as
science, but we of this day can repeat it as political and social truth. War passes the power
of all chemical solvents, breaking up the old
adhesions, and allowing the atoms of society to
take a new order. It is not the Government,
but the War, that has appointed the good
generals, sifted out the pedants, put in the new
and vigorous blood. The War has lifted many
other people besides Grant and Sherman into

their true places. Even Divine Providence, we may say, always seems to work after a certain military necessity. Every nation punishes the General who is not victorious. It is a rule in games of chance that the cards beat all the players, and revolutions disconcert and outwit all the insurgents.

The revolutions carry their own points, sometimes to the ruin of those who set them on foot. The proof that war also is within the highest right, is a marked benefactor in the hands of the Divine Providence, is its *morale*. The war gave back integrity to this erring and immoral nation. It charged with power, peaceful, amiable men, to whose life war and discord were abhorrent. What an infusion of character went out from this and other colleges! What an infusion of character down to the ranks! The experience has been uniform that it is the gentle soul that makes the firm hero after all. It is easy to recall the mood in which our young men, snatched from every peaceful pursuit, went to the war. Many of them had never handled a gun. They said, " It is not in me to resist. I go because I must. It is a duty which I shall never forgive myself if I decline. I do not know that I can make a soldier. I may be very clumsy. Perhaps I shall be timid ; but you can rely on me. Only one thing is certain, I can well die, but I cannot afford to misbehave."

In fact the infusion of culture and tender humanity from these scholars and idealists who went to the war in their own despite — God knows they had no fury for killing their old friends and countrymen — had its signal and lasting effect. It was found that enthusiasm was a more potent ally than science and munitions of war without it. "It is a principle of war," said Napoleon, "that when you can use the thunderbolt you must prefer it to the cannon." Enthusiasm was the thunderbolt. Here in this little Massachusetts, in smaller Rhode Island, in this little nest of New England republics it flamed out when the guilty gun was aimed at Sumter.

Mr. Chairman, standing here in Harvard College, the parent of all the colleges ; in Massachusetts, the parent of all the North ; when I consider her influence on the country as a principal planter of the Western States, and now, by her teachers, preachers, journalists and books, as well as by traffic and production, the diffuser of religious, literary and political opinion ; — and when I see how irresistible

the convictions of Massachusetts are in these
swarming populations, — I think the little state
bigger than I knew. When her blood is up, she
has a fist big enough to knock down an empire.
And her blood was roused. Scholars changed
the black coat for the blue. A single company
in the Forty-fourth Massachusetts Regiment
contained thirty-five sons of Harvard. You all
know as well as I the story of these dedicated
men, who knew well on what duty they went,
— whose fathers and mothers said of each
slaughtered son, "We gave him up when he
enlisted." One mother said, when her son was
offered the command of the first negro regiment,
" If he accepts it, I shall be as proud as if I had
heard that he was shot." ' These men, thus tender, thus high-bred, thus peaceable, were always
in the front and always employed. They might
say, with their forefathers the old Norse Vikings,
" We sung the mass of lances from morning
until evening." And in how many cases it
chanced, when the hero had fallen, they who
came by night to his funeral, on the morrow
returned to the war-path to show his slayers the
way to death !

Ah ' young brothers, all honor and gratitude
to you, — you, manly defenders, Liberty's and

Humanity's bodyguard! We shall not again disparage America, now that we have seen what men it will bear. We see — we thank you for it — a new era, worth to mankind all the treasure and all the lives it has cost; yes, worth to the world the lives of all this generation of American men, if they had been demanded.[1]

XVII

ADDRESS

AT THE DEDICATION OF THE SOLDIERS' MONUMENT IN CONCORD, APRIL 19, 1867

" THEY have shown what men may do,
They have proved how men may die, —
Count, who can, the fields they have pressed,
Each face to the solemn sky! ''

BROWNELL.

" THINK you these felt no charms
    In their gray homesteads and embowered farms ?
    In household faces waiting at the door
    Their evening step should lighten up no more ?
    In fields their boyish feet had known ?
    In trees their fathers' hands had set,
    And which with them had grown,
    Widening each year their leafy coronet ?
    Felt they no pang of passionate regret
    For those unsolid goods that seem so much our own ?
    These things are dear to every man that lives,
    And life prized more for what it lends than gives.
    Yea, many a tie, through iteration sweet,
    Strove to detain their fatal feet,
    And yet the enduring half they chose,
    Whose choice decides a man life's slave or king,
    The invisible things of God before the seen and known:
    Therefore their memory inspiration blows
    With echoes gathering on from zone to zone;
    For manhood is the one immortal thing
    Beneath Time's changeful sky,
    And, where it lightened once, from age to age,
    Men come to learn, in grateful pilgrimage,
    That length of days is knowing when to die "
                        LOWELL, *Concord Ode*

ADDRESS

DEDICATION OF SOLDIERS' MONUMENT IN CONCORD, APRIL 19, 1867

FELLOW CITIZENS: The day is in Concord doubly our calendar day, as being the anniversary of the invasion of the town by the British troops in 1775, and of the departure of the company of volunteers for Washington, in 1861. We are all pretty well aware that the facts which make to us the interest of this day are in a great degree personal and local here; that every other town and city has its own heroes and memorial days, and that we can hardly expect a wide sympathy for the names and anecdotes which we delight to record. We are glad and proud that we have no monopoly of merit. We are thankful that other towns and cities are as rich; that the heroes of old and of recent date, who made and kept America free and united, were not rare or solitary growths, but sporadic over vast tracts of the Republic. Yet, as it is a piece of nature and the common sense that the throbbing chord that

holds us to our kindred, our friends and our
town, is not to be denied or resisted, — no matter how frivolous or unphilosophical its pulses,
— we shall cling affectionately to our houses,
our river and pastures, and believe that our vis-
itors will pardon us if we take the privilege of
talking freely about our nearest neighbors as in
a family party ; — well assured, meantime, that
the virtues we are met to honor were directed on
aims which command the sympathy of every
loyal American citizen, were exerted for the
protection of our common country, and aided
its triumph.

The town has thought fit to signify its honor
for a few of its sons by raising an obelisk in the
square. It is a simple pile enough, — a few slabs
of granite, dug just below the surface of the soil,
and laid upon the top of it ; but as we have
learned that the upheaved mountain, from which
these discs or flakes were broken, was once a
glowing mass at white heat, slowly crystallized,
then uplifted by the central fires of the globe : so
the roots of the events it appropriately marks
are in the heart of the universe. I shall say of
this obelisk, planted here in our quiet plains,
what Richter says of the volcano in the fair landscape of Naples : " Vesuvius stands in this poem

of Nature, and exalts everything, as war does the age."

The art of the architect and the sense of the town have made these dumb stones speak; have, if I may borrow the old language of the church, converted these elements from a secular to a sacred and spiritual use; have made them look to the past and the future; have given them a meaning for the imagination and the heart. The sense of the town, the eloquent inscriptions the shaft now bears, the memories of these martyrs, the noble names which yet have gathered only their first fame, whatever good grows to the country out of the war, the largest results, the future power and genius of the land, will go on clothing this shaft with daily beauty and spiritual life. 'T is certain that a plain stone like this, standing on such memories, having no reference to utilities, but only to the grand instincts of the civil and moral man, mixes with surrounding nature, — by day with the changing seasons, by night the stars roll over it gladly, — becomes a sentiment, a poet, a prophet, an orator, to every townsman and passenger, an altar where the noble youth shall in all time come to make his secret vows.'

The old Monument, a short half-mile from

this house, stands to signalize the first Revolution, where the people resisted offensive usur-
pations, offensive taxes of the British Parliament,
claiming that there should be no tax without
representation. Instructed by events, after the
quarrel began, the Americans took higher
ground, and stood for political independence.
But in the necessities of the hour, they overlooked the moral law, and winked at a practical
exception to the Bill of Rights they had drawn
up. They winked at the exception, believing it
insignificant. But the moral law, the nature of
things, did not wink at it, but kept its eye wide
open It turned out that this one violation was
a subtle poison, which in eighty years corrupted
the whole overgrown body politic, and brought
the alternative of extirpation of the poison or
ruin to the Republic.'

This new Monument is built to mark the
arrival of the nation at the new principle, —
say, rather, at its new acknowledgment, for the
principle is as old as Heaven, — that only
that state can live, in which injury to the least
member is recognized as damage to the whole.

Reform must begin at home. The aim of the
hour was to reconstruct the South; but first
the North had to be reconstructed. Its own

theory and practice of liberty had got sadly
out of gear, and must be corrected. It was done
on the instant. A thunder-storm at sea sometimes reverses the magnets in the ship, and
south is north. The storm of war works the like
miracle on men. Every Democrat who went
South came back a Republican, like the governors who, in Buchanan's time, went to Kansas,
and instantly took the free-state colors. War,
says the poet, is

> " the arduous strife,
> To which the triumph of all good is given." [1]

Every principle is a war-note. When the rights
of man are recited under any old government,
every one of them is a declaration of war. War
civilizes, rearranges the population, distribut-
ing by ideas, — the innovators on one side, the
antiquaries on the other. It opens the eyes
wider. Once we were patriots up to the town-
bounds, or the state-line. But when you re-
place the love of family or clan by a principle,
as freedom, instantly that fire runs over the
state-line into New Hampshire, Vermont, New
York and Ohio, into the prairie and beyond,
leaps the mountains, bridges river and lake,
burns as hotly in Kansas and California as in
Boston, and no chemist can discriminate between

XI

one soil and the other. It lifts every population to an equal power and merit.

As long as we debate in council, both sides may form their private guess what the event may be, or which is the strongest. But the moment you cry " Every man to his tent, O Israel!" the delusions of hope and fear are at an end ; — the strength is now to be tested by the eternal facts. There will be no doubt more. The world is equal to itself. The secret architecture of things begins to disclose itself; the fact that all things were made on a basis of right ; that justice is really desired by all intelligent beings ; that opposition to it is against the nature of things ; and that, whatever may happen in this hour or that, the years and the centuries are always pulling down the wrong and building up the right.

The war made the Divine Providence credible to many who did not believe the good Heaven quite honest. Every man was an abolitionist by conviction, but did not believe that his neighbor was. The opinions of masses of men, which the tactics of primary caucuses and the proverbial timidity of trade had concealed, the war discovered ; and it was found, contrary to all popular belief, that the country was at

heart abolitionist, and for the Union was ready
to die.

As cities of men are the first effects of civilization, and also instantly causes of more civilization, so armies, which are only wandering
cities, generate a vast heat, and lift the spirit of
the soldiers who compose them to the boiling
point. The armies mustered in the North were
as much missionaries to the mind of the country
as they were carriers of material force, and had
the vast advantage of carrying whither they
marched a higher civilization. Of course, there
are noble men everywhere, and there are such
in the South; and the noble know the noble,
wherever they meet; and we have all heard
passages of generous and exceptional behavior
exhibited by individuals there to our officers
and men, during the war. But the common
people, rich or poor, were the narrowest and
most conceited of mankind, as arrogant as the
negroes on the Gambia River; and, by the way,
it looks as if the editors of the Southern press
were in all times selected from this class. The
invasion of Northern farmers, mechanics, engi-
neers, tradesmen, lawyers and students did more
than forty years of peace had done to educate
the South ' " This will be a slow business,"

writes our Concord captain home, " for we have
to stop and civilize the people as we go along."

It is an interesting part of the history, the
manner in which this incongruous militia were
made soldiers. That was done again on the
Kansas plan. Our farmers went to Kansas as
peaceable, God-fearing men as the members of
our school committee here. But when the
Border raids were let loose on their villages,
these people, who turned pale at home if called
to dress a cut finger, on witnessing the butchery
done by the Missouri riders on women and
babes, were so beside themselves with rage, that
they became on the instant the bravest soldiers
and the most determined avengers.' And the
first events of the war of the Rebellion gave
the like training to the new recruits.

All sorts of men went to the war, — the
roughs, men who liked harsh play and violence,
men for whom pleasure was not strong enough,
but who wanted pain, and found sphere at last
for their superabundant energy ; then the adventurous type of New Englander, with his
appetite for novelty and travel ; the village
politician, who could now verify his newspaper
knowledge, see the South, and amass what a
stock of adventures to retail hereafter at the

fireside, or to the well-known companions on
the Mill-dam; young men, also, of excellent education and polished manners, delicately brought
up; manly farmers, skilful mechanics, young
tradesmen, men hitherto of narrow opportunities of knowing the world, but well taught in
the grammar-schools. But perhaps in every one
of these classes were idealists, men who went
from a religious duty. I have a note of a conversation that occurred in our first company, the
morning before the battle of Bull Run. At a
halt in the march, a few of our boys were sitting
on a rail fence talking together whether it was
right to sacrifice themselves. One of them said,
'he had been thinking a good deal about it,
last night, and he thought one was never too
young to die for a principle.' One of our later
volunteers, on the day when he left home, in
reply to my question, How can you be spared
from your farm, now that your father is so ill?
said: "I go because I shall always be sorry if
I did not go when the country called me. I can
go as well as another." One wrote to his father
these words: "You may think it strange that
I, who have always naturally rather shrunk
from danger, should wish to enter the army;
but there is a higher Power that tunes the

hearts of men, and enables them to see their
duty, and gives them courage to face the dangers with which those duties are attended"
And the captain writes home of another of his
men, " B—— comes from a sense of duty and
love of country, and these are the soldiers you
can depend upon." [1]

None of us can have forgotten how sharp
a test to try our peaceful people with, was the
first call for troops. I doubt not many of our
soldiers could repeat the confession of a youth
whom I knew in the beginning of the war, who
enlisted in New York, went to the field, and
died early. Before his departure he confided to
his sister that he was naturally a coward, but
was determined that no one should ever find it
out ; that he had long trained himself by forc-
ing himself, on the suspicion of any near danger,
to go directly up to it, cost him what struggles
it might. Yet it is from this temperament of
sensibility that great heroes have been formed.

Our first company was led by an officer who
had grown up in this village from a boy.[2] The
older among us can well remember him at
school, at play and at work, all the way up, the
most amiable, sensible, unpretending of men ;
fair, blond, the rose lived long in his cheek ;

grave, but social, and one of the last men in this
town you would have picked out for the rough
dealing of war, — not a trace of fierceness, much
less of recklessness, or of the devouring thirst
for excitement ; tender as a woman in his care
for a cough or a chilblain in his men ; had
troches and arnica in his pocket for them. The
army officers were welcome to their jest on
him as too kind for a captain, and, later, as the
colonel who got off his horse when he saw
one of his men limp on the march, and told
him to ride. But *he* knew that his men had
found out, first that he was captain, then that
he was colonel, and neither dared nor wished to
disobey him. He was a man without conceit,
who never fancied himself a philosopher or a
saint ; the most modest and amiable of men,
engaged in common duties, but equal always
to the occasion ; and the war showed him still
equal, however stern and terrible the occasion
grew, — disclosed in him a strong good sense,
great fertility of resource, the helping hand, and
then the moral qualities of a commander, — a
patience not to be tired out, a serious devotion
to the cause of the country that never swerved,
a hope that never failed. He was a Puritan in
the army, with traits that remind one of John

Brown, — an integrity incorruptible, and an
ability that always rose to the need.

You will remember that these colonels, captains and lieutenants, and the privates too, are
domestic men, just wrenched away from their
families and their business by this rally of all
the manhood in the land. They have notes to
pay at home; have farms, shops, factories, affairs of every kind to think of and write home
about. Consider what sacrifice and havoc in
business arrangements this war-blast made.
They have to think carefully of every last resource at home on which their wives or mothers
may fall back; upon the little account in the
savings bank, the grass that can be sold, the
old cow, or the heifer. These necessities make
the topics of the ten thousand letters with
which the mail-bags came loaded day by day.
These letters play a great part in the war. The
writing of letters made the Sunday in every
camp: — meantime they are without the means
of writing. After the first marches there is no
letter-paper, there are no envelopes, no postage-
stamps, for these were wetted into a solid mass
in the rains and mud. Some of these letters are
written on the back of old bills, some on brown
paper, or strips of newspaper; written by fire-

light, making the short night shorter; written
on the knee, in the mud, with pencil, six words
at a time; or in the saddle, and have to stop
because the horse will not stand still. But the
words are proud and tender, — " Tell mother I
will not disgrace her;" "tell her not to worry
about me, for I know she would not have had
me stay at home if she could as well as not."
The letters of the captain are the dearest trea-
sures of this town. Always devoted, sometimes
anxious, sometimes full of joy at the deport-
ment of his comrades, they contain the sincere
praise of men whom I now see in this assembly. If Marshal Montluc's[1] Memoirs are the
Bible of soldiers, as Henry IV. of France said,
Colonel Prescott might furnish the Book of
Epistles.

He writes, " You don't know how one gets
attached to a company by living with them and
sleeping with them all the time. I know every
man by heart. I know every man's weak spot,
— who is shaky, and who is true blue." He
never remits his care of the men, aiming to
hold them to their good habits and to keep
them cheerful. For the first point, he keeps up
a constant acquaintance with them ; urges their
correspondence with their friends ; writes news

of them home, urging his own correspondent
to visit their families and keep them informed
about the men ; encourages a temperance society
which is formed in the camp. " I have not had
a man drunk, or affected by liquor, since we
came here." At one time he finds his company
unfortunate in having fallen between two companies of quite another class, — " 't is profanity
all the time ; yet instead of a bad influence on
our men, I think it works the other way, — it
disgusts them."

One day he writes, " I expect to have a time,
this forenoon, with the officer from West Point
who drills us. He is very profane, and I will not
stand it. If he does not stop it, I shall march my
men right away when he is drilling them. There
is a fine for officers swearing in the army, and
I have too many young men that are not used
to such talk. I told the colonel this morning
I should do it, and shall, — don't care what the
consequence is. This lieutenant seems to think
that these men, who never saw a gun, can drill
as well as he, who has been at West Point four
years." At night he adds : " I told that officer
from West Point, this morning, that he could
not swear at my company as he did yesterday ;
told him I would not stand it anyway. I told

him I had a good many young men in my company whose mothers asked me to look after
them, and I should do so, and not allow them
to hear such language, especially from an officer,
whose duty it was to set them a better example.
Told him I did not swear myself and would
not allow him to. He looked at me as much as
to say, *Do you know whom you are talking to?*
and I looked at him as much as to say., *Yes,
I do*. He looked rather ashamed, but went
through the drill without an oath." So much for
the care of their morals. His next point is to
keep them cheerful. 'T is better than medicine.
He has games of baseball, and pitching quoits,
and euchre, whilst part of the military discipline
is sham fights.

The best men heartily second him, and 'nvent
excellent means of their own. When, afterwards,
five of these men were prisoners in the Parish
Prison in New Orleans, they set themselves to
use the time to the wisest advantage, — formed
a debating-club, wrote a daily or weekly newspaper, called it " Stars and Stripes." It adver-
tises, " prayer-meeting at 7 o'clock, in cell No.
8, second floor," and their own printed record is
a proud and affecting narrative.

Whilst the regiment was encamped at Camp

Andrew, near Alexandria, in June, 1861, marching orders came. Colonel Lawrence sent for
eight wagons, but only three came. On these
they loaded all the canvas of the tents, but took
no tent-poles.

" It looked very much like a severe thunder-
storm," writes the captain, " and I knew the men
would all have to sleep out of doors, unless we
carried them. So I took six poles, and went to
the colonel, and told him I had got the poles for
two tents, which would cover twenty-four men,
and unless he ordered me not to carry them, I
should do so. He said he had no objection, only
thought they would be too much for me. We
only had about twelve men [the rest of the company being, perhaps, on picket or other duty],
and some of them have their heavy knapsacks
and guns to carry, so could not carry any poles.
We started and marched two miles without stop-
ping to rest, not having had anything to eat, and
being very hot and dry." At this time Captain
Prescott was daily threatened with sickness, and
suffered the more from this heat. " I told Lieutenant Bowers, this morning, that I could afford
to be sick from bringing the tent-poles, for it
saved the whole regiment from sleeping out-
doors; for they would not have thought of it, if

I had not taken mine. The major had tried to discourage me ; — said, 'perhaps, if I carried them over, some other company would get them ; ' — I told him, perhaps he did not think I was smart." He had the satisfaction to see the whole regiment enjoying the protection of these tents.'

In the disastrous battle of Bull Run this company behaved well, and the regimental officers believed, what is now the general conviction of the country, that the misfortunes of the day were not so much owing to the fault of the troops as to the insufficiency of the combinations by the general officers. It happened, also, that the Fifth Massachusetts was almost unofficered. The colonel was, early in the day, disabled by a casualty ; the lieutenant-colonel, the major and the adjutant were already transferred to new regiments, and their places were not yet filled. The three months of the enlistment expired a few days after the battle.

In the fall of 1861, the old artillery company of this town was reorganized, and Captain Richard Barrett received a commission in March, 1862, from the state, as its commander. This company, chiefly recruited here, was later embodied in the Forty-seventh Regiment, Massa-

chusetts Volunteers, enlisted as nine months'
men, and sent to New Orleans, where they were
employed in guard duty during their term of
service. Captain Humphrey H. Buttrick, lieutenant in this regiment, as he had been already
lieutenant in Captain Prescott's company in
1861, went out again in August, 1864, a captain
in the Fifty-ninth Massachusetts, and saw hard
service in the Ninth Corps, under General Burn-
side. The regiment being formed of veterans,
and in fields requiring great activity and exposure, suffered extraordinary losses ; Captain Buttrick and one other officer being the only officers
in it who were neither killed, wounded nor captured.' In August, 1862, on the new requisition
for troops, when it was becoming difficult to meet
the draft, — mainly through the personal example and influence of Mr. Sylvester Lovejoy,
twelve men, including himself, were enlisted for
three years, and, being soon after enrolled in the
Fortieth Massachusetts, went to the war; and
a very good account has been heard, not only
of the regiment, but of the talents and virtues of
these men.

After the return of the three months' company to Concord, in 1861, Captain Prescott
raised a new company of volunteers, and Cap-

tain Bowers another. Each of these companies included recruits from this town, and they formed part of the Thirty-second Regiment of Massachusetts Volunteers. Enlisting for three years, and remaining to the end of the war, these troops saw every variety of hard service which the war offered, and, though suffering at first some disadvantage from change of commanders, and from severe losses, they grew at last, under the command of Colonel Prescott, to an excellent reputation, attested by the names of the thirty battles they were authorized to inscribe on their flag, and by the important position usually assigned them in the field.

I have found many notes of their rough experience in the march and in the field. In McClellan's retreat in the Peninsula, in July, 1862, "it is all our men can do to draw their feet out of the mud. We marched one mile through mud, without exaggeration, one foot deep, — a good deal of the way over my boots, and with short rations ; on one day nothing but liver, blackberries, and pennyroyal tea."— "At Fredericksburg we lay eleven hours in one spot without moving, except to rise and fire." The next note is, "cracker for a day and

a half, — but all right." Another day, " had
not left the ranks for thirty hours, and the
nights were broken by frequent alarms. How
would Concord people," he asks, " like to pass
the night on the battle-field, and hear the dying
cry for help, and not be able to go to them?"
But the regiment did good service at Harrison's Landing, and at Antietam, under Colonel
Parker; and at Fredericksburg, in December,
Lieutenant-Colonel Prescott loudly expressed
his satisfaction at his comrades, now and then
particularizing names : " Bowers, Shepard and
Lauriat are as brave as lions." '

At the battle of Gettysburg, in July, 1863,
the brigade of which the Thirty-second Regiment formed a part, was in line of battle seventy-
two hours, and suffered severely. Colonel
Prescott's regiment went in with two hundred
and ten men, nineteen officers. On the second
of July they had to cross the famous wheat-
field, under fire from the rebels in front and
on both flanks. Seventy men were killed or
wounded out of seven companies. Here
Francis Buttrick, whose manly beauty all of us
remember,' and Sergeant Appleton, an excellent
soldier, were fatally wounded. The Colonel
was hit by three bullets. " I feel," he writes,

" I have much to be thankful for that my life is spared, although I would willingly die to have the regiment do as well as they have done. Our colors had several holes made, and were badly torn. One bullet hit the staff which the bearer had in his hand. The color-bearer is brave as a lion ; he will go anywhere you say, and no questions asked ; his name is Marshall Davis." The Colonel took evident pleasure in the fact that he could account for all his men. There were so many killed, so many wounded, — but no missing. For that word " missing " was apt to mean skulking. Another incident : " A friend of Lieutenant Barrow complains that we did not treat his body with respect, inasmuch as we did not send it home. I think we were very fortunate to save it at all, for in ten minutes after he was killed the rebels occupied the ground, and we had to carry him and all our wounded nearly two miles in blankets. There was no place nearer than Baltimore where we could have got a coffin, and I suppose it was eighty miles there. We laid him in two double blankets, and then sent off a long distance and got boards off a barn to make the best coffin we could, and gave him burial."

After Gettysburg, Colonel Prescott remarks

XI

that our regiment is highly complimented.
When Colonel Gurney, of the Ninth, came to
him the next day to tell him that " folks are
just beginning to appreciate the Thirty-second
Regiment : it always was a good regiment, and
people are just beginning to find it out; " Colonel Prescott notes in his journal, — " Pity they
have not found it out before it was all gone.
We have a hundred and seventy-seven guns
this morning."

Let me add an extract from the official report
of the brigade commander : " Word was sent
by General Barnes, that, when we retired, we
should fall back under cover of the woods.
This order was communicated to Colonel Prescott, whose regiment was then under the hottest
fire. Understanding it to be a peremptory
order to retire then, he replied, ' I don't want
to retire ; I am not ready to retire ; I can hold
this place ; ' and he made good his assertion.
Being informed that he misunderstood the
order, which was only to inform him how to
retire when it became necessary, he was satisfied, and he and his command held their ground
manfully." It was said that Colonel Prescott's
reply, when reported, pleased the Acting-Briga-
dier-General Sweitzer mightily.

After Gettysburg, the Thirty-second Regiment saw hard service at Rappahannock Station; and at Baltimore, in Virginia, where they were drawn up in battle order for ten days successively: crossing the Rapidan, and suffering from such extreme cold, a few days later, at Mine Run, that the men were compelled to break rank and run in circles to keep themselves from being frozen. On the third of December, they went into winter quarters.

I must not follow the multiplied details that make the hard work of the next year. But the campaign in the Wilderness surpassed all their worst experience hitherto of the soldier's life. On the third of May, they crossed the Rapidan for the fifth time. On the twelfth, at Laurel Hill, the regiment had twenty-one killed and seventy-five wounded, including five officers. "The regiment has been in the front and centre since the battle begun, eight and a half days ago, and is now building breastworks on the Fredericksburg road. This has been the hardest fight the world ever knew. I think the loss of our army will be forty thousand. Every day, for the last eight days, there has been a terrible battle the whole length of the line. One day they drove us; but it has been regular bull-dog fighting." On the twenty-first, they had been, for seventeen days and nights, under arms without rest. On the twenty-third, they crossed the North Anna, and achieved a great success. On the thirtieth, we learn, " Our regiment has never been in the second line since we crossed the Rapidan, on the third." On the night of the thirtieth, — " The hardest day we ever had. We have been in the first line twenty-six days, and fighting every day but two ; whilst your news- papers talk of the inactivity of the Army of the Potomac. If those writers could be here and fight all day, and sleep in the trenches, and be called up several times in the night by picket- firing, they would not call it inactive." June fourth is marked in the diary as " An awful day; — two hundred men lost to the command;" and not until the fifth of June comes at last a respite for a short space, during which the men drew shoes and socks, and the officers were able to send to the wagons and procure a change of clothes, for the first time in five weeks.

But from these incessant labors there was now to be rest for one head, — the honored and beloved commander of the regiment. On the sixteenth of June, they crossed the James River, and marched to within three miles of Petersburg

Early in the morning of the eighteenth they went
to the front, formed line of battle, and were ordered to take the Norfolk and Petersburg Railroad from the rebels. In this charge, Colonel
George L. Prescott was mortally wounded.
After driving the enemy from the railroad, crossing it, and climbing the farther bank to continue
the charge, he was struck, in front of his command, by a musket-ball which entered his breast
near the heart. He was carried off the field to
the division hospital, and died on the following
morning. On his death-bed, he received the
needless assurances of his general that "he had
done more than all his duty," — needless to a
conscience so faithful and unspotted. One of his
townsmen and comrades, a sergeant in his regiment, writing to his own family, uses these
words: "He was one of the few men who fight
for principle. He did not fight for glory, honor,
nor money, but because he thought it his duty.
These are not my feelings only, but of the whole
regiment."

On the first of January, 1865, the Thirty-
second Regiment made itself comfortable in log
huts, a mile south of our rear line of works
before Petersburg. On the fourth of February,
sudden orders came to move next morning at

daylight. At Dabney's Mills, in a sharp fight, they lost seventy-four in killed, wounded and missing. Here Major Shepard was taken prisoner. The lines were held until the tenth, with more than usual suffering from snow and hail and intense cold, added to the annoyance of the artillery fire. On the first of April, the regiment connected with Sheridan's cavalry, near the Five Forks, and took an important part in that battle which opened Petersburg and Richmond, and forced the surrender of Lee. On the ninth, they marched in support of the cavalry, and were advancing in a grand charge, when the white flag of General Lee appeared. The brigade of which the Thirty-second Regiment formed part was detailed to receive the formal surrender of the rebel arms. The homeward march began on the thirteenth, and the regiment was mustered out in the field, at Washington, on the twenty-eighth of June, and arrived in Boston on the first of July.

Fellow citizens: The obelisk records only the names of the dead. There is something partial in this distribution of honor. Those who went through those dreadful fields and returned not deserve much more than all the honor we can pay. But those also who went through the same fields, and returned alive, put just as much at hazard as those who died, and, in other countries, would wear distinctive badges of honor as long as they lived. I hope the disuse of such medals or badges in this country only signifies that everybody knows these men, and carries their deeds in such lively remembrance that they require no badge or reminder. I am sure I need not bespeak your gratitude to these fellow citizens and neighbors of ours. I hope they will be content with the laurels of one war.

But let me, in behalf of this assembly, speak directly to you, our defenders, and say, that it is easy to see that if danger should ever threaten the homes which you guard, the knowledge of your presence will be a wall of fire for their protection. Brave men! you will hardly be called to see again fields as terrible as those you have already trampled with your victories.

There are people who can hardly read the names on yonder bronze tablet, the mist so gathers in their eyes. Three of the names are of sons of one family.' A gloom gathers on this assembly, composed as it is of kindred men and women, for, in many houses, the dearest and noblest is gone from their hearth-stone. Yet it is tinged with light from heaven. A duty so severe has been discharged, and with such immense results of good, lifting private sacrifice to the sublime, that, though the cannon volleys have a sound of funeral echoes, they can yet hear through them the benedictions of their country and mankind.

APPENDIX

In the above Address I have been compelled to suppress more details of personal interest than I have used. But I do not like to omit the testimony to the character of the Commander of the Thirty-second Massachusetts Regiment, given in the following letter by one of his soldiers : —

NEAR PETERSBURG, VIRGINIA,
June 20, 1864

DEAR FATHER :

With feelings of deep regret, I inform you that Colonel Prescott, our brave and lamented leader, is no more. He was shot through the body, near the heart, on the eighteenth day of June, and died the following morning. On the morning of the eighteenth, our division was not in line. Reveille was at an early hour,

and before long we were moving to the front. Soon
we passed the ground where the Ninth Corps drove
the enemy from their fortified lines, and came upon and
formed our line in rear of Crawford's Division. In
front of us, and one mile distant, the Rebels' lines of
works could be seen. Between us and them, and in a
deep gulley, was the Norfolk and Petersburg Railroad.
Soon the order came for us to take the railroad from
the enemy, whose advance then held it. Four regiments of our brigade were to head the charge ; so the
32d Massachusetts, 62d, 91st and 155th Pennsylvania
regiments, under command of Colonel Gregory, moved
forward in good order, the enemy keeping up a steady
fire all the time. All went well till we reached the
road. The Rebels left when they saw us advance,
and, when we reached the road, they were running
away. But here our troubles began. The banks, on
each side of the road, were about thirty feet high,
and. being stiff clay, were nearly perpendicular. We
got down well enough, because we got started, and
were rolled to the bottom, a confused pile of Yanks.
Now to climb the other side ! It was impossible to
get up by climbing, for the side of it was like the
side of a house. By dint of getting on each other's
shoulders and making holes for our feet with bayonets,
a few of us got up ; reaching our guns down to the
others, we all finally got over. Meanwhile, a storm of
bullets was rained upon us. Through it all, Colonel
Prescott was cool and collected, encouraging the men

to do their best.   After we were almost all across, he
moved out in front of the line, and called the men out
to him, saying, " Come on, men ; form our line here."
The color-bearer stepped towards him, when a bullet
struck the Colonel, passed through him, and wounded
the color-bearer, Sergeant Giles of Company G.
Calmly the Colonel turned, and said, " I am wounded;
some one help me off."   A sergeant of Company B,
and one of the 21st Pennsylvania, helped him off.
This man told me, last night, all that the Colonel
said, while going off.   He was afraid we would be
driven back, and wanted these men to stick by him.
He said, " I die for my country."   He seemed to be
conscious that death was near to him, and said the
wound was near his heart ; wanted the sergeant of
Company B to write to his family, and tell them all
about him   He will write to Mrs. Prescott, probably ;
but if they do not hear from some one an account of
his death, I wish you would show this to Mrs. Prescott   He died in the division hospital, night before last,
and his remains will probably be sent to Concord.   We
lament his loss in the regiment very much.   He was
like a father to us, — always counselling us to be firm
in the path of duty, and setting the example himself.   I
think a more moral man, or one more likely to enter
the kingdom of heaven, cannot be found in the Army
of the Potomac.   No man ever heard him swear, or
saw him use liquor, since we were in the service.   I
wish there was some way for the regiment to pay some

tribute to his memory. But the folks at home must do this for the present. The Thirty-second Regiment has lost its leader, and calls on the people of Concord to console the afflicted family of the brave departed, by showing their esteem for him in some manner. He was one of the few men who fight for principle, — pure principle. He did not fight for glory, honor nor money but because he thought it his duty. These are not my feelings only, but of the whole regiment. I want you to show this to every one, so they can see what we thought of the Colonel, and how he died in front of his regiment. God bless and comfort his poor family. Perhaps people think soldiers have no feeling, but it is not so. We feel deep anxiety for the families of all our dear comrades.

CHARLES BARTLETT,
Sergeant Company G, 32d Mass. Vols.[1]

XVIII

EDITORS' ADDRESS

MASSACHUSETTS QUARTERLY REVIEW, DECEMBER, 1847

THE old men studied magic in the flowers,
And human fortunes in astronomy,
And an omnipotence in chemistry,
Preferring things to names, for these were men,
Were unitarians of the united world,
And, wheresoever their clear eye-beams fell,
They caught the footsteps of the Same. Our eyes
Are armed, but we are strangers to the stars,
And strangers to the mystic beast and bird,
And strangers to the plant and to the mine.
The injured elements say, ' Not in us ; '
And night and day, ocean and continent,
Fire, plant and mineral say, ' Not in us; '
And haughtily return us stare for stare
For we invade them impiously for gain;
We devastate them unreligiously,
And coldly ask their pottage, not their love.
Therefore they shove us from them, yield to us
Only what to our griping toil is due;
But the sweet affluence of love and song,
The rich results of the divine consents
Of man and earth, of world beloved and loved,
The nectar and ambrosia are withheld.

EDITORS' ADDRESS

THE American people are fast opening their own destiny. The material basis is of such extent that no folly of man can quite subvert it; for the territory is a considerable fraction of the planet, and the population neither loath nor inexpert to use their advantages. Add, that this energetic race derive an unprecedented material power from the new arts, from the expansions effected by public schools, cheap postage and a cheap press, from the telescope, the telegraph, the railroad, steamship, steam-ferry, steam-mill; from domestic architecture, chemical agriculture, from ventilation, from ice, ether, caoutchouc, and innumerable inventions and manufactures.

A scholar who has been reading of the fabulous magnificence of Assyria and Persia, of Rome and Constantinople, leaves his library and takes his seat in a railroad-car, where he is importuned by newsboys with journals still wet from Liverpool and Havre, with telegraphic despatches not yet fifty minutes old from Buffalo and Cincinnati. At the screams of the steam-whistle, the train quits city and suburbs, darts away into the interior, drops every man at his estate as it whirls along, and shows our traveller what tens of thousands of powerful and weaponed men, science-armed and society-armed, sit at large in this ample region, obscure from their numbers and the extent of the domain He reflects on the power which each of these plain republicans can employ; how far these chains of intercourse and travel reach, interlock and ramify; what levers, what pumps, what exhaustive analyses are applied to Nature for the benefit of masses of men. Then he exclaims, What a negro-fine royalty is that of Jamschid and Solomon! What a substantial sovereignty does my townsman possess! A man who has a hundred dollars to dispose of — a hundred dollars over his bread — is rich beyond the dreams of the Cæsars.

Keep our eyes as long as we can on this pic-ture, we cannot stave off the ulterior question, — the famous question of Cineas to Pyrrhus,'— the WHERE TO of all this power and population, these surveys and inventions, this taxing and tabulating, mill-privilege, roads, and mines. The aspect this country presents is a certain maniacal activity, an immense apparatus of cunning machinery which turns out, at last, some Nuremberg toys. Has it generated, as great interests do, any intellectual power? Where are the works of the imagination — the surest test of a national genius? At least as far as the purpose and genius of America is yet reported in any book, it is a sterility and no genius.

One would say there is nothing colossal in the country but its geography and its material activities; that the moral and intellectual effects are not on the same scale with the trade and production. There is no speech heard but that of auctioneers, newsboys, and the caucus. Where is the great breath of the New World, the voice of aboriginal nations opening new eras with hymns of lofty cheer? Our books and fine arts are imitations; there is a fatal in- curiosity and disinclination in our educated men to new studies and the interrogation of Nature. We have taste, critical talent, good professors, good commentators, but a lack of male energy. What more serious calamity can befall a people than a constitutional dulness and limitation? The moral influence of the intellect is wanting. We hearken in vain for any profound voice speaking to the American heart, cheering timid good men, animating the youth, consoling the

XI

defeated, and intelligently announcing duties which clothe life with joy, and endear the face of land and sea to men.' It is a poor considera- tion that the country wit is precocious, and, as we say, practical; that political interests on so broad a scale as ours are administered by little men with some saucy village talent, by deft partisans, good cipherers; strict economists, quite empty of all superstition.

Conceding these unfavorable appearances, it would yet be a poor pedantry to read the fates of this country from these narrow data. On the contrary, we are persuaded that moral and ma- terial values are always commensurate. Every material organization exists to a moral end, which makes the reason of its existence. Here are no books, but who can see the continent with its inland and surrounding waters, its temperate climates, its west-wind breathing vigor through all the year, its confluence of races so favorable to the highest energy, and the infinite glut of their production, without putting new queries to Destiny as to the pur- pose for which this muster of nations and this sudden creation of enormous values is made?

This is equally the view of science and of patriotism. We hesitate to employ a word so much abused as *patriotism*, whose true sense is almost the reverse of its popular sense. We have no sympathy with that boyish egotism, hoarse with cheering for one side, for one state, for one town : the right patriotism consists in the delight which springs from contributing our peculiar and legitimate advantages to the benefit of humanity. Every foot of soil has its proper quality ; the grape on two sides of the same fence has new flavors ; and so every acre on the globe, every family of men, every point of climate, has its distinguishing virtues. Certainly then this country does not lie here in the sun causeless ; and though it may not be easy to define its influence, men feel already its emancipating quality in the careless self-reliance of the manners, in the freedom of thought, in the direct roads by which grievances are reached and redressed, and even in the reckless and sinister politics, not less than in purer expressions. Bad as it is, this freedom leads onward and upward, — to a Columbia of thought and art, which is the last and endless end of Columbus's adventure.

Lovers of our country, but not always approvers of the public counsels, we should certainly be glad to give good advice in politics. We have not

been able to escape our national and endemic
habit, and to be liberated from interest in the
elections and in public affairs. Nor have we
cared to disfranchise ourselves. We are more
solicitous than others to make our politics clear
and healthful, as we believe politics to be nowise
accidental or exceptional, but subject to the same
laws with trees, earths and acids. We see that
reckless and destructive fury which characterizes
the lower classes of American society, and which
is pampered by hundreds of profligate presses.
The young intriguers who drive in bar-rooms
and town-meetings the trade of politics, sagacious only to seize the victorious side, have put
the country into the position of an overgrown
bully, and Massachusetts finds no heart or head
to give weight and efficacy to her contrary judgment. In hours when it seemed only to need one
just word from a man of honor to have vindicated the rights of millions, and to have given a
true direction to the first steps of a nation, we
have seen the best understandings of New England, the trusted leaders of her counsels, consti-
tuting a snivelling and despised opposition,
clapped on the back by comfortable capitalists
from all sections, and persuaded to say, We are
too old to stand for what is called a New England

sentiment any longer. Rely on us for commercial representatives, but for questions of ethics,
— who knows what markets may be opened?
We are not well, we are not in our seats, when
justice and humanity are to be spoken for.

We have a bad war, many victories, each of
which converts the country into an immense
chanticleer ; and a very insincere political opposition.[1] The country needs to be extricated from
its delirium at once. Public affairs are chained
in the same law with private ; the retributions
of armed states are not less sure and signal than
those which come to private felons. The facility
of majorities is no protection from the natural
sequence of their own acts. Men reason badly,
but Nature and Destiny are logical.[2]

But, whilst we should think our pains well bestowed if we could cure the infatuation of statesmen, and should be sincerely pleased if we could
give a direction to the Federal politics, we are far
from believing politics the primal interest of
men. On the contrary, we hold that the laws and
governors cannot possess a commanding interest for any but vacant or fanatical people ; for
the reason that this is simply a formal and superficial interest ; and men of a solid genius are only
interested in substantial things.

The State, like the individual, should rest on an ideal basis. Not only man but Nature is injured by the imputation that man exists only to be fattened with bread, but he lives in such connection with Thought and Fact that his bread is surely involved as one element thereof, but is not its end and aim. So the insight which commands the laws and conditions of the true polity precludes forever all interest in the squabbles of parties. As soon as men have tasted the enjoyment of learning, friendship and virtue, for which the State exists, the prizes of office appear polluted, and their followers outcasts.

A journal that would meet the real wants of this time must have a courage and power sufficient to solve the problems which the great groping society around us, stupid with perplexity, is dumbly exploring. Let it now show its astuteness by dodging each difficult question and arguing diffusely every point on which men are long ago unanimous. Can it front this matter of Socialism, to which the names of Owen and Fourier have attached, and dispose of that question? Will it cope with the allied questions of Government, Nonresistance, and all that belongs under that category? Will it measure itself with the chapter on Slavery, in some sort the special

enigma of the time, as it has provoked against it
a sort of inspiration and enthusiasm singular in
modern history? There are literary and philosophical reputations to settle. The name of
Swedenborg has in this very time acquired new
honors, and the current year has witnessed the
appearance, in their first English translation, of
his manuscripts. Here is an unsettled account
in the book of Fame; a nebula to dim eyes, but
which great telescopes may yet resolve into a
magnificent system. Here is the standing problem of Natural Science, and the merits of her
great interpreters to be determined; the ency-
clopædical Humboldt, and the intrepid general-
izations collected by the author of the Vestiges
of Creation. Here is the balance to be adjusted
between the exact French school of Cuvier, and
the genial catholic theorists, Geoffroy St.-Hilaire,
Goethe, Davy and Agassiz. Will it venture into
the thin and difficult air of that school where the
secrets of structure are discussed under the topics
of mesmerism and the twilights of demonology?

What will easily seem to many a far higher
question than any other is that which respects
the embodying of the Conscience of the period.
Is the age we live in unfriendly to the highest
powers; to that blending of the affections with

the poetic faculty which has distinguished the
Religious Ages? We have a better opinion of
the economy of Nature than to fear that those
varying phases which humanity presents ever
leave out any of the grand springs of human
action. Mankind for the moment seem to be
in search of a religion. The Jewish *cultus* is
declining; the Divine, or, as some will say, the
truly Human, hovers, now seen, now unseen,
before us. This period of peace, this hour when
the jangle of contending churches is hushing or
hushed, will seem only the more propitious to
those who believe that man need not fear the
want of religion, because they know his religious
constitution, — that he must rest on the moral
and religious sentiments, as the motion of
bodies rests on geometry. In the rapid decay
of what was called religion, timid and unthink-
ing people fancy a decay of the hope of man.
But the moral and religious sentiments meet
us everywhere, alike in markets as in churches.
A God starts up behind cotton bales also. The
conscience of man is regenerated as is the atmosphere, so that society cannot be debauched.
The health which we call Virtue is an equipoise
which easily redresses itself, and resembles
those rocking stones which a child's finger can

move, and a weight of many hundred tons cannot overthrow.

With these convictions, a few friends of good letters have thought fit to associate themselves for the conduct of a new journal. We have obeyed the custom and convenience of the time in adopting this form of a Review, as a mould into which all metal most easily runs. But the form shall not be suffered to be an impediment. The name might convey the impression of a book of criticism, and that nothing is to be found here which was not written expressly for the Review; but good readers know that inspired pages are not written to fill a space, but for inevitable utterance; and to such our journal is freely and solicitously open, even though everything else be excluded. We entreat the aid of every lover of truth and right, and let these principles entreat for us. We rely on the talents and industry of good men known to us, but much more on the magnetism of truth, which is multiplying and educating advocates for itself and friends for us. We rely on the truth foi and against ourselves.

XIX

ADDRESS TO KOSSUTH

AT CONCORD, MAY 11, 1852

God said, I am tired of kings,
I suffer them no more;
Up to my ear the morning brings
The outrage of the poor.

My angel, — his name is Freedom, —
Choose him to be your king;
He shall cut pathways east and west,
And fend you with his wing.

ADDRESS TO KOSSUTH

SIR, — The fatigue of your many public visits, in such unbroken succession as may compare with the toils of a campaign, forbid us to detain you long. The people of this town share with their countrymen the admiration of valor and perseverance ; they, like their compatriots, have been hungry to see the man whose extraordinary eloquence is seconded by the splendor and the solidity of his actions. But, as it is the privilege of the people of this town to keep a hallowed mound which has a place in the story of the country ; as Concord is one of the monuments of freedom ; we knew beforehand that you could not go by us ; you could not take all your steps in the pilgrimage of American liberty, until you had seen with your eyes the ruins of the bridge where a handful of brave farmers opened our Revolution. Therefore, we sat and waited for you.

And now, Sir, we are heartily glad to see you, at last, in these fields. We set no more value than you do on cheers and huzzas. But we think that the graves of our heroes around us throb to-day to a footstep that sounded like their own : —

" The mighty tread
Brings from the dust the sound of liberty." [1]

Sir, we have watched with attention your progress through the land, and the varying feeling with which you have been received, and the unvarying tone and countenance which you have maintained. We wish to discriminate in our regard. We wish to reserve our honor for actions of the noblest strain. We please ourselves that in you we meet one whose temper was long since tried in the fire, and made equal to all events ; a man so truly in love with the greatest future, that he cannot be diverted to any less.

It is our republican doctrine, too, that the wide variety of opinions is an advantage. I believe I may say of the people of this country at large, that their sympathy is more worth, because it stands the test of party. It is not a blind wave ; it is a living soul contending with living souls. It is, in every expression, antagonized. No opinion will pass but must stand the tug of war. As you see, the love you win is worth something ; for it has been argued through ; its foundation searched ; it has proved sound and whole ; it may be avowed ; it will last, and it will draw all opinion to itself.

We have seen, with great pleasure, that there is nothing accidental in your attitude. We have seen that you are organically in that cause you plead. The man of Freedom, you are also the man of Fate. You do not elect, but you are elected by God and your genius to the task. We do not, therefore, affect to thank you. We only see in you the angel of freedom, crossing sea and land; crossing parties, nationalities, private interests and self-esteems; dividing populations where you go, and drawing to your part only the good. We are afraid that you are growing popular, Sir; you may be called to the dangers of prosperity. But, hitherto, you have had in all centuries and in all parties only the men of heart. I do not know but you will have the million yet. Then, may your strength be equal to your day. But remember, Sir, that everything great and excellent in the world is in minorities.[1]

Far be from us, Sir, any tone of patronage; we ought rather to ask yours. We know the austere condition of liberty — that it must be reconquered over and over again; yea, day by day; that it is a state of war; that it is always slipping from those who boast it to those who fight for it: and you, the foremost soldier of freedom in this age,— it is for us to crave your judgment; who are we that we should dictate to you? You have won your own. We only affirm it. This country of workingmen greets in you a worker. This republic greets in you a republican. We only say, ' Well done, good and faithful.' — You have earned your own nobility at home. We admit you *ad eundem* (as they say at College). We admit you to the same degree, without new trial. We suspend all rules before so paramount a merit. You may well sit a doctor in the college of liberty. You have achieved your right to interpret our Washington. And I speak the sense not only of every generous American, but the law of mind, when I say that it is not those who live idly in the city called after his name, but those who, all over the world, think and act like him, who can claim to explain the sentiment of Washington.

Sir, whatever obstruction from selfishness, indifference, or from property (which always sympathizes with possession) you may encounter, we congratulate you that you have known how to convert calamities into powers, exile into a campaign, present defeat into lasting victory. For this new crusade which you preach

to willing and to unwilling ears in America is a
seed of armed men. You have got your story
told in every palace and log hut and prairie
camp, throughout this continent. And, as the
shores of Europe and America approach every
month, and their politics will one day mingle,
when the crisis arrives it will find us all instructed beforehand in the rights and wrongs of
Hungary, and parties already to her freedom.

XI

XX

WOMAN

A LECTURE READ BEFORE THE WOMAN'S RIGHTS CONVENTION, BOSTON, SEPTEMBER 20, 1855

THE politics are base,
   The letters do not cheer,
And 't is far in the deeps of history,
   The voice that speaketh clear.

Yet there in the parlor sits
   Some figure in noble guise, —
Our Angel in a stranger's form;
   Or Woman's pleading eyes.

"Lo, when the Lord made North and South.
    And sun and moon ordained he,
Forth bringing each by word of mouth
    In order of its dignity,
Did man from the crude clay express
    By sequence, and, all else decreed,
He formed the woman; nor might less
    Than Sabbath such a work succeed."

COVENTRY PATMOR

WOMAN

AMONG those movements which seem to be, now and then, endemic in the public mind, — perhaps we should say, sporadic, — rather than the single inspiration of one mind, is that which has urged on society the benefits of action having for its object a benefit to the position of Woman. And none is more seriously interesting to every healthful and thoughtful mind.

In that race which is now predominant over all the other races of men, it was a cherished belief that women had an oracular nature. They are more delicate than men, — delicate as iodine to light, — and thus more impressionable. They are the best index of the coming hour. I share this belief. I think their words are to be weighed; but it is their inconsiderate word, — according to the rule, 'take their first advice, not the second:' as Coleridge was wont to apply to a lady for her judgment in questions of taste, and accept it; but when she added — "I think so, because —" "Pardon me, madam," he said, "leave me to find out the reasons for myself." In this sense, as more delicate mer-

curies of the imponderable and immaterial influences, what they say and think is the shadow
of coming events. Their very dolls are indic-
ative. Among our Norse ancestors, Frigga was
worshipped as the goddess of women. "Weirdes
all," said the Edda, "Frigga knoweth, though
she telleth them never." That is to say, all wis-
doms Woman knows; though she takes them
for granted, and does not explain them as discoveries, like the understanding of man. Men
remark figure: women always catch the expression. They inspire by a look, and pass with us
not so much by what they say or do, as by
their presence. They learn so fast and convey
the result so fast as to outrun the logic of their
slow brother and make his acquisitions poor.'
'T is their mood and tone that is important.
Does their mind misgive them, or are they firm
and cheerful? 'T is a true report that things
are going ill or well. And any remarkable opinion or movement shared by woman will be the
first sign of revolution.

Plato said, Women are the same as men in
faculty, only less in degree. But the general
voice of mankind has agreed that they have
their own strength; that women are strong by
sentiment; that the same mental height which

their husbands attain by toil, they attain by
sympathy with their husbands. Man is the will,
and Woman the sentiment. In this ship of
humanity, Will is the rudder, and Sentiment the
sail: when Woman affects to steer, the rudder
is only a masked sail. When women engage in
any art or trade, it is usually as a resource, not
as a primary object. The life of the affections
is primary to them, so that there is usually no
employment or career which they will not with
their own applause and that of society quit for
a suitable marriage. And they give entirely to
their affections, set their whole fortune on the
die, lose themselves eagerly in the glory of
their husbands and children. Man stands astonished at a magnanimity he cannot pretend to.
Mrs. Lucy Hutchinson, one of the heroines
of the English Commonwealth, who wrote the
life of her husband, the Governor of Notting-
ham, says, " If he esteemed her at a higher rate
than she in herself could have deserved, he was
the author of that virtue he doted on, while she
only reflected his own glories upon him. All
that she was, was *him*, while he was hers, and
all that she is now, at best, but his pale shade."
As for Plato's opinion, it is true that, up to recent times, in no art or science, nor in painting,

poetry or music, have they produced a master-
piece. Till the new education and larger opportunities of very modern times, this position,
with the fewest possible exceptions, has always
been true. Sappho, to be sure, in the Olympic
Games, gained the crown over Pindar. But, in
general, no mastery in either of the fine arts —
which should, one would say, be the arts of
women — has yet been obtained by them, equal
to the mastery of men in the same. The part
they play in education, in the care of the young
and the tuition of older children, is their organic
office in the world. So much sympathy as they
have makes them inestimable as the mediators
between those who have knowledge and those
who want it . besides, their fine organization,
their taste and love of details, makes the knowledge they give better in their hands.

But there is an art which is better than painting, poetry, music, or architecture, — better
than botany, geology, or any science ; namely,
Conversation. Wise, cultivated, genial conversation is the last flower of civilization and the
best result which life has to offer us, — a cup
for gods, which has no repentance. Conversation is our account of ourselves. All we have,
all we can, all we know, is brought into play,

and as the reproduction, in finer form, of all
our havings.

Women are, by this and their social influence,
the civilizers of mankind. What is civilization?
I answer, the power of good women. It was
Burns's remark when he first came to Edinburgh that between the men of rustic life and
the polite world he observed little difference;
that in the former, though unpolished by fashion
and unenlightened by science, he had found
much observation and much intelligence; but
a refined and accomplished woman was a being
almost new to him, and of which he had formed
a very inadequate idea. " I like women," said
a clear-headed man of the world; " they are so
finished." They finish society, manners, language. Form and ceremony are their realm.
They embellish trifles. All these ceremonies
that hedge our life around are not to be despised,
and when we have become habituated to them,
cannot be dispensed with. No woman can
despise them with impunity. Their genius de-
lights in ceremonies, in forms, in decorating life
with manners, with properties, order and grace.
They are, in their nature, more relative; the
circumstance must always be fit; out of place
they lose half their weight, out of place they are

disfranchised. Position, Wren said, is essential
to the perfecting of beauty ; — a fine building
is lost in a dark lane ; a statue should stand in
the air ; much more true is it of woman.

We commonly say that easy circumstances
seem somehow necessary to the finish of the
female character : but then it is to be remembered that they create these with all their might.
They are always making that civilization which
they require ; that state of art, of decoration,
that ornamental life in which they best appear.

The spiritual force of man is as much shown
in taste, in his fancy and imagination, — attach-
ing deep meanings to things and to arbitrary inventions of no real value, — as in his perception
of truth. He is as much raised above the beast
by this creative faculty as by any other. The
horse and ox use no delays ; they run to the
river when thirsty, to the corn when hungry,
and say no thanks, but fight down whatever
opposes their appetite. But man invents and
adorns all he does with delays and degrees, paints
it all over with forms, to please himself better ;
he invented majesty and the etiquette of courts
and drawing-rooms ; architecture, curtains,
dress, all luxuries and adornments, and the ele-
gance of privacy, to increase the joys of society.

He invented marriage ; and surrounded by religion, by comeliness, by all manner of dignities
and renunciations, the union of the sexes.

And how should we better measure the gulf
between the best intercourse of men in old
Athens, in London, or in our American capitals,
— between this and the hedgehog existence of
diggers of worms, and the eaters of clay and offal,
— than by signalizing just this department of
taste or comeliness ? Herein woman is the
prime genius and ordainer. There is no grace
that is taught by the dancing-master, no style
adopted into the etiquette of courts, but was first
the whim and the mere action of some brilliant
woman, who charmed beholders by this new
expression, and made it remembered and copied.
And I think they should magnify their ritual
of manners.[1] Society, conversation, decorum,
flowers, dances, colors, forms, are their homes
and attendants. They should be found in fit
surroundings — with fair approaches, with agreeable architecture, and with all advantages which
the means of man collect:

> " The far-fetched diamond finds its home
>   Flashing and smouldering in her hair.
> For her the seas their pearls reveal,
>   Art and strange lands her pomp supply

With purple, chrome and cochineal,
　　Ochre and lapis lazuli.
The worm its golden woof presents.
　　Whatever runs, flies, dives or delves
All doff for her their ornaments,
　　Which suit her better than themselves." [1]

There is no gift of Nature without some draw-
back. So, to women, this exquisite structure
could not exist without its own penalty. More
vulnerable, more infirm, more mortal than men,
they could not be such excellent artists in this
element of fancy if they did not lend and give
themselves to it. They are poets who believe
their own poetry. They emit from their pores
a colored atmosphere, one would say, wave upon
wave of rosy light, in which they walk evermore,
and see all objects through this warm-tinted
mist that envelops them.

But the starry crown of woman is in the
power of her affection and sentiment, and the
infinite enlargements to which they lead. Beautiful is the passion of love, painter and adorner
of youth and early life : but who suspects, in
its blushes and tremors, what tragedies, hero-
isms and immortalities are beyond it? The
passion, with all its grace and poetry, is profane
to that which follows it. All these affections

are only introductory to that which is beyond,
and to that which is sublime.

We men have no right to say it, but the omnipotence of Eve is in humility. The instincts
of mankind have drawn the Virgin Mother —

> " Created beings all in lowliness
> Surpassing, as in height above them all.''[1]

This is the Divine Person whom Dante and
Milton saw in vision. This is the victory of
Griselda, her supreme humility. And it is
when love has reached this height that all our
pretty rhetoric begins to have meaning. When
we see that, it adds to the soul a new soul, it is
honey in the mouth, music in the ear and balsam
in the heart.

> " Far have I clambered in my mind,
>   But nought so great as Love I find.
>   What is thy tent, where dost thou dwell ?
> ' My mansion is humility,
>   Heaven's vastest capability.'
>   The further it doth downward tend,
>   The higher up it doth ascend ''[2]

The first thing men think of, when they love,
is to exhibit their usefulness and advantages to
the object of their affection. Women make light
of these, asking only love. They wish it to be
an exchange of nobleness.

There is much in their nature, much in their social position which gives them a certain power of divination. And women know, at first sight, the characters of those with whom they converse. There is much that tends to give them a religious height which men do not attain. Their sequestration from affairs and from the injury to the moral sense which affairs often inflict, aids this. And in every remarkable religious development in the world, women have taken a leading part. It is very curious that in the East, where Woman occupies, nationally, a lower sphere, where the laws resist the education and emancipation of women, — in the Mohammedan faith, Woman yet occupies the same leading position, as a prophetess, that she has among the ancient Greeks, or among the Hebrews, or among the Saxons. This power, this religious character, is everywhere to be remarked in them.'

The action of society is progressive. In barbarous society the position of women is always low — in the Eastern nations lower than in the West. "When a daughter is born," says the Shiking, the old Sacred Book of China, " she sleeps on the ground, she is clothed with a wrapper, she plays with a tile; she is incapable of

evil or of good." And something like that
position, in all low society, is the position of
woman ; because, as before remarked, she is
herself its civilizer. With the advancements of
society, the position and influence of woman
bring her strength or her faults into light. In
modern times, three or four conspicuous instru-
mentalities may be marked. After the deification
of Woman in the Catholic Church, in the sixteenth or seventeenth century, — when her religious nature gave her, of course, new importance,
— the Quakers have the honor of having first
established, in their discipline, the equality in the
sexes. It is even more perfect in the later sect
of the Shakers, where no business is broached
or counselled without the intervention of one
elder and one elderess.

A second epoch for Woman was in France,
— entirely civil ; the change of sentiment from
a rude to a polite character, in the age of Louis
XIV., — commonly dated from the building of
the Hôtel de Rambouillet.' I think another
important step was made by the doctrine of
Swedenborg, a sublime genius who gave a scientific exposition of the part played severally by
man and woman in the world, and showed the
difference of sex to run through nature and

through thought. Of all Christian sects this is
at this moment the most vital and aggressive.

Another step was the effect of the action of
the age in the antagonism to Slavery. It was
easy to enlist Woman in this ; it was impossible
not to enlist her. But that Cause turned out
to be a great scholar. He was a terrible meta-
physician. He was a jurist, a poet, a divine.
Was never a University of Oxford or Gottingen
that made such students. It took a man from
the plough and made him acute, eloquent, and
wise, to the silencing of the doctors. There
was nothing it did not pry into, no right it did
not explore, no wrong it did not expose. And
it has, among its other effects, given Woman
a feeling of public duty and an added self-
respect.

One truth leads in another by the hand ; one
right is an accession of strength to take more.
And the times are marked by the new attitude
of Woman ; urging, by argument and by association, her rights of all kinds, — in short, to
one half of the world ; — as the right to education, to avenues of employment, to equal rights
of property, to equal rights in marriage, to the
exercise of the professions and of suffrage.

Of course, this conspicuousness had its inconveniences. But it is cheap wit that has been spent on this subject; from Aristophanes, in whose comedies I confess my dulness to find good joke, to Rabelais, in whom it is monstrous exaggeration of temperament, and not borne out by anything in nature, — down to English Comedy, and, in our day, to Tennyson,[1] and the American newspapers. In all, the body of the joke is one, namely, to charge women with temperament; to describe them as victims of temperament; and is identical with Mahomet's opinion that women have not a sufficient moral or intellectual force to control the perturbations of their physical structure. These were all drawings of morbid anatomy, and such satire as might be written on the tenants of a hospital or on an asylum for idiots. Of course it would be easy for women to retaliate in kind, by painting men from the dogs and gorillas that have worn our shape. That they have not, is an eulogy on their taste and self-respect. The good easy world took the joke which it liked. There is always the want of thought; there is always credulity. There are plenty of people who believe women to be incapable of anything but to cook, incapable of interest in affairs. There are plenty of people who believe that the world is

XI

governed by men of dark complexions, that
affairs are only directed by such, and do not see
the use of contemplative men, or how ignoble
would be the world that wanted them. And so
without the affection of women.

But for the general charge : no doubt it is
well founded. They are victims of the finer
temperament. They have tears, and gayeties, and
faintings, and glooms and devotion to trifles.
Nature's end, of maternity for twenty years, was
of so supreme importance that it was to be
secured at all events, even to the sacrifice of the
highest beauty. They are more personal. Men
taunt them that, whatever they do, say, read or
write, they are thinking of themselves and their
set. Men are not to the same degree tempera-
mented, for there are multitudes of men who
live to objects quite out of them, as to politics,
to trade, to letters or an art, unhindered by
any influence of constitution.

The answer that lies, silent or spoken, in the
minds of well-meaning persons, to the new
claims, is this : that though their mathematical
justice is not to be denied, yet the best women
do not wish these things ; they are asked for
by people who intellectually seek them, but

who have not the support or sympathy of the
truest women ; and that, if the laws and customs
were modified in the manner proposed, it would
embarrass and pain gentle and lovely persons
with duties which they would find irksome and
distasteful. Very likely. Providence is always
surprising us with new and unlikely instruments.
But perhaps it is because these people have been
deprived of education, fine companions, opportunities, such as they wished, — because they
feel the same rudeness and disadvantage which
offends you, — that they have been stung to say,
' It is too late for us to be polished and fash-
ioned into beauty, but, at least, we will see that
the whole race of women shall not suffer as we
have suffered.'

They have an unquestionable right to their
own property. And if a woman demand votes,
offices and political equality with men, as among
the Shakers an Elder and Elderess are of equal
power, — and among the Quakers, — it must
not be refused. It is very cheap wit that finds
it so droll that a woman should vote. Educate
and refine society to the highest point, — bring
together a cultivated society of both sexes, in a
drawing-room, and consult and decide by voices
on a question of taste or on a question of right, and

is there any absurdity or any practical difficulty in obtaining their authentic opinions? If not, then there need be none in a hundred companies, if you educate them and accustom them to judge. And, for the effect of it, I can say, for one, that all my points would sooner be carried in the State if women voted. On the questions that are important, — whether the government shall be in one person, or whether representative, or whether democratic; whether men shall be holden in bondage, or shall be roasted alive and eaten, as in Typee, or shall be hunted with bloodhounds, as in this country; whether men shall be hanged for stealing, or hanged at all; whether the unlimited sale of cheap liquors shall be allowed; — they would give, I suppose, as intelligent a vote as the voters of Boston or New York.

We may ask, to be sure, — Why need you vote? If new power is here, of a character which solves old tough questions, which puts me and all the rest in the wrong, tries and condemns our religion, customs, laws, and opens new careers to our young receptive men and women, you can well leave voting to the old dead people. Those whom you teach, and those whom you half teach, will fast enough make themselves considered and

strong with their new insight, and votes will
follow from all the dull.

The objection to their voting is the same as
is urged, in the lobbies of legislatures, against
clergymen who take an active part in politics;
— that if they are good clergymen they are
unacquainted with the expediencies of politics,
and if they become good politicians they are
worse clergymen. So of women, that they cannot enter this arena without being contaminated
and unsexed.

Here are two or three objections : first, a want
of practical wisdom ; second, a too purely ideal
view ; and, third, danger of contamination. For
their want of intimate knowledge of affairs, I do
not think this ought to disqualify them from voting at any town-meeting which I ever attended.
I could heartily wish the objection were sound.
But if any man will take the trouble to see how
our people vote, — how many gentlemen are
willing to take on themselves the trouble of
thinking and determining for you, and, standing
at the door of the polls, give every innocent citizen his ticket as he comes in, informing him
that this is the vote of his party ; and how the
innocent citizen, without further demur, goes
and drops it in the ballot-box, — I cannot but

think he will agree that most women might vote as wisely.

For the other point, of their not knowing the world, and aiming at abstract right without allowance for circumstances, — that is not a disqualification, but a qualification. Human society is made up of partialities. Each citizen has an interest and a view of his own, which, if followed out to the extreme, would leave no room for any other citizen. One man is timid and another rash ; one would change nothing, and the other is pleased with nothing ; one wishes schools, another armies, one gunboats, another public gardens. Bring all these biases together and something is done in favor of them all.

Every one is a half vote, but the next elector behind him brings the other or corresponding half in his hand : a reasonable result is had Now there is no lack, I am sure, of the expediency, or of the interests of trade or of imperative class interests being neglected. There is no lack of votes representing the physical wants ; and if in your city the uneducated emigrant vote numbers thousands, representing a brutal ignorance and mere animal wants, it is to be corrected by an educated and religious vote, representing the wants and desires of honest and refined persons.

If the wants, the passions, the vices, are allowed
a full vote through the hands of a half-brutal
intemperate population, I think it but fair that
the virtues, the aspirations should be allowed a
full vote, as an offset, through the purest part of
the people.

As for the unsexing and contamination, —
that only accuses our existing politics, shows
how barbarous we are, — that our policies are
so crooked, made up of things not to be spoken,
to be understood only by wink and nudge;
this man to be coaxed, that man to be bought,
and that other to be duped. It is easy to see
that there is contamination enough, but it rots
the men now, and fills the air with stench. Come
out of that: it is like a dance-cellar. The fairest
names in this country in literature, in law, have
gone into Congress and come out dishonored.
And when I read the list of men of intellect,
of refined pursuits, giants in law, or eminent
scholars, or of social distinction, leading men of
wealth and enterprise in the commercial community, and see what they have voted for and
suffered to be voted for, I think no community
was ever so politely and elegantly betrayed.

I do not think it yet appears that women wish

this equal share in public affairs. But it is they and not we that are to determine it. Let the laws be purged of every barbarous remainder, every barbarous impediment to women. Let the public donations for education be equally shared by them, let them enter a school as freely as a church, let them have and hold and give their property as men do theirs; — and in a few years it will easily appear whether they wish a voice in making the laws that are to govern them. If you do refuse them a vote, you will also refuse to tax them, — according to our Teutonic principle, No representation, no tax.

All events of history are to be regarded as growths and offshoots of the expanding mind of the race, and this appearance of new opinions, their currency and force in many minds, is itself the wonderful fact. For whatever is popular is important, shows the spontaneous sense of the hour. The aspiration of this century will be the code of the next. It holds of high and distant causes, of the same influences that make the sun and moon. When new opinions appear, they will be entertained and respected, by every fair mind, according to their reasonableness, and not according to their convenience, or their fitness to shock our customs. But let us deal with

them greatly; let them make their way by the
upper road, and not by the way of manufacturing public opinion, which lapses continually into
expediency, and makes charlatans. All that is
spontaneous is irresistible, and forever it is individual force that interests. I need not repeat to
you — your own solitude will suggest it — that
a masculine woman is not strong, but a lady is.
The loneliest thought, the purest prayer, is rushing to be the history of a thousand years.

Let us have the true woman, the adorner, the
hospitable, the religious heart, and no lawyer
need be called in to write stipulations, the cunning clauses of provision, the strong investitures;
— for woman moulds the lawgiver and writes the
law. But I ought to say, I think it impossible
to separate the interests and education of the
sexes. Improve and refine the men, and you
do the same by the women, whether you will or
no. Every woman being the wife or the daughter
of a man, — wife, daughter, sister, mother, of a
man, she can never be very far from his ear,
never not of his counsel, if she has really something to urge that is good in itself and agreeable
to nature. Slavery it is that makes slavery:
freedom, freedom. The slavery of women happened when the men were slaves of kings. The

melioration of manners brought their melioration of course. It could not be otherwise, and
hence the new desire of better laws. For there
are always a certain number of passionately loving fathers, brothers, husbands and sons who
put their might into the endeavor to make a
daughter, a wife, or a mother happy in the way
that suits best. Woman should find in man her
guardian. Silently she looks for that, and when
she finds that he is not, as she instantly does,
she betakes her to her own defences, and does
the best she can. But when he is her guardian,
fulfilled with all nobleness, knows and accepts
his duties as her brother, all goes well for both.

The new movement is only a tide shared by
the spirits of man and woman; and you may
proceed in the faith that whatever the woman's
heart is prompted to desire, the man's mind is
simultaneously prompted to accomplish.'

XXI

ADDRESS

TO THE INHABITANTS OF CONCORD AT THE
CONSECRATION OF SLEEPY HOLLOW
SEPTEMBER 29, 1855

SLEEPY HOLLOW

No abbey's gloom, nor dark cathedral stoops,
  No winding torches paint the midnight air;
Here the green pines delight, the aspen droops
  Along the modest pathways, and those fair
Pale asters of the season spread their plumes
Around this field, fit garden for our tombs

And shalt thou pause to hear some funeral-bell
  Slow stealing o'er the heart in this calm place,
Not with a throb of pain, a feverish knell,
  But in its kind and supplicating grace,
It says, Go, pilgrim, on thy march, be more
Friend to the friendless than thou wast before;

Learn from the loved one's rest serenity;
  To-morrow that soft bell for thee shall sound,
And thou repose beneath the whispering tree,
  One tribute more to this submissive ground, —
Prison thy soul from malice, bar out pride,
Nor these pale flowers nor this still field deride:

Rather to those ascents of being turn
  Where a ne'er-setting sun illumes the year
Eternal, and the incessant watch-fires burn
  Of unspent holiness and goodness clear, —
Forget man's littleness, deserve the best,
God's mercy in thy thought and life confest "
                    WILLIAM ELLERY CHANNING.

ADDRESS

CITIZENS AND FRIENDS: The committee to whom was confided the charge of carrying out the wishes of the town in opening the cemetery, having proceeded so far as to enclose the ground, and cut the necessary roads, and having laid off as many lots as are likely to be wanted at present, have thought it fit to call the inhabitants together, to show you the ground, now that the new avenues make its advantages appear ; and to put it at your disposition.

They have thought that the taking possession of this field ought to be marked by a public meeting and religious rites : and they have requested me to say a few words which the serious and tender occasion inspires.

And this concourse of friendly company assures me that they have rightly interpreted your wishes. [Here followed, in the address, about three pages of matter which Mr. Emerson used later in his essay on Immortality, which may be found in the volume *Letters and Social Aims*,

beginning on page 324, "The credence of
men," etc., and ending on pages 326–27 with
the sentence, "Meantime the true disciples saw,
through the letters, the doctrine of eternity
which dissolved the poor corpse and nature also,
and gave grandeur to the passing hour."]

In these times we see the defects of our old
theology ; its inferiority to our habit of thoughts.
Men go up and down ; Science is popularized ;
the irresistible democracy — shall I call it ? — of
chemistry, of vegetation, which recomposes for
new life every decomposing particle, — the race
never dying, the individual never spared, — have
impressed on the mind of the age the futility of
these old arts of preserving. We give our earth
to earth. We will not jealously guard a few atoms
under immense marbles, selfishly and impos-
sibly sequestering it from the vast circulations
of Nature, but, at the same time, fully admitting
the divine hope and love which belong to our
nature, wishing to make one spot tender to our
children, who shall come hither in the next
century to read the dates of these lives.

Our people accepting this lesson from science,
yet touched by the tenderness which Christianity
breathes, have found a mean in the consecration
of gardens. A simultaneous movement has, in

a hundred cities and towns in this country, selected some convenient piece of undulating ground with pleasant woods and waters ; every family chooses its own clump of trees ; and we lay the corpse in these leafy colonnades.

A grove of trees, — what benefit or ornament is so fair and great ? they make the landscape ; they keep the earth habitable ; their roots run down, like cattle, to the water-courses ; their heads expand to feed the atmosphere. The life of a tree is a hundred and a thousand years ; its decays ornamental ; its repairs self-made : they grow when we sleep, they grew when we were unborn. Man is a moth among these longevities. He plants for the next millennium. Shadows haunt them ; all that ever lived about them cling to them. You can almost see behind these pines the Indian with bow and arrow lurking yet exploring the traces of the old trail.

Modern taste has shown that there is no ornament, no architecture alone, so sumptuous as well disposed woods and waters, where art has been employed only to remove superfluities, and bring out the natural advantages. In cultivated grounds one sees the picturesque and opulent effect of the familiar shrubs, barberry, lilac, privet and thorns, when they are disposed in

masses, and in large spaces. What work of man
will compare with the plantation of a park? It
dignifies life. It is a seat for friendship, counsel,
taste and religion. I do not wonder that they
are the chosen badge and point of pride of
European nobility. But how much more are
they needed by us, anxious, overdriven Americans, to stanch and appease that fury of temperament which our climate bestows!

This tract fortunately lies adjoining to the
Agricultural Society's ground, to the New Burial
Ground, to the Court House and the Town
House, making together a large block of public
ground, permanent property of the town and
county, — all the ornaments of either adding so
much value to all.

I suppose all of us will readily admit the value
of parks and cultivated grounds to the pleasure
and education of the people, but I have heard it
said here that we would gladly spend for a park
for the living, but not for a cemetery; a garden
for the living, a home of thought and friendship.
Certainly the living need it more than the dead;
indeed, to speak precisely, it is given to the dead
for the reaction of benefit on the living. But if
the direct regard to the living be thought expedient, that is also in your power. This ground

is happily so divided by Nature as to admit of
this relation between the Past and the Present.
In the valley where we stand will be the Monuments. On the other side of the ridge, towards
the town, a portion of the land is in full view of
the cheer of the village and is out of sight of the
Monuments ; it admits of being reserved for
secular purposes ; for games, — not such as the
Greeks honored the dead with, but for games of
education ; the distribution of school prizes ;
the meeting of teachers ; patriotic eloquence, the
utterance of the principles of national liberty to
private, social, literary or religious fraternities.
Here we may establish that most agreeable
of all museums, and agreeable to the temper of
our times, — an *Arboretum*, — wherein may be
planted, by the taste of every citizen, one tree,
with its name recorded in a book ; every tree
that is native to Massachusetts, or will grow in
it ; so that every child may be shown growing,
side by side, the eleven oaks of Massachusetts ;
and the twenty willows ; the beech, which we
have allowed to die out of the eastern counties ;
and here the vast firs of California and Oregon.

This spot for twenty years has borne the name
of *Sleepy Hollow*. Its seclusion from the village
in its immediate neighborhood had made it to

XI

all the inhabitants an easy retreat on a Sabbath
day, or a summer twilight, and it was inevitably
chosen by them when the design of a new cemetery was broached, if it did not suggest the
design, as the fit place for their final repose. In
all the multitudes of woodlands and hillsides,
which within a few years have been laid out with
a similar design, I have not known one so fitly
named. *Sleepy Hollow*. In this quiet valley, as
in the palm of Nature's hand, we shall sleep well
when we have finished our day. What is the
Earth itself but a surface scooped into nooks and
caves of slumber — according to the Eastern
fable, a bridge full of holes, into one or other of
which all the passengers sink to silence? Nay,
when I think of the mystery of life, its round
of illusions, our ignorance of its beginning or its
end, the speed of the changes of that glittering
dream we call existence, — I think sometimes
that the vault of the sky arching there upward,
under which our busy being is whirled, is only
a Sleepy Hollow, with path of Suns, instead of
foot-paths; and Milky Ways, for truck-roads.

The ground has the peaceful character that
belongs to this town; — no lofty crags, no glittering cataracts; — but I hold that every part of
Nature is handsome when not deformed by bad

Art. Bleak sea-rocks and sea-downs and blasted heaths have their own beauty; and though we make much ado in our praises of Italy or Andes. Nature makes not so much difference. The morning, the moonlight, the spring day, are magical painters, and can glorify a meadow or a rock.

But we must look forward also, and make ourselves a thousand years old; and when these acorns, that are falling at our feet, are oaks overshadowing our children in a remote century, this mute green bank will be full of history: the good, the wise and great will have left their names and virtues on the trees; heroes, poets, beauties, sanctities, benefactors, will have made the air timeable and articulate.

And hither shall repair, to this modest spot of God's earth, every sweet and friendly influence; the beautiful night and beautiful day will come in turn to sit upon the grass. Our use will not displace the old tenants. The well-beloved birds will not sing one song the less, the high-holding woodpecker, the meadow-lark, the oriole, robin, purple finch, bluebird, thrush and red-eyed warbler, the heron, the bittern will find out the hospitality and protection from the gun of this asylum, and will seek the waters of the meadow; and in the grass, and by the pond, the locust, the cricket and the hyla, shall shrilly play.

We shall bring hither the body of the dead, but how shall we catch the escaped soul? Here will burn for us, as the oath of God, the sublime belief. I have heard that death takes us away from ill things, not from good. I have heard that when we pronounce the name of man, we pronounce the belief of immortality. All great natures delight in stability; all great men find eternity affirmed in the promise of their faculties. Why is the fable of the Wandering Jew agreeable to men, but because they want more time and land to execute their thoughts in? Life is not long enough for art, nor long enough for friendship. The evidence from intellect is as valid as the evidence from love. The being that can share a thought and feeling so sublime as confidence in truth is no mushroom. Our dissatisfaction with any other solution is the blazing evidence of immortality.

XXII

ROBERT BURNS

SPEECH DELIVERED AT THE CELEBRATION OF
THE BURNS CENTENARY, BOSTON
JANUARY 25, 1859

"His was the music to whose tone
    The common pulse of man keeps time
In cot or castle's mirth or moan,
    In cold or sunny clime.

Praise to the bard! his words are driven,
    Like flower-seeds by the far winds sown,
Where'er, beneath the sky of heaven,
    The birds of fame have flown."

HALLECK

ROBERT BURNS

MR. PRESIDENT, AND GENTLEMEN:
I do not know by what untoward accident it has chanced, and I forbear to inquire,
that, in this accomplished circle, it should fall
to me, the worst Scotsman of all, to receive
your commands, and at the latest hour too, to
respond to the sentiment just offered, and
which indeed makes the occasion. But I am
told there is no appeal, and I must trust to
the inspirations of the theme to make a fitness
which does not otherwise exist. Yet, Sir, I
heartily feel the singular claims of the occasion.
At the first announcement, from I know not
whence, that the 25th of January was the hundredth anniversary of the birth of Robert Burns,
a sudden consent warmed the great English race,
in all its kingdoms, colonies and states, all over
the world, to keep the festival. We are here to
hold our parliament with love and poesy, as men
were wont to do in the Middle Ages. Those
famous parliaments might or might not have
had more stateliness and better singers than
we, — though that is yet to be known, — but
they could not have better reason. I can only

explain this singular unanimity in a race which
rarely acts together, but rather after their watch-
word, Each for himself, — by the fact that
Robert Burns, the poet of the middle class, represents in the mind of men to-day that great
uprising of the middle class against the armed
and privileged minorities, that uprising which
worked politically in the American and French
Revolutions, and which, not in governments
so much as in education and social order, has
changed the face of the world.

In order for this destiny, his birth, breeding
and fortunes were low. His organic sentiment
was absolute independence, and resting as it
should on a life of labor. No man existed who
could look down on him. They that looked
into his eyes saw that they might look down the
sky as easily.[1] His muse and teaching was common sense, joyful, aggressive, irresistible. Not
Latimer, nor Luther struck more telling blows
against false theology than did this brave singer.
The Confession of Augsburg, the Declaration
of Independence, the French Rights of Man,
and the Marseillaise, are not more weighty documents in the history of freedom than the songs
of Burns. His satire has lost none of its edge.
His musical arrows yet sing through the air.

He is so substantially a reformer that I find his grand plain sense in close chain with the greatest masters, — Rabelais, Shakspeare in comedy, Cervantes, Butler, and Burns. If I should add another name, I find it only in a living country-man of Burns.[1]

He is an exceptional genius. The people who care nothing for literature and poetry care for Burns. It was indifferent — they thought who saw him — whether he wrote verse or not : he could have done anything else as well. Yet how true a poet is he ! And the poet, too, of poor men, of gray hodden and the guernsey coat and the blouse. He has given voice to all the experiences of common life; he has endeared the farmhouse and cottage, patches and poverty, beans and barley ; ale, the poor man's wine ; hardship ; the fear of debt; the dear society of weans and wife, of brothers and sisters, proud of each other, knowing so few and finding amends for want and obscurity in books and thoughts.[2] What a love of Nature, and, shall I say it? of middle-class Nature. Not like Goethe, in the stars, or like Byron, in the ocean, or Moore, in the luxurious East, but in the homely landscape which the poor see around them, — bleak leagues of pasture and stubble, ice and sleet and

rain and snow-choked brooks; birds, hares,
field-mice, thistles and heather, which he daily
knew. How many "Bonny Doons" and "John
Anderson my jo's" and "Auld lang synes" all
around the earth have his verses been applied to!
And his love-songs still woo and melt the youths
and maids; the farm-work, the country holiday,
the fishing-cobble are still his debtors to-day.

And as he was thus the poet of the poor,
anxious, cheerful, working humanity, so had he
the language of low life. He grew up in a rural
district, speaking a *patois* unintelligible to all but
natives, and he has made the Lowland Scotch a
Doric dialect of fame. It is the only example in
history of a language made classic by the genius
of a single man. But more than this. He had
that secret of genius to draw from the bottom of
society the strength of its speech, and astonish
the ears of the polite with these artless words,
better than art, and filtered of all offence through
his beauty. It seemed odious to Luther that
the devil should have all the best tunes; he
would bring them into the churches; and Burns
knew how to take from fairs and gypsies, black-
smiths and drovers, the speech of the market
and street, and clothe it with melody. But I am
detaining you too long. The memory of Burns,

— I am afraid heaven and earth have taken too good care of it to leave us anything to say. The west winds are murmuring it. Open the windows behind you, and hearken for the incoming tide, what the waves say of it. The doves perching always on the eaves of the Stone Chapel opposite, may know something about it. Every name in broad Scotland keeps his fame bright. The memory of Burns, — every man's, every boy's and girl's head carries snatches of his songs, and they say them by heart, and, what is strangest of all, never learned them from a book, but from mouth to mouth. The wind whispers them, the birds whistle them, the corn, barley, and bulrushes hoarsely rustle them, nay, the music-boxes at Geneva are framed and toothed to play them; the hand-organs of the Savoyards in all cities repeat them, and the chimes of bells ring them in the spires. They are the property and the solace of mankind.[1]

XXIII

REMARKS

AT THE CELEBRATION OF THE THREE HUNDREDTH
ANNIVERSARY OF THE BIRTH OF SHAKSPEARE
BY THE SATURDAY CLUB AT THE
REVERE HOUSE, BOSTON, 1864

ENGLAND's genius filled all measure
Of heart and soul, of strength and pleasure,
Gave to mind its emperor
And life was larger than before;
And centuries brood, nor can attain
The sense and bound of Shakspeare's brain.
The men who lived with him became
Poets, for the air was fame.

SHAKSPEARE

T IS not our fault if we have not made
this evening's circle still richer than it is.
We seriously endeavored, besides our brothers
and our seniors, on whom the ordinary lead
of literary and social action falls — and falls
because of their ability — to draw out of their
retirements a few rarer lovers of the muse —
" seld-seen flamens "—whom this day seemed to
elect and challenge. And it is to us a painful disappointment that Bryant and Whittier as guests,
and our own Hawthorne, — with the best will
to come, — should have found it impossible at
last ; and again, that a well-known and honored
compatriot, who first in Boston wrote elegant
verse, and on Shakspeare, and whose American
devotion through forty or fifty years to the
affairs of a bank, has not been able to bury the
fires of his genius, — Mr. Charles Sprague, —
pleads the infirmities of age as an absolute bar
to his presence with us.

We regret also the absence of our members
Sumner and Motley.

We can hardly think of an occasion where

so little need be said. We are all content to let Shakspeare speak for himself. His fame is settled on the foundations of the moral and intellectual world. Wherever there are men, and in the degree in which they are civil — have power of mind, sensibility to beauty, music, the secrets of passion, and the liquid expression of thought, he has risen to his place as the first poet of the world.

Genius is the consoler of our mortal condition, and Shakspeare taught us that the little world of the heart is vaster, deeper and richer than the spaces of astronomy. What shocks of surprise and sympathetic power, this battery, which he is, imparts to every fine mind that is born! We say to the young child in the cradle, ' Happy, and defended against Fate! for here is Nature, and here is Shakspeare, waiting for you !'

'T is our metre of culture. He is a cultivated man — who can tell us something new of Shakspeare. All criticism is only a making of rules out of his beauties. He is as superior to his countrymen, as to all other countrymen. He fulfilled the famous prophecy of Socrates, that the poet most excellent in tragedy would be most excellent in comedy, and more than fulfilled it by making tragedy also a victorious melody which healed its own wounds. In short, Shakspeare is the one resource of our life on which no gloom gathers; the fountain of joy which honors him who tastes it; day without night; pleasure without repentance; the genius which, in unpoetic ages, keeps poetry in honor and, in sterile periods, keeps up the credit of the human mind.

His genius has reacted on himself. Men were so astonished and occupied by his poems that they have not been able to see his face and condition, or say, who was his father and his brethren; or what life he led; and at the short distance of three hundred years he is mythical, like Orpheus and Homer, and we have already seen the most fantastic theories plausibly urged, as that Raleigh and Bacon were the authors of the plays.

Yet we pause expectant before the genius of Shakspeare — as if his biography were not yet written; until the problem of the whole English race is solved.

I see, among the lovers of this catholic genius, here present, a few, whose deeper knowledge invites me to hazard an article of my literary creed; that Shakspeare, by his transcendant

XI

reach of thought, so unites the extremes, that, whilst he has kept the theatre now for three centuries, and, like a street-bible, furnishes sayings to the market, courts of law, the senate, and common discourse, — he is yet to all wise men the companion of the closet. The student finds the solitariest place not solitary enough to read him ; and so searching is his penetration, and such the charm of his speech, that he still agitates the heart in age as in youth, and will, until it ceases to beat.

Young men of a contemplative turn carry his sonnets in the pocket. With that book, the shade of any tree, a room in any inn, becomes a chapel or oratory in which to sit out their happiest hours. Later they find riper and manlier lessons in the plays.

And secondly, he is the most robust and potent thinker that ever was. I find that it was not history, courts and affairs that gave him lessons, but he that gave grandeur and prestige to them. There never was a writer who, seeming to draw every hint from outward history, the life of cities and courts, owed them so little. You shall never find in this world the barons or kings he depicted. 'T is fine for Englishmen to say, they only know history by Shakspeare.

The palaces they compass earth and sea to enter,
the magnificence and personages of royal and
imperial abodes, are shabby imitations and cari-
catures of his, — clumsy pupils of his instruction. There are no Warwicks, no Talbots, no
Bolingbrokes, no Cardinals, no Harry Fifth, in
real Europe, like his. The loyalty and royalty
he drew were all his own. The real Elizabeths,
Jameses and Louises were painted sticks before
this magician.

The unaffected joy of the comedy, — he lives
in a gale, — contrasted with the grandeur of the
tragedy, where he stoops to no contrivance, no
pulpiting, but flies an eagle at the heart of the
problem ; where his speech is a Delphi, — the
great Nemesis that he is and utters. What a
great heart of equity is he! How good and
sound and inviolable his innocency, that is never
to seek, and never wrong, but speaks the pure
sense of humanity on each occasion. He dwarfs
all writers without a solitary exception. No
egotism. The egotism of men is immense. It
concealed Shakspeare for a century. His mind
has a superiority such that the universities
should read lectures on him, and conquer the
unconquerable if they can.

There are periods fruitful of great men; others, barren; or, as the world is always equal to itself, periods when the heat is latent, — others when it is given out.

They are like the great wine years, — the vintage of 1847, is it? or 1835? — which are not only noted in the carte of the table d'hôte, but which, it is said, are always followed by new vivacity in the politics of Europe. His birth marked a great wine year when wonderful grapes ripened in the vintage of God, when Shakspeare and Galileo were born within a few months of each other, and Cervantes was his exact contemporary, and, in short space before and after, Montaigne, Bacon, Spenser, Raleigh and Jonson. Yet Shakspeare, not by any inferiority of theirs, but simply by his colossal proportions, dwarfs the geniuses of Elizabeth as easily as the wits of Anne, or the poor slipshod troubadours of King René.

In our ordinary experience of men there are some men so born to live well that, in whatever company they fall, — high or low, — they fit well, and lead it! but, being advanced to a higher class, they are just as much in their element as before, and easily command: and being again preferred to selecter companions, find no obstacle to ruling these as they did their earlier mates; I suppose because they have more humanity than talent, whilst they have quite as much of the last as any of the company. It would strike you as comic, if I should give my own customary examples of this elasticity, though striking enough to me. I could name in this very company — or not going far out of it — very good types, but in order to be parliamentary, Franklin, Burns and Walter Scott are examples of the rule; and king of men, by this grace of God also, is Shakspeare.

The Pilgrims came to Plymouth in 1620. The plays of Shakspeare were not published until three years later. Had they been published earlier, our forefathers, or the most poetical among them, might have stayed at home to read them.

XXIV

HUMBOLDT

AN ABSTRACT OF MR. EMERSON'S REMARKS MADE
AT THE CELEBRATION OF THE CENTENNIAL ANNI-
VERSARY OF THE BIRTH OF ALEXANDER VON
HUMBOLDT, SEPTEMBER 14, 1869

'If a life prolonged to an advanced period bring with it several inconveniences to the individual, there is a compensation in the delight of being able to compare older states of knowledge with that which now exists, and to see great advances in knowledge develop themselves under our eyes in departments which had long slept in inactivity."

HUMBOLDT, *Letter to Ritter.*

HUMBOLDT

HUMBOLDT was one of those wonders of the world, like Aristotle, like Julius Cæsar, like the Admirable Crichton, who appear from time to time, as if to show us the possibilities of the human mind, the force and the range of the faculties, — a universal man, not only possessed of great particular talents, but they were symmetrical, his parts were well put together. As we know, a man's natural powers are often a sort of committee that slowly, one at a time, give their attention and action; but Humboldt's were all united, one electric chain, so that a university, a whole French Academy, travelled in his shoes. With great propriety, he named his sketch of the results of science Cosmos. There is no other such survey or surveyor. The wonderful Humboldt, with his solid centre and expanded wings, marches like an army, gathering all things as he goes. How he reaches from science to science, from law to law, folding away moons and asteroids and solar systems in the clauses and parentheses of his encyclopædic paragraphs! There is no book like it; none indicating such a battalion of powers. You could not put him on any sea or shore but his instant recollection of every other sea or shore illuminated this.

He was properly a man of the world; you could not lose him ; you could not detain him ; you could not disappoint him, for at any point on land or sea he found the objects of his researches. When he was stopped in Spain and could not get away, he turned round and interpreted their mountain system, explaining the past history of the continent of Europe. He belonged to that wonderful German nation, the foremost scholars in all history, who surpass all others in industry, space and endurance. A German reads a literature whilst we are reading a book. One of their writers warns his countrymen that it is not the Battle of Leipsic, but the Leipsic Fair Catalogue, which raises them above the French. I remember Cuvier tells us of fossil elephants ; that Germany has furnished the greatest number ; — not because there are more elephants in Germany, — oh no; but because in that empire there is no canton without some well-informed person capable of making researches and publishing interesting results. I know that we have been accustomed to think they were too good scholars, that because they reflect, they never resolve, that "in a crisis no plan-maker was to be found in the empire;" but we have lived to see now, for the second time in the history of Prussia, a statesman of the first class, with a clear head and an inflexible will.

XXV

WALTER SCOTT

REMARKS AT THE CELEBRATION BY THE MASSACHU
SETTS HISTORICAL SOCIETY OF THE CENTENNIAL
ANNIVERSARY OF HIS BIRTH,
AUGUST 15, 1871

Scott, the delight of generous boys.

As far as Sir Walter Scott aspired to be known for a fine gentleman, so far our sympathies leave him. . . . Our concern is only with the residue, where the man Scott was warmed with a divine ray that clad with beauty every sheet of water, every bald hill in the country he looked upon, and so reanimated the well-nigh obsolete feudal history and illustrated every hidden corner of a barren and disagreeable territory.

Lecture, " Being and Seeing," 1838.

WALTER SCOTT

THE memory of Sir Walter Scott is dear
to this Society, of which he was for ten
years an honorary member. If only as an
eminent antiquary who has shed light on the
history of Europe and of the English race, he
had high claims to our regard. But to the rare
tribute of a centennial anniversary of his birthday, which we gladly join with Scotland, and
indeed with Europe, to keep, he is not less entitled — perhaps he alone among literary men
of this century is entitled — by the exceptional
debt which all English-speaking men have gladly
owed to his character and genius. I think no
modern writer has inspired his readers with such
affection to his own personality. I can well remember as far back as when The Lord of the
Isles was first republished in Boston, in 1815,
— my own and my school-fellows' joy in the
book.' Marmion and The Lay had gone before, but we were then learning to spell. In
the face of the later novels, we still claim that
his poetry is the delight of boys. But this means
that when we reopen these old books we all
consent to be boys again. We tread over our

youthful grounds with joy. Critics have found
them to be only rhymed prose. But I believe
that many of those who read them in youth,
when, later, they come to dismiss finally their
school-days' library, will make some fond exception for Scott as for Byron.

It is easy to see the origin of his poems.
His own ear had been charmed by old ballads
crooned by Scottish dames at firesides, and written down from their lips by antiquaries; and
finding them now outgrown and dishonored by
the new culture, he attempted to dignify and
adapt them to the times in which he lived.
Just so much thought, so much picturesque
detail in dialogue or description as the old ballad
required, so much suppression of details and
leaping to the event, he would keep and use,
but without any ambition to write a high poem
after a classic model. He made no pretension
to the lofty style of Spenser, or Milton, or
Wordsworth. Compared with their purified
songs, purified of all ephemeral color or material, his were *vers de société*. But he had the
skill proper to *vers de société*, — skill to fit his
verse to his topic, and not to write solemn
pentameters alike on a hero or a spaniel. His
good sense probably elected the ballad to make

his audience larger. He apprehended in advance the immense enlargement of the reading public, which almost dates from the era of his books, — which his books and Byron's inaugurated ; and which, though until then unheard of, has become familiar to the present time.

If the success of his poems, however large, was partial, that of his novels was complete. The tone of strength in Waverley at once announced the master, and was more than justified by the superior genius of the following romances, up to the Bride of Lammermoor, which almost goes back to Æschylus for a counterpart as a painting of Fate, — leaving on every reader the impression of the highest and purest tragedy.'.

His power on the public mind rests on the singular union of two influences. By nature, by his reading and taste an aristocrat, in a time and country which easily gave him that bias, he had the virtues and graces of that class, and by his eminent humanity and his love of labor escaped its harm. He saw in the English Church the symbol and seal of all social order ; in the historical aristocracy the benefits to the state which Burke claimed for it; and in his own reading and research such store of legend and

XI

renown as won his imagination to their cause.
Not less his eminent humanity delighted in the
sense and virtue and wit of the common people.
In his own household and neighbors he found
characters and pets of humble class, with whom
he established the best relation,— small farmers
and tradesmen, shepherds, fishermen, gypsies,
peasant-girls, crones, — and came with these
into real ties of mutual help and good will.
From these originals he drew so genially his
Jeanie Deans, his Dinmonts and Edie Ochil-
trees, Caleb Balderstones and Fairservices, Cud-
die Headriggs, Dominies, Meg Merrilies, and
Jenny Rintherouts, full of life and reality ;
making these, too, the pivots on which the
plots of his stories turn ; and meantime without
one word of brag of this discernment, — nay,
this extreme sympathy reaching down to every
beggar and beggar's dog, and horse and cow. In
the number and variety of his characters he
approaches Shakspeare. Other painters in verse
or prose have thrown into literature a few type-
figures ; as Cervantes, De Foe, Richardson,
Goldsmith, Sterne and Fielding ; but Scott
portrayed with equal strength and success every
figure in his crowded company.

His strong good sense saved him from the

faults and foibles incident to poets, — from nervous egotism, sham modesty or jealousy. He played ever a manly part.[1] With such a fortune and such a genius, we should look to see what heavy toll the Fates took of him, as of Rousseau or Voltaire, of Swift or Byron. But no : he had no insanity, or vice, or blemish. He was a thoroughly upright, wise and great-hearted man, equal to whatever event or fortune should try him. Disasters only drove him to immense exertion. What an ornament and safeguard is humor! Far better than wit for a poet and writer. It is a genius itself, and so defends from the insanities.

Under what rare conjunction of stars was this man born, that, wherever he lived, he found superior men, passed all his life in the best company, and still found himself the best of the best! He was apprenticed at Edinburgh to a Writer to the Signet, and became a Writer to the Signet, and found himself in his youth and manhood and age in the society of Mackintosh, Horner, Jeffrey, Playfair, Dugald Stewart, Sydney Smith, Leslie, Sir William Hamilton, Wilson, Hogg, De Quincey, — to name only some of his literary neighbors, and, as soon as he died all this brilliant circle was broken up.

XXVI

SPEECH

AT BANQUET IN HONOR OF THE CHINESE EMBASSY
BOSTON, 1868

NATURE creates in the East the uncontrollable yearning to escape from limitation into the vast and boundless, to use a freedom of fancy which plays with all works of Nature, great or minute, galaxy or grain of dust, as toys and words of the mind; inculcates a beatitude to be found in escape from all organization and all personality, and makes ecstasy an institution.

SPEECH

AT THE BANQUET IN HONOR OF
THE CHINESE EMBASSY

MR. MAYOR: I suppose we are all of
one opinion on this remarkable occasion
of meeting the embassy sent from the oldest
Empire in the world to the youngest Republic.
All share the surprise and pleasure when the
venerable Oriental dynasty— hitherto a romantic legend to most of us — suddenly steps into
the fellowship of nations. This auspicious event,
considered in connection with the late innova-
tions in Japan, marks a new era, and is an irresistible result of the science which has given us
the power of steam and the electric telegraph.
It is the more welcome for the surprise. We
had said of China, as the old prophet said of
Egypt, " Her strength is to sit still." Her
people had such elemental conservatism that
by some wonderful force of race and national
manners, the wars and revolutions that occur
in her annals have proved but momentary swells
or surges on the pacific ocean of her history,
leaving no trace. But in its immovability this
race has claims. China is old, not in time only,

but in wisdom, which is gray hair to a nation, —
or, rather, truly seen, is eternal youth.   As we
know, China had the magnet centuries before
Europe ; and block-printing or stereotype, and
lithography, and gunpowder, and vaccination,
and canals ; had anticipated Linnæus's nomen-
clature of plants ; had codes, journals, clubs,
hackney coaches, and, thirty centuries before
New York, had the custom of New Year's calls
of comity and reconciliation.   I need not mention its useful arts, — its pottery indispensable
to the world, the luxury of silks, and its tea, the
cordial of nations.   But I must remember that
she has respectable remains of astronomic science, and historic records of forgotten time, that
have supplied important gaps in the ancient history of the western nations.   Then she has philosophers who cannot be spared.   Confucius has
not yet gathered all his fame.   When Socrates
heard that the oracle declared that he was the
wisest of men, he said, it must mean that other
men held that they were wise, but that he knew
that he knew nothing. Confucius had already
affirmed this of himself : and what we call the
GOLDEN RULE of Jesus, Confucius had uttered
in the same terms five hundred years before.
His morals, though addressed to a state of

society unlike ours, we read with profit to-day. His rare perception appears in his GOLDEN MEAN, his doctrine of Reciprocity, his unerring insight, — putting always the blame of our misfortunes on ourselves ; as when to the governor who complained of thieves, he said, " If you, sir, were not covetous, though you should reward them for it, they would not steal." His ideal of greatness predicts Marcus Antoninus. At the same time, he abstained from paradox, and met the ingrained prudence of his nation by saying always, " Bend one cubit to straighten eight."

China interests us at this moment in a point of politics. I am sure that gentlemen around me bear in mind the bill which the Hon. Mr. Jenckes of Rhode Island has twice attempted to carry through Congress, requiring that candidates for public offices shall first pass examinations on their literary qualifications for the same. Well, China has preceded us, as well as England and France, in this essential correction of a reckless usage ; and the like high esteem of education appears in China in social life, to whose distinctions it is made an indispensable passport.

It is gratifying to know that the advantages

of the new intercourse between the two countries are daily manifest on the Pacific coast.
The immigrants from Asia come in crowds.
Their power of continuous labor, their versatil-
ity in adapting themselves to new conditions,
their stoical economy, are unlooked-for virtues.
They send back to their friends, in China,
money, new products of art, new tools, machinery, new foods, etc., and are thus establishing a
commerce without limit. I cannot help adding,
after what I have heard to-night, that I have
read in the journals a statement from an English source, that Sir Frederic Bruce attributed to
Mr. Burlingame the merit of the happy reform
in the relations of foreign governments to China.
I am quite sure that I heard from Mr. Burlingame in New York, in his last visit to America,
that the whole merit of it belonged to Sir Frederic Bruce. It appears that the ambassadors
were emulous in their magnanimity. It is certainly the best guaranty for the interests of
China and of humanity.

XXVII

REMARKS

AT THE MEETING FOR ORGANIZING THE FREE
RELIGIOUS ASSOCIATION, BOSTON
MAY 30, 1867

In many forms we try
To utter God's infinity,
But the Boundless hath no form,
And the Universal Friend
Doth as far transcend
An angel as a worm.

The great Idea baffles wit,
Language falters under it,
It leaves the learned in the lurch;
Nor art, nor power, nor toil can find
The measure of the eternal Mind,
Nor hymn nor prayer nor church.

REMARKS

AT THE MEETING FOR ORGANIZING
THE FREE RELIGIOUS ASSOCIATION

MR. CHAIRMAN : I hardly felt, in finding this house this morning, that I had
come into the right hall. I came, as I supposed myself summoned, to a little committee
meeting, for some practical end, where I should
happily and humbly learn my lesson ; and I
supposed myself no longer subject to your call
when I saw this house. I have listened with
great pleasure to the lessons which we have
heard. To many, to those last spoken, I have
found so much in accord with my own thought
that I have little left to say. I think that it does
great honor to the sensibility of the committee
that they have felt the universal demand in the
community for just the movement they have begun. I say again, in the phrase used by my friend,
that we began many years ago, — yes, and many
ages before that. But I think the necessity very
great, and it has prompted an equal magnanimity, that thus invites all classes, all religious men,
whatever their connections, whatever their spe-
cialties, in whatever relation they stand to the

Christian Church, to unite in a movement of benefit to men, under the sanction of religion. We are all very sensible — it is forced on us every day — of the feeling that churches are outgrown; that the creeds are outgrown; that a technical theology no longer suits us. It is not the ill will of people — no, indeed, but the incapacity for confining themselves there. The church is not large enough for the man; it cannot inspire the enthusiasm which is the parent of everything good in history, which makes the romance of history. For that enthusiasm you must have something greater than yourselves, and not less.

The child, the young student, finds scope in his mathematics and chemistry or natural history, because he finds a truth larger than he is; finds himself continually instructed. But, in churches, every healthy and thoughtful mind finds itself in something less; it is checked, cribbed, confined. And the statistics of the American, the English and the German cities, showing that the mass of the population is leaving off going to church, indicate the necessity, which should have been foreseen, that the Church should always be new and extemporized, because it is eternal and springs from the sentiment

of men, or it does not exist.¹ One wonders sometimes that the churches still retain so many vo-
taries, when he reads the histories of the Church.
There is an element of childish infatuation in
them which does not exalt our respect for man.
Read in Michelet, that in Europe, for twelve or
fourteen centuries, God the Father had no temple and no altar. The Holy Ghost and the Son
of Mary were worshipped, and in the thirteenth
century the First Person began to appear at the
side of his Son, in pictures and in sculpture, for
worship, but only through favor of his Son.
These mortifying puerilities abound in religious
history. But as soon as every man is apprised
of the Divine Presence within his own mind, —
is apprised that the perfect law of duty corresponds with the laws of chemistry, of vegetation,
of astronomy, as face to face in a glass ; that the
basis of duty, the order of society, the power of
character, the wealth of culture, the perfection
of taste, all draw their essence from this moral
sentiment, then we have a religion that exalts,
that commands all the social and all the private
action.

What strikes me in the sudden movement
which brings together to-day so many separated friends, — separated but sympathetic, —

and what I expected to find here, was some
practical suggestions by which we were to re-
animate and reorganize for ourselves the true
Church, the pure worship. Pure doctrine always bears fruit in pure benefits. It is only
by good works, it is only on the basis of active
duty, that worship finds expression. What
is best in the ancient religions was the sacred
friendships between heroes, the Sacred Bands,
and the relations of the Pythagorean disciples.
Our Masonic institutions probably grew from
the like origin. The close association which
bound the first disciples of Jesus is another
example; and it were easy to find more. The
soul of our late war, which will always be remembered as dignifying it, was, first, the desire
to abolish slavery in this country, and secondly, to abolish the mischief of the war itself,
by healing and saving the sick and wounded
soldiers, — and this by the sacred bands of
the Sanitary Commission. I wish that the various beneficent institutions which are spring-
ing up, like joyful plants of wholesomeness,
all over this country, should all be remembered as within the sphere of this committee, —
almost all of them are represented here, — and
that within this little band that has gathered

here to-day, should grow friendship. The interests that grow out of a meeting like this should
bind us with new strength to the old eternal
duties.

xi

XXVIII

SPEECH

AT THE SECOND ANNUAL MEETING OF THE FREE
RELIGIOUS ASSOCIATION, AT TREMONT TEMPLE
FRIDAY, MAY 28, 1869

Thou metest him by centuries,
And lo! he passes like the breeze;
Thou seek'st in globe and galaxy,
He hides in pure transparency;
Thou ask'st in fountains and in fires,
He is the essence that inquires.

SPEECH

AT SECOND ANNUAL MEETING OF THE FREE RELIGIOUS ASSOCIATION

FRIENDS: I wish I could deserve anything of the kind expression of my friend, the President, and the kind good will which the audience signifies, but it is not in my power to-day to meet the natural demands of the occasion, and, quite against my design and my will, I shall have to request the attention of the audience to a few written remarks, instead of the more extensive statement which I had hoped to offer them.

I think we have disputed long enough. I think we might now relinquish our theological controversies to communities more idle and ignorant than we. I am glad that a more realistic church is coming to be the tendency of society, and that we are likely one day to forget our obstinate polemics in the ambition to excel each other in good works. I have no wish to proselyte any reluctant mind, nor, I think, have I any curiosity or impulse to intrude on those whose ways of thinking differ from mine. But as my friend, your presiding officer, has asked

me to take at least some small part in this day's
conversation, I am ready to give, as often befoie,
the fiist simple foundation of my belief, that the
Author of Nature has not left himself without a
witness in any sane mind : that the moral sentiment speaks to every man the law after which
the Universe was made ; that we find parity,
identity of design, through Nature, and benefit
to be the uniform aim : that there is a force
always at work to make the best better and the
worst good.' We have had not long since presented us by Max Muller a valuable paragraph
from St. Augustine, not at all extraordinary in
itself, but only as coming from that eminent
Father in the Church, and at that age, in which
St. Augustine writes : "That which is now
called the Christian religion existed among the
ancients, and never did not exist from the planting of the human race until Christ came in the
flesh, at which time the true religion which
already existed began to be called Christianity."
I believe that not only Christianity is as old as
the Creation, — not only every sentiment and
precept of Christianity can be paralleled in other
religious writings, — but more, that a man of
religious susceptibility, and one at the same time
conversant with many men, — say a much-

travelled man, — can find the same idea in num-
berless conversations. The religious find religion
wherever they associate. When I find in people
narrow religion, I find also in them narrow
reading. Nothing really is so self-publishing, so
divulgatory, as thought. It cannot be confined
or hid. It is easily carried ; it takes no room ;
the knowledge of Europe looks out into Persia
and India, and to the very Kaffirs. Every proverb, every fine text, every pregnant jest, trav-
els across the line ; and you will find it at Cape
Town, or among the Tartars. We are all believ-
ers in natural religion ; we all agree that the
health and integrity of man is self-respect, self-
subsistency, a regard to natural conscience. All
education is to accustom him to trust himself,
discriminate between his higher and lower
thoughts, exert the timid faculties until they are
robust, and thus train him to self-help, until he
ceases to be an underling, a tool, and becomes a
benefactor. I think wise men wish their religion
to be all of this kind, teaching the agent to go
alone, not to hang on the world as a pensioner,
a permitted person, but an adult, self-searching
soul, brave to assist or resist a world: only
humble and docile before the source of the
wisdom he has discovered within him.

As it is, every believer holds a different creed; that is, all the churches are churches of one member. All our sects have refined the point of difference between them. The point of difference that still remains between churches, or between classes, is in the addition to the moral code, that is, to natural religion, of somewhat positive and historical. I think that to be, as Mr. Abbot has stated it in his form, the one difference remaining. I object, of course, to the claim of miraculous dispensation, — certainly not to the *doctrine* of Christianity.' This claim impairs, to my mind, the soundness of him who makes it, and indisposes us to his communion. This comes the wrong way; it comes from without, not within. This positive, historical, authoritative scheme is not consistent with our experience or our expectations. It is something not in Nature : it is contrary to that law of Nature which all wise men recognize ; namely, never to require a larger cause than is necessary to the effect. George Fox, the Quaker, said that, though he read of Christ and God, he knew them only from the like spirit in his own soul. We want all the aids to our moral training. We cannot spare the vision nor the virtue of the saints ; but let it be by pure sympathy, not with any personal or official claim. If you are childish, and exhibit your saint as a worker of wonders, a thaumaturgist, I am repelled. That claim takes his teachings out of logic and out of nature, and permits official and arbitrary senses to be grafted on the teachings. It is the praise of our New Testament that its teachings go to the honor and benefit of humanity, — that no better lesson has been taught or incarnated. Let it stand, beautiful and wholesome, with whatever is most like it in the teaching and practice of men; but do not attempt to elevate it out of humanity, by saying, 'This was not a man,' for then you confound it with the fables of every popular religion, and my distrust of the story makes me distrust the doctrine as soon as it differs from my own belief.

Whoever thinks a story gains by the prodigious, by adding something out of nature, robs it more than he adds. It is no longer an example, a model; no longer a heart-stirring hero, but an exhibition, a wonder, an anomaly, removed out of the range of influence with thoughtful men. I submit that in sound frame of mind, we read or remember the religious sayings and oracles of other men, whether Jew or Indian, or Greek or Persian, only for friendship, only for joy in the social identity which they open to us, and that these words would have no weight with us if we had not the same conviction already. I find something stingy in the unwilling and disparaging admission of these foreign opinions — opinions from all parts of the world — by our churchmen, as if only to enhance by their dimness the superior light of Christianity. Meantime, observe, you cannot bring me too good a word, too dazzling a hope, too penetrating an insight from the Jews. I hail every one with delight, as showing the riches of my brother, my fellow soul, who could thus think and thus greatly feel. Zealots eagerly fasten their eyes on the differences between their creed and yours, but the charm of the study is in finding the agreements, the identities, in all the religions of men.'

I am glad to hear each sect complain that they do not now hold the opinions they are charged with. The earth moves, and the mind opens. I am glad to believe society contains a class of humble souls who enjoy the luxury of a religion that does not degrade ; who think it the highest worship to expect of Heaven the most and the best; who do not wonder that there was a Christ, but that there were not

a thousand; who have conceived an infinite
hope for mankind; who believe that the history of Jesus is the history of every man, written large.[1]

XXIX

ADDRESS

AT THE OPENING OF THE CONCORD FREE
PUBLIC LIBRARY

THE bishop of Cavaillon, Petrarch's friend, in a playful experiment locked up the poet's library, intending to exclude him from it for three days, but the poet's misery caused him to restore the key on the first evening "And I verily believe I should have become insane," says Petrarch, "if my mind had longer been deprived of its necessary nourishment."

ADDRESS

AT THE OPENING OF THE CONCORD
FREE PUBLIC LIBRARY

THE people of Massachusetts prize the
simple political arrangement of towns, each
independent in its local government, electing
its own officers, assessing its taxes, caring for its
schools, its charities, its highways. That town is
attractive to its native citizens and to immigrants
which has a healthy site, good land, good roads,
good sidewalks, a good hotel; still more, if it
have an adequate town hall, good churches,
good preachers, good schools, and if it avail
itself of the Act of the Legislature authorizing
towns to tax themselves for the establishment
of a public library. Happier, if it contain citizens who cannot wait for the slow growth of
the population to make these advantages adequate to the desires of the people, but make
costly gifts to education, civility and culture,
as in the act we are met to witness and acknowledge to-day.

I think we cannot easily overestimate the
benefit conferred. In the details of this munificence, we may all anticipate a sudden and

lasting prosperity to this ancient town, in the
benefit of a noble library, which adds by the
beauty of the building, and its skilful arrangement, a quite new attraction, — making readers
of those who are not readers, — making scholars
of those who only read newspapers or novels
until now; and whilst it secures a new and
needed culture to our citizens, offering a strong
attraction to strangers who are seeking a country home to sit down here. And I am not sure
that when Boston learns the good deed of Mr.
Munroe, it will not be a little envious, nor
rest until it has annexed Concord to the city.
Our founder has found the many admirable
examples which have lately honored the country,
of benefactors who have not waited to bequeath
colleges and hospitals, but have themselves
built them, reminding us of Sir Isaac Newton's
saving, " that they who give nothing before
their death, never in fact give at all."

I think it is not easy to exaggerate the utility
of the beneficence which takes this form. If you
consider what has befallen you when reading
a poem, or a history, or a tragedy, or a novel,
even, that deeply interested you, — how you
forgot the time of day, the persons sitting in the
room, and the engagements for the evening, you

will easily admit the wonderful property of books to make all towns equal: that Concord Library makes Concord as good as Rome, Paris or London, for the hour; — has the best of each of those cities in itself. Robinson Crusoe, could he have had a shelf of our books, could almost have done without his man Friday, or even the arriving ship.

Every faculty casts itself into an art, and memory into the art of writing, that is, the book. The sedge *Papyrus*, which gave its name to our word paper, is of more importance to history than cotton, or silver, or gold. Its first use for writing is between three and four thousand years old, and though it hardly grows now in Egypt, where I lately looked for it in vain, I always remember with satisfaction that I saw that venerable plant in 1833, growing wild at Syracuse, in Sicily, near the fountain of Arethusa.

The chairman of Mr. Munroe's trustees has told you how old is the foundation of our village library, and we think we can trace in our modest records a correspondent effect of culture amidst our citizens. A deep religious sentiment is, in all times, an inspirer of the intellect, and that was not wanting here. The town was settled by

XI

a pious company of non-conformists from England, and the printed books of their pastor and leader, Rev. Peter Bulkeley, sometime fellow of Saint John's College in Cambridge, England, testify the ardent sentiment which they shared. " There is no people," said he to his little flock of exiles, " but will strive to excel in something. What can we excel in if not in holiness ? If we look to number, we are the fewest ; if to strength, we are the weakest ; if to wealth and riches, we are the poorest of all the people of God through the whole world. We cannot excel, nor so much as equal other people in these things, and if we come short in grace and holiness too, we are the most despicable people under heaven. Strive we therefore herein to excel, and suffer not this crown to be taken away from us." [1]

The religious bias of our founders had its usual effect to secure an education to read their Bible and hymn-book, and thence the step was easy for active minds to an acquaintance with history and with poetry. Peter Bulkeley sent his son John to the first class that graduated at Harvard College in 1642, and two sons to later classes. Major Simon Willard's son Samuel graduated at Harvard in 1659, and was for six years, from 1701 to 1707, vice-president of the college ; and his son Joseph was president of the college from 1781 to 1804; and Concord counted fourteen graduates of Harvard in its first century, and its representation there increased with its gross population.[1]

I possess the manuscript journal of a lady, native of this town (and descended from three of its clergymen), who removed into Maine, where she possessed a farm and a modest income. She was much addicted to journeying and not less to reading, and whenever she arrived in a town where was a good minister who had a library, she would persuade him to receive her as a boarder, and would stay until she had looked over all his volumes which were to her taste. On a very cold day, she writes in her diary, " Life truly resembles a river — ever the same — never the same ; and perhaps a greater variety of internal emotions would be felt by remaining with books in one place than pursuing the waves which are ever the same. Is the melancholy bird of night, covered with the dark foliage of the willow and cypress, less gratified than the gay lark amid the flowers and suns ? I think that you never enjoy so much as in solitude with a book that meets the feelings," and in reference to her favorite authors, she adds, " The delight

in others' superiority is my best gift from
God."[1]

Lemuel Shattuck, by his history of the town,
has made all of us grateful to his memory as a
careful student and chronicler; but events so
important have occurred in the forty years since
that book was published, that it now needs a
second volume.

Henry Thoreau we all remember as a man
of genius, and of marked character, known to
our farmers as the most skilful of surveyors, and
indeed better acquainted with their forests and
meadows and trees than themselves, but more
widely known as the writer of some of the best
books which have been written in this country,
and which, I am persuaded, have not yet
gathered half their fame. He, too, was an
excellent reader. No man would have rejoiced
more than he in the event of this day. In a
private letter to a lady, he writes, " Do you read
any noble verses ? For my part, they have been
the only things I remembered, — or that which
occasioned them, — when all things else were
blurred and defaced.' All things have put on
mourning but they: for the elegy itself is some
victorious melody in you, escaping from the
wreck. It is a relief to read some true books

wherein all are equally dead, equally alive. I
think the best parts of Shakspeare would only
be enhanced by the most thrilling and affecting
events. I have found it so : and all the more,
that they are not intended for consolation."

Nathaniel Hawthorne's residence in the
Manse gave new interest to that house whose
windows overlooked the retreat of the British
soldiers in 1775, and his careful studies of Concord life and history are known wherever the
English language is spoken.'

I know the word literature has in many ears
a hollow sound. It is thought to be the harmless entertainment of a few fanciful persons, and
not at all to be the interest of the multitude.
To these objections, which proceed on the cheap
notion that nothing but what grinds corn, roasts
mutton and weaves cotton, is anything worth, I
have little to say. There are utilitarians who
prefer that Jesus should have wrought as a
carpenter, and Saint Paul as a tent-maker. But
literature is the record of the best thoughts.
Every attainment and discipline which increases
a man's acquaintance with the invisible world
lifts his being. Everything that gives him a new
perception of beauty multiplies his pure enjoy-
ments. A river of thought is always running

out of the invisible world into the mind of man.
Shall not they who received the largest streams
spread abroad the healing waters?

It was the symbolical custom of the ancient
Mexican priests, after the annual extinction of
the household fires of their land, to procure in
the temple fire from the sun, and thence distrib-
ute it as a sacred gift to every hearth in the nation. It is a just type of the service rendered to
mankind by wise men. Homer and Plato and
Pindar and Shakspeare serve many more than
have heard their names. Thought is the most
volatile of all things. It cannot be contained in
any cup, though you shut the lid never so tight.
Once brought into the world, it runs over the
vessel which received it into all minds that love
it. The very language we speak thinks for us
by the subtle distinctions which already are
marked for us by its words, and every one of
these is the contribution of the wit of one and
another sagacious man in all the centuries of
time.

Consider that it is our own state of mind at
any time that makes our estimate of life and the
world. If you sprain your foot, you will presently come to think that Nature has sprained
hers. Everything begins to look so slow and

inaccessible. And when you sprain your mind, by gloomy reflection on your failures and vexations, you come to have a bad opinion of life. Think how indigent Nature must appear to the blind, the deaf, and the idiot. Now if you can kindle the imagination by a new thought, by heroic histories, by uplifting poetry, instantly you expand, — are cheered, inspired, and become wise, and even prophetic. Music works this miracle for those who have a good ear; what omniscience has music! so absolutely impersonal, and yet every sufferer feels his secret sorrow reached. Yet to a scholar the book is as good or better. There is no hour of vexation which on a little reflection will not find diversion and relief in the library. His companions are few: at the moment, he has none: but, year by year, these silent friends supply their place. Many times the reading of a book has made the fortune of the man, — has decided his way of life. It makes friends. 'T is a tie between men to have been delighted with the same book. Every one of us is always in search of his friend, and when unexpectedly he finds a stranger enjoying the rare poet or thinker who is dear to his own solitude, — it is like finding a brother. Dr. Johnson hearing that Adam Smith, whom he had once met, relished rhyme, said, "If I had known that, I should have hugged him."

We expect a great man to be a good reader, or in proportion to the spontaneous power should be the assimilating power. There is a wonderful agreement among eminent men of all varieties of character and condition in their estimate of books. Julius Cæsar, when ship-wrecked, and forced to swim for life, did not gather his gold, but took his Commentaries between his teeth and swam for the shore. Even the wild and warlike Arab Mahomet said, "Men are either learned or learning : the rest are block-heads." The great Duke of Marlborough could not encamp without his Shakspeare. The Duch-ess d'Abrantes, wife of Marshal Junot, tells us that Bonaparte, in hastening out of France to join his army in Germany, tossed his journals and books out of his travelling carriage as fast as he had read them, and strewed the highway with pamphlets. Napoleon's reading could not be large, but his criticism is sometimes admir-able, as reported by Las Casas ; and Napoleon was an excellent writer. Montesquieu, one of the greatest minds that France has produced, writes : " The love of study is in us almost the only eternal passion. All the others quit us in proportion as this miserable machine which gives them to us approaches its ruin. Study has been for me the sovereign remedy against the disgusts of life, never having had a chagrin which an hour of reading has not put to flight." Hear the testimony of Seldon, the oracle of the English House of Commons in Cromwell's time. " Patience is the chiefest fruit of study. A man, that strives to make himself a different thing from other men by much reading gains this chiefest good, that in all fortunes he hath something to entertain and comfort himself withal."

I have found several humble men and women who gave as affectionate, if not as judicious testimony to their readings. One curious witness was that of a Shaker who, when showing me the houses of the Brotherhood, and a very modest bookshelf, said there was Milton's Paradise Lost, and some other books in the house, and added " that he knew where they were, but he took up a sound cross in not reading them."

In 1618 (8th March) John Kepler came upon the discovery of the law connecting the mean distances of the planets with the periods of their revolution about the sun, that the squares of the times vary as the cubes of the

distances. And he writes, " It is now eighteen
months since I got the first glimpse of light, —
three months since the dawn, — very few days
since the unveiled sun, most admirable to gaze
on, burst out upon me. Nothing holds me.
I will indulge in my sacred fury. I will triumph
over mankind by the honest confession that I
have stolen the golden vases of the Egyptians
to build up a tabernacle for my God far away
from the confines of Egypt. If you forgive me,
I rejoice ; if you are angry, I can bear it : the
die is cast ; the book is written ; to be read
either now or by posterity. I care not which.
It may well wait a century for a reader, since
God has waited six thousand years for an ob-
server like myself."

In books I have the history or the energy
of the past. Angels they are to us of entertainment, sympathy and provocation. With them
many of us spend the most of our life, — these
silent guides, — these tractable prophets, histo-
rians, and singers, whose embalmed life is the
highest feat of art ; who now cast their moonlight illumination over solitude, weariness and
fallen fortunes. You say, 't is a languid pleasure. Yes, but its tractableness, coming and
going like a dog at our bidding, compensates

the quietness, and contrasts with the slowness of fortune and the inaccessibleness of persons.

You meet with a man of science, a good thinker or good wit, — but you do not know how to draw out of him that which he knows. But the book is a sure friend, always ready at your first leisure, — opens to the very page you desire, and shuts at your first fatigue, — as possibly your professor might not.

It is a tie between men to have read the same book, and it is a disadvantage not to have read the book your mates have read, or not to have read it at the same time, so that it may take the place in your culture it does in theirs, and you shall understand their allusions to it, and not give it more or less emphasis than they do. Yet the strong character does not need this sameness of culture. The imagination knows its own food in every pasture, and if it has not had the Arabian Nights, Prince Le Boo, or Homer or Scott, has drawn equal delight and terror from haunts and passages which you will hear of with envy.

In saying these things for books, I do not for a moment forget that they are secondary, mere means, and only used in the off-hours, only in the pause, and, as it were, the sleep, or passive state of the mind. The intellect reserves all its rights. Instantly, when the mind itself wakes, all books, all past acts are forgotten, huddled aside as impertinent in the august presence of the creator. Their costliest benefit is that they set us free from themselves; for they wake the imagination and the sentiment, — and in their inspirations we dispense with books. Let me add then, — read proudly; put the duty of being read invariably on the author. If he is not read, whose fault is it? I am quite ready to be charmed, — but I shall not make believe I am charmed.

But there is no end to the praise of books, to the value of the library. Who shall estimate their influence on our population where all the millions read and write? It is the joy of nations that man can communicate all his thoughts, discoveries and virtues to records that may last for centuries.

But I am pleading a cause which in the event of this day has already won: and I am happy in the assurance that the whole assembly to whom I speak entirely sympathize in the feeling of this town in regard to the new Library, and its honored Founder.

XXX

THE FORTUNE OF THE REPUBLIC

" There is a mystery in the soul of state
Which hath an operation more divine
Than breath or pen can give expression to."

THE FORTUNE OF THE REPUBLIC

IT is a rule that holds in economy as well as in hydraulics that you must have a source higher than your tap. The mills, the shops, the theatre and the caucus, the college and the church, have all found out this secret. The sailors sail by chronometers that do not lose two or three seconds in a year, ever since Newton explained to Parliament that the way to improve navigation was to get good watches, and to offer public premiums for a better time-keeper than any then in use. The manufacturers rely on turbines of hydraulic perfection ; the carpet-mill, on mordants and dyes which exhaust the skill of the chemist ; the calico print, on designers of genius who draw the wages of artists, not of artisans. Wedgwood, the eminent potter, bravely took the sculptor Flaxman to counsel, who said, "Send to Italy, search the museums for the forms of old Etruscan vases, urns, water-pots, domestic and sacrificial vessels of all kinds." They built great works and called their manufacturing village Etruria. Flaxman, with his Greek taste, selected and combined the loveliest forms, which were executed in English clay ; sent boxes of these as gifts to every court of Europe, and formed the taste of the world. It was a renaissance of the break-fast-table and china-closet. The brave manu-facturers made their fortune. The jewellers imitated the revived models in silver and gold.

The theatre avails itself of the best talent of poet, of painter, and of amateur of taste, to make the *ensemble* of dramatic effect. The marine insurance office has its mathematical counsellor to settle averages ; the life-assurance, its table of annuities. The wine-merchant has his analyst and taster, the more exquisite the better. He has also, I fear, his debts to the chemist as well as to the vineyard.

Our modern wealth stands on a few staples, and the interest nations took in our war was ex-asperated by the importance of the cotton trade. And what is cotton? One plant out of some two hundred thousand known to the botanist, vastly the larger part of which are reckoned weeds. What is a weed? A plant whose virtues have not yet been discovered, — every one of the two hundred thousand probably yet to be of utility in the arts. As Bacchus of the vine, Ceres of the wheat, as Arkwright and Whitney were the demi-gods of cotton, so prolific Time will yet bring an inventor to every plant. There is not a property in Nature but a mind is born to seek and find it. For it is not the plants or the animals, innumerable as they are, nor the whole magazine of material nature that can give the sum of power, but the infinite applicability of these things in the hands of thinking man, every new application being equivalent to a new material.[1]

Our sleepy civilization, ever since Roger Bacon and Monk Schwartz invented gunpowder, has built its whole art of war, all fortification by land and sea, all drill and military education, on that one compound, — all is an extension of a gun-barrel, — and is very scornful about bows and arrows, and reckons Greeks and Romans and Middle Ages little better than Indians and bow-and-arrow times. As if the earth, water, gases, lightning and caloric had not a million energies, the discovery of any one of which could change the art of war again, and put an end to war by the exterminating forces man can apply.

Now, if this is true in all the useful and in the fine arts, that the direction must be drawn from a superior source or there will be no good work, does it hold less in our social and civil life?

In our popular politics you may note that each aspirant who rises above the crowd, however at first making his obedient apprenticeship in party tactics, if he have sagacity, soon learns that it is by no means by obeying the vulgar weathercock of his party, the resentments, the fears and whims of it, that real power is gained, but that he must often face and resist the party, and abide by his resistance, and put them in fear; that the only title to their permanent respect, and to a larger following, is to see for himself what is the real public interest, and to stand for that; — that is a principle, and all the cheering and hissing of the crowd must by and by accommodate itself to it. Our times easily afford you very good examples.

The law of water and all fluids is true of wit. Prince Metternich said, "Revolutions begin in the best heads and run steadily down to the populace." It is a very old observation; not truer because Metternich said it, and not less true.

There have been revolutions which were not in the interest of feudalism and barbarism, but in that of society. And these are distinguished not by the numbers of the combatants nor the numbers of the slain, but by the motive. No interest now attaches to the wars of York and Lancaster, to the wars of German, French and Spanish emperors, which were only dynastic wars, but to those in which a principle was involved. These are read with passionate interest and never lose their pathos by time. When the cannon is aimed by ideas, when men with religious convictions are behind it, when men die for what they live for, and the mainspring that works daily urges them to hazard all, then the cannon articulates its explosions with the voice of a man, then the rifle seconds the cannon and the fowling-piece the rifle, and the women make the cartridges, and all shoot at one mark; then gods join in the combat; then poets are born, and the better code of laws at last records the victory.

Now the culmination of these triumphs of humanity — and which did virtually include the extinction of slavery — is the planting of America.

At every moment some one country more than any other represents the sentiment and the future of mankind. None will doubt that America occupies this place in the opinion of nations, as is proved by the fact of the vast immigration into this country from all the nations of Western and Central Europe. And when the adventurers have planted themselves and looked about, they send back all the money they can spare to bring their friends.

Meantime they find this country just passing through a great crisis in its history, as necessary as lactation or dentition or puberty to the human individual. We are in these days settling for ourselves and our descendants questions which, as they shall be determined in one way or the other, will make the peace and prosperity or the calamity of the next ages. The questions of Education, of Society, of Labor, the direction of talent, of character, the nature and habits of the American, may well occupy us, and more the question of Religion.

The new conditions of mankind in America are really favorable to progress, the removal of absurd restrictions and antique inequalities The mind is always better the more it is used, and here it is kept in practice. The humblest is daily challenged to give his opinion on practical questions, and while civil and social freedom exists, nonsense even has a favorable effect. Cant is good to provoke common sense. . . .

The trance-mediums, the rebel paradoxes, exasperate the common sense. The wilder the paradox, the more sure is Punch to put it in the pillory.

The lodging the power in the people, as in republican forms, has the effect of holding things closer to common sense; for a court or an aristocracy, which must always be a small minority, can more easily run into follies than a republic, which has too many observers — each with a vote in his hand — to allow its head to be turned by any kind of nonsense: since hunger, thirst, cold, the cries of children and debt are always holding the masses hard to the essential duties.

One hundred years ago the American people attempted to carry out the bill of political rights to an almost ideal perfection. They have made great strides in that direction since. They are now proceeding, instructed by their success and by their many failures, to carry out, not the bill of rights, but the bill of human duties.

And look what revolution that attempt involves. Hitherto government has been that of the single person or of the aristocracy. In this country the attempt to resist these elements, it is asserted, must throw us into the government not quite of mobs, but in practice of an inferior class of professional politicians, who by means of newspapers and caucuses really thrust their unworthy minority into the place of the old aristocracy on the one side, and of the good, industrious, well-taught but unambitious population on the other, win the posts of power and give their direction to affairs. Hence liberal congresses and legislatures ordain, to the surprise of the people, equivocal, interested and vicious measures. The men themselves are suspected and charged with lobbying and being lobbied. No measure is attempted for itself, but the opinion of the people is courted in the first place, and the measures are perfunctorily carried through as secondary. We do not choose our own candidate, no, nor any other man's first choice, — but only the available candidate, whom, perhaps, no man loves. We do not speak what we think, but grope after the practicable and available. Instead of character, there is a studious exclusion of character. The people are feared and flattered. They are not reprimanded. The country is governed in bar-rooms, and in the mind of bar-rooms. The low can best win the low, and each aspirant for power vies with his rival which can stoop lowest, and depart widest from himself.

The partisan on moral, even on religious questions, will choose a proven rogue who can answer the tests, over an honest, affectionate, noble gentleman; the partisan ceasing to be a man that he may be a sectarian.

The spirit of our political economy is low and degrading. The precious metals are not so precious as they are esteemed. Man exists for his own sake, and not to add a laborer to the state. The spirit of our political action, for the most part, considers nothing less than the sacredness of man. Party sacrifices man to the measure.[1]

We have seen the great party of property and education in the country drivelling and huckstering away, for views of party fear or advantage, every principle of humanity and the dearest hopes of mankind; the trustees of power only energetic when mischief could be done, imbecile as corpses when evil was to be prevented.

Our great men succumb so far to the forms of the day as to peril their integrity for the sake of adding to the weight of their personal character the authority of office, or making a real government titular. Our politics are full of adventurers, who having by education and social innocence a good repute in the state, break away from the law of honesty and think they can afford to join the devil's party. 'T is odious, these offenders in high life. You rally to the support of old charities and the cause of literature, and there, to be sure, are these brazen faces. In this innocence you are puzzled how to meet them ; must shake hands with them, under protest.' We feel toward them as the minister about the Cape Cod farm, — in the old time when the minister was still invited, in the spring, to make a prayer for the blessing of a piece of land, — the good pastor being brought to the spot, stopped short : " No, this land does not want a prayer, this land wants manure."

> " 'T is virtue which they want, and wanting it,
> Honor no garment to their backs can fit." [2]

Parties keep the old names, but exhibit a surprising fugacity in creeping out of one snake-skin into another of equal ignominy and lubricity, and the grasshopper on the turret of Faneuil Hall gives a proper hint of the men below.

Everything yields. The very glaciers are

viscous, or relegate into conformity, and the stiffest patriots falter and compromise; so that *will* cannot be depended on to save us.

How rare are acts of will! We are all living according to custom; we do as other people do, and shrink from an act of our own. Every such act makes a man famous, and we can all count the few cases — half a dozen in our time — when a public man ventured to act as he thought without waiting for orders or for public opinion. John Quincy Adams was a man of an audacious independence that always kept the public curiosity alive in regard to what he might do. None could predict his word, and a whole congress could not gainsay it when it was spoken. General Jackson was a man of will, and his phrase on one memorable occasion, " I will take the responsibility," is a proverb ever since.'

The American marches with a careless swagger to the height of power, very heedless of his own liberty or of other peoples', in his reckless confidence that he can have all he wants, risking all the prized charters of the human race, bought with battles and revolutions and religion, gambling them all away for a paltry selfish gain.

He sits secure in the possession of his vast

domain, rich beyond all experience in resources, sees its inevitable force unlocking itself in elemental order day by day, year by year; looks from his coal-fields, his wheat-bearing prairie, his gold-mines, to his two oceans on either side, and feels the security that there can be no famine in a country reaching through so many latitudes, no want that cannot be supplied, no danger from any excess of importation of art or learning into a country of such native strength, such immense digestive power.

In proportion to the personal ability of each man, he feels the invitation and career which the country opens to him. He is easily fed with wheat and game, with Ohio wine, but his brain is also pampered by finer draughts, by political power and by the power in the railroad board, in the mills, or the banks. This elevates his spirits, and gives, of course, an easy self-reliance that makes him self-willed and unscrupulous.

I think this levity is a reaction on the people from the extraordinary advantages and invitations of their condition. When we are most disturbed by their rash and immoral voting, it is not malignity, but recklessness. They are careless of politics, because they do not entertain the possibility of being seriously caught in meshes of legislation. They feel strong and irresistible. They believe that what they have enacted they can repeal if they do not like it. But one may run a risk once too often. They stay away from the polls, saying that one vote can do no good! Or they take another step, and say 'One vote can do no harm!' and vote for something which they do not approve, because their party or set votes for it. Of course this puts them in the power of any party having a steady interest to promote which does not conflict manifestly with the pecuniary interest of the voters. But if they should come to be interested in themselves and in their career, they would no more stay away from the election than from their own counting-room or the house of their friend.

The people are right-minded enough on ethical questions, but they must pay their debts, and must have the means of living well, and not pinching. So it is useless to rely on them to go to a meeting, or to give a vote, if any check from this must-have-the-money side arises. If a customer looks grave at their newspaper, or damns their member of Congress, they take another newspaper, and vote for another man. They must have money, for a certain style of living fast becomes necessary; they must take wine at the hotel, first, for the look of it, and second, for the purpose of sending the bottle to two or three gentlemen at the table ; and presently because they have got the taste, and do not feel that they have dined without it.

The record of the election now and then alarms people by the all but unanimous choice of a rogue and a brawler. But how was it done? What lawless mob burst into the polls and threw in these hundreds of ballots in defiance of the magistrates? This was done by the very men you know, — the mildest, most sensible, best-natured people. The only account of this is, that they have been scared or warped into some association in their mind of the candidate with the interest of their trade or of their property.

Whilst each cabal urges its candidate, and at last brings, with cheers and street demonstrations, men whose names are a knell to all hope of progress, the good and wise are hidden in their active retirements, and are quite out of question.

"These we must join to wake, for these are of the strain
    That justice dare defend, and will the age maintain." [1]

Yet we know, all over this country, men of integrity, capable of action and of affairs, with the deepest sympathy in all that concerns the public, mortified by the national disgrace, and quite capable of any sacrifice except of their honor.

Faults in the working appear in our system, as in all, but they suggest their own remedies. After every practical mistake out of which any disaster grows, the people wake and correct it with energy. And any disturbances in politics, in civil or foreign wars, sober them, and instantly show more virtue and conviction in the popular vote. In each new threat of faction the ballot has been, beyond expectation, right and decisive.

It is ever an inspiration, God only knows whence ; a sudden, undated perception of eternal right coming into and correcting things that were wrong ; a perception that passes through thousands as readily as through one.

The gracious lesson taught by science to this country is that the history of Nature from first to last is incessant advance from less to more, from rude to finer organization, the globe of matter thus conspiring with the principle of undying hope in man. Nature works in immense time, and spends individuals and races prodigally to prepare new individuals and races. The lower kinds are one after one extinguished ; the

higher forms come in.' The history of civilization, or the refining of certain races to wonderful
power of performance, is analogous; but the
best civilization yet is only valuable as a ground
of hope.

Ours is the country of poor men. Here is
practical democracy; here is the human race
poured out over the continent to do itself justice; all mankind in its shirt-sleeves; not grimacing like poor rich men in cities, pretending to
be rich, but unmistakably taking off its coat
to hard work, when labor is sure to pay.' This
through all the country. For really, though you
see wealth in the capitals, it is only a sprinkling
of rich men in the cities and at sparse points;
the bulk of the population is poor. In Maine,
nearly every man is a lumberer. In Massachusetts, every twelfth man is a shoemaker, and
the rest, millers, farmers, sailors, fishermen.

Well, the result is, instead of the doleful experience of the European economist, who tells
us, " In almost all countries the condition of the
great body of the people is poor and miserable,"
here that same great body has arrived at a sloven
plenty, — ham and corn-cakes, tight roof and
coals enough have been attained; an unbuttoned
comfort, not clean, not thoughtful, far from

polished, without dignity in his repose ; the man awkward and restless if he have not something to do, but honest and kind for the most part, understanding his own rights and stiff to maintain them, and disposed to give his children a better education than he received.

The steady improvement of the public schools in the cities and the country enables the farmer or laborer to secure a precious primary education. It is rare to find a born American who cannot read and write. The facility with which clubs are formed by young men for discussion of social, political and intellectual topics secures the notoriety of the questions.

Our institutions, of which the town is the unit, are all educational, for responsibility educates fast. The town-meeting is, after the high-school, a higher school.' The legislature, to which every good farmer goes once on trial, is a superior academy.

The result appears in the power of invention, the freedom of thinking, in the readiness for reforms, eagerness for novelty, even for all the follies of false science ; in the antipathy to secret societies, in the predominance of the democratic party in the politics of the Union, and in the voice of the public even when irregular and vicious, — the voice of mobs, the voice of lynch law, — because it is thought to be, on the whole, the verdict, though badly spoken, of the greatest number.

All this forwardness and self-reliance, cover self-government ; proceed on the belief that as the people have made a government they can make another ; that their union and law are not in their memory, but in their blood and condition. If they unmake a law, they can easily make a new one. In Mr. Webster's imagination the American Union was a huge Prince Rupert's drop, which will snap into atoms if so much as the smallest end be shivered off. Now the fact is quite different from this. The people are loyal, law-abiding. They prefer order, and have no taste for misrule and uproar.

America was opened after the feudal mischief was spent, and so the people made a good start. We began well. No inquisition here, no kings, no nobles, no dominant church. Here heresy has lost its terrors. We have eight or ten religions in every large town, and the most that comes of it is a degree or two on the thermometer of fashion ; a pew in a particular church gives an easier entrance to the subscription ball.

We began with freedom, and are defended

from shocks now for a century by the facility
with which through popular assemblies every
necessary measure of reform can instantly be carried. A congress is a standing insurrection, and
escapes the violence of accumulated grievance.
As the globe keeps its identity by perpetual
change, so our civil system, by perpetual appeal
to the people and acceptance of its reforms.

The government is acquainted with the opinions of all classes, knows the leading men in the
middle class, knows the leaders of the humblest
class. The President comes near enough to
these; if he does not, the caucus does, the
primary ward and town-meeting, and what is
important does reach him.

The men, the women, all over this land shrill
their exclamations of impatience and indignation
at what is short-coming or is unbecoming in
the government, — at the want of humanity, of
morality, — ever on broad grounds of general
justice, and not on the class-feeling which nar-
rows the perception of English, French, German
people at home.

In this fact, that we are a nation of individuals,
that we have a highly intellectual organization,
that we can see and feel moral distinctions, and
that on such an organization sooner or later the

moral laws must tell, to such ears must speak,
— in this is our hope. For if the prosperity of
this country has been merely the obedience
of man to the guiding of Nature, — of great
rivers and prairies, — yet is there fate above
fate, if we choose to spread this language; or if
there is fate in corn and cotton, so is there fate
in thought, — this, namely, that the largest
thought and the widest love are born to victory,
and must prevail.

The revolution is the work of no man, but the
eternal effervescence of Nature. It never did not
work. And we say that revolutions beat all the
insurgents, be they never so determined and
politic; that the great interests of mankind,
being at every moment through ages in favor of
justice and the largest liberty, will always, from
time to time, gain on the adversary and at last
win the day. Never country had such a fortune,
as men call fortune, as this, in its geography, its
history, and in its majestic possibilities.

We have much to learn, much to correct, —
a great deal of lying vanity. The spread eagle
must fold his foolish wings and be less of a peacock; must keep his wings to carry the thunderbolt when he is commanded. We must realize
our rhetoric and our rituals. Our national flag

is not affecting, as it should be, because it does not represent the population of the United States, but some Baltimore or Chicago or Cincinnati or Philadelphia caucus; not union or justice, but selfishness and cunning. If we never put on the liberty-cap until we were freemen by love and self-denial, the liberty-cap would mean something. I wish to see America not like the old powers of the earth, grasping, exclusive and narrow, but a benefactor such as no country ever was, hospitable to all nations, legislating for all nationalities. Nations were made to help each other as much as families were; and all advancement is by ideas, and not by brute force or mechanic force.

In this country, with our practical understanding, there is, at present, a great sensualism, a headlong devotion to trade and to the conquest of the continent, — to each man as large a share of the same as he can carve for himself, — an extravagant confidence in our talent and activity, which becomes, whilst successful, a scornful materialism, — but with the fault, of course, that it has no depth, no reserved force whereon to fall back when a reverse comes.

That repose which is the ornament and ripeness of man is not American. That repose which indicates a faith in the laws of the universe, — a faith that they will fulfil themselves, and are not to be impeded, transgressed or accelerated. Our people are too slight and vain. They are easily elated and easily depressed. See how fast they extend the fleeting fabric of their trade, — not at all considering the remote reaction and bankruptcy, but with the same abandonment to the moment and the facts of the hour as the Esquimau who sells his bed in the morning. Our people act on the moment, and from external impulse. They all lean on some other, and this superstitiously, and not from insight of his merit. They follow a fact; they follow success, and not skill. Therefore, as soon as the success stops and the admirable man blunders, they quit him; already they remember that they long ago suspected his judgment, and they transfer the repute of judgment to the next prosperous person who has not yet blundered. Of course this levity makes them as easily despond. It seems as if history gave no account of any society in which despondency came so readily to heart as we see it and feel it in ours. Young men at thirty and even earlier lose all spring and vivacity, and if they fail in their first enterprise throw up the game.

The source of mischief is the extreme difficulty with which men are roused from the torpor
of every day. Blessed is all that agitates the mass,
breaks up this torpor, and begins motion. *Cor-
pora non agunt nisi soluta;* the chemical rule is
true in mind. Contrast, change, interruption,
are necessary to new activity and new combinations.

If a temperate wise man should look over our
American society, I think the first danger that
would excite his alarm would be the European
influences on this country. We buy much of
Europe that does not make us better men; and
mainly the expensiveness which is ruining that
country. We import trifles, dancers, singers,
laces, books of patterns, modes, gloves and
cologne, manuals of Gothic architecture, steam-
made ornaments. America is provincial. It is
an immense Halifax. See the secondariness and
aping of foreign and English life, that runs
through this country, in building, in dress, in
eating, in books. Every village, every city, has
its architecture, its costume, its hotel, its private
house, its church, from England.

Our politics threaten her. Her manners
threaten us. Life is grown and growing so costly
that it threatens to kill us. A man is coming,

here as there, to value himself on what he can buy. Worst of all, his expense is not his own, but a far-off copy of Osborne House or the Elysée. The tendency of this is to make all men alike; to extinguish individualism and choke up all the channels of inspiration from God in man. We lose our invention and descend into imitation. A man no longer conducts his own life It is manufactured for him. The tailor makes your dress; the baker your bread; the upholsterer, from an imported book of patterns, your furniture; the Bishop of London your faith.

In the planters of this country, in the seventeenth century, the conditions of the country, combined with the impatience of arbitrary power which they brought from England, forced them to a wonderful personal independence and to a certain heroic planting and trading. Later this strength appeared in the solitudes of the West, where a man is made a hero by the varied emergencies of his lonely farm, and neighborhoods must combine against the Indians, or the horse-thieves, or the river rowdies, by organizing themselves into committees of vigilance. Thus the land and sea educate the people, and bring out presence of mind, self-reliance, and hundred-handed activity. These are the people for an emergency. They are not to be surprised, and can find a way out of any peril. This rough and ready force becomes them, and makes them fit citizens and civilizers. But if we found them clinging to English traditions, which are graceful enough at home, as the English Church, and entailed estates, and distrust of popular election, we should feel this reactionary, and absurdly out of place.

Let the passion for America cast out the passion for Europe. Here let there be what the earth waits for, — exalted manhood. What this country longs for is personalities, grand persons, to counteract its materialities. For it is the rule of the universe that corn shall serve man, and not man corn.

They who find America insipid — they for whom London and Paris have spoiled their own homes — can be spared to return to those cities. I not only see a career at home for more genius than we have, but for more than there is in the world.

The class of which I speak make themselves merry without duties. They sit in decorated club-houses in the cities, and burn tobacco and play whist; in the country they sit idle in stores and bar-rooms, and burn tobacco, and gossip and sleep. They complain of the flatness of American life; "America has no illusions, no romance." They have no perception of its destiny. They are not Americans.

The felon is the logical extreme of the epicure and coxcomb. Selfish luxury is the end of both, though in one it is decorated with refinements, and in the other brutal. But my point now is, that this spirit is not American.

Our young men lack idealism. A man for success must not be pure idealist, then he will practically fail; but he must have ideas, must obey ideas, or he might as well be the horse he rides on. A man does not want to be sun-dazzled, sun-blind; but every man must have glimmer enough to keep him from knocking his head against the walls. And it is in the interest of civilization and good society and friendship, that I dread to hear of well-born, gifted and amiable men, that they have this indifference, disposing them to this despair.

Of no use are the men who study to do exactly as was done before, who can never understand that to-day is a new day. There never was such a combination as this of ours, and the rules to meet it are not set down in any history. We want men of original perception and original action, who can open their eyes wider than to a nationality, — namely, to considerations of benefit to the human race, — can act in the interest of civilization; men of elastic, men of moral mind, who can live in the moment and take a step forward. Columbus was no back-ward-creeping crab, nor was Martin Luther, nor John Adams, nor Patrick Henry, nor Thomas Jefferson; and the Genius or Destiny of Amer-ica is no log or sluggard, but a man incessantly advancing, as the shadow on the dial's face, or the heavenly body by whose light it is marked.

The flowering of civilization is the finished man, the man of sense, of grace, of accomplish-ment, of social power, — the gentleman. What hinders that he be born here? The new times need a new man, the complemental man, whom plainly this country must furnish. Freer swing his arms; farther pierce his eyes; more forward and forthright his whole build and rig than the Englishman's, who, we see, is much imprisoned in his backbone.

'T is certain that our civilization is yet in-complete, it has not ended nor given sign of ending in a hero. 'T is a wild democracy; the riot of mediocrities and dishonesties and fudges.

Ours is the age of the omnibus, of the third person plural, of Tammany Hall. Is it that Nature has only so much vital force, and must dilute it if it is to be multiplied into millions? The beautiful is never plentiful. Then Illinois and Indiana, with their spawning loins, must needs be ordinary.

It is not a question whether we shall be a multitude of people. No, that has been conspicuously decided already; but whether we shall be the new nation, the guide and lawgiver of all nations, as having clearly chosen and firmly held the simplest and best rule of political society.

Now, if the spirit which years ago armed this country against rebellion, and put forth such gigantic energy in the charity of the Sanitary Commission, could be waked to the conserving and creating duty of making the laws just and humane, it were to enroll a great constituency of religious, self-respecting, brave, tender, faithful obeyers of duty, lovers of men, filled with loyalty to each other, and with the simple and sublime purpose of carrying out in private and in public action the desire and need of mankind.

Here is the post where the patriot should plant himself; here the altar where virtuous young men, those to whom friendship is the dearest covenant, should bind each other to loyalty; where genius should kindle its fires and bring forgotten truth to the eyes of men.

It is not possible to extricate yourself from the questions in which your age is involved. Let the good citizen perform the duties put on him here and now. It is not by heads reverted to the dying Demosthenes, or to Luther, or to Wallace, or to George Fox, or to George Washington, that you can combat the dangers and dragons that beset the United States at this time. I believe this cannot be accomplished by dunces or idlers, but requires docility, sympathy, and religious receiving from higher principles; for liberty, like religion, is a short and hasty fruit, and like all power subsists only by new rallyings on the source of inspiration.

Power can be generous. The very grandeur of the means which offer themselves to us should suggest grandeur in the direction of our expenditure. If our mechanic arts are unsurpassed in usefulness, if we have taught the river to make shoes and nails and carpets, and the bolt of heaven to write our letters like a Gillot pen, let these wonders work for honest humanity, for the poor, for justice, genius and the public good.' Let us realize that this country, the last found, is the great charity of God to the human race.

America should affirm and establish that in no instance shall the guns go in advance of the present right. We shall not make *coups d'état* and afterwards explain and pay, but shall proceed like William Penn, or whatever other Christian or humane person who treats with the Indian or the foreigner, on principles of honest trade and mutual advantage. We can see that the Constitution and the law in America must be written on ethical principles, so that the entire power of the spiritual world shall hold the citizen loyal, and repel the enemy as by force of nature. It should be mankind's bill of rights, or Royal Proclamation of the Intellect ascending the throne, announcing its good pleasure that now, once for all, the world shall be governed by common sense and law of morals.

The end of all political struggle is to establish morality as the basis of all legislation. 'T is not free institutions, 't is not a democracy that is the end, — no, but only the means. Morality is the object of government. We want a state of things in which crime will not pay; a state of things which allows every man the largest liberty compatible with the liberty of every other man.

Humanity asks that government shall not be ashamed to be tender and paternal, but that democratic institutions shall be more thoughtful for the interests of women, for the training of children, and for the welfare of sick and unable persons, and serious care of criminals, than was ever any the best government of the Old World.

The genius of the country has marked out our true policy, — opportunity. Opportunity of civil rights, of education, of personal power, and not less of wealth; doors wide open. If I could have it, — free trade with all the world without toll or custom-houses, invitation as we now make to every nation, to every race and skin, white men, red men, yellow men, black men; hospitality of fair field and equal laws to all.¹ Let them compete, and success to the strongest, the wisest and the best. The land is wide enough, the soil has bread for all.

I hope America will come to have its pride in being a nation of servants, and not of the served. How can men have any other ambition where the reason has not suffered a disastrous eclipse? Whilst every man can say I serve, — to the whole extent of my being I apply my faculty to the service of mankind in my especial place, — he therein sees and shows a reason for his being in the world, and is not a moth or incumbrance in it.

The distinction and end of a soundly constituted man is his labor. Use is inscribed on all his faculties. Use is the end to which he exists. As the tree exists for its fruit, so a man for his work. A fruitless plant, an idle animal, does not stand in the universe. They are all toiling, however secretly or slowly, in the province assigned them, and to a use in the economy of the world; the higher and more complex organizations to higher and more catholic service. And man seems to play, by his instincts and activity, a certain part that even tells on the general face of the planet, drains swamps, leads rivers into dry countries for their irrigation, perforates forests and stony mountain chains with roads, hinders the inroads of the sea on the continent, as if dressing the globe for happier races

On the whole, I know that the cosmic results

will be the same, whatever the daily events may
be. Happily we are under better guidance than
of statesmen. Pennsylvania coal-mines and New
York shipping and free labor, though not idealists, gravitate in the ideal direction. Nothing
less large than justice can keep them in good
temper. Justice satisfies everybody, and justice
alone. No monopoly must be foisted in, no
weak party or nationality sacrificed, no coward compromise conceded to a strong partner.
Every one of these is the seed of vice, war and
national disorganization. It is our part to carry
out to the last the ends of liberty and justice.
We shall stand, then, for vast interests ; north
and south, east and west will be present to our
minds, and our vote will be as if they voted,
and we shall know that our vote secures the
foundations of the state, good will, liberty
and security of traffic and of production, and
mutual increase of good will in the great
interests.

Our helm is given up to a better guidance
than our own ; the course of events is quite too
strong for any helmsman, and our little wherry
is taken in tow by the ship of the great Admi-
ral which knows the way, and has the force to
draw men and states and planets to their good.

Such and so potent is this high method by which the Divine Providence sends the chiefest benefits under the mask of calamities, that I do not think we shall by any perverse ingenuity prevent the blessing.

In seeing this guidance of events, in seeing this felicity without example that has rested on the Union thus far, I find new confidence for the future.

I could heartily wish that our will and endeavor were more active parties to the work. But I see in all directions the light breaking. Trade and government will not alone be the favored aims of mankind, but every useful, every elegant art, every exercise of the imagination, the height of reason, the noblest affection, the purest religion will find their home in our institutions, and write our laws for the benefit of men.

NOTES

NOTES

THE LORD'S SUPPER

MR. EMERSON did not wish to have his sermons pub lished. All that was worth saving in them, he said, would be found in the Essays. Yet it seemed best, to Mr. Cabot and to Mr. Emerson's family, that this one sermon should be preserved. A record of a turning-point in his life, it showed at once his thought and his character; for he not only gives the reasons why he believes the rite not authoritatively enjoined, and hence recommends its modification or discontin-uance, but with serenity and sweetness renders back his trust into his people's hands, since he cannot see his way longer to exercise it as most of them desire.

In the month of June, 1832, Mr. Emerson had proposed to the church, apparently with hope of their approval, that the Communion be observed only as a festival of commemoration, without the use of the elements. The committee to whom the proposal was referred made a report expressing confidence in him, but declining to advise the change, as the matter was one which they could not properly be called upon to decide.

The question then came back to the pastor, whether he was willing to remain in his place and administer the rite in the usual form.

He went alone to the White Mountains, then seldom vis-ited, to consider the grave question whether he was prepared, rather than to continue the performance of a part of his priestly office from which his instincts and beliefs recoiled, to sacrifice a position of advantage for usefulness to his people to whom he was bound by many ties, and in preparation for which he had

spent long years. He wrote, at Conway, New Hampshire:
"Here among the mountains the pinions of thought should
be strong, and one should see the errors of men from a calmer
height of love and wisdom." His diary at Ethan Allan Crawford's contains his doubts and questionings, which Mr. Cabot
has given in his Memoir. Yet there was but one answer for
him, and after a fortnight, he came back clear in his mind to
give his decision, embodied in this sermon, to his people. On
the same day that it was preached, he formally resigned his
pastorate. The church was loth to part with him. It was hoped
that some other arrangement might be made. Mr. Cabot
learned that "several meetings were held and the proprietors
of pews were called in, as having 'an undoubted right to retain
Mr. Emerson as their pastor, without reference to the opposition of the church.' At length, after two adjournments and
much discussion, it was decided by thirty votes against twenty-
four to accept his resignation. It was voted at the same time
to continue his salary for the present."

Thus Mr. Emerson and his people parted in all kindness,
but, as Mr. Cabot truly said, their difference of views on this
rite "was in truth only the symptom of a deeper difference
which would in any case sooner or later have made it impossible
for him to retain his office; a disagreement not so much about
particular doctrines or observances as about their sanction, the
authority on which all doctrines and observances rest."

In the farewell letter which Mr. Emerson wrote to the
people of his church, he said: —

"I rejoice to believe that my ceasing to exercise the pastoral office among you does not make any real change in our
spiritual relation to each other. Whatever is most desirable
and excellent therein remains to us. For, truly speaking, whoever provokes me to a good act or thought has given me a

pledge of his fidelity to virtue, — he has come under bonds to
adhere to that cause to which we are jointly attached. And
so I say to all you who have been my counsellors and coöp-
erators in our Christian walk, that I am wont to see in your
faces the seals and certificates of our mutual obligations. If we
have conspired from week to week in the sympathy and expression of devout sentiments; if we have received together the
unspeakable gift of God's truth; if we have studied together
the sense of any divine word; or striven together in any charity; or conferred together for the relief or instruction of any
brother; if together we have laid down the dead in a pious
hope; or held up the babe into the baptism of Christianity;
above all, if we have shared in any habitual acknowledgment
of the benignant God, whose omnipresence raises and glorifies
the meanest offices and the lowest ability, and opens heaven
in every heart that worships him, — then indeed we are united,
we are mutually debtors to each other of faith and hope, engaged to persist and confirm each other's hearts in obedience to
the Gospel. We shall not feel that the nominal changes and
little separations of this world can release us from the strong
cordage of this spiritual bond. And I entreat you to consider
how truly blessed will have been our connection if, in this
manner, the memory of it shall serve to bind each one of us
more strictly to the practice of our several duties."

Page 18, note 1. The doctrine of the offices of Jesus, even
in the Unitarianism of Dr. Channing, was never congenial to
Mr. Emerson's mind. He notes the same with regard to his
father, and even to his Aunt Mary, in spite of her Calvinism.
Any interposed personality between the Creator and the cre
ated was repugnant to him. Even in March, 1831, he is
considering in his journal that his hearers will say, "To what

purpose is this attempt to explain away so safe and holy a doctrine as that of the Holy Spirit? Why unsettle or disturb a
faith which presents to many minds a helpful medium by which
they approach the idea of God?" and he answers, "And
this question I will meet. It is because I think the popular
views of this principle are pernicious, because it does put a
medium, because it removes the idea of God from the mind.
It leaves some events, some things, some thoughts, out of the
power of Him who causes every event, every flower, every
thought. The tremendous idea, as I may well call it, of God
is screened from the soul. . . . And least of all can we
believe — Reason will not let us — that the presiding Creator
commands all matter and never descends into the secret
chambers of the Soul. There he is most present. The Soul
rules over matter. Matter may pass away like a mote in the
sunbeam, may be absorbed into the immensity of God, as a
mist is absorbed into the heat of the Sun — but the soul is the
kingdom of God, the abode of love, of truth, of virtue."

Page 19, note 1. In the hope of satisfying those of his
people who held to the letter of the Scriptural Law, Mr.
Emerson made the foregoing clear statement with regard to
the authority for the rite, from the professional point of
view. It seems quite unlike his usual method, and there is
little doubt that in it appears the influence of his elder
brother, William, whose honest doubts had led him to abandon
even earlier the profession of his fathers. In the introductory
note to the chapter on Goethe, in *Representative Men,* is
given an account of his unsuccessful pilgrimage to Weimar, in
hopes that the great mind of Germany could solve these
doubts. There is a letter still preserved, written by William,
soon after his return, to his venerable kinsman at Concord,
Dr. Ripley, in which he explains with great clearness his

own reasons for not believing that the Communion rite was enjoined by Jesus for perpetual observance. The argument on scriptural grounds there clearly stated is substantially the same as that which his younger brother makes use of in the beginning of this sermon. Thus far he has spoken of outward authority; from this point onward he speaks from within — the way native to him.

Page 25, note 1. Mr. Emerson left the struggles of the Past behind, and did not care to recall them. Thus, writing of Lucretia Mott, whom he met when giving a course of lectures in Philadelphia, in January, 1843, he said: —

" Me she taxed with living out of the world, and I was not much flattered that her interest in me respected my rejection of an ordinance, sometime, somewhere. Also yesterday — for Philadelphian ideas, like love, do creep where they cannot go — I was challenged on the subject of the Lord's Supper, and with great slowness and pain was forced to recollect the grounds of my dissent in that particular. You may be sure I was very tardy with my texts."

Mr. Emerson's journal during the period of trial and decision, in the mountains, shows that he was reading with great interest the life of George Fox. The simplicity of the Society of Friends, their aversion to forms and trust in the inward light, always appealed to him.

In his essay on The Preacher he says: —

" The supposed embarrassments to young clergymen exist only to feeble wills. . . . That gray deacon, or respectable matron with Calvinistic antecedents, you can readily see, would not have presented any obstacle to the march of St. Bernard or of George Fox, of Luther or of Theodore Parker." This hints at the help he had found in the Quaker's history in his time of need.

HISTORICAL DISCOURSE AT CONCORD

Mr. Emerson's Discourse was printed soon after its delivery, and with it, in an Appendix, the following notice of the celebration of the second centennial anniversary of the incorporation of the town, sent to him by "a friend who thought it desirable to preserve the remembrance of some particulars of this historical festival."

"At a meeting of the town of Concord, in April last, it was voted to celebrate the Second Centennial Anniversary of the settlement of the town, on the 12th September following. A committee of fifteen were chosen to make the arrangements. This committee appointed Ralph Waldo Emerson, Orator, and Rev. Dr. Ripley and Rev. Mr. Wilder, Chaplains of the Day. Hon. John Keyes was chosen President of the Day.

"On the morning of the 12th September, at half past 10 o'clock, the children of the town, to the number of about 500, moved in procession to the Common in front of the old church and court-house and there opened to the right and left, awaiting the procession of citizens. At 11 o'clock, the Concord Light Infantry, under Captain Moore, and the Artillery under Captain Buttrick, escorted the civic procession, under the direction of Moses Prichard as Chief Marshal, from Shepherd's hotel through the lines of children to the Meeting-house. The South gallery had been reserved for ladies, and the North gallery for the children; but (it was a good omen) the children overran the space assigned for their accommodation, and were sprinkled throughout the house, and ranged on seats along the aisles. The old Meeting-house, which was propped to sustain the unwonted weight of the multitude within its walls, was built in 1712, thus having stood for more than half the period to which our history goes back. Prayers were offered and the Scriptures read by the aged minister of the town, Rev. Ezra Ripley, now in the 85th year of his age; —another interesting feature in this scene of reminiscences. A very pleasant and impressive part of the services in the church was the singing of the 107th psalm, from the New England version of the psalms made by Eliot, Mather, and others, in 1639, and used in the church in this town in the days of Peter Bulkeley. The psalm was read a line at a time, after the ancient fashion, from the Deacons' seat, and so sung to the tune of St. Martin's by the whole congregation standing.

"Ten of the surviving veterans who were in arms at the Bridge, on the 19th April, 1775, honored the festival with their presence. Their names are Abel Davis, Thaddeus Blood, Tilly Buttrick, John Hosmer, of *Concord;* Thomas Thorp, Solomon Smith, John Oliver, Aaron Jones, of *Acton;* David Lane, of *Bedford;* Amos Baker, of *Lincoln.*

"On leaving the church, the procession again formed, and moved to a large tent nearly opposite Shepherd's hotel, under which dinner was prepared, and the company sat down to the tables, to the number of four hundred. We were honored with the presence of distinguished guests, among whom were Lieutenant-Governor Armstrong, Judge Davis, Alden Bradford (descended from the 2d governor of Plymouth Colony), Hon. Edward Everett, Hon. Stephen C. Phillips of Salem, Philip Hone, Esq., of New York, General Dearborn, and Lieutenant-Colonel R. C. Winthrop (descended from the 1st governor of Massachusetts). Letters were read from several gentlemen expressing their regret at being deprived of the pleasure of being present on the occasion. The character of the speeches and sentiments at the dinner were manly and affectionate, in keeping with the whole temper of the day.

"On leaving the dinner-table, the invited guests, with
many of the citizens, repaired to the court-house to pay their
respects to the ladies of Concord, who had there, with their
friends, partaken of an elegant collation, and now politely
offered coffee to the gentlemen. The hall, in which the collation was spread, had been decorated by fair hands with fes-
toons of flowers, and wreaths of evergreen, and hung with
pictures of the Fathers of the Town. Crowded as it was with
graceful forms and happy faces, and resounding with the hum
of animated conversation, it was itself a beautiful living picture.
Compared with the poverty and savageness of the scene which
the same spot presented two hundred years ago, it was a brilliant reverse of the medal; and could scarcely fail, like all the
parts of the holiday, to lead the reflecting mind to thoughts of
that Divine Providence, which, in every generation, has been
our tower of defence and horn of blessing.

"At sunset the company separated and retired to their
homes; and the evening of this day of excitement was as quiet
as a Sabbath throughout the village."

Within the year, Mr. Emerson had come to make his
home for life in the ancestral town, and had become a house-
holder. Two days after the festival, he drove to Plymouth in
a chaise, and was there married to Lidian Jackson, and immediately brought his bride to her Concord home.

His aged step-grandfather was the senior chaplain at the
Celebration, and his brother Charles, who was to live with him
in the new home, was one of the marshals.

In preparation for this address Mr. Emerson made diligent
examination of the old town records, and spent a fortnight in
Cambridge consulting the works on early New England in
the College Library. I reproduce most of his references to his

authorities exactly, although there are, no doubt, newer editions of some of the works.

Page 30, note 1. This story is from Bede's *Ecclesiastical
History* (chapter xiii., Bohn's *Antiquarian Library*). Mr.
Emerson used it in full as the exordium of his essay on Im-
mortality, in *Letters and Social Aims.*

Page 30, note 2. The poem "Hamatreya," wherein
appear the names of many of these first settlers, might well be
read in connection with the opening passages of this address.

Mr. Emerson's right of descent to speak as representative of Peter Bulkeley, who was the spiritual arm of the settlement, as Simon Willard was its sword-arm, may here be
shown : Rev. Joseph Emerson of Mendon (son of Thomas
of Ipswich, the first of the name in this country) married
Elizabeth, daughter of Rev. Edward Bulkeley, who succeeded
his father, the Rev. Peter Bulkeley, as minister of Concord.·
Edward, the son of Joseph of Mendon and Elizabeth Bulkeley, was father of Rev. Joseph Emerson of Malden, who
was father of Rev. William Emerson of Concord, who was
father of Rev. William Emerson of Harvard and Boston, the
father of Ralph Waldo Emerson.

Page 31, note 1. Neal's *History of New England*, vol. i.,
p. 132.

Page 31, note 2. Neal, vol. i., p. 321.

Page 31, note 3. Shattuck's *History of Concord*, p. 158.

Page 32, note 1. On September 2, 1635, the General
Court passed this order : ——

"It is ordered that there shalbe a plantačon att Muskete-
quid & that there shalbe 6 myles of land square to belong to
it, & that the inhabitants thereof shall have three yeares immunities from all publ[ic] charges except traineings; Further, that

when any that plant there shall have occačon of carryeing of goods thither, they shall repaire to two of the nexte magistrates where the teames are, whoe shall have the power for a yeare to presse draughts, att reasonable rates, to be payed by the owners of the goods, to transport their goods thither att seasonable tymes & the name of the place is changed & here after to be called Concord.''

Page 32, note 2. Shattuck, p 5.

Page 33, note 1. In his lecture on Boston (published in the volume *Natural History of Intellect*) Mr. Emerson gives an amusing enumeration of some troubles which seemed so great to the newcomers from the Old World· he mentions their fear of lions, the accident to John Smith from '' the most poisonous tail of a fish called a sting-ray,'' the circumstance of the overpowering effect of the sweet fern upon the Concord party, and the intoxicating effect of wild grapes eaten by the Norse explorers, and adds: '' Nature has never again indulged in these exasperations. It seems to have been the last outrage ever committed by the sting-rays, or by the sweet fern, or by the fox-grapes They have been of peaceable behavior ever since.''

Page 34, note 1 Johnson's *Wonder-Working Providence,* chap. xxxv. Mr. Emerson abridged and slightly altered some sentences.

Page 35, note 1. Mourt, *Beginning of Plymouth,* 1621, p 60.

Page 35, note 2. Johnson, p. 56. Josselyn, in his *New England's Rarities Discovered,* speaks with respect of '' Squashes, but more truly squontersquashes; a kind of mellon, or rather gourd; . . . some of these are green; some yellow; some longish like a gourd; others round, like an apple: all of them pleasant food, boyled and buttered, and seasoned with spice·

But the yellow squash — called an apple-squash (because like an apple) and about the bigness of a pome-water is the best kind." Wood, in his *New England Prospect*, says: " In summer, when their corn is spent, isquotersquashes is their best bread, a fruit much like a pumpion."

Page 36, note 1. Nashawtuck, a small and shapely hill between the Musketaquid and the Assabet streams, at their point of union, was a pleasant and convenient headquarters for a sagamore of a race whose best roadway for travel and transportation was a deep, quiet stream, the fish of which they ate, and also used for manure for their cornfields along the bluffs. Indian graves have been found on this hill.

Page 36, note 2. Josselyn's *Voyages to New England,* 1638.

Page 36, note 3. Hutchinson's *History of Massachusetts,* vol. i., chap. 6.

Page 36, note 4. Thomas Morton, *New England Canaan,* p. 47.

Page 37, note 1. Shattuck, p. 6.

The old Middlesex Hotel, which stood during the greater part of the nineteenth century on the southwest side of the Common, opposite the court- and town-houses, had fallen into decay in 1900, and was bought and taken down by the town as an improvement to the public square to commemorate the one hundred and twenty-fifth anniversary of Concord Fight. It is probable that Jethro's Oak, under which the treaty was made, stood a little nearer the house of Rev. Peter Bulkeley, the site of which, about one hundred paces distant on the Lowell road, is now marked by a stone and bronze tablet.

Page 38, note 1. Depositions taken in 1684, and copied in the first volume of the Town Records.

Page 39, note 1. Johnson's *Wonder-Working Providence.*

Page 39, note 2. *New England's Plantation.*

Page 39, note 3. E. W.'s Letter in Mourt, 1621.

Page 40, note 1. Peter Bulkeley's *Gospel Covenant;* preached at Concord in New England. 2d edition, London, 1651, p. 432.

Page 41, note 1. See petition in Shattuck's *History*, p. 14.

Page 41, note 2. Shattuck, p. 14. This was the meadow and upland on the Lowell road, one mile north of Concord, just beyond the river. On the farm stands the unpainted "lean-to" house, now owned by the daughters of the late Edmund Hosmer.

Page 42, note 1. Concord Town Records.

Page 43, note 1. Bancroft, *History of the United States,* vol. i., p. 389.

Page 44, note 1. Savage's *Winthrop*, vol. i., p. 114.

Page 44, note 2. Colony Records, vol. i.

Page 44, note 3. See Hutchinson's *Collection*, p. 287.

Page 46, note 1. Winthrop's *Journal*, vol. i., pp. 128, 129, and the editor's note.

Page 46, note 2. Winthrop's *Journal*, vol. ii., p. 160

Page 48, note 1. Town Records.

With the exception of the anecdotes in this and the following sentence, almost the whole of this account of the theory and practice of the New England town-meeting was used by Mr. Emerson in his oration, given in December, 1870, before the New England Society in New York. The greater part of the matter used in that address is included in the lecture on Boston, in the volume *Natural History of Intellect.*

The New England Society of New York recently published the Orations delivered before it previous to 1871, including Mr. Emerson's, as far as it could be recovered from the scattered manuscript, and the newspaper reports of the time.

Page 50, note 1. Hutchinson's *Collection*, p. 27.

Page 51, note 1. Shattuck, p. 20. "The Government, 13 Nov., 1644, ordered the county courts to take care of the Indians residing within their several shires, to have them civilized, and to take order, from time to time, to have them instructed in the knowledge of God."

Page 52, note 1. Shepard's *Clear Sunshine of the Gospel,* London, 1648.

Page 52, note 2. These rules are given in Shattuck's *History,* pp. 22–24, and were called " Conclusions and orders made and agreed upon by divers Sachems and other principal men amongst the Indians at Concord in the end of the eleventh Month (called January) An. 1646."

The following are interesting specimens of these: —

Rule 2. "That there shall be no more Powwawing amongst the Indians. And if any shall hereafter powwaw, both he that shall powwaw, and he that shall procure him to powwaw, shall pay twenty shillings apiece."

Rule 4. " They desire they may understand the wiles of Satan, and grow out of love with his suggestions and temtations."

Rule 5. " That they may fall upon some better course to improve their time than formerly."

Rule 15. "They will wear their haire comely, as the English do, and whosoever shall offend herein shall pay four shillings."

Rule 23. " They shall not disguise themselves in their mournings as formerly, nor shall they keep a great noyse by howling."

Rule 24. "The old ceremony of a maide walking alone and living apart so many days, [fine] twenty shillings."

Page 53, note 1. Shepard, p. 9.

Page 54, note 1. Wilson's Letter, 1651.

Page 54, note 2. *News from America*, p. 22.

Page 54, note 3. Winthrop, vol. ii., p. 2.

Page 55, note 1. Hutchinson, vol. i., p. 90.

Page 55, note 2. Hutchinson, vol. i., p. 112.

Page 55, note 3. Winthrop, vol. ii., p. 21.

Page 55, note 4. Hutchinson, vol. i., p. 94.

Page 55, note 5. Bulkeley's *Gospel Covenant*, p. 209.

Page 55, note 6. Winthrop, vol. ii., p. 94.

Page 56, note 1. *Gospel Covenant*, p. 301.

Page 57, note 1. Shattuck, p. 45.

Page 57, note 2. Hutchinson, vol. i., p. 172.

Page 57, note 3. See his instructions from the Commissioners, his narrative, and the Commissioners' letter to him, in Hutchinson's *Collection*, pp. 261–270.

Page 58, note 1. Hutchinson's *History*, vol. i., p. 254.

Page 58, note 2. Hubbard's *Indian Wars*, p. 119, ed 1801

Mr. Charles H. Walcott, in his *Concord in the Colonial Period* (Estes & Lauriat, Boston, 1884), gives a very interesting account of the Brookfield fight.

Page 58, note 3. Hubbard, p. 201.

Page 59, note 1. Hubbard, p. 185.

Page 59, note 2. Hubbard, p. 245.

Page 60, note 1. Shattuck, p. 55.

Page 60, note 2. Hubbard, p. 260.

Page 61, note 1. Neal's *History of New England*, vol. i., p. 321.

Page 61, note 2. Mather, *Magnalia Christi*, vol. i., p. 363.

Page 61, note 3. "Tradition has handed down the following anecdote. A consultation among the Indian chiefs took place about this time on the high lands in Stow, and, as they cast their eyes towards Sudbury and Concord, a question arose which they should attack first. The decision was made to attack the former. One of the principal chiefs said: ' We no prosper if we go to Concord — the Great Spirit love that people — the evil spirit tell us not to go — they have a great man there — he *great pray*.' The Rev. Edward Bulkeley was then minister of the town, and his name and distinguished character were known even to the red men of the forest." — Shattuck's *History*, p. 59, note.

Page 61, note 4. On this occasion the name of Hoar, since honored in Concord through several generations, came to the front. John Hoar, the first practitioner of law in Concord, an outspoken man of sturdy independence, who, for uttering complaints that justice was denied him in the courts, had been made to give bonds for good behavior and " disabled to plead any cases but his oune in this jurisdiction," who had been fined £10 for saying that " the Blessing which his Master Bulkeley pronounced in dismissing the publique Assembly was no more than vane babling," and was twice fined for non-attendance at public worship, proved to be the only man in town who was willing to take charge of the Praying Indians of Nashobah, whom the General Court ordered moved to Concord during Philip's War. The magistrates who had persecuted him had to turn to him, and he made good provision on his own place for the comfort and safe-keeping of these unfortunates, and their employment, when public opinion was directed against them with the cruelty of fear. Soon, however, Captain Mosley, who had been secretly sent for by some citizens, came with soldiers into the meeting-house, announced to the congregation that he had heard that " there were some heathen in town committed to one Hoar, who, he was informed, were a trouble and disquiet to them;" therefore, if the people desired it, he would remove them to Boston. No one made objection, so he went to Mr. Hoar's house, counted the Indians and set a guard, Hoar vigorously protesting. He came next day; Hoar bravely refused to give them up, so Mosley removed them by violence and carried the Indians to Deer Island, where they suffered much during the winter. See Walcott's *Concord in the Colonial Period.*

Page 62, note 1. Sprague's *Centennial Ode.*

Page 62, note 2. Shattuck, chap iii. Walcott, chap. iii.

Page 63, note 1. Hutchinson's *Collection*, p. 484.

Page 63, note 2. Hutchinson's *Collection*, pp. 543, 548, 557, 566.

Page 63, note 3. Hutchinson's *History*, vol. i., p. 336.

The month of April has been fateful for Concord, especially its nineteenth day On that day the military company under Lieutenant Heald marched to Boston to take part in the uprising of the freemen of the colony against Andros. On that same day, in 1775, the minute-men and militia of Concord, promptly reinforced by the soldiers of her daughter and sister towns, marched down to the guarded North Bridge and returned the fire of the Royal troops in the opening battle of the Revolution Again on the nineteenth of April, 1861, the "Concord Artillery" (so-called, although then a company of the Fifth Infantry, M. V. M.) left the village for the front in the War of the Rebellion; and yet again in the last days of April, 1898, the same company, then, as now, attached to the Sixth Regiment, M. V. M., marched from the village green to bear its part in the Spanish War.

Page 64, note 1. Town Records.

Page 64, note 2 The following minutes from the Town Records in 1692 may serve as an example. —

"John Craggin, aged about 63 years, and Sarah his wife, aet. about 63 years, do both testify upon oath that about 2 years ago John Shepard, sen. of Concord, came to our house in Obourne, to treat with us, and give us a visit, and carried the said Sary Craggin to Concord with him, and there discoursed us in order to a marriage between his son, John Shepard, jun. and our daughter, Eliz. Craggin, and, for our incouragement, and before us, did promise that, upon the consummation of the said marriage, he, the said John Shepard, sen. would give to his son, John Shepard, jun. the one half of his dwelling house, and the old barn, and the pasture before the barn; the old plow-land, and the old horse, when his colt was fit to ride, and his old oxen, when his steers were fit to work. All this he promised upon marriage as above said, which marriage was consummated upon March following, which is two years ago, come next March. Dated Feb. 25, 1692. Taken on oath before me.   Wm. Johnson."

Page 64, note 3. Town Records, July, 1698.

Page 64, note 4. Records, Nov. 1711.

Page 65, note 1. Records, May, 1712.

Page 66, note 1. Records, 1735.

Page 66, note 2. Whitfield in his journal wrote: "About noon I reached Concord. Here I preached to some thousands in the open air; and comfortable preaching it was. The hearers were sweetly melted down. . . . The minister of the town being, I believe, a true child of God, I chose to stay all night at his house that we might rejoice together. The Lord was with us. The Spirit of the Lord came upon me and God gave me to wrestle with him for my friends, especially those then with me. . . . Brother B——s, the minister, broke into floods of tears, and we had reason to cry out it was good for us to be here."

Page 67, note 1. Church Records, July, 1792.

Page 67, note 2. The Rev. Daniel Bliss has left the name of having been an earnest, good man, evidently emotional. His zealous and impassioned preaching gave offence to some of the cooler and more conservative clergy, and indeed bred discord in the church of Concord. The "aggrieved brethren" withdrew, and, for want of a church, held public worship at a tavern where was the sign of a black horse, hence were called "the Black Horse Church." Their complaints preferred against Mr. Bliss resulted in councils which drew in most of the churches of Middlesex into their widening vortex. Yet he remained the honored pastor of the town until his death. His daughter Phebe married the young William Emerson, his successor; he was therefore Mr. Emerson's great-grandfather.

Page 67, note 3. Town Records.

Page 70, note 1. Town Records.

Page 71, note 1. Town Records

Page 71, note 2. The spirited protest of this County Convention, presided over by Hon. James Prescott of Groton, is given in full in Shattuck's *History*, pp. 82–87

Page 72, note 1 General Gage, the Governor, having refused to convene the General Court at Salem, the Provincial Congress of delegates from the towns of Massachusetts was called by conventions of the various counties to meet at Concord, October 11, 1774. The delegates assembled in the meeting-house, and organized, with John Hancock as President, and Benjamin Lincoln as Secretary. Called together to maintain the rights of the people, this Congress assumed the government of the province, and by its measures prepared the way for the Revolution.

Page 72, note 2. This eloquent sermon to the volunteers

of 1775, still preserved in MS., is very interesting. The young minister shows them the dignity of their calling, warns them of the besetting sins of New England soldiery, explains to them the invasion of their rights and that they are not rebels, tells them that he believes their fathers foresaw the evil day and did all in their power to guard the infant state from encroachments of unconstitutional power, and implores the sons to be true to their duty to their posterity. He fully admits the utter gloom of the prospect, humanly considered: would Heaven hold him innocent, he would counsel submission, but as an honest man and servant of Heaven he dare not do so, and with great spirit bids his injured countrymen "Arise! and plead even with the sword, the firelock and the bayonet, the birthright of Englishmen . . . and if God does not help, it will be because your sins testify against you, otherwise *you may be assured.*"

Page 74, note 1. Journal, July, 1835. " It is affecting to see the old man's [Thaddeus Blood] memory taxed for facts occurring 60 years ago at Concord fight. ' It is hard to bring them up;' he says, ' the truth never will be known.' The Doctor [Ripley], like a keen hunter, unrelenting, follows him up and down, barricading him with questions. Yet cares little for the facts the man can tell, but much for the confirmation of the printed History. ' Leave me, leave me to repose.' "

Thaddeus Blood, who was only twenty years old at the time of Concord fight, later became a schoolmaster, hence was always known as " Master Blood." He was one of the Concord company stationed at Hull, in 1776, which took part in the capture of Lieutenant-Colonel Campbell and his battalion of the 71st (Frazer) Highlanders as they sailed into Boston Harbor, not being aware of the evacuation of the town. They were confined at Concord until their exchange. See *Sir*

*Archibald Campbell of Inverneill, sometime Prisoner of War
in the Jail at Concord, Massachusetts.* By Charles H.
Walcott, Boston, 1898.

Page 74, note 2 In his poem in memory of his brother
Edward, written by the riverside near the battle-ground, Mr.
Emerson alluded to

> Yon stern headstone,
> Which more of pride than pity gave
> To mark the Briton's friendless grave.
> Yet it is a stately tomb,
> The grand return
> Of eve and morn,
> The year's fresh bloom,
> The silver cloud,
> Might grace the dust that is most proud.

Page 76, note 1. Captain Miles commanded the Concord
company that joined the Northern Army at Ticonderoga in
August, 1776, as part of Colonel Reed's regiment.

Page 77, note 1. Judge John S. Keyes, who clearly remembers the incidents of this celebration, seen from a boy's
coign of vantage, the top of one of the inner doors of the
church, tells me that the ten aged survivors of the battle, who
sat in front of the pulpit, bowed in recognition of this
compliment by the orator, and then the audience all bowed to
them. The sanctity of the church forbade in those days cheering or applause even at a civic festival.

Page 77, note 2. The following was Mr. Emerson's note
concerning his authorities —

"The importance which the skirmish at Concord Bridge
derived from subsequent events, has, of late years, attracted
much notice to the incidents of the day. There are, as might

be expected, some discrepancies in the different narratives of the fight. In the brief summary in the text, I have relied mainly on the depositions taken by order of the Provincial Congress within a few days after the action, and on the other contemporary evidence. I have consulted the English narrative in the Massachusetts Historical Collections, and in the trial of Horne (*Cases adjudged in King's Bench;* London, 1800, vol. ii., p. 677); the inscription made by order of the legislature of Massachusetts on the two field-pieces presented to the Concord Artillery; Mr. Phinney's *History of the Battle at Lexington;* Dr. Ripley's *History of Concord Fight;* Mr. Shattuck's narrative in his *History*, besides some oral and some manuscript evidence of eye-witnesses. The following narrative, written by Rev. William Emerson, a spectator of the action, has never been published. A part of it has been in my possession for years: a part of it I discovered, only a few days since, in a trunk of family papers: —

" ' 1775, 19 April. This morning, between 1 and 2 o'clock, we were alarmed by the ringing of the bell, and upon examination found that the troops, to the number of 800, had stole their march from Boston, in boats and barges, from the bottom of the Common over to a point in Cambridge, near to Inman's Farm, and were at Lexington Meeting-house, half an hour before sunrise, where they had fired upon a body of our men, and (as we afterward heard) had killed several. This intelligence was brought us at first by Dr. Samuel Prescott, who narrowly escaped the guard that were sent before on horses, purposely to prevent all posts and messengers from giving us timely information. He, by the help of a very fleet horse, crossing several walls and fences, arrived at Concord at the time above mentioned; when several posts were immedi-

ately despatched, that returning confirmed the account of the
regulars' arrival at Lexington, and that they were on their way
to Concord. Upon this, a number of our minute-men belong-
ing to this town, and Acton, and Lyncoln, with several others
that were in readiness, marched out to meet them; while the
alarm company were preparing to receive them in the town.
Captain Minot, who commanded them, thought it proper to
take possession of the hill above the meeting-house, as the most
advantageous situation. No sooner had our men gained it,
than we were met by the companies that were sent out to
meet the troops, who informed us, that they were just upon
us, and that we must retreat, as their number was more than
treble ours. We then retreated from the hill near the Liberty
Pole, and took a new post back of the town upon an eminence, where we formed into two battalions, and waited the
arrival of the enemy. Scarcely had we formed, before we saw
the British troops at the distance of a quarter of a mile, glittering in arms, advancing towards us with the greatest celerity.
Some were for making a stand, notwithstanding the superiority of their number; but others more prudent thought best
to retreat till our strength should be equal to the enemy's by
recruits from neighboring towns that were continually coming
in to our assistance. Accordingly we retreated over the bridge,
when the troops came into the town, set fire to several car-
riages for the artillery, destroyed 60 bbls. flour, rifled several
houses, took possession of the town-house, destroyed 500 lb.
of balls, set a guard of 100 men at the North Bridge, and sent
up a party to the house of Colonel Barrett, where they were in
expectation of finding a quantity of warlike stores. But these
were happily secured, just before their arrival, by transportation into the woods and other by-places. In the mean time,
the guard set by the enemy to secure the pass at the North

Bridge were alarmed by the approach of our people, who had retreated, as mentioned before, and were now advancing with special orders not to fire upon the troops unless fired upon. These orders were so punctually observed that we received the fire of the enemy in three several and separate discharges of their pieces before it was returned by our commanding officer; the firing then soon become general for several minutes, in which skirmish two were killed on each side, and several of the enemy wounded. It may here be observed, by the way, that we were the more cautious to prevent beginning a rupture with the King's troops, as we were then uncertain what had happened at Lexington, and knew [not][1] that they had began the quarrel there by first firing upon our people, and killing eight men upon the spot. The three companies of troops soon quitted their post at the bridge, and retreated in the greatest disorder and confusion to the main body, who were soon upon the march to meet them. For half an hour, the enemy, by their marches and counter-marches, discovered great fickleness and inconstancy of mind, sometimes advancing, sometimes returning to their former posts, till, at length they quitted the town, and retreated by the way they came. In the mean time, a party of our men (150) took the back way through the Great Fields into the east quarter, and had placed themselves to advantage, lying in ambush behind walls, fences and buildings, ready to fire upon the enemy on their retreat.'"

Page 78, note 1. Fifty years after his death the town erected a cenotaph to the memory of its brave young minister, whose body lies by the shore of Otter Creek, near Rutland, Vermont. On it they wrote: —

[1] Mr. Emerson believed the "not" had been accidentally omitted, and it can hardly be questioned that he was right in his supposition.

" Enthusiastic, eloquent, affectionate and pious, he loved his family, his people, his God and his Country, and to this last he yielded the cheerful sacrifice of his life."

Page 78, note 2. Town Records, Dec. 1775.

Page 79, note 1. These facts are recorded by Shattuck in his History.

Page 79, note 2. Bradford's *History of Massachusetts,* vol. ii., p. 113.

Page 79, note 3. Shattuck.

Page 80, note 1. Town Records, May 3, 1782

Page 81, note 1. Town Records, Sept. 9, and Bradford's *History,* vol 1, p. 266.

Page 81, note 2. The Rev. Grindall Reynolds, late pastor of the First Church in Concord, wrote an interesting account of Shays's Rebellion, and various papers concerning his adopted town which are included in his *Historical and Other Papers,* published by his daughter in 1895.

Page 81, note 3. Town Records, Oct. 21.

Page 82, note 1. Town Records, May 7.

Page 82, note 2. Town Records, 1834 and 1835. In 1903-4 the town, with a population of about 5000, appropriated for public purposes $65,752, the amount for school purposes being $28,000.

Page 82, note 3. The Unitarian and the " Orthodox " (as the Trinitarian Congregationalist society has always been called in Concord) churches have for a century been good neighbors, and for many years have held union meetings on Thanksgiving Day. At the time of Mr. Emerson's discourse it is doubtful if Concord contained a single Catholic or Episcopalian believer. The beginning of the twentieth century finds a larger body of Catholic worshippers than the four other societies contain. Yet all live in charity with one another.

Page 83, note 1. Mr. Emerson's honored kinsman, Rev. Ezra Ripley, who sat in the pulpit that day, was eighty-four years old, and when, six years later, he died, he had been pastor of the Concord church for sixty-three years.

Page 83, note 2. Lemuel Shattuck, author of the excellent *History of Concord*, which was published before the end of the year.

Page 85, note 1. In Mr. Emerson's lecturing excursions during the following thirty-five years, he found with pleasure and pride the sons of his Concord neighbors important men in the building up the prairie and river towns, or the making and operating the great highways of emigration and trade.

LETTER TO PRESIDENT VAN BUREN

April 19, 1838, Mr. Emerson made this entry in his Journal: —

"This disaster of the Cherokees, brought to me by a sad friend to blacken my days and nights! I can do nothing; why shriek ? why strike ineffectual blows ? I stir in it for the sad reason that no other mortal will move, and if I do not, why, it is left undone. The amount of it, to be sure, is merely a scream; but sometimes a scream is better than a thesis.

.   .   .   .

"Yesterday wrote the letter to Van Buren, — a letter hated of me, a deliverance that does not deliver the soul. I write my journal, I read my lecture with joy; but this stirring in the philanthropic mud gives me no peace. I will let the republic alone until the republic comes to me. I fully sympathize, be sure, with the sentiments I write; but I accept it rather from

mv friends than dictate it   It is not my impulse to say it, and
therefore my genius deserts me; no muse befriends; no music
of thought or word accompanies."

Yet his conscience then, and many a time later, brought
him to do the brave, distasteful duty.

ADDRESS ON EMANCIPATION IN THE BRITISH
WEST INDIES

The tenth anniversary of the emancipation by Act of Parliament of all slaves in the insular possessions of Great Britain
in the West Indies was celebrated in Concord, in the year
1844, by citizens of thirteen Massachusetts towns, and they
invited Mr. Emerson to make the Address. The Rev. Dr.
Channing, on whose mind the wrongs of the slave had weighed
ever since he had seen them in Santa Cruz, had spoken on
Slavery in Faneuil Hall in 1837, had written on the subject,
and his last public work had been a speech on the anniversary
of the West Indian Emancipation in 1842, in the village of
Lenox. The public conscience was slowly becoming aroused,
especially among the country people, who had not the mercantile
and social relations with the Southerner which hampered the
action of many people in the cities   Yet even in Concord the
religious societies appear to have closed their doors against the
philanthropists who gathered to celebrate this anniversary in
1844, but the energy of the young Thoreau, always a champion of Freedom, secured the use of the Court-House, and
he himself rang the bell to call the people together.

It is said that Mr. Emerson, while minister of the Second
Church in Boston, had held his pulpit open to speakers on
behalf of liberty, and to his attitude in 1835 Harriet Martineau

bears witness in her Autobiography. After speaking of the temperamental unfitness of these brother scholars, Charles and Waldo, to become active workers in an Abolitionist organiza- tion, she says: "Yet they did that which made me feel that I knew them through the very cause in which they did not implicate themselves. At the time of the hubbub against me in Boston, Charles Emerson stood alone in a large company and declared that he would rather see Boston in ashes than that I or anybody should be debarred in any way from perfectly free speech. His brother Waldo invited me to be his guest in the midst of my unpopularity, and during my visit told me his course about this matter of slavery. He did not see that there was any particular thing for him to do in it then; but when, in coaches or steamboats or anywhere else, he saw people of color ill treated, or heard bad doctrine or sentiment propounded, he did what he could, and said what he thought. Since that date he has spoken more abundantly and boldly, the more crit- ical the times became; and he is now, and has long been, iden- tified with the Abolitionists in conviction and sentiment, though it is out of his way to join himself to their organization."

Mr. Cabot in his Memoir [1] gives several pages of extracts from Mr. Emerson's journal showing his feelings at this time, before the slave power, aggressive and advancing, left him, as a lover of Freedom, no choice but to fight for her as he could, by tongue and pen, in seasons of peril.

This Address was printed in England, as well as in Amer- ica, the autumn after its delivery here. In a letter to Carlyle written September 1, Mr. Emerson says he is sending proof to the London publisher.

"Chapman wrote to me by the last steamer, urging me to send him some manuscript that had not yet been published in

[1] Vol. ii., pp. 424–433.

America [hoping for copyright, and promising half profits]
. . . The request was so timely, since I was not only printing a book, but also a pamphlet, that I came to town yesterday
and hastened the printers, and have now sent him proofs
of all the Address, and of more than half of the book.'' He
requests Carlyle to have an eye to its correct reproduction,
to which his friend faithfully attended.

Page 100, note 1. It was characteristic of Mr. Emerson
that, as a corrective to the flush of righteous wrath that man
should be capable of

> laying hands on another
> To coin his labor and sweat,

came his sense of justice, and the power of seeing the planter's
side, born into such a social and political condition, by breeding and climatic conditions unable to toil, and with his whole
inheritance vested in slaves In a speech in New York in
1855, Mr Emerson urged emancipation with compensation
to the owners, by general sacrifices to this great end by old
and young throughout the North, not as the planters' due,
but as recognizing their need and losses. Yet with all due consideration for the planters' misfortune of condition, he said,
on the main question, '' It is impossible to be a gentleman and
not be an abolitionist.''

Page 103, note 1.

> Sole estate his sire bequeathed, —
> Hapless sire to hapless son, —
> Was the wailing song he breathed,
> And his chain when life was done.

These lines from '' Voluntaries '' in the *Poems*, and the stanza
which there follows them, are recalled by this passage.

Page 106, note 1. Granville Sharp (1734–1813) was a broad-minded scholar and determined philanthropist. He left the study of law to go into the ordnance office, which he left, when the American Revolution came on, disapproving of the course of the government. In the case of one of the slaves whom he defended, the Lord Mayor discharged the negro, but his master would not give him up. The case then went before the Court of Kings Bench, and the twelve judges decided in 1772 that a man could not be held in, or transported from, England. In June, 1787, Sharp with Clarkson and ten others, nine of whom were Quakers, formed a committee " for effecting the abolition of the slave trade;" Sharp was chairman. Defeated in Parliament in 1788 and 1789, they were joined by Pitt and Fox in 1790. In 1793 the Commons passed an act for gradual abolition of the trade, which was rejected by the Peers This occurred again in 1795 and 1804. In 1806, the Fox and Grenville Ministry brought forward abolition of the trade as a government measure. It was carried in 1807. Then the enemies of slavery began to strive for its gradual abolition throughout the British dominions, Clarkson, Wilberforce and Buxton being the principal leaders. The course of events, however, showed that immediate emancipation would be a better measure. The government brought this forward in 1823, modified by an apprenticeship system. The bill with this feature and some compensation to owners was passed in 1833.

Page 108, note 1. In the essay on Self-Reliance Mr. Emerson said: " An institution is the lengthened shadow of one man; as Monachism, of the Hermit Antony; the Reformation, of Luther; Quakerism, of Fox; Methodism, of Wesley; Abolition, of Clarkson."

Page 112, note 1. The " prædials " seem to have been

the slaves born into captivity, as distinguished from imported slaves.

Page 115, note 1. *Emancipation in the West Indies: A Six Months' Tour in Antigua, Barbadoes and Jamaica, in the year 1837.* By J A. Thome and J. H. Kimball, New York, 1838.

Page 120, note 1. This was very soon after the coronation of the young Queen Victoria, which occurred in the previous year

Page 125, note 1. "All things are moral, and in their boundless changes have an unceasing reference to spiritual nature. Therefore is nature glorious with form, color and motion, that every globe in the remotest heaven, every chemical change from the rudest crystal up to the laws of life . every animal function from the sponge up to Hercules, shall hint or thunder to man the laws of right and wrong, and echo the Ten Commandments." — *Nature, Addresses and Lectures,* p. 40. See also the last sentence in "Prudence," *Essays, First Series.*

Page 131, note 1. "For he [a ruler] is the minister of God to thee for good But if thou do that which is evil, be afraid; for he beareth not the sword in vain for he is the minister of God, a revenger to execute wrath upon him that doeth evil." *Epistle to the Romans,* xiii. 4.

Page 132, note 1. The cause for Mr. Emerson's indignation was great and recent. His honored townsman, Samuel Hoar, Esq., sent by the State of Massachusetts as her commissioner to South Carolina to investigate the seizures, imprisonments, punishments, and even sale of colored citizens of Massachusetts who had committed no crime, had been expelled with threats of violence from the city of Charleston. (See "Samuel Hoar," in *Lectures and Biographical Sketches.*)

Page 133, note 1.

> A union then of honest men,
> Or union never more again.
>
> " Boston." *Poems.*

Page 134, note 1. John Quincy Adams, who, though disapproving, as untimely, the legislation urged on Congress by the abolitionists, yet fought strongly and persistently against the rules framed to check their importunity, as inconsistent with the right of petition itself.

Page 144, note 1. Here comes in the doctrine of the Survival of the Fittest that appears in the " Ode inscribed to W. H. Channing," but, even more than there, tempered by faith in the strength of humanity. See the " Lecture on the Times," given in 1841 (*Nature, Addresses and Lectures,* p. 220), for considerations on slavery more coolly philosophical than Mr. Emerson's warm blood often admitted of, during the strife for liberty in the period between the Mexican and Civil Wars.

Page 145, note 1.

> To-day unbind the captive,
> So only are ye unbound;
> Lift up a people from the dust,
> Trump of their rescue, sound!
>
> " Boston Hymn," *Poems.*

Page 146, note 1. In the early version of the " Boston ' poem were these lines: —

> O pity that I pause!
> The song disdaining shuns
> To name the noble sires, because
> Of the unworthy sons.

> .   .   .   .   .   °

Your town is full of gentle names,
   By patriots once were watchwords made;
Those war-cry names are muffled shames
   On recreant sons mislaid.

WAR

In the winter and early spring of 1838, the American Peace Society held a course of lectures in Boston. This lecture was the seventh in the course. Mr. Alcott wrote in his diary at that time: —

"I heard Emerson's lecture on *Peace*, as the closing discourse of a series delivered at the Odeon before the American Peace Society. . . . After the lecture I saw Mr. Garrison, who is at this time deeply interested in the question of Peace, as are many of the meekest and noblest souls amongst us. He expressed his great pleasure in the stand taken by Mr. Emerson and his hopes in him as a man of the new age. This great topic has been brought before the general mind as a direct consequence of the agitation of the abolition of slavery."

The lecture was printed in 1849 in *Æsthetic Papers*, edited by Miss Elizabeth P. Peabody.

Although the chronicles of the campaigns and acts of prowess of the masterly soldiers were always attractive reading to Mr. Emerson, — much more acts of patriotic devotion in the field, — and he was by no means committed as a non-resistant, he saw that war had been a part of evolution, and that its evils might pave the way for good, as flowers spring up next year on a field of carnage. He knew that evolution required an almost divine patience, yet his good hope was strengthened by the signs of the times, and he desired to hasten the great upward step in civilization.

It is evident from his words and course of action during the outrages upon the peaceful settlers of Kansas, and when Sumter was fired upon and Washington threatened, that he recognized that the hour had not yet come. He subscribed lavishly from his limited means for the furnishing Sharp's rifles to the " Free State men." In the early days of the War of the Rebellion he visited Charlestown Navy-Yard to see the preparations, and said, " Ah! sometimes gunpowder smells good." In the opening of his address at Tufts College, in 'uly, 1861, he said, " The brute noise of cannon has a most poetic echo in these days, as instrument of the primal sentiments of humanity." Several speeches included in this volume show that at that crisis his feeling was, as he had said of the forefathers' " deed of blood " at Concord Bridge, —

> Even the serene Reason says
> It was well done.

But all this was only a postponement of hope.

Page 152, note 1. With regard to schooling a man's courage for whatever may befall, Mr. Emerson said " Our culture therefore must not omit the arming of the man. Let him hear in season that he is born into the state of war, and that the commonwealth and his own well-being require that he should not go dancing in the weeds of peace, but warned, self-collected and neither defying nor dreading the thunder, let him take both reputation and life in his hand, and with perfect urbanity dare the gibbet and the mob by the absolute truth of his speech and the rectitude of his behavior." — " Heroism," *Essays, First Series.*

" A state of war or anarchy, in which law has little force, is so far valuable that it puts every man on trial." — " The Conservative," *Nature, Addresses and Lectures.*

Page 156, note 1. Mr. Emerson used to take pleasure in a story illustrating this common foible of mankind A returned Arctic explorer, in a lecture, said, " In this wilderness among the ice-floes, I had the fortune to see a terrible conflict between two Polar bears — " " Which beat ?" cried an excited voice from the audience

Page 160, note 1. In his description of the Tower of London in the journal of 1834, it appears that the suits of armor there set up affected Mr. Emerson unpleasantly, suggesting half-human destructive lobsters and crabs. It is, I believe, said that Benvenuto Cellini learned to make the cunning joints in armor for men from those of these marine warriors

In the opening paragraphs of the essay on Inspiration Mr. Emerson congratulates himself that the doleful experiences of the aboriginal man were got through with long ago. " They combed his mane, they pared his nails, cut off his tail, set him on end, sent him to school and made him pay taxes, before he could begin to write his sad story for the compassion or the repudiation of his descendants, who are all but unanimous to disown him. We must take him as we find him," etc.

Page 162, note 1. In *English Traits,* at the end of the chapter on Stonehenge, Mr Emerson gave a humorous account of his setting forth the faith or hope of the non-resistants and idealists in New England, to the amazed and shocked ears of Carlyle and Arthur Helps.

Page 164, note 1. " As the solidest rocks are made up of invisible gases, as the world is made of thickened light and arrested electricity, so men know that ideas are the parents of men and things; there was never anything that did not proceed from a thought." — " The Scholar," *Lectures and Biographical Sketches.*

Page 164, note 2. In " The Problem" he says of the Parthenon and England's abbeys that

> out of Thought's interior sphere
> These wonders rose to upper air.

Page 167, note 1. Mr. Emerson in his conversation frankly showed that he was not yet quite prepared to be a non-resistant. He would have surely followed his own counsel where he says, " Go face the burglar in your own house," and he seemed to feel instinctive sympathy with what Mr. Dexter, the counsel, said in the speech which he used to read me from the Selfridge trial· —

" And may my arm drop powerless when it fails to defend my honor ! "

He exactly stated his own position in a later passage, where he says that " in a given extreme event Nature and God will instruct him in that hour."

Page 172, note 1. Thoreau lived frankly and fearlessly up to this standard.

Page 173, note 1. This same view is even more attractively set forth in " Aristocracy" (*Lectures and Biographical Sketches,* pp. 36–40).

Rev. Dr. Cyrus A. Bartol, in an interesting paper on " Emerson's Religion," [1] gives, among other reminiscences, the following. " I asked him if he approved of war. ' Yes,' he said, ' in one born to fight.' "

---

[1] *The Genius and Character of Emerson; Lectures at the Concord School of Philosophy,* edited by F. B Sanborn. Boston: James R Osgood & Co . 1885

THE FUGITIVE SLAVE LAW, CONCORD, 1851

The opening passages of this speech to his friends and neigh-bors show how deeply Mr. Emerson was moved. He could no longer be philosophical, as in the " Ode " inscribed to his friend William Channing, and in earlier addresses. The time had come when he might at any moment be summoned to help the marshal's men seize and return to bondage the poor fugitive who had almost reached the safety of England's pro-tection. Such men were frequently passing through Concord, concealed and helped by the good Bigelow, the blacksmith, and his wife, the Thoreaus, Mrs. Brooks, and even once at a critical moment by her husband, the law-abiding " 'Squire " himself.

Mr. Emerson instantly took his stand, and did not hesitate to run atilt against the dark giant, once so honored. The question of secession for conscience' sake had come up among the Abolitionists. Mr. Emerson had stood for Union, yet felt that there could be nothing but shame in Union until the humiliating statute was repealed. Meanwhile he fell back on the reserve-right of individual revolution as the duty of honest men. The Free-Soilers soon after renominated Dr. John Gorham Palfrey for a seat in Congress, and in his campaign Mr. Emerson delivered this speech in several Middlesex towns. In Cambridge he was interrupted by young men from the college, Southerners, it was said, but it appears that the dis-turbance was quite as much due to " Northern men who were eager to keep up a show of fidelity to the interest of the South," as a Southern student said in a dignified disclaimer. Mr. Cabot

in his Memoir gives an interesting account by Professor James
B. Thayer of Mr. Emerson's calm ignoring of the rude and
hostile demonstration.

Writing to Carlyle, in the end of July, 1857, Mr. Emerson said: "In the spring, the abomination of our Fugitive
Slave Bill drove me to some writing and speech-making, without hope of effect, but to clear my own skirts."

This was the reaction which could not but be felt by him
where he had been forced to descend into the dust and conflict of the arena from the serene heights. He wrote in his
journal next year: —

"Philip Randolph [a valued friend] was surprised to find
me speaking to the politics of anti-slavery in Philadelphia. I
suppose because he thought me a believer in general laws and
that it was a kind of distrust of my own general teachings to
appear in active sympathy with these temporary heats. He is
right so far as it is becoming in the scholar to insist on central
soundness rather than on superficial applications. I am to give
a wise and just ballot, though no man else in the republic doth.
I am to demand the absolute right, affirm that, and do that;
but not push Boston into a showy and theatrical attitude,
endeavoring to persuade her she is more virtuous than she is.
Thereby I am robbing myself more than I am enriching the
public. After twenty, fifty, a hundred years, it will be quite
easy to discriminate who stood for the right, and who for the
expedient."

Yet however hard the duty of the hour might be, Mr.
Emerson never failed in his duty as a good citizen to come
to the front in dark days.

"In spite of all his gracefulness and reserve and love of the
unbroken tranquillity of serene thought, he was by the right
of heredity a belligerent in the cause of Freedom."

Page 181, note 1. Shadrach was hurried to Concord after his rescue, and by curious coincidence Edwin Bigelow, the good village blacksmith who there harbored him and drove him to the New Hampshire line, was one of the jurors in the trial of another rescue case.

Page 183, note 1. Mr. Emerson wrote in his journal, after Mr. Hoar's return —

"The position of Massachusetts seems to me to be better for Mr. Hoar's visit to South Carolina in this point, that one illusion is dispelled. Massachusetts was dishonored before, but she was credulous in the protection of the Constitution, and either did not believe, or affected not to believe in that she was dishonored. Now all doubt on that subject is removed, and every Carolina boy will not fail to tell every Massachusetts boy whenever they meet how the fact stands. The Boston merchants would willingly salve the matter over, but they cannot hereafter receive Southern gentlemen at their tables without a consciousness of shame."

Page 192, note 1. Apparently from Vattel, book 1., ch. 1., p. 79.

Page 201, note 1.

But there was chaff within the flour,
    And one was false in ten,
And reckless clerks in lust of power
    Forgot the rights of men;
Cruel and blind did file their mind,
And sell the blood of human kind.

Your town is full of gentle names
    By patriots once were watchwords made;
Those war-cry names are muffled shames
    On recreant sons mislaid.

What slave shall dare a name to wear
Once Freedom's passport everywhere?
                      See note to poem " Boston."

Mr. Charles Francis Adams's *Life of Richard H. Dana*
gives light on the phrase used in the first of these verses. The
following passage is from Mr. Dana's journal during the trial
of Anthony Burns, the fugitive: —

"Choate, I had an amusing interview with. I asked him
to make one effort in favor of freedom, and told him that the
1850 delusion was dispelled and all men were coming round,
the Board of Brokers and Board of Aldermen were talking
treason, and that he must come and act. He said he should
be glad to make an effort on our side, but that he had given
written opinions against us in the Sims case on every point,
and that he could not go against them.

"'You corrupted your mind in 1850.'
"'Yes. Filed my mind.'
"'I wish you would file it in court for our benefit.'"

Shakspeare said, —

"For Banquo's issue have I filed my mind."

Page 202, note 1. Mr. F. B. Sanborn, in his *Life of
Thoreau*, says that Webster gave, as a reason for not visiting
Concord in his later years, that "Many of those whom I so
highly esteemed in your beautiful and quiet village have become a good deal estranged, to my great grief, by abolitionism,
free-soilism, transcendentalism and other notions which I cannot but regard as so many vagaries of the imagination."

Page 204, note 1.

Or who, with accent bolder,
Dare praise the freedom-loving mountaineer?

I found by thee, O rushing Contoocook!
And in thy valleys, Agiochook!
The jackals of the negro-holder.

. . . .

Virtue palters, Right is hence;
Freedom praised, but hid;
Funeral eloquence
Rattles the coffin-lid.
                    Poems, " Ode," inscribed to W. H. Channing.

See also what is said of " the treachery of scholars " in the
last pages of " The Man of Letters," *Lectures and Biographical Sketches.*

Page 209, note 1. This appeal for a general movement in
the free states to free the slaves and to recompense the planters, unhappily brought up to the institution, for their loss, was so
much better in an anti-slavery address in New York, in 1855,
than in the Concord speech four years earlier, that I have sub-
stituted the later version here. In Mr. Cabot's Memoir,
pp. 558–593, a portion of the New York speech, including
this paragraph, is given.

THE FUGITIVE SLAVE LAW, NEW YORK, 1854

Writing to his friend Carlyle on March 11, 1854, Mr.
Emerson said : —

" One good word closed your letter in September . . .
namely, that you might come westward when Frederic was
disposed of Speed Frederic, then, for all reasons and for this !
America is growing furiously, town and state; new Kansas,
new Nebraska looming up in these days, vicious politicians

seething a wretched destiny for them already at Washington.
The politicians shall be sodden, the States escape, please God!
The fight of slave and freeman drawing nearer, the question is
sharply, whether slavery or whether freedom shall be abolished.
Come and see.''

Four days before thus writing, he had given this address, to a
fairly large audience, in the " Tabernacle " in New York City,
for, however dark the horizon looked, the very success of the
slave power was working its ruin. Encouraged by the submission of the North to the passage of the evil law to pacify them,
they had resolved to repeal the Missouri Compromise, which
confined slavery to a certain latitude. It was repealed within
a few days of the time Mr. Emerson made this address. During the debate, Charles Sumner said to Douglas, '' Sir, the
bill you are about to pass is at once the worst and the best on
which Congress has ever acted. . . . It is the worst bill
because it is a present victory for slavery. . . . Sir, it is the
best bill on which Congress has ever acted, *for it annuls all
past compromises with slavery and makes any future compromises impossible*. Thus it puts Freedom and Slavery face to
face and bids them grapple. Who can doubt the result ? ''
The rendition to slavery of Anthony Burns from Boston in
May wrought a great change in public feeling there. Even
the commercial element in the North felt the shame.

Though not a worker in the anti-slavery organization, Mr.
Emerson had always been the outspoken friend of freedom for
the negroes. Witness his tribute in 1837 to Elijah Lovejoy,
the martyr in their cause (see " Heroism," *Essays, First
Series*, p. 262, and note). But the narrow and uncharitable
speech and demeanor of many " philanthropists " led him to
such reproofs as the one quoted by Dr. Bartol, '' Let them
first be anthropic,'' or that in " Self-Reliance '' to the angry

bigot: " Go love thy infant; love thy wood-chopper; be good-natured and modest; have that grace; and never varnish your hard, uncharitable ambition with this incredible tenderness for black folk a thousand miles off."

But now the foe was at the very gate The duty to resist was instant and commanding. Mr. Emerson wrote in his journal, soon after. —

" Why do we not say, We are abolitionists of the most absolute abolition, as every man that is a man must be ? . . . We do not try to alter your laws in Alabama, nor yours in Japan, or in the Feejee Islands; but we do not admit them, or permit a trace of them here. Nor shall we suffer you to carry your Thuggism, north, south, east or west into a single rod of territory which we control. We intend to set and keep a *cordon sanitaire* all around the infected district, and by no means suffer the pestilence to spread.

" It is impossible to be a gentleman, and not be an abolitionist, for a gentleman is one who is fulfilled with all nobleness, and imparts it, is the natural defender and raiser of the weak and oppressed."

With Mr. Emerson's indignation at Webster's fall was mingled great sorrow. From his youth he had admired and revered him. The verses about him printed in the Appendix to the *Poems* show the change of feeling. He used to quote Browning's " Lost Leader " as applying to him, and admired Whittier's fine poem " Ichabod " (" The glory is departed," I. Samuel, iv., 21, 22) on his apostasy.

Mr. Emerson's faithfulness to his sense of duty, leading him, against his native instincts, into the turmoil of politics, striving to undo the mischief that a leader once revered had wrought in the minds of Americans, is shown in the extract from his journal with regard to this lecture. —

"At New York Tabernacle, on the 7th March, I saw the great audience with dismay, and told the bragging secretary that I was most thankful to those that staid at home; every auditor was a new affliction, and if all had staid away, by rain or preoccupation, I had been best pleased."

Page 217, note 1. In *Lectures and Biographical Sketches,* in the essay on Aristocracy, and also in that on The Man of Letters, the duty of loyalty to his thought and his order is urged as a trait of the gentleman and the scholar, and in the latter essay, the scholar's duty to stand for what is generous and free.

Page 219, note 1. Mr. Emerson in his early youth did come near slavery for a short time. His diary at St. Augustine, quoted by Mr. Cabot in his Memoir, mentions that, while he was attending a meeting of the Bible Society, a slave-auction was going on outside, but it does not appear that he actually saw it.

Page 221, note 1. Carlyle described Webster as "a magnificent specimen. . . . As a Logic-fencer, Advocate, or Parliamentary Hercules, one would incline to back him at first sight against all the extant world. The tanned complexion, that amorphous, crag-like face, the dull black eyes under their precipice of brows, like dull anthracite furnaces needing only to be blown, the mastiff-mouth, accurately closed: —I have not traced as much of *silent Berserkir-rage,* that I remember of, in any other man." [1]

Page 225, note 1. Mr. James S. Gibbons (of the *New York Tribune*) in a letter written to his son two days after this speech was delivered, says, referring evidently to this passage: —

"Emerson gave us a fine lecture on Webster. He made

[1] *Correspondence of Carlyle and Emerson,* vol i., pp 260, 261.

him stand before us in the proportions of a giant, and then with one word crushed him to powder.''

Page 226, note 1. Professor John H. Wright of Harvard University has kindly furnished me with the passage from Dio Cassius, xlvii. 49, where it is said of Brutus. —

Καὶ ἀναβοήσας τοῦτο δὴ ‘Ηράκλειον

ὦ τλῆμον ἀρετή, λόγος ἄρ’ ἦσθ’, ἐγὼ δέ σε

ὡς ἔργον ἤσκουν· σὺ δ’ ἄρ’ ἐδούλευες τύχῃ, —

παρακάλεσέ τινα τῶν συνόντων, ἵν’ αὐτὸν ἀποκτείνῃ, —

which he renders, '' He cried out this sentiment of Heracles, ‘ O wretched Virtue, after all, thou art a name, but I cherished thee as a fact. Fortune's slave wast thou; ’ and called upon one of those with him to slay him.''

Professor Wright adds that Theodorus Prodromus, a Byzantine poet of the twelfth century, said, '' What Brutus says (O Virtue, etc.) I pronounce to be ignoble and unworthy of Brutus's soul.'' It seems very doubtful whence the Greek verses came.

Page 233, note 1. Just ten years earlier, Hon. Samuel Hoar, the Commissioner of Massachusetts, sent to Charleston, South Carolina, in the interests of our colored citizens there constantly imprisoned and ill used, had been expelled from that state with a show of force. See *Lectures and Biographical Sketches.*

Page 234, note 1. The sending back of Onesimus by Paul was a precedent precious in the eyes of pro-slavery preachers, North and South, in those days, ignoring, however, Paul's message, '' Not now as a servant, but above a servant, a brother beloved, specially to me, but how much more unto thee, both in the flesh and in the Lord. If thou count me therefore a partner, receive him as myself.'' [1]

[1] *Epistle of Paul to Philemon,* i. 16, 17.

Page 235, note 1. The hydrostatic paradox has been before alluded to as one of Mr. Emerson's favorite symbols, the balancing of the ocean by a few drops of water. In many places he dwells on the power of minorities — a minority of one. In " Character " (*Lectures and Biographical Sketches*) he says, " There was a time when Christianity existed in one child." For the value and duty of minorities, see *Conduct of Life,* pp. 249 ff.*, Letters and Social Aims,* pp. 219, 220.

Page 236, note 1. This was a saying of Mahomet. What follows, with regard to the divine sentiments always soliciting us, is thus rendered in " My Garden: "

> Ever the words of the gods resound;
> But the porches of man's ear
> Seldom in this low life's round
> Are unsealed, that he may hear.

Page 236, note 2. This is the important key to the essay on Self-Reliance.

Page 238, note 1. In the " Sovereignty of Ethics " Mr. Emerson quotes an Oriental poet describing the Golden Age as saying that God had made justice so dear to the heart of Nature that, if any injustice lurked anywhere under the sky, the blue vault would shrivel to a snake-skin, and cast it out by spasms.

Page 240, note 1. There seems to be some break in the construction here probably due to the imperfect adjustment of lecture-sheets. It would seem that the passage should read. " Liberty is never cheap. It is made difficult because freedom is the accomplishment and perfectness of man — the finished man; earning and bestowing good; " etc.

Page 241, note 1. See *Lectures and Biographical Sketches,* pp. 246 and 251.

Page 242, note 1. The occasion alluded to was Hon. Robert C. Winthrop's speech to the alumni of Harvard College on Commencement Day in 1852. What follows is not an abstract, but Mr. Emerson's rendering of the spirit of his address.

THE ASSAULT UPON MR. SUMNER

One evening in May, Judge Hoar came to Mr Emerson's house, evidently deeply stirred, and told in a few words the startling news that the great Senator from Massachusetts had been struck down at his desk by a Representative from South Carolina, and was dangerously hurt. The news was heard with indignant grief in Concord, and a public meeting was held four days later in which Mr. Emerson and others gave vent to this feeling.

Among Mr. Emerson's papers are the fragmentary notes on Sumner, given below, without indication as to when they were used.

CHARLES SUMNER

Clean, self-poised, great-hearted man, noble in person, incorruptible in life, the friend of the poor, the champion of the oppressed.

Of course Congress must draw from every part of the country swarms of individuals eager only for private interests, who could not love his stern justice. But if they gave him no high employment, he made low work high by the dignity of honesty and truth. But men cannot long do without faculty and perseverance, and he rose, step by step, to the mastery of all affairs intrusted to him, and by those lights and upliftings with which the spirit that makes the Universe rewards labor and brave truth. He became learned, and adequate to the highest questions, and the counsellor of every correction of old errors, and of every noble reform. How nobly he bore himself in disastrous times. Every reform he led or assisted. In the shock of the war his patriotism never failed. A man of varied learning and accomplishments.

He held that every man is to be judged by the horizon of his mind, and Fame he defined as the shadow of excellence, but that which follows him, not which he follows after.

Tragic character, like Algernon Sydney, man of conscience and courage, but without humor. Fear did not exist for him. In his mind the American idea is no crab, but a man incessantly advancing, as the shadow of the dial or the heavenly body that casts it. The American idea is emancipation, to abolish kingcraft, feudalism, black-letter monopoly, it pulls down the gallows, explodes priestcraft, opens the doors of the sea to all emigrants, extemporizes government in new country.

Sumner has been collecting his works. They will be the history of the Republic for the last twenty-five years, as told by a brave, perfectly honest and well instructed man, with social culture and relation to all eminent persons. Diligent and able workman, with rare ability, without genius, without humor, but with persevering study, wide reading, excellent memory, high stand of honor (and pure devotion to his country), disdaining any bribe, any compliances, and incapable of falsehood. His singular advantages of person, of manners, and a statesman's conversation impress every one favorably. He has the foible of most public men, the egotism which seems almost unavoidable at Washington. I sat in his room once at Washington whilst he wrote a weary procession of letters, — he writing without pause as fast as if he were copying. He outshines all his mates in historical conversation, and is so public in his regards that he cannot be relied on to push an office-seeker, so that he is no favorite with politicians. But wherever I have met with a dear lover of the country and its moral interests, he is sure to be a supporter of Sumner.

It characterizes a man for me that he hates Charles Sumner: for it shows that he cannot discriminate between a foible and a vice. Sumner's moral instinct and character are so exceptionally pure that he must have perpetual magnetism for honest men; his ability and working energy such, that every good friend of the Republic must stand by him. Those who come near him and are offended by his egotism, or his foible (if you please) of using classic quotations, or other bad tastes, easily forgive these whims, if themselves are good, or magnify them into disgust, if they themselves are incapable of his virtue.

And when he read one night in Concord a lecture on Lafayette we felt that of all Americans he was best entitled by his own character and fortunes to read that eulogy.

Every Pericles must have his Cleon: Sumner had his adversaries, his wasps and back-biters. We almost wished that he had not stooped to answer them. But he condescended to give them truth and patriotism, without asking whether they could appreciate the instruction or not.

A man of such truth that he can be truly described: he needs no exaggerated praise. Not a man of extraordinary genius, but a man of great heart, of a perpetual youth, with the highest sense of honor, incapable of any fraud, little or large; loving his friend and loving his country, with perfect steadiness to his purpose, shunning no labor that his aim required, and his works justified him by their scope and thoroughness.

He had good masters, who quickly found that they had a good scholar. He read law with Judge Story, who was at the head of the Law School at Harvard University, and who speedily discovered the value of his pupil, and called him to his assistance in the Law School. He had a great talent for labor, and spared no time and no research to make himself master of his subject. His treatment of every question was faithful and exhaustive, and marked always by the noble sentiment.

Page 252, *note 1*. With this message of comfort to Sumner, struck down for his defence of Liberty, may be contrasted what is said of Webster when he abandoned her cause: —

" Those to whom his name was once dear and honored, as the manly statesman to whom the choicest gifts of Nature had been accorded, disown him: . . . he who was their pride in the woods and mountains of New England is now their mortification, — they have torn his picture from the wall, they have thrust his speeches into the chimney," etc. — " Address on the Fugitive Slave Law," at Concord, 1851.

SPEECH ON AFFAIRS IN KANSAS

By an act of Congress, passed in May, 1854, the territories of Kansas and Nebraska were organized, and in a section of that act it was declared that the Constitution and all the laws of the United States should be in force in these territories, except the Missouri Compromise Act of 1820, which was declared inoperative and void. The act thereby repealed had confined slavery to the region of the Louisiana Purchase south of latitude 36°, 30′ North. Foreseeing the probable success of this measure to increase the area of slavery, Emigrant Aid Societies had been formed in Massachusetts first, and later, in Connecticut, which assisted Northern emigrants to the settlement of this fertile region. Settlers from the Northwestern States also poured in, and also from Missouri, the latter bringing slaves with them. A fierce struggle, lasting for some years and attended with bloodshed and barbarities, began at once, hordes of armed men from the border state of Missouri constantly voting at Kansas elections and intimidating the free state settlers, and even driving parties of immigrants out of the state. Franklin Pierce was then President, and threw the influence and power of the administration on the side of the pro-slavery party in Kansas. Despairing of redress from Washington, the settlers from the free states appealed in their distress to their friends at home, and sent Mr. Whitman, Rev. Mr. Nute, and later, John Brown, to make known to them their wrongs, and ask moral and material aid, especially arms to defend their rights, and reinforcements of brave settlers. Meetings were held, not only in the cities, but in the country towns, and, certainly in the latter, were well attended by earnest people who gave, a few from their wealth, but many from their poverty, large sums to help "bleeding Kansas." In response to the petitions of the friends of Freedom, who urged the Legislature of Massachusetts to come to the rescue, a joint committee was appointed by the General Court to consider the petitions for a state appropriation of ten thousand dollars to protect the interests of the North and the rights of her citizens in Kansas, should they be again invaded by Southern marauders. John Brown addressed this committee

in February, 1856. He made a clear and startling statement
of the outrages he had witnessed and the brave struggles of
the settlers, and told of the murder and imprisonment and
maltreatment of his sons, seven of whom were in Kansas
with him during the struggle.[1]

Mr. Emerson always attended the meetings in aid of Kansas
in Concord, gave liberally to the cause, and spoke there and
elsewhere when called upon.

Page 263, note 1. George Bancroft, the historian, said of
the conclusion of this speech: —

"Emerson as clearly as any one, perhaps more clearly than
any one at the time, saw the enormous dangers that were gathering over the Constitution. . . . It would certainly be difficult, perhaps impossible, to find any speech made in the same
year that is marked with so much courage and foresight as this
of Emerson. . . . Even after the inauguration of Lincoln
several months passed away before his Secretary of State or
he himself saw the future so clearly as Emerson had fore-
shadowed it in 1856."[2]

[1] See the report of this speech in Redpath's *Life of Captain John Brown.*
Boston: Thayer & Eldridge, 1860
[2] "Review of Holmes's Life of Emerson," *North American Review,*
February, 1885.

JOHN BROWN: SPEECH AT BOSTON

Mr. F B. Sanborn, in his *Familiar Letters of Thoreau,* says that he introduced John Brown to Thoreau in March, 1857, and Thoreau introduced him to Emerson. This was at the time when Brown came on to awaken the people of Massachusetts to the outrages which the settlers and their families were suffering, and procure aid for them. His clear-cut face, smooth-shaven and bronzed, his firmly shut mouth and mild but steady blue eyes, gave him the appearance of the best type of old New England farmers; indeed he might well have passed for a rustic brother of Squire Hoar Mr. Emerson was at once interested in him and the story of the gallant fight that the Free-State men in Kansas were making, though Brown was very modest about his own part and leadership Indeed he claimed only to be a fellow worker and adviser. I think that soon after this time, on one of his visits to Concord, he stayed at Mr. Emerson's house; certainly he spent the evening there. The last time he came to Concord he was a changed man, all the pleasant look was gone. His gray hair, longer and brushed upright, his great gray beard and the sharpening of his features by exposure and rude experiences gave him a wild, fierce expression. His speech in the Town Hall was excited, and when he drew a huge sheath-knife from under his coat and showed it as a symbol of Missouri civilization, and last drew from his bosom a horse-chain and clanked it in air, telling that his son had been bound with this and led bareheaded under a burning sun beside their horses, by United States dragoons, and in the mania brought on by this inhuman treatment had worn the rusty chain bright, — the old man

recalled the fierce Balfour of Burley in Scott's *Old Mortality*.
It was a startling sight and sent a thrill through his hearers.
Yet on earlier occasions his speech had been really more effective, when a quiet farmer of mature years, evidently self-con-
tained, intelligent, truthful and humane, simply told in New
England towns what was going on in Kansas, the outrages
committed upon the settlers, the violation of their elementary
rights under the Constitution, — and all this connived at by
the general government. He opened the eyes of his hearers,
even against their wills, to the alarming pass into which the
slave power had brought the affairs of the country.

But now wrong and outrage, not only on others but ter-
ribly suffered in his own family, had made Brown feel that
not he but " Slavery was an outlaw " against which he " held
a commission direct from God Almighty " to act. A friend
quoted him as having said, " The loss of my family and the
troubles in Kansas have shattered my constitution, and I am
nothing to the world but to defend the right, and that, by
God's help, I have done and will do."

The people were not ready to follow him in revolutionary
measures, but when on his own responsibility he had precipi-
tated the inevitable conflict by breaking with a government,
then so unrighteous, and offered his life as a sacrifice for
humanity, they could not but do homage to him as a hero, who
was technically a traitor. He had cut the Gordian knot which
they had suffered to be tied tighter.

Of course Mr. Emerson had known nothing of John Brown's
plan for a raid into the slave states. It was the motive and
courage he honored, not the means. He wrote: " I wish
we should have health enough to know virtue when we see it,
and not cry with the fools and the newspapers, ' Madman! '
when a hero passes."

On the first day of November, John Brown had been sentenced to death. This meeting in Boston, to give aid to his
family, was held on the eighteenth, just two weeks before his
execution.

The verses which serve as motto are from Mr. Edmund
Clarence Stedman's poem written at the time, which Mr.
Emerson used to read aloud to his family and friends with
much pleasure.

Page 269, note 1. " This court acknowledges, I suppose,
the validity of the Law of God. I see a book kissed here
which I suppose to be the Bible, or, at least, the New Testament That teaches me that all things ' whatsoever I would
that men should do unto me, I should do even so to them.'
It teaches me further to ' remember them which are in bonds
as bound with them ' I endeavored to act up to that instruction I say I am yet too young to understand that God is any
respecter of persons. I believe that to have interfered as I have
done, as I have always freely admitted that I have done, in
behalf of His despised poor, was not wrong, but right. Now,
if it is deemed necessary that I should forfeit my life for the
furtherance of the ends of justice, and mingle my blood further
with the blood of my children, and with the blood of millions
in this slave country whose rights are disregarded by wicked,
cruel and unjust enactments — I submit: so let it be done."
From the Speech of John Brown to the Court.

Page 270, note 1. Among the sheets of the lecture
" Courage " is one which seems to have been used at that
time —

" Governor Wise and Mr. Mason no doubt have some
right to their places. It is some superiority of working brain
that put them there, and the aristocrats in every society. But

when they come to deal with Brown, they find that he speaks
their own speech, — has whatever courage and directness they
have, and a great deal more of the same; so that they feel
themselves timorous little fellows in his hand; he outsees, out-
thinks, outacts them, and they are forced to shuffle and stam-
mer in their turn.

"'They painfully feel this, that he is their governor and superior, and the only alternative is to kneel to him if they are
truly noble, or else (if they wish to keep their places), to
put this fact which they know, out of sight of other people,
as fast as they can. Quick, drums and trumpets strike up!
Quick, judges and juries, silence him, by sentence and execution of sentence, and hide in the ground this alarming fact.
For, if everything comes to its right place, he goes up, and
we down.''

Page 271, note 1. Commodore Hiram Paulding, in 1857,
had broken up Walker's filibustering expedition at Nicaragua.
The arrest of Walker on foreign soil the government did not
think it wise wholly to approve.

Page 272, note 1. The allusion is to the trials of the fugitives Shadrach, Sims and Burns in Boston. The story of these
humiliations is told in full and in a most interesting manner in
the diary of Richard H. Dana,[1] whose zeal in the cause of
these poor men did him great honor.

During the trial of Sims, a chain was put up, as a barrier
against the crowd, around the United States Court-House, and

---

[1] *Richard Henry Dana; a Biography* By Charles Francis Adams
Houghton, Mifflin & Co , 1890. In chapter viii. of this book is a very
remarkable account of John Brown and his family at their home at North
Elba in 1849, when Mr Dana and a friend, lost in the Adirondac woods,
chanced to come out upon the Brown clearing and were kindly received and
aided.

the stooping of the judges to creep under this chain in order to enter the court-house was considered symbolic of their abject attitude towards the aggressive slave power.

JOHN BROWN· SPEECH AT SALEM

The second of December, on which day John Brown was executed at Charlestown, Virginia, was bright in that State, but in New England was of a strange sultriness with a wind from the south and a lowering sky At noon, the hour appointed for his death, in Concord (as in many New England towns) the men and women who honored his character and motives gathered and made solemn observance of a day and event which seemed laden with omens There was a prayer, I think offered by the Rev. Edmund Sears of Wayland,[1] Mr. Emerson read William Allingham's beautiful poem "The Touchstone" which is used as the motto to this speech, Thoreau read with sad bitterness Sir Walter Raleigh's "The Soule's Errand." Hon. John S. Keyes read some appropriate verses from Aytoun's "Execution of Montrose" and Mr. Sanborn a poem which he had written for the occasion.

Page 279, note 1. Here, as often in Mr. Emerson's speech

[1] While waiting for the services to begin, Mr. Sears wrote some verses The following lines, which Mrs Emerson saw him write, were a prophecy literally fulfilled within three years by the Union armies singing the John Brown song. —

> "But not a pit six feet by two
> Can hold a man like thee ;
> John Brown shall tramp the shaking earth
> From Blue Ridge to the sea."

and writing, is shown his respect for the old religion of New England and its effect on the thought and character of her people. As Lowell said of them in his Concord Ode in 1875: —

" And yet the enduring half they chose,
  Whose choice decides a man life's slave or king,
  The invisible things of God before the seen and known."

Page 279, note 2 I well remember the evening, in my school-boy days, when John Brown, in my father's house, told of his experiences as a sheep-farmer, and his eye for animals and power over them. He said he knew at once a strange sheep in his flock of many hundred, and that he could always make a dog or cat so uncomfortable as to wish to leave the room, simply by fixing his eyes on it.

Page 281, note 1. " Heroism feels and never reasons, and therefore is always right; and although a different breeding, different religion and greater intellectual activity would have modified or even reversed the particular action, yet, for the hero, that thing he does is the highest deed, and is not open to the censure of philosophers and divines." — " Heroism," *Essays, First Series.*

" I can leave to God the time and means of my death, for I believe now that the sealing of my testimony before God and man with my blood will do far more to further the cause to which I have earnestly devoted myself than anything else I have done in my life." — Letter of John Brown to a friend.

THEODORE PARKER

Theodore Parker, worn by his great work in defence of liberal religion and in every cause of suffering humanity, had succumbed to disease and died in Florence in May, 1860, not quite fifty years of age. Born in the neighbor town of Lexington when Emerson was seven years old, they had been friends probably from the time when the latter, soon after settling in Concord, preached for the society at East Lexington, from 1836 for two years. Parker was, during this period, studying divinity, and was settled as pastor of the West Roxbury church in 1837. In that year he is mentioned by Mr. Alcott as a member of the Transcendental Club and attending its meetings in Boston. When, in June, 1838, Mr. Emerson fluttered the conservative and the timid by his Divinity School Address, the young Parker went home and wrote, " It was the most inspiring strain I ever listened to. . . . My soul is roused, and this week I shall write the long-meditated sermons on the state of the church and the duties of these times."

Mr. Parker was one of those who attended the gathering in Boston which gave birth to the *Dial*, to which he was a strong contributor. Three years after its death, he, with the help of Mr. James Elliot Cabot and Mr. Emerson, founded the *Massachusetts Quarterly Review*, vigorous though short-lived, of which he was the editor. Parker frequently visited Emerson, and the two, unlike in their method, worked best apart in the same great causes. Rev. William Gannett says, " What Emerson uttered without plot or plan, Theodore

Parker elaborated to a system. Parker was the Paul of transcendentalism.''

Mr. Edwin D. Mead, in his chapter on Emerson and
Theodore Parker,[1] gives the following pleasant anecdote: —

" At one of Emerson's lectures in Boston, when the storm
against Parker was fiercest, a lecture at which a score of the
religious and literary leaders of the city were present, Emerson,
as he laid his manuscript upon the desk and looked over the
audience, after his wont, observed Parker; and immediately
he stepped from the platform to the seat near the front where
Parker sat, grasping his hand and standing for a moment's
conversation with him. It was not ostentation, and it was
not patronage: it was admiring friendship, — and that fortification and stimulus Parker in those times never failed to feel.
It was Emerson who fed his lamp, he said; and Emerson said
that, be the lamp fed as it might, it was Parker whom the
time to come would have to thank for finding the light burning.''

Parker dedicated to Emerson his *Ten Sermons on Religion*.
In acknowledging this tribute, Mr. Emerson thus paid tribute
to Parker's brave service: —

" We shall all thank the right soldier whom God gave
strength to fight for him the battle of the day.''

When Mr. Parker's failing forces made it necessary for him
to drop his arduous work and go abroad for rest, Mr. Emerson was frequently called to take his place in the Music Hall
on Sundays. I think that this was the only pulpit he went
into to conduct Sunday services after 1838.

It is told that Parker, sitting, on Sunday morning, on the
deck of the vessel that was bearing him away, never to return,

[1] In the very interesting work *The Influence of Emerson*, published in
Boston in 1903, by the American Unitarian Association.

smiled and said: " Emerson is preaching at Music Hall to-
day."

Page 286, note 1. Mr. Emerson wrote in his journal: —
" The Duc de Brancas said, ' Why need I read the Encyclo-
pédie? Rivarol visits me.' I may well say it of Theodore
Parker."

Page 290, note 1. Richard H. Dana wrote in his diary,
November 3, 1852: —
" It is now ten days since Webster's death. . . . Strange
that the best commendation that has appeared yet, the most
touching, elevated, meaning eulogy, with all its censure, should
have come from Theodore Parker! Were I Daniel Webster,
I would not have that sermon destroyed for all that had been
said in my favor as yet."

Page 293, note 1 I copy from Mr. Emerson's journal at
the time of Mr. Parker's death these sentences which precede
some of those included in this address. —
" Theodore Parker has filled up all his years and days and
hours. A son of the energy of New England; restless, eager,
manly, brave, early old, contumacious, clever. I can well
praise him at a spectator's distance, for our minds and methods
were unlike, — few people more unlike. All the virtues are
solitaires Each man is related to persons who are not related
to each other, and I saw with pleasure that men whom I
could not approach, were drawn through him to the admiration of that which I admire."

AMERICAN CIVILIZATION

On January 31, 1862, Mr. Emerson lectured at the Smith-
sonian Institution in Washington on American Civilization.
Just after the outbreak of war in the April preceding, he had
given a lecture, in a course in Boston on Life and Literature,
which he called " Civilization at a Pinch," the title suggesting how it had been modified by the crisis which had suddenly
come to pass. In the course of the year the flocking of slaves
to the Union camps, and the opening vista of a long and bitter
struggle, with slavery now acknowledged as its root, had
brought the question of Emancipation as a war-measure to the
front. Of course Mr. Emerson saw hope in this situation of
affairs, and when he went to Washington with the chance
of being heard by men in power there, he prepared himself
to urge the measure, as well on grounds of policy as of right.
So the Boston lecture was much expanded to deal with the
need of the hour. There is no evidence that President Lincoln
heard it; it is probable that he did not; nor is it true that Mr.
Emerson had a long and earnest conversation with him on the
subject next day, both of which assertions have been made in
print. Mr. Emerson made an unusual record in his journal of
the incidents of his stay in Washington, and though he tells
of his introduction to Mr. Lincoln and a short chat with him,
evidently there was little opportunity for serious conversation.
The President's secretaries had, in 1886, no memory of his
having attended the lecture, and the Washington papers do
not mention his presence there. The following notice of the
lecture, however, appeared in one of the local papers: " The

audience received it, as they have the other anti-slavery lectures of the course, with unbounded enthusiasm. It was in many respects a wonderful lecture, and those who have often heard Mr. Emerson said that he seemed inspired through nearly the whole of it, especially the part referring to slavery and the war.''

A gentleman in Washington, who took the trouble to look up the question as to whether Mr. Lincoln and other high officials heard it, says that Mr. Lincoln could hardly have attended lectures then: —

'' He was very busy at the time, Stanton the new war secretary having just come in, and storming like a fury at the business of his department   The great operations of the war for the time overshadowed all the other events. . . . It is worth remarking that Mr. Emerson in this lecture clearly fore-shadowed the policy of Emancipation some six or eight months in advance of Mr. Lincoln   He saw the logic of events lead ing up to a crisis in our affairs, to ' emancipation as a platform with compensation to the loyal owners ' (his words as reported in the *Star*). The notice states that the lecture was very fully attended.''

Very possibly it may be with regard to this address that we have the interesting account given of the effect of Mr. Emerson's speaking on a well-known English author. Dr. Garnett, in his *Life of Emerson*, says: —

'' A shrewd judge, Anthony Trollope, was particularly struck with the note of sincerity in Emerson when he heard him address a large meeting during the Civil War. Not only was the speaker terse, perspicuous, and practical to a degree amazing to Mr. Trollope's preconceived notions, but he commanded his hearers' respect by the frankness of his dealing with them. ' You make much of the American eagle,' he

said, ' you do well But beware of the American peacock.'
When shortly afterwards Mr. Trollope heard the consum-
mate rhetorician, ——— ——— he discerned at once that
oratory was an end with him, instead of, as with Emerson, a
means. He was neither bold nor honest, as Emerson had
been, and the people knew that while pretending to lead
them he was led by them."

Mr. Emerson revised the lecture and printed it in the *Atlantic Monthly* for April, 1862. It was afterwards separated
into the essay " Civilization," treating of the general and permanent aspects of the subject (printed in *Society and Solitude*),
and this urgent appeal for the instant need.

The few lines inspired by the Flag are from one of the
verse-books.

Page 298, note 1. Mr. Emerson himself was by no means
free from pecuniary anxieties and cares in those days.

Journal, 1862. " Poverty, sickness, a lawsuit, even bad,
dark weather, spoil a great many days of the scholar's year,
hinder him of the frolic freedom necessary to spontaneous flow
of thought."

Page 300, note 1. This was during the days of apparent
inaction when, after the first reverses or minor successes of
the raw Northern armies, the magnitude of the task before
them and the energy of their opponents was realized, and
recruiting, fortification, organization was going on in earnest
in preparation for the spring campaign. General Scott had resigned; General McClellan was doing his admirable work of
creating a fit army, and Secretary Cameron had been succeeded
by the energetic and impatient Stanton. But the government
was still very shy of meddling with slavery for fear of disaf-
fecting the War Democrats and especially the Border States.

xi

Page 307, note 1. A short time before this address was delivered Mr. Moncure D. Conway (a young Virginian, who, for conscience' sake, had left his charge as a Methodist preacher and had abandoned his inheritance in slaves, losing in so doing the good will of his parents, and become a Unitarian minister and an abolitionist) had read in Concord an admirable and eloquent lecture called " The Rejected Stone " This stone, slighted by the founders, although they knew it to be a source of danger, had now " become the head of the corner," and its continuance in the national structure threatened its stability. Mr. Emerson had been much struck with the excellence and cogency of Mr. Conway's arguments, based on his knowledge of Southern economics and character, and in this lecture made free use of them.

Page 308, note 1. Mason and Slidell, the emissaries sent by the Confederacy to excite sympathy in its cause in Europe, had been taken off an English vessel at the Bermudas by Commodore Wilkes, and were confined in Fort Warren in Boston Harbor. President Lincoln's action in surrendering them at England's demand had been a surprise to the country, but was well received.

Page 309, note 1. From the Veeshnoo Sarma.

Page 309, note 2. See in the address on Theodore Parker the passage commending him for insisting " that the essence of Christianity is its practical morals; it is there for use or nothing," etc.

Page 311, note 1. In the agitation concerning the abolition of slavery in the British colonies, gradual emancipation was at first planned, as more reasonable and politic, but, in the end, not only the reformers but the planters came in most cases to see that immediate emancipation was wiser.

THE EMANCIPATION PROCLAMATION

On the 22d of September, President Lincoln at last spoke the word so long earnestly desired by the friends of Freedom and the victims of slavery, abolishing slavery on the first day of the coming year in those states which should then be in rebellion against the United States.

At a meeting held in Boston in honor of this auspicious utterance, Mr. Emerson spoke, with others.

The address was printed in its present form in the *Atlantic Monthly* for November, 1862.

Page 316, note 1. It may be interesting in this connection to recall the quiet joy with which Mr. Emerson in his poem "The Adirondacs" celebrates man's victory over matter, and its promise to human brotherhood, when the Atlantic Cable was supposed to be a success in 1858.

Page 320, note 1. Milton, "Comus."

Page 321, note 1. It is pleasant to contrast this passage with the tone of sad humiliation which prevails in the address on the Fugitive Slave Law given in Concord in 1851.

Page 324, note 1. See the insulting recognition of this disgraceful attitude of the North by John Randolph, quoted by Mr. Emerson in his speech on the Fugitive Slave Law in Concord in 1851.

Page 326, note 1. Shakspeare, Sonnet cvii.

Page 326, note 2. The tragedy of the negro is tenderly told in the poem "Voluntaries," which was written just after they had gallantly stood the test of battle in the desperate attack on Fort Wagner.

On the first day of the year 1863, when Emancipation became a fact throughout the United States, a joyful meeting was held in Boston, and there Mr. Emerson read his " Boston Hymn."

ABRAHAM LINCOLN

In the year 1865, the people of Concord gathered on the Nineteenth of April, as had been their wont for ninety years, but this time not to celebrate the grasping by the town of its great opportunity for freedom and fame. The people came together in the old meeting-house to mourn for their wise and good Chief Magistrate, murdered when he had triumphantly finished the great work which fell to his lot. Mr. Emerson, with others of his townsmen, spoke.

Page 331, note 1. On the occasion of his visit to Washington in January, 1862, Mr Emerson had been taken to the White House by Mr Sumner and introduced to the President. Mr. Lincoln's first remark was, " Mr. Emerson, I once heard you say in a lecture that a Kentuckian seems to say by his air and manners, ' Here am I; if you don't like me, the worse for you.' "

The interview with Mr. Lincoln was necessarily short, but he left an agreeable impression on Mr. Emerson's mind The full account of this visit is printed in the *Atlantic Monthly* for July, 1904, and will be included among the selections from the journals which will be later published

Page 332, note 1. Mr. Emerson's poem, "The Visit," shows how terrible the devastation of the day of a public man would have seemed to him.

Page 336, note 1. The brave retraction by Thomas Taylor of the hostile ridicule which *Punch* had poured on Lincoln in earlier days contained these verses: —

"   Beside this corpse, that bears for winding-sheet
          The Stars and Stripes he lived to rear anew,
     Between the mourners at his head and feet,
          Say, scurrile jester, is there room for *you ?*

"   Yes, he had lived to shame me from my sneer,
          To lame my pencil, and confute my pen; —
     To make me own this hind of princes peer,
          This rail-splitter a true-born king of men."

The whole poem is included in Mr. Emerson's collection *Parnassus.*

Page 337, note 1. This thought is rendered more fully in the poem "Spiritual Laws," and in the lines in "Worship," —

          This is he men miscall Fate,
          Threading dark ways, arriving late,
          But ever coming in time to crown
          The truth, and hurl wrong-doers down.

Page 338, note 1. The following letter was written by Mr. Emerson in November, 1863, to his friend, Mr. George P. Bradford, who, as Mr. Cabot says, came nearer to being a "crony" than any of the others: —

                                                CONCORD.

DEAR GEORGE, — I hope you do not need to be reminded

that we rely on you at 2 o'clock on Thanksgiving Day.
Bring all the climate and all the memories of Newport with
you. Mr. Lincoln in fixing this day has in some sort bound
himself to furnish good news and victories for it   If not, we
must comfort each other with the good which already is, and
with that which must be.

Yours affectionately,

R. W. EMERSON

A year later, he wrote to the same friend —

" I give you joy of the Election. Seldom in history was so
much staked on a popular vote — i suppose never in history.

" One hears everywhere anecdotes of late, very late, remorse
overtaking the hardened sinners and just saving them from final
reprobation."

Journal, 1864–65. " Why talk of President Lincoln's
equality of manners to the elegant or titled men with whom
Everett or others saw him ? A sincerely upright and intelligent man as he was, placed in the chair, has no need to
think of his manners or appearance. His work day by day
educates him rapidly and to the best. He exerts the enormous
power of this continent in every hour, in every conversation,
in every act, — thinks and decides under this pressure, forced
to see the vast and various bearings of the measures he adopts.
he cannot palter, he cannot but carry a grace beyond his own,
a dignity, by means of what he drops, e. g., all pretension
and trick, and arrives, of course, at a simplicity, which is the
perfection of manners."

HARVARD COMMEMORATION SPEECH

It was a proud and sad, and yet a joyful day, when Harvard welcomed back those of her sons who had survived the war. All who could come were there, from boys to middle-aged men, from private soldier to general, some strong and brown, and others worn and sick and maimed, but all on that day proud and happy. The names of the ninety-three of Harvard's sons who had fallen in the war were inscribed on six tablets and placed where all could see.

In the church, where then the college exercises were held, the venerable ex-president, Dr. Walker, read the Scriptures, Rev. Phillips Brooks offered prayer, a hymn by Robert Lowell was sung, and the address was made by the Rev. George Putnam. In the afternoon the alumni, civic and military, with their guests, were marshalled by Colonel Henry Lee into a great pavilion behind Harvard Hall, where they dined. Hon. Charles G. Loring presided ; Governor Andrew, General Meade, General Devens and other distinguished soldiers spoke, and poems by Dr. Holmes and Mrs. Julia Ward Howe were read. The president of the day called on Mr. Emerson as representative of the poets and scholars whose thoughts had been an inspiration to Harvard's sons in the field.

Page 344, note 1. This was the mother of Robert Gould Shaw, who lost his life a few months later, leading his dusky soldiers up the slopes of Fort Wagner. It was in his honor that Mr. Emerson wrote in the " Voluntaries," —

Stainless soldier on the walls,
Knowing this, — and knows no more, —
Whoever fights, whoever falls,
Justice conquers evermore,
Justice after as before, —
And he who battles on her side,
God, though he were ten times slain,
Crowns him victor glorified,
Victor over death and pain.

Page 345, note 1.

"O Beautiful! my Country! ours once more!

.   .   .   .

What words divine of lover or of poet
Could tell our love and make thee know it,
Among the Nations bright beyond compare ?
What were our lives without thee ?
What all our lives to save thee ?
We reck not what we gave thee,
We will not dare to doubt thee,
But ask whatever else, and we will dare!"
            Lowell, "Commemoration Ode."

ADDRESS AT THE DEDICATION OF THE SOL-DIERS' MONUMENT IN CONCORD

In 1836, the "Battle Monument" to commemorate "the First organized Resistance to British Aggression" had been erected "in Gratitude to God and Love of Freedom" on "the spot where the first of the Enemy fell in the War which gave Independence to the United States." Thirty-three years later, on the Nineteenth day of April, with its threefold patri-otic memories for Concord,[1] the people gathered on the village common to see their new memorial to valor. The inscription on one of its bronze tablets declared that

THE TOWN OF CONCORD

BUILDS THIS MONUMENT

IN HONOR OF

THE BRAVE MEN

WHOSE NAMES IT BEARS:

AND RECORDS

WITH GRATEFUL PRIDE

THAT THEY FOUND HERE

A BIRTHPLACE, HOME OR GRAVE.

The inscription on the other tablet is the single sentence, —

THEY DIED FOR THEIR COUNTRY

IN THE WAR OF THE REBELLION

with the forty-four names.

Hon. John S. Keyes as President of the Day opened the

[1] See note 3 to page 63 of the "Historical Discourse."

ceremonies with a short address. The Rev. Grindall Rey-
nolds made the prayer. An Ode written by Mr. George B.
Bartlett was sung to the tune of *Auld Lang Syne*. Hon.
Ebenezer Rockwood Hoar, the Chairman of the Monument
Committee, read the Report, in itself an eloquent and moving
speech. This was followed by Mr. Emerson's Address.
Mr F. B. Sanborn contributed a Poem, and afterwards short
speeches were made by Senator George S. Boutwell, William
Schouler, the efficient Adjutant-General of the State, and by
Colonels Parker and Marsh respectively of the Thirty-second
and Forty-seventh regiments of Massachusetts Volunteers, in
which the Concord companies had served. The exercises were
concluded by the reading of a poem by Mr. Sampson Mason,
an aged citizen of the town

It was a beautiful spring day. The throng was too large
for the town hall, so, partly sheltered from the afternoon sun
by the town elm, thickening with its brown buds, they gathered around the town-house steps, which served as platform for
the speakers.

Page 351, note 1 Compare, in the *Poems*, the lines in
"The Problem" on the adoption by Nature of man's devo-
tional structures

Page 352, note 1

> Great men in the Senate sate,
> Sage and hero, side by side,
> Building for their sons the State,
> Which they shall rule with pride.
> They forbore to break the chain
> Which bound the dusky tribe,
> Checked by the owners' fierce disdain,
> Lured by "Union" as the bribe.

Destiny sat by, and said,
' Pang for pang your seed shall pay,
Hide in false peace your coward head,
I bring round the harvest day.'

Page 353, note 1. Wordsworth's Sonnet, No. xiv., in
" Poems dedicated to National Independence," part ii.

Page 355, note 1. Mr. Emerson had in mind the aston-
ishing fertility of resource in difficulties shown by the Eighth
Massachusetts Regiment in the march from Annapolis to Wash-
ington, as told by Major Theodore Winthrop in " New York
Seventh Regiment. Our march to Washington " (*Atlantic
Monthly,* June, 1861). See " Resources," *Letters and Social
Aims,* p. 143.

Judge Hoar in his report on this occasion said, " Two
names [on the tablet] recall the unutterable horrors of Andersonville, and will never suffer us to forget that our armies conquered barbarism as well as treason."

Page 356, note 1. Between 1856 and 1859 John Brown
and other Free-State men, Mr. Whitman, Mr. Nute and
Preacher Stewart, had told the sad story of Kansas to the
Concord people and received important aid.

Page 358, note 1. This was Captain Charles E. Bowers,
a shoemaker, and Mr. Emerson's next neighbor, much respected by him, whose forcible speaking at anti-slavery and
Kansas aid meetings he often praised. When the war came,
Mr. Bowers, though father of a large family, and near the
age-limit of service, volunteered as a private in the first company, went again as an officer in the Thirty-second Massachusetts Regiment, and served with credit in the Army of the
Potomac until discharged for disability.

Page 358, note 2. George L. Prescott, a lumber dealer

and farmer, later Colonel of the Thirty-second Regiment, U. S. V. He was of the same stock as Colonel William Prescott, the hero of Bunker Hill.

Judge Hoar said of him, "An only son, an only brother, a husband and a father, with no sufficient provision made for his wife and children, he had everything to make life dear and desirable, and to require others to hesitate for him, but he did not hesitate himself."

Page 361, note 1. Blaise de Montluc, a Gascon officer of remarkable valor, skill and fidelity, under Francis I. and several succeeding kings of France.

Page 365, note 1. It was well said by Judge Hoar. "His instinctive sympathies taught him from the outset, what many higher in command were so slow and so late to learn, that it is the first duty of an officer to take care of his men as much as to lead them. His character developed new and larger proportions, with new duties and larger responsibilities"

Page 366, note 1 The Buttricks were among the original settlers of Concord, and the family has given good account of itself for nearly two hundred and seventy years, and still owns the farm on the hill whence Major John led the yeomen of Middlesex down to force the passage of the North Bridge Seven representatives of that family of sturdy democrats volunteered at the beginning of the War of the Rebellion. Two were discharged as physically unfit, but the others served in army or navy with credit, and two of them lost their lives in the service. Alden Buttrick had fought the Border Ruffians in Kansas. Humphrey, a mason by trade, but a mighty hunter, left his wife and little children at the first call, and was first sergeant of Prescott's company. Mr. Emerson omits to state that he was commissioned lieutenant in the Forty-seventh Regiment the following year. His service, especially as captain in the Fifty-ninth Regiment, was arduous and highly creditable.

Page 368, note 1. Edward O. Shepard, who had been master of the Concord High School, afterwards a successful lawyer, had an excellent war record, and rose to be lieutenant-colonel of the Thirty-second Regiment.

George Lauriat left the gold-beater's shop of Ephraim W. Bull (the producer of the Concord Grape) to go to the war in Concord's first company. Modest and brave, he became an excellent officer and returned captain and brevet-major of the Thirty-second Regiment.

Page 368, note 2. Francis Buttrick, younger brother of Humphrey, a handsome and attractive youth, had lived at Mr. Emerson's home to carry on the farm for him.

Page 375, note 1. These three were Asa, John and Samuel Melvin. Asa died of wounds received before Petersburg; both his brothers of sickness, Samuel after long suffering in the prison-pen at Andersonville. They came of an old family of hunter-farmers in Concord. Close by the wall next the street of the Old Hill Burying Ground is the stone in memory of one of their race, whose " Martial Genius early engaged him in his Country's cause under command of the valiant Captain Lovel in that hazardous Enterprise where our hero, his Commander, with many brave and valiant Men bled and died."

Page 379, note 1. The writer of this letter, a quiet, handsome school-boy the year before the war broke out, lived just across the brook behind Mr. Emerson's house. He was an excellent soldier in the Thirty-second Regiment, and reenlisted as a veteran in 1864.

EDITORS' ADDRESS, MASSACHUSETTS QUARTERLY REVIEW

Mr. Cabot, in his Memoir, says that just before Mr. Emerson sailed for Europe in 1847, Theodore Parker, Dr. S. G. Howe and others (Mr. Cabot was one of these) met to consider whether there could not be " a new quarterly review which should be more alive than was the *North American* to the questions of the day." Charles Sumner and Thoreau are mentioned as having been present. Colonel Higginson says that Mr. Parker wished it to be " the *Dial* with a beard." It was decided that the undertaking should be made. Mr. Parker wished Mr. Emerson to be editor, but he declined. A committee was chosen — Emerson, Parker and Howe — to draft a manifesto to the public. Mr. Emerson wrote the paper here printed, but when the first number of the Review came to him in England, was annoyed at finding his name set down as one of the editors. I think that the only paper he ever wrote for it, beyond the " Address to the Public," was a notice of " Some Oxford Poetry," — the recently published poems of John Sterling and Arthur Hugh Clough.

Theodore Parker was the real editor. During its three years of life the *Massachusetts Quarterly* — now hard to obtain — was a brave, independent and patriotic magazine, and, like the *Dial*, gives the advancing thought of the time in literary and social matters, and also in religion and politics.

Page 384, note 1. Plutarch tells that Cineas, the wise counsellor of Pyrrhus, king of the Epirots, asked his monarch when he set forth to conquer Rome what he should do afterwards Pyrrhus said he could then become master of Sicily. "And then ?" asked Cineas. The king told of further dreams of conquest of Carthage and Libya. "But when we have conquered all that, what are we to do then ?" "Why then, my friend," said Pyrrhus, laughing, "we will take our ease, and drink and be merry." Cineas, having brought him thus far, replied, "And what hinders us from drinking and taking our ease now, when we have already those things in our hands at which we propose to arrive through seas of blood, through infinite toils and dangers, innumerable calamities which we must both cause and suffer ?"

Page 386, note 1. "To live without duties is obscene." — "Aristocracy," *Lectures and Biographical Sketches.*

Page 389, note 1. This was shortly after the annexation of Texas, and during the successful progress of the Mexican War. The slave power, although awakening opposition by its insatiable demands, was still on the increase. Charles Sumner, though a rising statesman, had not yet entered Congress.

Page 389, note 2.

> For Destiny never swerves,
> Nor yields to men the helm.
>
> "The World-Soul," *Poems.*

ADDRESS TO KOSSUTH

On a beautiful day in May, 1852, Louis Kossuth, the exiled governor of Hungary, who had come to this country to solicit her to interfere in European politics on behalf of his oppressed people, visited the towns of Lexington and Concord, and spoke to a large assemblage in each place.

Kossuth was met at the Lexington line by a cavalcade from

Concord, who escorted him to the village, where he received a cordial welcome. The town hall was crowded with people. The Hon. John S. Keyes presided, and Mr. Emerson made the address of welcome.

Kossuth, in his earnest appeal for American help, addressed Mr Emerson personally in the following passages, after alluding to Concord's part in the struggle for Freedom in 1775. —

"It is strange, indeed, how every incident of the present bears the mark of a deeper meaning around me. There is meaning in the very fact that it is you, sir, by whom the representative of Hungary's ill-fated struggle is so generously welcomed . . . to the shrine of martyrs illumined by victory. You are wont to dive into the mysteries of truth and disclose mysteries of right to the eyes of men. Your honored name is Emerson; and Emerson was the name of a man who, a minister of the gospel, turned out with his people, on the 19th of April of eternal memory, when the alarm-bell first was rung. . . . I take hold of that augury, sir. Religion and Philosophy, you blessed twins, — upon you I rely with my hopes to America. Religion, the philosophy of the heart, will make the Americans generous; and philosophy, the religion of the mind, will make the Americans wise, and all that I claim is a generous wisdom and a wise generosity."

Page 398, note 1. I am unable to find the source of these lines.

Page 399, note 1. For the power of minorities, see "Progress of Culture," *Letters and Social Aims,* pp. 216–219, and "Considerations by the Way," *Conduct of Life,* pp. 248, 249.

WOMAN

Perhaps the pleasantest word Mr. Emerson ever spoke about women was what he said at the end of the war: "Everybody has been wrong in his guess except good women, who never despair of an ideal right."

Mr. Emerson's habitual treatment of women showed his real feeling towards them. He held them to their ideal selves by his courtesy and honor. When they called him to come to their aid, he came. Men must not deny them any right that they desired; though he never felt that the finest women would care to assume political functions in the same way that men did.

Mr. Cabot gives in his Memoir (p. 455) a letter which Mr. Emerson wrote, five years before this speech was made, to a lady who asked him to join in a call for a Woman's Suffrage Convention. His distaste for the scheme clearly appears, and though perhaps felt in a less degree as time went on, never quite disappeared. At the end of the notes on this address is given the greater part of a short speech which he wrote many years later, but which he seems never to have delivered. Colonel Thomas Wentworth Higginson is reported in the *Woman's Journal* as having said at the New England Women's Club, May 16, 1903, that Mr. Cabot put into his Memoir what Mr. Emerson said in his early days, when he was opposed to woman's suffrage (the letter above alluded to), and "left out all those warm and cordial sentences that he wrote later in regard to it, culminating in his assertion that, whatever might be said of it as an abstract question, all his

measures would be carried sooner if women could vote." This
last assertion, though not in the Memoir, Mr. Cabot printed
in its place in the present address, and the only other address
on the subject which is known to exist, Mr. Cabot did not
print probably because Mr. Emerson never delivered it.

Page 406, note 1. This passage from the original is omitted: —

"A woman of genius said, 'I will forgive you that you
do so much, and you me that I do nothing.'"

Page 411, note 1. This sentence originally ended, "And
their convention should be holden in a sculpture-gallery."

Page 412, note 1. From *The Angel in the House,* by
Coventry Patmore.

Page 413, note 1. Milton, *Paradise Lost.*

Because of the high triumph of Humility, his favorite virtue, Mr. Emerson, though commonly impatient of sad stories,
had always a love for the story of Griselda, as told by Chau-
cer, alluded to below. In spite of its great length, he would
not deny it a place in his collection *Parnassus.*

Page 413, note 2. From "Love and Humility," by
Henry More (1614–87).

Page 414, note 1. These anecdotes followed in the original speech: —

"'I use the Lord of the Kaaba; what is the Kaaba to
me?' said Rabia. 'I am so near to God that his word,
"Whoso nears me by a span, to him come I a mile," is
true for me.' A famed Mahometan theologian asked her,
'How she had lifted herself to this degree of the love of God?'
She replied, 'Hereby, that all things which I had found, I
have lost in him.' The other said, 'In what way or method
hast thou known him?' She replied, 'O Hassan! thou know-

est him after a certain art and way, but I without art and
way.' When once she was sick, three famed theologians
came to her, Hassan Vasri, Malek and Balchi. Hassan said,
' He is not upright in his prayer who does not endure th
blows of his Lord.' Balchi said, ' He is not upright in hi
prayer who does not rejoice in the blows of his Lord.' Bu
Rabia, who in these words detected some trace of egoism,
said, ' He is not upright in his prayer, who, when he be-
holds his Lord, forgets not that he is stricken.' ''

Page 415, note 1. See " Clubs," in *Society and Solitude*, p. 243.

Page 417, note 1. " The Princess " is the poem alluded
to. Mr. Emerson liked it, but used to say it was sad to hear
it end with, *Go home and mind your mending.*

Page 426, note 1. The internal evidence shows that the
short speech given below was written after the war. All that
is important is here given. There were one or two paragraphs that essentially were the same as those of the 1855
address.

On the manuscript is written, apparently in Mr. Emerson's
hand, in pencil, " Never read," and evidently in his hand,
the title, thus: —

Discours Manqué

WOMAN

I consider that the movement which unites us to-day is
no whim, but an organic impulse, — a right and proper
inquiry, — honoring to the age. And among the good signs
of the times, this is of the best.

The distinctions of the mind of Woman we all recognize;
their affectionate, sympathetic, religious, oracular nature; their
swifter and finer perception; their taste, or love of order and

beauty, influencing or creating manners. We commonly say, Man represents Intellect; and Woman, Love Man looks for hard truth. Woman, with her affection for goodness, benefit. Hence they are religious. In all countries and creeds the temples are filled by women, and they hold men to religious rites and moral duties. And in all countries the man — no matter how hardened a reprobate he is — likes well to have his wife a saint. It was no historic chance, but an instinct, which softened in the Middle Ages the terror of the superstitious, by gradually lifting their prayers to the Virgin Mary and so adopting the Mother of God as the efficient Intercessor. And now, when our religious traditions are so far outgrown as to require correction and reform, 't is certain that nothing can be fixed and accepted which does not commend itself to Woman

I suppose women feel in relation to men as 't is said geniuses feel among energetic workers, that, though overlooked and thrust aside in the press, they outsee all these noisy masters: and we, in the presence of sensible women, feel overlooked, judged, — and sentenced.

They are better scholars than we at school, and the reason why they are not better than we twenty years later may be because men can turn their reading to account in the professions, and women are excluded from the professions.

These traits have always characterized women. We are a little vain of our women, as if we had invented them. I think we exaggerate the effect of Greek, Roman and even Oriental institutions on the character of woman. Superior women are rare anywhere, as superior men are. But the anecdotes of every country give like portraits of womanhood, and every country in its Roll of Honor has as many women as men. The high sentiment of women appears in the Hebrew, the

Hindoo; in Greek women in Homer, in the tragedies, and Roman women in the histories. Their distinctive traits, grace, vivacity, and surer moral sentiment, their self-sacrifice, their courage and endurance, have in every nation found respect and admiration.

Her gifts make woman the refiner and civilizer of her mate. Civilization is her work. Man is rude and bearish in colleges, in mines, in ships, because there is no woman. Let good women go passengers in the ship, and the manners at once are mended; in schools, in hospitals, in the prairie, in California, she brings the same reform. . . .

Her activity in putting an end to Slavery; and in serving the hospitals of the Sanitary Commission in the war, and in the labors of the Freedman's Bureau, have opened her eyes to larger rights and duties. She claims now her full rights of all kinds, — to education, to employment, to equal laws of property. Well, now in this country we are suffering much and fearing more from the abuse of the ballot and from fraudulent and purchased votes. And now, at the moment when committees are investigating and reporting the election frauds, woman asks for her vote. It is the remedy at the hour of need. She is to purify and civilize the voting, as she has the schools, the hospitals and the drawing-rooms. For, to grant her request, you must remove the polls from the tavern and rum-shop, and build noble edifices worthy of the State, whose halls shall afford her every security for deliberate and sovereign action.

'T is certainly no new thing to see women interest themselves in politics. In England, in France, in Germany, Italy, we find women of influence and administrative capacity, — some Duchess of Marlborough, some Madame de Longueville, Madame Roland, — centres of political power and intrigue. . . . But we have ourselves seen the great political enter-

prise of our times, the abolition of Slavery in America, under-
taken by a society whose executive committee was composed
of men and women, and which held together until this object
was attained And she may well exhibit the history of that as
her voucher that she is entitled to demand power which she
has shown she can use so well.

'T is idle to refuse them a vote on the ground of incompetency.
I wish our masculine voting were so good that we had any
right to doubt their equal discretion. They could not easily
give worse votes, I think, than we do.

CONSECRATION OF SLEEPY HOLLOW
CEMETERY

Within a quarter of a mile of Concord Common was a
natural amphitheatre, carpeted in late summer with a purple
bloom of wild grass, and girt by a horseshoe-shaped glacial
moraine clothed with noble pines and oaks. It was part of
Deacon Brown's farm, and reached by a lane, with a few
houses on it, cut through a low part of the ridge of hills which
sheltered the old town. When the Deacon died, the town
laid out a new road to Bedford, cutting off this " Sleepy
Hollow " (as the townspeople who enjoyed strolling there
had named it) from the rest of the farm. Mr. John S. Keyes
saw the fitness of the ground for a beautiful cemetery, and
induced the town to buy it for that purpose; and as chairman
of the committee, laid out the land. The people of the village — for Concord had nothing suburban about it then —
gathered there one beautiful September afternoon to choose
their resting-places and consecrate the ground. Mr. Emerson

made the address on the slope just below the place where, beneath a great pine, the tree he loved best, he had chosen the spot for his own grave.

Much of his essay on Immortality was originally a part of this discourse, and therefore that portion is omitted here, its place in the essay being indicated.

ROBERT BURNS

It is pleasant to be able to let Dr. Holmes, who was present at the Burns Festival, speak for himself and Lowell and Judge Hoar of Mr. Emerson's speech on that day. I have heard the Judge tell the story of his friend's success with the same delight.

"On the 25th of January, 1859, Emerson attended the Burns Festival, held at the Parker House in Boston, on the Centennial Anniversary of the poet's birth. He spoke, after the dinner, to the great audience with such beauty and eloquence that all who listened to him have remembered it as one of the most delightful addresses they ever heard. Among his hearers was Mr. Lowell, who says of it that 'every word seemed to have just dropped down to him from the clouds.' Judge Hoar, who was another of his hearers, says that, though he has heard many of the chief orators of his time, he never witnessed such an effect of speech upon men. I was myself present on that occasion, and underwent the same fascination that these gentlemen and the varied audience before the speaker experienced. His words had a passion in them not usual in the calm, pure flow most natural to his uttered thoughts; white-hot iron we are familiar with, but white-hot silver is what we do not often look upon, and his inspiring address glowed like silver fresh from the cupel.''

The strange part of all the accounts given by the hearers is that Mr Emerson seemed to speak *extempore*, which can hardly have been so

No account of the Festival, or Mr. Emerson's part therein, appears in the journals, except a short page of praise of the felicitous anecdotes introduced by other after-dinner speakers.

Page 440, note 1. Here comes out that respect for labor which affected all Mr. Emerson's relations to the humblest people he met. In the Appendix to the *Poems* it appears in the verses beginning, —

Said Saadi, When I stood before
Hassan the camel-driver's door.

Page 441, note 1. Thomas Carlyle.

Page 441, note 2. Mr. Emerson here recalls his childhood and that of his brothers, as in the passage in '' Domestic Life,'' in *Society and Solitude*, that has been often referred to in these notes.

Page 443, note 1. Among some stray lecture-sheets was the following on the scholar or poet: —

'' Given the insight, and he will find as many beauties and heroes and strokes of genius close by him as Dante or Shakspeare beheld. It was in a cold moor farm, in a dingy country inn, that Burns found his fancy so sprightly. You find the times and places mean. Stretch a few threads over an Æolian harp, and put it in the window and listen to what it says of the times and of the heart of Nature. You shall not believe the miracle of Nature is less, the chemical power worn out. Watch the breaking morning, or the enchantments of the sunset.''

SHAKSPEARE

The following notes on Shakspeare were written by Mr. Emerson for the celebration in Boston by the Saturday Club of the Three Hundredth Anniversary of the poet's birth.

In Mr. Cabot's *Memoir of Emerson*, vol. ii., page 621, apropos of Mr. Emerson's avoidance of impromptu speech on public occasions, is this statement: —

"I remember his getting up at a dinner of the Saturday Club on the Shakspeare anniversary in 1864, to which some guests had been invited, looking about him tranquilly for a minute or two, and then sitting down; serene and unabashed, but unable to say a word upon a subject so familiar to his thoughts from boyhood."

Yet on the manuscript of this address Mr. Emerson noted that it was read at the Club's celebration on that occasion, and at the Revere House. ("Parker's" was the usual gathering-place of the Club.) The handwriting of this note shows that Mr. Emerson wrote it in his later years, so it is very possible that Mr. Cabot was right. Mr. Emerson perhaps forgot to bring his notes with him to the dinner, and so did not venture to speak. And the dinner may have been at "Parker's."

ALEXANDER VON HUMBOLDT

The Boston Society of Natural History celebrated the One Hundredth Anniversary of the birth of Humboldt. Dr Robert C Waterston presided at the Music Hall, where Agassiz made the address. In the evening there was a reception in Horticultural Hall. The occasion was made memorable by the Society by the founding of a Humboldt and Agassiz scholarship in the Museum of Comparative Zoology in Cambridge

Poems by Dr. Holmes and Mrs. Howe were read. Professor E. J. Young and Dr. Charles T. Jackson gave reminiscences of Humboldt; Colonel Higginson, the Rev. Dr Hedge and others spoke. Mr. Emerson's remarks are taken from an abstract given in the account of the celebration published by the Society.

WALTER SCOTT

Although Mr. Emerson, in the period between 1838 and 1848 especially, when considering the higher powers of poetry, spoke slightingly of Scott, — in the *Dial* papers as "objective" and "the poet of society, of patrician and conventional Europe," or in *English Traits* as a writer of "a rhymed travellers' guide to Scotland," — he had always honor for the noble man, and affectionate remembrance for the poems as well as the novels. In the poem "The Harp," when enumerating poets, he calls Scott "the delight of generous boys," but the *generosus puer* was his own delight; the hope of the generation lay in him, and his own best audience was made up of such. In the essay " Illusions," he says that the boy " has no better friend than Scott, Shakspeare, Plutarch and Homer. The man lives to other objects, but who dare affirm that they are more real ? " In the essay " Aristocracy," he names among the claims of a superior class, " Genius, the power to affect the Imagination," and presently speaks of " those who think and paint and laugh and weep in their eloquent closets, and then convert the world into a huge whispering-gallery, to report the tale to all men and win smiles and tears from many generations," and gives Scott and Burns among the high company whom he instances.

Mr. Emerson's children can testify how with regard to Scott he always was ready to become a boy again. As we walked in the woods, he would show us the cellar-holes of the Irish colony that came to Concord to build the railroad, and he named these deserted villages Derncleugh and Ellangowan. The sight recalled Meg Merrilies' pathetic lament to the laird at the eviction of the gypsies, which he would then recite. " Alice Brand," the " Sair Field o' Harlaw," which old Elspeth sings to the children in *The Antiquary*, and " Helvellyn " were again and again repeated to us with pleasure on both sides. With special affection in later years when we walked in Walden woods he would croon the lines from " The Dying Bard," —

" Dinas Emlinn, lament, for the moment is nigh,
   When mute in the woodlands thine echoes shall die."

Perhaps he had foreboding for his loved woods, beginning to be desecrated with rude city picnics, and since burned over repeatedly by the fires from the railroad, —

" When half of their charms with Cadwallon shall die."

Of this poem he wrote in the journal of 1845: —

" ' Dinas Emlinn ' of Scott, like his ' Helvellyn,' shows how near to a poet he was. All the Birmingham part he had, and what taste and sense! Yet never rose into the creative region As a practitioner or professional poet he is unrivalled in modern times." Yet he immediately adds, "In lectures on Poetry almost all Scott would be to be produced "

Page 463, note 1 Mr Emerson took especial pleasure in the passage in the *Lord of the Isles* where the old abbot, rising to denounce excommunicated Bruce to his foes, is inspired against his will to bless him and prophesy his triumph as Scotland's deliverer.

Mr. Emerson, writing in his journal in 1842 of his impatience of superficial city life, during a visit to New York, alludes to the renewed comfort he had in the *Lord of the Isles:*

" Life goes headlong Each of us is always to be found hurrying headlong in the chase of some fact, hunted by some fear or command behind us Suddenly we meet a friend. We pause. Our hurry and *empressement* look ridiculous. . . . When I read the *Lord of the Isles* last week at Staten Island, and when I meet my friend, I have the same feeling of shame at having allowed myself to be a mere huntsman and follower "

His boyish love for the *Lay of the Last Minstrel* remained through life. As we walked on Sunday afternoons he recited to his children the stanzas about " the custom of Branksome Hall," and the passage where the Ladye of Branksome defies the spirits of the flood and fell; and the bleak mile of road between Walden woods and home would often call out from him

> " The way was long, the wind was cold,
>   The Minstrel was infirm and old," etc.

NOTES 637

Page 465, note 1. The *Bride of Lammermoor* was the only dreary tale that Mr. Emerson could abide, except *Griselda.*

Journal, 1856. "Eugène Sue, Dumas, etc., when they begin a story, do not know how it will end, but Walter Scott, when he began the *Bride of Lammermoor*, had no choice; nor Shakspeare, nor Macbeth."

Page 467, note 1. Journal. "We talked of Scott. There is some greatness in defying posterity and writing for the hour."

SPEECH AT THE BANQUET IN HONOR OF THE CHINESE EMBASSY

When the Chinese Embassy visited Boston in the summer of 1868 a banquet was given them at the St. James Hotel, on August 21. The young Emerson, sounding an early note of independence of the past, had written in 1824: —

I laugh at those who, while they gape and gaze,
The bald antiquity of China praise; —

but later he learned to revere the wisdom of Asia. About the time when the *Dial* appeared, many sentences of Chinese wisdom are found in his journal, and also in the magazine among the "Ethnical Scriptures."

REMARKS AT THE ORGANIZATION OF THE
FREE RELIGIOUS ASSOCIATION

In the spring of 1867, a call for a public meeting was issued
by Octavius B. Frothingham, William J. Potter and Rowland
Connor " to consider the conditions, wants and progress of Free
Religion in America." The response was so large as to sur-
prise the committee, and Horticultural Hall was completely
filled on May 30. Rev. Octavius B. Frothingham presided.
The committee had invited as speakers the Rev. H. Blanchard
of Brooklyn from the Universalists, Lucretia Mott from the
Society of Friends, Robert Dale Owen from the Spiritualists,
the Rev. John Weiss from the Left Wing of the Unitarians,
Oliver Johnson from the Progressive Friends, Francis E.
Abbot, editor of the *Index;* and also David A. Wasson,
Colonel T. W. Higginson and Mr. Emerson. The meeting
was very successful and the Free Religious Association was
founded.

Mr. Emerson's genial and affirmative attitude at this meeting was helpful and important. He wished the new movement
to be neither aggressive towards the beliefs of others, nor merely
a religion of works, purely beneficently utilitarian. Doubtless
there were many young and active radicals strong for destructive criticism. Mr. Emerson wished to see that in their zeal
to destroy the dry husk of religion they should not bruise the
white flower within. His counsel to young men was, " Omit
all negative propositions. It will save ninety-nine one hun-
dredths of your labor, and increase the value of your work in
the same measure."

Page 479, note 1. In the journal of 1837 he said, "Why rake up old manuscripts to find therein a man's soul? You do not look for conversation in a corpse." And elsewhere, "In religion the sentiment is all, the ritual or ceremony indifferent."

SPEECH AT THE SECOND ANNUAL MEETING OF THE FREE RELIGIOUS ASSOCIATION

Page 486, note 1. Mrs. Julia Ward Howe writes of Mr. Emerson, —

"He knew from the first the victory of good over evil; and when he told me, to my childish amazement, that the angel must always be stronger than the demon, he gave utterance to a thought most familiar to him, though at the time new to me." [1]

Page 488, note 1. In the essay on Character (*Lectures and Biographical Sketches*), he says, "The establishment of Christianity in the world does not rest on any miracle but the miracle of being the broadest and most humane doctrine."

"The word Miracle, as pronounced by Christian churches, gives a false impression; it is Monster. It is not one with the blowing clover and the falling rain." — "Address in Divinity College," *Nature, Addresses and Lectures.*

Page 490, note 1. Mr. Emerson's doctrine was not to attack beliefs, but give better: "True genius will not impoverish, but will liberate." In a letter to one of his best friends who had joined the Church of Rome he said, perhaps

[1] "Emerson's Relation to Society," in *The Genius and Character of Emerson*, Lectures at the Concord School of Philosophy, edited by F. B Sanborn. Boston: J. R. Osgood & Co., 1885.

in 1858: " To old eyes how supremely unimportant the form under which we celebrate the justice, love and truth, the attributes of the deity and the soul!"

Page 491, note 1. Dr. Holmes, in his tribute to his friend, after his death, read before the Massachusetts Historical Society, said: —

" What could we do with this unexpected, unprovided for, unclassified, half unwelcome newcomer, who had been for a while potted, as it were, in our Unitarian cold greenhouse, but had taken to growing so fast that he was lifting off its glass roof and letting in the hail-storms ? Here was a protest that outflanked the extreme left of liberalism, yet so calm and serene that its radicalism had the accents of the gospel of peace. Here was an iconoclast without a hammer, who took down our idols from their pedestals so tenderly that it seemed like an act of worship."

ADDRESS AT THE OPENING OF THE CONCORD FREE PUBLIC LIBRARY

The Town of Concord, in the year 1782, chose a committee of ten leading citizens to give instructions to its selectmen. The third of the seventeen articles proposed by them read thus: " That care be taken of the Books of Marters and other bookes, and that they be kept from abusive usage, and not lent to persons more than one month at one time." This indicates the root of a town library. A constitution of a Library Company, dated 1784, is extant. In 1806 a Social Library was incorporated, which was merged in the Town Library in 1851. The books were kept in a room in the Town House which was open for borrowers on Saturdays.

William Munroe, son of a Concord tradesman who vied with the Thoreaus in the manufacture of lead pencils, after leaving the Concord schools went into business, and later into the manufacture of silk. His intelligence and force of character secured prosperity. He loved Concord, and, to use his own words, "desired to testify my regard to my native town by doing something to promote the education and intelligence, and thus the welfare and prosperity of its people." He gave to Concord a lot of land in the heart of the town and a building for a Free Public Library, which, with great care and thoroughness, he had built thereon and duly furnished; and made handsome provision for care of the land and the extension of the building later. He added a generous gift for books of reference and standard works. The town thankfully accepted the gift, placed their books in it, and chose their library committee. On a fine autumn day in 1873, the library was opened with public ceremonies. Mr. Munroe in a short and modest speech explained his purpose; Mr. H. F. Smith, on behalf of the new library committee, reported its action and the gifts which had poured in; Judge Hoar received the property on behalf of the Board of Corporation, and Mr. Emerson, but lately returned with improved health from his journey to the Nile, made the short address. Writing was now very difficult for him, but the occasion pleased and moved him, and his notes on books and on Concord, and the remembrance of his friends the Concord authors but lately gone, served him, and the day passed off well.

Page 498, note 1. The Gospel Covenant, printed in London in 1646, and quoted by Mr. Emerson in the "Historical Discourse."

Page 499, note 1. Major Simon Willard, a Kentish mer-

xi

chant was Peter Bulkeley's strong coadjutor in the founding of Concord. He also is alluded to in the " Historical Discourse."

Page 500, note 1. These extracts are from the diary of Miss Mary Moody Emerson.

Page 500, note 2. This letter was written not long after the death of John Thoreau, Henry's dearly loved brother, and also of little Waldo Emerson, to whom he became greatly attached while he was a member of Mr. Emerson's household

Page 501, note 1 Mr. Emerson here speaks for others. He could not read Hawthorne because of the gloom of his magic mirror, but the man interested and attracted him, though even as neighbors they seldom met.

Page 506, note 1. Mr Emerson notes that this is an allusion to the " Harmonies of Ptolemy."

THE FORTUNE OF THE REPUBLIC

In 1863, during the dark days of the Civil War, before the tide had fully turned in the field, while disaffection showed itself in the North, and England and France threatened intervention, Mr. Emerson gave a hopeful lecture, the basis of the present discourse, on the Fortune of the Republic. After the war it was adapted to the new and happier conditions. On the 30th of March, 1878, six years after Mr. Emerson had withdrawn from literary work, and but four years before his death, he was induced to read the lecture in the Old South Church, in a course planned by the committee, to save the venerable building. The church was filled, Mr. Emerson's delivery was good, and he seemed to enjoy the occasion. It was probably his last speech in public, and so fitly closes the volume.

Page 513, note 1. This passage occurred in the early lecture: —

" It is the distinction of man to think, and all the few men who, since the beginning of the world, have done anything for us were men who did not follow the river, or ship the cotton, or pack the pork, but who thought for themselves. What the country wants is personalities, — grand persons, — to counteract its materialities, for it is the rule of the universe that corn shall serve man, and not man, corn."

Page 519, note 1. Here followed: " What we call ' Kentucky,' or ' Vallandigham,' or ' Fernando Wood ' is really the ignorance and nonsense in us, stolid stupidity which gives the strength to those names. . . . It is our own vice which takes form, or gives terror with which these persons affect us."

Page 520, note 1. This refers to a young Massachusetts scholar, of promise and beauty, whom Mr. Emerson had been pleased with, as a fellow voyager. He soon was corrupted by politics. Coming up, at a reception, to shake hands with Mr. Emerson he was thus greeted: " If what I hear of your recent action be true, I must shake hands with you under protest." Soon after, this aspirant for power attended the dinner given to Brooks after his cowardly assault on Sumner; but the moment the Emancipation Proclamation had been approved by the people, he became an ornamental figurehead at Republican and reform gatherings.

Page 520, note 2. From the last scene of *Cynthia's Revels,* by Ben Jonson.

Page 521, note 1 "The one serious and formidable thing in Nature is a will." — "Fate," *Conduct of Life*, p. 30.

See also "Aristocracy," in *Lectures and Biographical Sketches*, p. 50.

Page 524, note 1. Ben Jonson, *The Golden Age Restored*.

Page 526, note 1.

> She spawneth men as mallows fresh.
> "Nature," II., *Poems*.

See also the "Song of Nature," in the *Poems*

Page 526, note 2. In the earlier lecture was this passage: —

"The roots of our success are in our poverty, our Calvinism, our thrifty habitual industry, — in our snow and east wind, and farm-life and sea-life. . . .

"There is in this country this immense difference from Europe, that, whereas all their systems of government and society are historical, our politics are almost ideal. We wish to treat man as man, without regard to rank, wealth, race, color, or caste, — simply as human souls. We lie near to Nature, we are pensioners on Nature, draw on inexhaustible resources, and we interfere the least possible with individual freedom."

Page 527, note 1. In the "Historical Discourse" in this volume, Mr. Emerson tells of the evolution of the town-meeting of New England and its working excellence, and of the latter also in "Social Aims" and "Eloquence," in *Letters and Social Aims*.

Page 540, note 1.

> For you can teach the lightning speech,
> And round the globe your voices reach.
> "Boston," *Poems*.

Page 541, note 1.

> I will divide my goods;
> Call in the wretch and slave:
> None shall rule but the humble,
> And none but Toil shall have.
>
> "Boston Hymn," *Poems.*

Page 544, note 1. The following passages came from the earlier lecture: —

"I must be permitted to read a quotation from De Tocqueville, whose censure is more valuable, as it comes from one obviously very partial to the American character and institutions: —

"'I know no country in which there is so little true independence of opinion and freedom of discussion as in America' (vol. i., p. 259)."

"I am far from thinking it late. I don't despond at all whilst I hear the verdicts of European juries against us — Renan says this; Arnold says that. That does not touch us.

"'T is doubtful whether London, whether Paris can answer the questions which now rise in the human mind. But the humanity of all nations is now in the American Union. Europe, England is historical still. Our politics, our social frame are almost ideal. We have got suppled into a state of melioration. When I see the emigrants landing at New York, I say, There they go — to school.

"In estimating nations, potentiality must be considered as well as power; not what to-day's actual performance is, but what promise is in the mind which a crisis will bring out."

"The war has established a chronic hope, for a chronic despair. It is not a question whether we shall be a nation, or only a multitude of people No, that has been conspicuously decided already; but whether we shall be the new nation, guide and lawgiver of all nations, as having clearly chosen and firmly held the simplest and best rule of political society.

" Culture, be sure, is in some sort the very enemy of nationality and makes us citizens of the world, and yet it is essential that it should have the flavor of the soil in which it grew, and combine this with universal sympathies. Thus in this country are new traits and distinctions not known to former history. Colonies of an old country, but in new and commanding conditions. Colonies of a small and crowded island, but planted on a continent and therefore working it in small settlements, where each man must count for ten, and is put to his mettle to come up to the need. . . .

" Pray leave these English to form their opinions. 'T is a matter of absolute insignificance what those opinions are. They will fast enough run to change and retract them on their knees when they know who you are. . . .

" I turn with pleasure to the good omen in the distinguished reception given in London to Mr. Beecher It was already prepared by the advocacy of Cobden, Bright and Forster, Mill, Newman, Cairnes and Hughes, and by the intelligent Americans already sent to England by our Government to communicate with intelligent men in the English Government and out of it. But Mr. Beecher owed his welcome to himself. He fought his way to his reward. It is one of the memorable exhibitions of the force of eloquence, — his evening at Exeter Hall. The consciousness of power shown in his broad good sense, in his jocular humor and entire presence of mind, the surrender of the English audience on recognizing the true master. He steers the Behemoth, sits astride him, strokes his fur, tickles his ear, and rides where he will. And I like

the well-timed compliment there paid to our fellow citizen
when the stormy audience reminds him to tell England that
Wendell Phillips is the first orator of the world. One orator had a right to speak of the other, — Byron's thunder-
storm, where

> " ' Jura answers from his misty shroud
> Back to the joyous Alps who call to him aloud.'

" The young men in America to-day take little thought of
what men in England are thinking or doing. That is the point
which decides the welfare of a people, — *which way does it
look?* If to any other people, it is not well with them. If
occupied in its own affairs, and thoughts, and men, with a
heat which excludes almost the notice of any other people, —
as the Jews, as the Greeks, as the Persians, as the Romans, the
Arabians, the French, the English, at their best times have
done, — they are sublime; and we know that in this abstrac-
tion they are executing excellent work. Amidst the calamities
that war has brought on our Country, this one benefit has
accrued, — that our eyes are withdrawn from England, withdrawn from France, and look homeward. We have come to
feel that

> " ' By ourselves our safety must be bought; '

to know the vast resources of the continent; the good will that
is in the people; their conviction of the great moral advantages
of freedom, social equality, education and religious culture, and
their determination to hold these fast, and by these hold fast
the Country, and penetrate every square inch of it with this
American civilization. . . .

" Americans — not girded by the iron belt of condition,
not taught by society and institutions to magnify trifles, not

victims of technical logic, but docile to the logic of events; not, like English, worshippers of fate; with no hereditary upper house, but with legal, popular assemblies, which constitute a perpetual insurrection, and by making it perpetual save us from revolutions.''

The Riverside Press
CAMBRIDGE · MASSACHUSETTS
U · S · A